general editor John M. MacKenzie

Established in the belief that imperialism as a cultural phenomenon had as significant an effect on the dominant as on the subordinate societies, Studies in Imperialism seeks to develop the new socio-cultural approach which has emerged through cross-disciplinary work on popular culture, media studies, art history, the study of education and religion, sports history and children's literature. The cultural emphasis embraces studies of migration and race, while the older political and constitutional, economic and military concerns will never be far away. It incorporates comparative work on European and American empire-building, with the chronological focus primarily, though not exclusively, on the nineteenth and twentieth centuries, when these cultural exchanges were most powerfully at work.

The French empire at war 1940–45

MANCHESTER
UNIVERSITY PRESS

STUDIES IN
IMPERIALISM

Geography and imperialism, 1820–1940
ed. Morag Bell, Robin Butlin and Michael Heffernan

Acts of supremacy
The British Empire and the stage, 1790–1930
J. S. Bratton *et al.*

Britannia's children
Reading colonialism through children's books and magazines
Kathryn Castle

Western medicine as contested knowledge
ed. Andrew Cunningham and Bridie Andrews

Unfit for heroes
Reconstruction and soldier settlement in the Empire between the wars
Kent Fedorowich

Empire and sexuality
The British experience
Ronald Hyam

'An Irish Empire?'
Aspects of Ireland and the British Empire
ed. Keith Jeffery

The language of empire
Myths and metaphors of popular imperialism, 1880–1918
Robert H. MacDonald

The empire of nature
Hunting, conservation and British imperialism
John M. MacKenzie

Propaganda and empire
The manipulation of British public opinion, 1880–1960
John M. MacKenzie

Imperialism and popular culture
ed. John M. MacKenzie

Popular imperialism and the military, 1850–1950
ed. John M. MacKenzie

Gender and imperialism
Clare Midgley

Colonial masculinity
The 'manly Englishman' and the 'effeminate Bengali'
Mrinalini Sinha

The French empire at war, 1940–45
Martin Thomas

Asia in Western fiction
ed. Robin W. Winks and James R. Rush

Travellers in Africa
British travelogues, 1850–1900
Tim Youngs

The French empire at war 1940–45

Martin Thomas

MANCHESTER
UNIVERSITY PRESS
Manchester and New York

Distributed exclusively in the USA by
ST. MARTIN'S PRESS

Published by **MANCHESTER UNIVERSITY PRESS**
OXFORD ROAD, MANCHESTER M13 9NR, UK
and ROOM 400, 175 FIFTH AVENUE, NEW YORK, NY 10010, USA

Distributed exclusively in the USA by
ST. MARTIN'S PRESS, INC.
175 FIFTH AVENUE, NEW YORK, NY 10010, USA

Distributed exclusively in Canada by
UBC PRESS, UNIVERSITY OF BRITISH COLUMBIA,
6344 MEMORIAL ROAD, VANCOUVER, BC, CANADA V6T 1Z2

British Library Cataloguing-in-Publication Data
A catalogue record for this book is available from the British Library

Library of Congress Cataloging-in-Publication Data applied for

ISBN 0 7190 5034 0 *hardback*

First published in 1998

02 01 00 99 98 10 9 8 7 6 5 4 3 2 1

Typeset in Trump Medieval
by Northern Phototypesetting Co Ltd, Bolton
Printed in Great Britain
by Redwood Books, Trowbridge

For Suzy and my parents

CONTENTS

GENERAL EDITOR'S INTRODUCTION

No one has ever doubted the profound effects of the Second World War upon European imperialism. But they have often been studied primarily in political, diplomatic and military terms, an approach which tends to highlight specific events and turning points. Moreover, there has frequently been a gulf between global and regional studies and a time lag in scholarly approaches to the various empires, particularly those of the British and the French. Only comparatively recently has there been a more profound appreciation of the underlying economic and social transformations which were necessarily rooted in the years between the two great wars of the twentieth century, but which were powerfully affected by the intensive demands, disruptions and regional destabilisations of the Second World War period.

This book constitutes a major contribution to this debate. Firmly based on primary research in France and Britain, it offers the first comprehensive account of the turbulent events in the French empire in the 1940s, a time when francophone imperial territories became the setting for strife between the competing claims of the Vichy government and de Gaulle's Free French movement, and various pragmatic positions in between. It explores the manner in which the empire constitutes, in complex and destructive ways, one of the launch pads for the liberation of France, a focal point for the conflicts between and among the Axis powers and the Western Allies, and a setting for the working out of a wide variety of ideological ambitions. The resulting economic and social strains produced much suffering for indigenous peoples, fertile ground for the emergence of many forms of resistance movement.

The scope and depth of Martin Thomas's work enable him not only to range across the French empire from the Caribbean and North America to Africa, the Middle East, the Indian Ocean and Indo-China, but also to deal with the economic and the social dimensions of these processes as much as the political and military. In addition to capturing the idiom and often extreme conservatism of French imperial politics, he demonstrates a profound sympathy for the aspirations, only dimly understood by the French, of colonised peoples. This book will contribute greatly to the study of the impact of the Second World War on greater France and its enforced decolonisation. It should also act as a foundation for further studies of elite and popular reactions to empire in twentieth-century France, as well as the processes of social change and identity formation which disrupted the characteristic French imperial ambitions to assimilation and association.

John M. MacKenzie

ACKNOWLEDGEMENTS

The research and writing of this book have been an all-consuming affair, and I owe a good deal to the archives, funding agencies and friends that have helped me to complete it. Most of the research was done in France, where diffuse archival sources, requests for restricted files and weighty cartons of documents can be, at once, inspiring and frustrating. As a result, I have often relied upon the staffs at the Vincennes military, naval and air force archives, the Foreign Ministry archive at the Quai d'Orsay, the Archives Nationales in Paris and the Centre des Archives d'Outre-mer in Aix-en-Provence. In all these archives, I have received generous help with often obscure problems. I am also grateful to Mme Worms de Romilly for permission to consult René Pleven's papers and to General Mourrut for granting access to the private papers of General Maxime Weygand at the Service Historique de l'Armée de Terre. In Britain, the personnel of the Public Record Office at Kew, the Churchill College archive in Cambridge, the Liddell Hart Centre at King's College, London, the St Antony's College Middle East Centre and the Bodleian and Rhodes House Libraries in Oxford have provided much valuable assistance. I am grateful for permission to quote from the following collections in their care: the Alfred Duff Cooper papers, Lord Lloyd papers, Major-general Edward Spears papers, Lord Strang and Earl of Swinton papers - all at Churchill College archive; the Major-general Edward Spears and Neville Barbour papers at St Antony's College; and the papers of Major-general F. H. N. Davidson, Admiral Sir Gerald Dickens and General Sir Douglas Gracey at the Liddell Hart Centre for Military Archives. All quotations from Crown copyright material are with the permission of the Controller of Her Majesty's Stationary Office. I would also like to thank the staff of the National Archives of Canada in Ottawa for a warm welcome and considerable help with Canadian source material. My thanks to Mme Thérèse Vanier for permission to quote from the Georges Vanier papers.

None of this research would have been possible without funding support. I am indebted to the British Academy, the Scouloudi Foundation and the Nuffield Foundation for providing grants to underpin work in Paris and Aix-en-Provence. The Canadian High Commission and the Canadian Department of Foreign Affairs and International Trade provided an invaluable grant to support work in Ottawa. The UWE Humanities Faculty Research Committee has also provided vital assistance.

Some of the material contained in the book has appeared within articles published in different form elsewhere. Chapter two includes a short segment of an article published in *Diplomacy and Statecraft* in 1995. Within chapter four the analysis of the St Pierre and Miquelon affair summarises some of the points made in an article published in the *International History Review* in 1997. In the same chapter, the discussion of the invasion of Madagascar in

1942 is based upon an article published in the *Historical Journal* in 1996. Full details of these articles are given in the bibliography. I am indebted to these journals for permission to reproduce some of this earlier work here.

Several people have helped me with this project, either reading drafts, discussing details or simply having the patience to listen to tales of the French empire. I am duly grateful to all of them. Kent Fedorowich and Glyn Stone provided valuable criticism of draft chapters. Robert Aldrich, Martin Shipway, Chris Goscha, Alan Dobson, David Woolner and Martin Alexander have all provided valuable insights into French policy-making or its effects on other nations. The British International History Group and the University of London Imperialism Seminar gave me opportunities to air papers on Madagascar and French imperial defence. Chris Hearmon of the UWE Geography Department kindly produced the maps. Finally, my wife Suzy has lent support, indulgence and good humour in equal measure.

M.T.

LIST OF ABBREVIATIONS

Territories, parties and organisations

AEF	Afrique Equatoriale Française ((Middle) Congo, Gabon, Oubangui-Chari and Chad)
AFN	Afrique Française du Nord (Morocco, Algeria, Tunisia)
AML	Amis du Manifeste et de la Liberté (Algerian nationalist party, formed 1944)
AOF	Afrique Occidentale Française (Senegal, Mauritania, French Guinea, French Sudan, Côte d'Ivoire (Ivory Coast), Niger and Dahomey)
BCRA	Bureau Central de Renseignements et d'Action (Free French secret service)
CCDC	Comité Consultatif de la Défense des Colonies
CCOS	Combined Chiefs of Staff (Anglo-American)
CFR	Committee on Foreign (Allied) Resistance
CLI	Corps Léger d'Intervention (Free French commando force for Indo-China)
COS	Chiefs of Staff (British)
EMGDN	Etat-Major Général de la Défense Nationale (post-Liberation General Staff)
ENA	Etoile Nord-Africaine (Algerian nationalist party, formed 1926)
FCNL	French Committee of National Liberation (based in Algiers)
FFI	Forces Françaises de l'Intérieur (French resistance army)
FIDES	Fonds d'Investissement pour le Développement Economique et Social (Colonial Investment Fund)
FLN	Front de Libération Nationale (Algerian nationalist front, formed 1954)
FMF	Forces Maritimes Françaises (Vichy navy)
FNFL	Forces Navales de la France Libre (Free French navy)
GPRF	Gouvernement Provisoire de la République Française (post-Liberation French provisional government)
Istiqlal	Moroccan independence party (formed January 1944)
JSM	Joint Staff Mission (Washington)
Néo-Destour	Tunisian nationalist party (formed 1934)
OSS	Office of Strategic Services (American)

PCF	Parti Communiste Français
PPA	Parti Populaire Algérien (Algerian (Messalist) nationalist party, formed 1937)
PPF	Parti Populaire Français (fascistic party led by Jacques Doriot)
PSF	Parti Social Français (ultra-right party, hier to the Croix de Feu)
SAA	Syndicat Agricole Africaine (planters' union formed in Côte d'Ivoire, 1944)
SEAC	South East Asia Command (British)
SOE	Special Operations Executive (British)
SOL	Service d'Ordre Légionnaire (Vichyite)
Viet Minh	League for the Independence of Vietnam (coalition, formed 1942)
VNQDD	Viet Nam Quoc Dan Dong (Vietnam National Party, formed 1927)

Archives and published documents

AN	Archives Nationales
ANCOM	Archives Nationales Centre des Archives d'Outre-Mer
DDF	*Documents Diplomatiques Français*
FRUS	*Foreign Relations of the United States*
MAE	Ministère des Affaires Etrangères (Quai d'Orsay)
NAC	National Archives of Canada
PRO	Public Record Office
SHAT	Service Historique de l'Armée de Terre
SHM	Service Historique de la Marine

Terms and expressions

Carlton Gardens	London headquarters of Free French movement/French National Committee.
Free France/ Fighting France	From Bastille Day 1942, Free France (France Libre) adopted the appellation Fighting France (France Combattante). For convenience, Free France is the preferred term in this book, although Fighting France appears in chapters dealing with the latter stages of the war.
Maghreb	region encompassing the French North African territories.
ralliement	literally, the 'rallying' of territory to Free France.

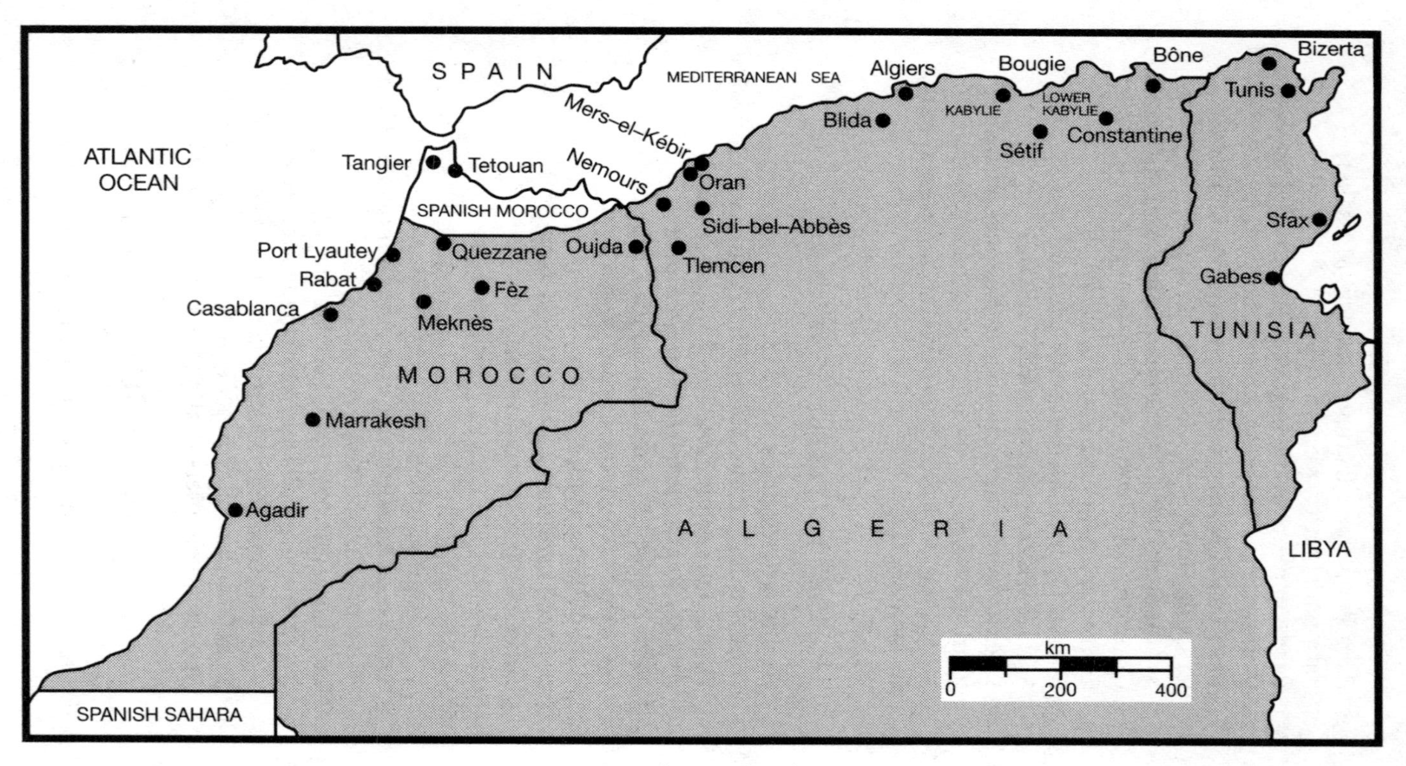

1 French North Africa

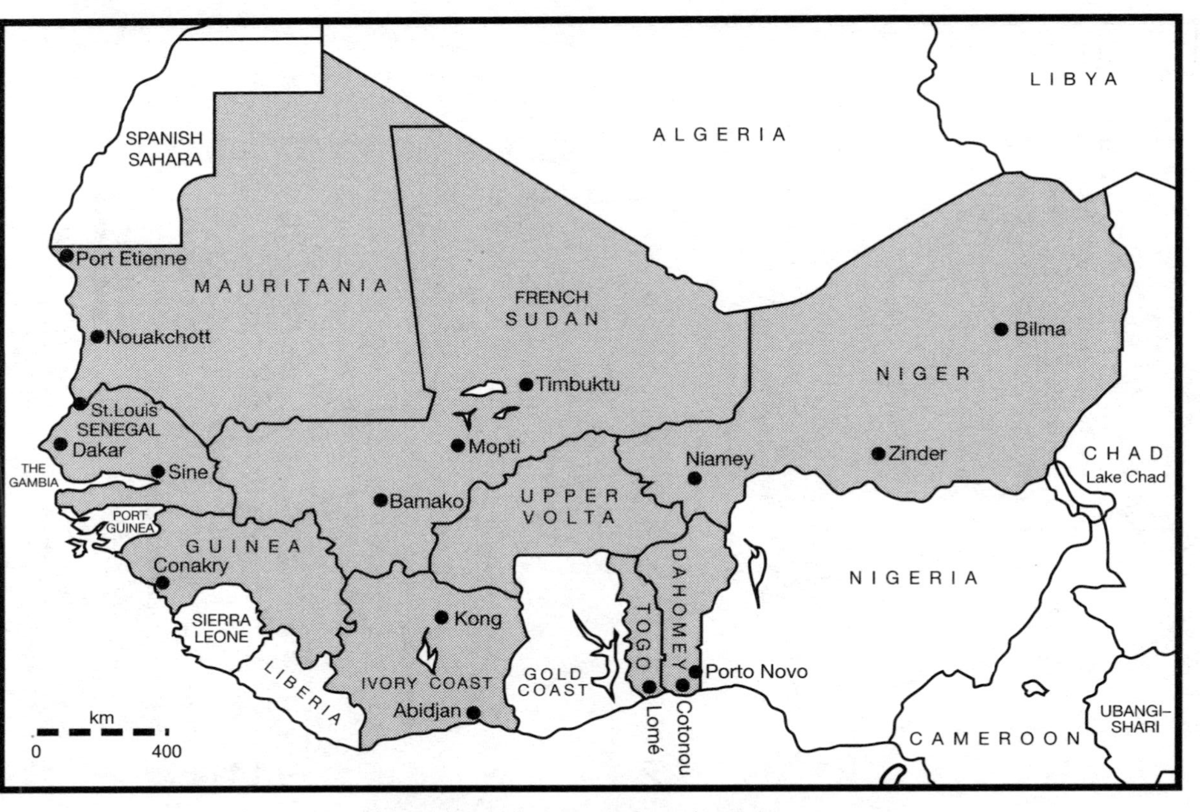

2 French West Africa (AOF)

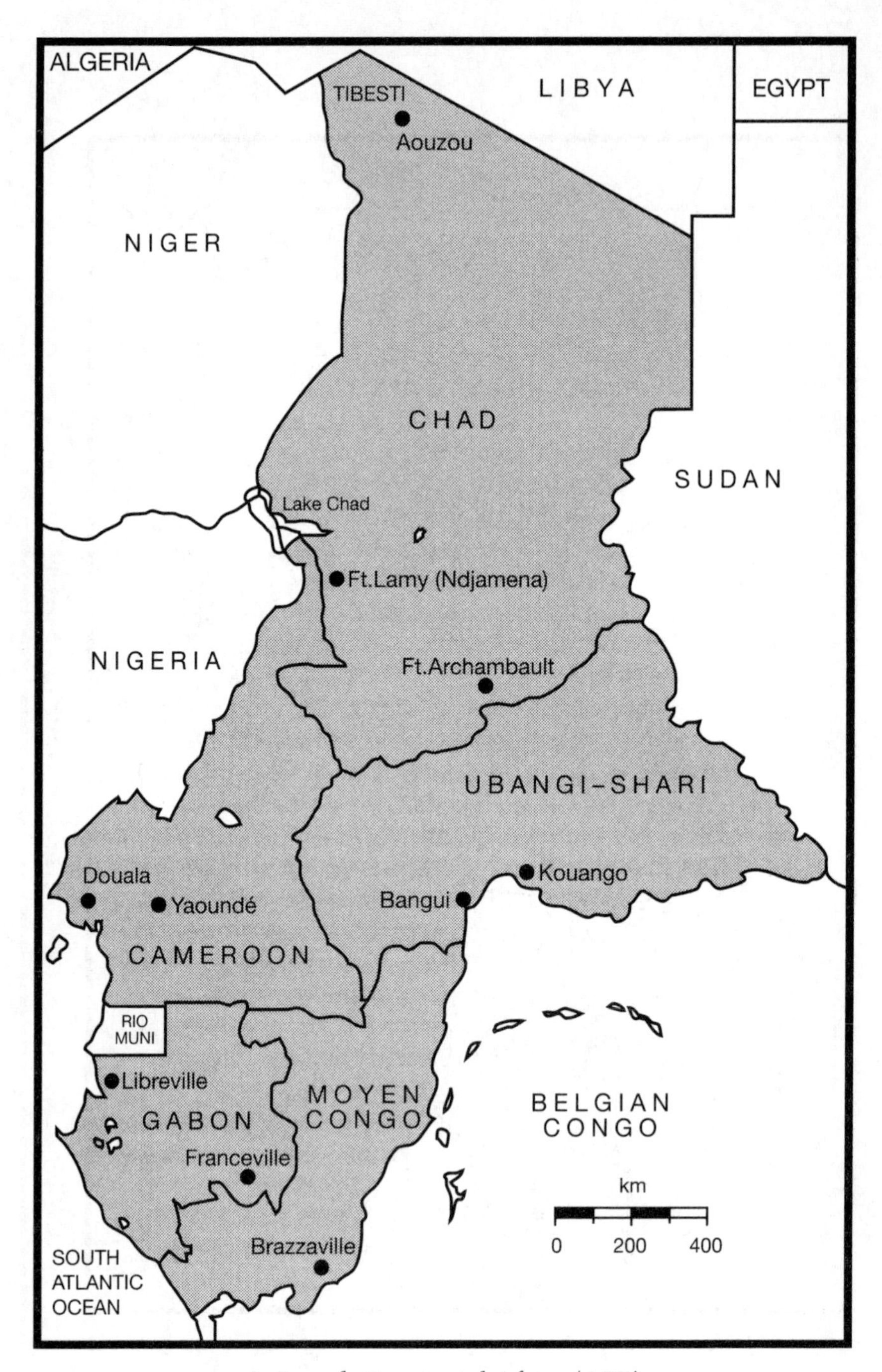

3 French Equatorial Africa (AEF)

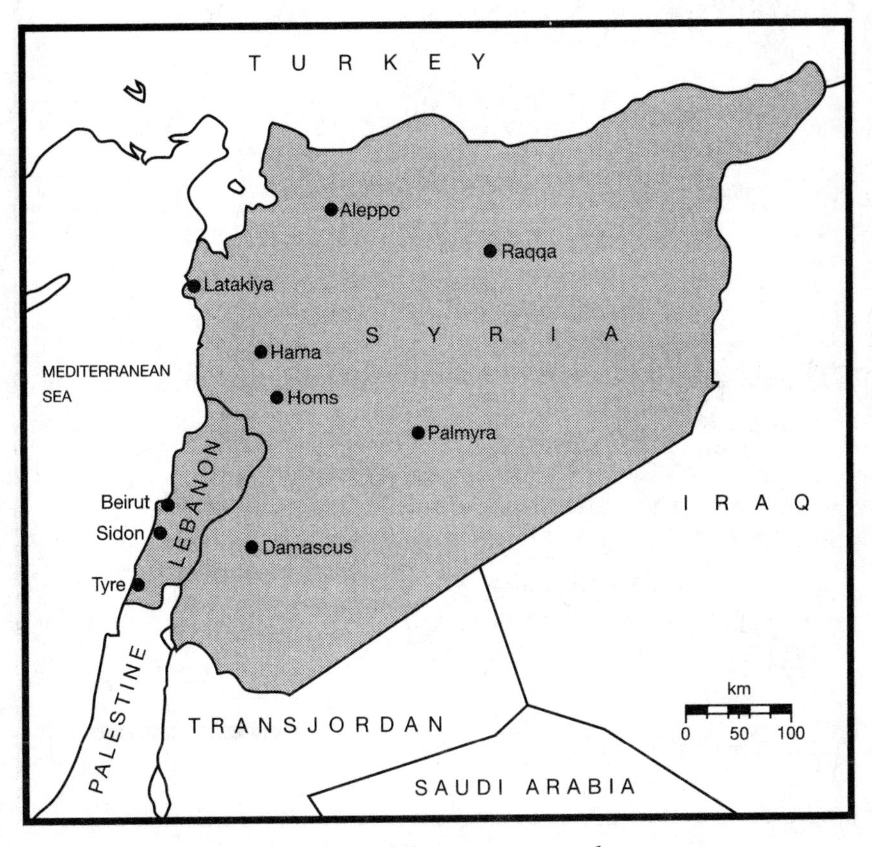

4 French Middle Eastern mandates

5 French Indo-China

INTRODUCTION

Between 1940 and 1945 the French empire divided against itself. To be more precise, the administrative, military and settler elites that ran French imperial affairs became adversaries in the contest between Vichy loyalism and Free French republicanism. Although no colony remained openly committed to the discredited Vichy regime by 1944, vestiges of reactionary 'Pétainism' certainly persisted to war's end: the rediscovered imperial unity of France's colonial rulers and settlers in 1945 was actually a weak reed. France's wartime imperial split was unique. After Germany's western onslaught in May–June 1940, the Belgian Congo and the Dutch East Indies, for example, remained faithful to their respective governments-in-exile, even though these territories were, to a considerable degree, isolated in practice. Although the stresses of war nourished colonial nationalism and protest within several British colonies, Britain's empire none the less contributed significantly to the country's war effort throughout 1939–45. Nationalist organisation in the French colonies was also transformed by the humiliation of the colonial power, vigorous suppression of organised protest and the economic constraints imposed by the Second World War. But for the rulers of France's empire, the Vichy–Free French division was perhaps more significant as a portent of the entrenched settler and military conservatism that would divide France and its empire once more during the Algerian rebellion of 1954–62.

This book traces this period of wartime French imperial division, setting it within the wider international politics of the Second World War. Neither the Vichy nor the Free French imperial authorities were masters of their own destiny. A truism perhaps – under Marshal Philippe Pétain, the Vichy regime established in July 1940 governed only part of a defeated country under the gaze of the fascist powers. Charles de Gaulle's Free French movement, fashioned in London in defiance of Pétain's capitulation, initially derived sustenance from its British patron. Nevertheless, once the extent of France's weakness is recognised, it becomes clear that a history of its wartime empire must be placed within the broader framework of the Second World War. Transfers of imperial authority were frequently the result of events outside French control. Hence the common thread linking such diverse events as New Caledonia's Australian-assisted declaration for Free France in August 1940, the British-led invasions of Syria and Madagascar in 1941 and 1942, the American landings in French North

Africa in November 1942 and Japan's increasing grip upon Indo-China from 1940 onwards.

In consequence, the principal causes of the abrupt changes of French political allegiance across France's wartime empire were more often the product of hostile military intervention than of shifting public attitudes towards Vichy or Free France. Vichy ideology and that regime's acute instinct for self-preservation certainly made their impact upon France's colonial rulers. So, too, the spirit of Free French resistance and the appeal of de Gaulle's rhetoric swayed numerous officials, soldiers and settlers across the empire. But only in 1940 were the conflicts of French politics generally decisive in tipping individual colonial governments one way or the other. As the war progressed, the French empire was increasingly re-fashioned piecemeal by the initiatives of the major combatant powers. Even the nationalist oppositions which gathered their momentum against French authority during wartime derived much of their capacity for action from the manner in which the war affected their particular territory, whether economically, politically or militarily. As a result, the direct intrusion or the close proximity of the war was a major dynamic to longer-term political change within the French empire. Some North African nationalists drew upon the German example in their assertion of Arab national unity and their consequent repudiation of French rights in the Maghreb territories of Morocco, Algeria and Tunisia. Others, such as Ferhat Abbas in Algeria and Habib Bourguiba in Tunisia, saw much to admire in declared US war aims, calculating that the eventual application of the Atlantic Charter would ensure greater freedom for colonial peoples. In the Levant states, the British government was enlisted as accomplice in the reassertion of Syrian and Lebanese treaty rights at French expense. In Indo-China, the Viet Minh nationalist coalition developed its political programme and refined its military skills in opposition to Japan's de facto control. Other Vietnamese nationalist groups judged that Japan's regional supremacy presented an unprecedented opportunity to undermine the French colonial presence in collaboration with the Japanese. In all these cases, the French effort to maintain colonial control was reactive and rarely went unchallenged.

In spite of these common threads, what emerges from the chapters which follow is that there is less overarching unity in the history of the French empire at war between 1940 and 1945 than might be supposed. Certainly, the force of Vichy authority declined over time, much as the Gaullist star rose. Clearly, too, the war did lasting harm both to French imperial prestige and to the credibility of France's distinctive philosophy of colonial assimilationism whereby certain colonial subjects were expected to identify with French cultural values.

Whether subject to Vichy or Free French administration, colonial nationalists were understandably unenthusiastic about a return to untrammelled French rule in peacetime, not least because it was widely anticipated that a weakened France might actually prove less restrained in its efforts to reimpose local control. Nevertheless, France's wartime imperial history remains inherently fragmentary. Much as individual colonies were to varying extents isolated, so too the historical bonds linking them together were often more imagined than real. The Federation of French West Africa – Afrique Occidentale Française (AOF) – is a case in point. Ruled in theory as a homogeneous unit from the federal administrative centre of Dakar, AOF was in fact as unwieldy as it was massive and diverse.[1] While Senegal and Côte d'Ivoire offered the richest economic rewards, the huge landlocked territories in the north of the Federation – from Mauritania in the west, through French Sudan to Niger in the East – provided vital links with Morocco, Algeria and French Equatorial Africa (Afrique Equatoriale Française (AEF)).[2] Although subservient to the same colonial authority, many of the subject peoples of AOF were as diffuse in culture, language, religion and economic activity as they were supposedly united by the shared experience of French rule. In short, outside the confines of French colonial administration, there was less substance to the concept of 'federation' than the French cared to admit. As Christopher Harrison puts it in reference to the immediate post-1919 period, at one extreme, 'AOF represented a federation of parochial governments, isolated parish councils whose perception of policy and strategic interest was necessarily limited and for whom the dictates of the imperial bureaucrats in Paris may well have been meaningless.'[3] The Second World War and France's defeat changed many of the rules of colonial governance but it did little to make the empire a more coherent whole.

In writing a strategic and international history of empire, one thus challenges an assumption which underlies much of the French writing on the wartime empire: namely, that competing French elites determined the complexion of colonial loyalties. This is not to suggest that those actors directly involved in Vichy and Free French government were in any way insignificant. Indeed, the decade after 1945 saw the publication of a host of popular memoirs and war diaries written by many of the leading characters in the leadership of both the Vichy state and the Free French movement. From an imperial perspective, this body of work is immediately striking for three main reasons. Firstly, without exception, the recollections of France's wartime leaders pay far more attention to questions of empire than any comparable set of politicians' writings from the preceding era of the Third Republic. Secondly, although the lines of political division are plainly apparent between Gaullists and unreconstructed Pétainists, there is, none the less, a remarkable consensus regarding the vital importance of empire to the salvation of French national dignity in 1940, and to the post-war reconstruction of France as a major power. Finally, the great majority of this writing is deeply conservative. There is little treatment of bold imperial reform, far more attention being devoted to the role of colonies within the authors' visions of a resurrected and powerful France. Detailed discussion of colonial populations and conditions is largely confined to the work of Ministry of Colonies administrators, Ecole Coloniale personnel or specialist academics, of whom Robert Delavignette and Charles-André Julien are obvious examples.[4] Among the pro-consuls of the Free French empire, such as Adolphe Sicé in AEF and Georges Catroux in the Levant and North Africa, the challenges of 'native affairs' appear as a distraction from the real business of contributing to the liberation of France. Elsewhere, France's subject peoples, especially in black Africa, are frequently portrayed in stereotypical terms – as loyal, martial and, depending on the politics of the author, either grateful for, or uninterested in, the politics of Gaullism.[5]

It is thus tempting to add a fourth aspect to this body of literature – its strongly metropolitan bias. Empire is presented as a tool in the service of France's revival, or, more broadly, as the arena in which the peculiar French political rivalries of the Second World War were played out.[6] What emerges only occasionally, if at all, from such works is the rising force of colonial opinion and the structural frailties of French imperial control. Put bluntly, few French memoirs convey the popular animosity towards French colonial administration which is writ large within the archival records of the period. In one sense, this is unsurprising. Former Vichyite administrators, like their erstwhile Free French opponents, moved within the narrow confines of a governing elite. The French officers on both sides, often well versed in imperial policing and in daily contact with colonial troops, were not inclined to dwell on more intangible questions of public mood unless it was their job to report on the subject. The exceptions to this are perhaps Morocco, Algeria and Tunisia, where regular administrative assessment of Muslim opinion was already well established by 1940.

It would be remarkable indeed if former governors and colonial generals emerged in their writings as having been enlightened opponents of empire. But what does bear emphasis is that French memoir histories of the empire at war became immersed in the polemics of the Fourth Republic as the post-war regime struggled to come to terms with the Vichy past and with the violence of decolonisation in Indo-China and, above all, Algeria. Conversely, neither the terms of the

1946 French Union, nor the human and material costs of the Indo-China war aroused as much debate in post-war France as issues closer to home such as French economic reconstruction and the revival of German power. Instead, the manner in which the wartime empire had first divided and was then reunited under de Gaulle became something of an allegory. Wartime recollections of empire were employed either as an object lesson in the decadence of French Republican democracy and the divisiveness of Gaullism or as proof of the lasting strengths of the Republican ideal and the virtues of inspired leadership.[7]

Control of the French empire was vital to the competing French leaderships of 1940–44. The empire was a physical embodiment of what limited independence remained to the Vichy regime. Preservation of imperial control helped Vichy governments withstand Germano-Italian pressure for concessions in metropolitan France, and was pivotal to Vichy's claim to be more than the mouthpiece of a defeated nation. The national revolution espoused by the supporters of Marshal Pétain was enthusiastically endorsed in many regions of the empire from North and West Africa to the French West Indies. The dual-track nature of the armistice disarmament provisions which distinguished between metropolitan France and Vichy's overseas territories ensured that the Armée d'Afrique in French North Africa, and the colonial units stationed in black Africa and elsewhere, became the vanguard of Vichy land forces and a powerful symbol of supposed national and colonial renewal. Furthermore, the Vichy navy, the one service which escaped many armistice restrictions, devoted itself to imperial defence and became the sharpest element of the Vichy armed services. For Free France, too, the empire had a political and symbolic importance which far outweighed its material significance. The early declarations of colonial support – or *ralliements* – underpinned de Gaulle's claim to legitimacy, while the colonies themselves provided the core of Free French forces and a vital source of sterling income. Possession of imperial territory also gave the Free French a greater voice in their dealings with the British government. Much as Vichy-administered territories were supposed to represent the ideal of loyal service to the nation, so too Free French colonies were vital to the Gaullist themes of resistance, republican legitimacy and constitutional renaissance.

Although this study is primarily an international history of the wartime French empire, in order to evaluate the stability, the value and the strength of the empire, consideration is also given to the nature of Vichy and Free French colonial rule and the impact of that authority upon the local populations concerned. In certain territories – the French West Indies, Syria and Indo-China, for example – the manifest shortcomings of French colonial government were instrumental in the overthrow of wartime regimes or the growth of nationalist sentiment during the war itself. But it would be simplistic and misleading to attribute gathering opposition to colonial rule to the failures of Vichy as an imperial power. Colonial manpower was vital to both Vichy and Free France and, in many respects, this contribution was better acknowledged by Vichy than by de Gaulle and his followers. More basically, since many Vichy colonies lived under the restrictions of British naval blockade, the incentive to exploit African labour in pursuit of export revenue was sometimes diminished by force of circumstance. By contrast, Gaullist colonial governors strove hard to meet ambitious export targets in pursuit of a Free French 'war effort'.[8] Where it is contended that the fate of individual colonies or groups of colonies was determined by events beyond French control, this is illustrated by discussion of local colonial conditions. In French West Africa, for instance, Governor Pierre Boisson built up a federation of Vichyite administrations which was more cohesive than the far richer territories of French North Africa. Even so, the work accomplished by Boisson in West Africa, Charles-Auguste Noguès in Morocco or, on the Gaullist side, Henri Catroux in Syria, was quickly undermined by the intervention of combatant states whose actions were driven by their strategic requirements.

Prior to the fall of France several Ministries played a role in supervising French colonial administration. The demarcation of authority between the Ministry of Colonies, the Foreign Ministry and the Ministry of the Interior prefigured political divisions which were to emerge after June 1940. The French residency in Tunisia, responsible to the Quai d'Orsay, did not produce the same enthusiastic support for Vichy as was evident among the Algiers administration which reported directly to the Ministry of the Interior. By contrast, Morocco and much of black Africa, though with civil administrations responsible to the Quai d'Orsay and Ministry of Colonies respectively, were in practice largely run as military governorships. But the War Ministry spared little time for imperial matters. Only the Ministry of Marine consistently placed empire at the heart of its strategic planning before June 1940. These points are crucial to what follows in two respects. Firstly, to the army staff the empire was viewed primarily as a vital manpower reserve for use in the defence of metropolitan France. Only later did Vichy exploit the high concentration of colonial troops in the armistice armies in order to represent colonial forces and subject peoples as loyal servants and capable martial races devoted to the defence of imperial territory. Secondly, the navy's broader strategic outlook acquired lasting importance under Vichy as foreign and colonial policy fell under the sway of Admirals Jean-François Darlan, Charles Platon and Henri Bléhaut. To the military establishment as a whole, both before and after the 1940 armistice agreements, the empire's anticipated contribution to France was fashioned by memories of the First World War. It is to this earlier period that we now turn.

Notes

1 AOF comprised Senegal, Mauritania, French Guinea, French Sudan, Côte d'Ivoire (Ivory Coast), Niger and Dahomey. The French-administered section of the former German mandate of Togo was also treated as an adjunct to AOF. Upper Volta was partitioned among other AOF colonies in 1912 before its re-establishment in 1948: see Yves Person, 'French West Africa and Decolonization' in Prosser Gifford and William Roger Louis (eds), *The Transfer of Power in Africa. Decolonization, 1940–1960*, (New Haven, Conn., Yale University Press, 1982), p. 141.
2 French Equatorial Africa (AEF) was federated in 1910 to include the French (Middle) Congo, Gabon, Oubangui-Chari and Chad. As in the case of Togo and AOF, the former German mandate of Cameroon was sometimes treated as an adjunct to AEF.
3 Christopher Harrison, *France and Islam in West Africa, 1860–1960* (Cambridge, Cambridge University Press, 1988), p. 5.
4 See, for example, Robert Delavignette and Charles-André Julien, *Les Constructeurs de la France d'Outre-mer* (Paris, Presses Universitaires de France, 1946).
5 Adolphe Sicé, *L'Afrique équatoriale française et le Cameroun au service de la France* (Paris, Presses Universitaires de France, 1946); Georges Catroux, *Dans la bataille de la Méditerranée. Egypte–Levant–Afrique du Nord, 1940–1944* (Paris, Julliard, 1949). Vichy's Indo-China Governor, Admiral Jean Decoux, devoted only two short chapters to his social policies, see his *A la Barre de l'Indochine. Histoire de mon gouvernement général (1940–1945)* (Paris, Plon, 1949), pp. 384–411.
6 Two more recent examples of this trend are: René Cassin, *Les Hommes partis de rien. Le réveil de la France abattue (1940–1941)* (Paris, Plon, 1975); and Gaston Palewski, *Mémoires d'action, 1924–1974* (Paris, Plon, 1988). Cassin was de Gaulle's principal legal adviser in 1940. Palewski supported de Gaulle's call for army reform in the 1930s and served with Free French forces in East Africa in 1941–42.
7 Henry Rousso, *The Vichy Syndrome. History and Memory in France since 1944* (Cambridge, Mass., Harvard University Press, 1991), pp. 60, 75–80.
8 Frederick Cooper, *Decolonization and African Society. The Labor Question in French and British Africa* (Cambridge, Cambridge University Press, 1996), pp. 147–51.

PART I

The inter-war background

CHAPTER ONE

The inter-war empire and French defence

The legacy of the First World War

In the imperial history of inter-war France, memories of the First World War should figure large. The experience of the Great War shaped inter-war French attitudes to empire more than any other single event. Once the western front stalemate took shape in the early autumn of 1914, it became increasingly apparent that France's war against the central powers was likely to be long-fought. In spite of the military alliances with Russia and Britain, the French army saw itself in the van of the struggle against imperial Germany. Both during its bloody course and in the twenty years of peace which followed, the Great War was both proof and reminder of France's demographic inferiority next to the German state. Colonial manpower and resources helped to restore the balance. Much as France's nineteenth century colonial *conquistadors*, General Louis Faidherbe and Marshal Joseph Galliéni, saw the potential for employing West African troops in further imperial conquests in the 1890s, so in 1914 the French military staff turned eagerly to black Africans to assist in the defence of France itself. Where West African riflemen (Tirailleurs) had helped conquer Madagascar twenty years earlier, they were later called upon to man French trenches in 1916.[1]

Directed by the Governor-general of Afrique Occidentale Française (AOF), William Ponty, and encouraged by the Senegalese Deputy, Blaise Daigny, French colonial administrators in West Africa pursued ambitious First World War recruitment drives. Infamous within French West Africa as an *impôt du sang* – or blood tax – which prompted tens of thousands of potential conscripts to flee to neighbouring British colonies, and which led directly to three major outbreaks of colonial disorder between 1915 and 1917 (in French Sudan, in Dahomey and in Upper Volta), the colonial contribution to French victory in 1918 was nevertheless remembered fondly in France as a triumph of military and economic mobilisation. Common service in war was portrayed as a testament to the vitality of empire.[2]

In Indo-China, too, similar efforts were made. Here, the colony's *garde indigène* dated its history back to an ordinance of July 1888 which established the first 'civil guard' in Indo-China. After a series of decrees passed between 1895 and 1904, the *garde indigène* was reorganised into formal regiments, officered by specialist French soldiers selected primarily for their linguistic ability. Though criticised in the French Senate between 1911 and 1913 for general unruliness and a doubtful ability to maintain civil order, the garde proved highly valuable once war broke out. It remained an effective force although large numbers of its French officers were promptly recalled to the western front. The recruitment of further native troops in Indo-China was strongly supported by Albert Sarraut, appointed Governor-general of the Indo-China federation in 1917.[3]

In total, according to Sarraut, who was made Minister of Colonies in January 1920, the empire provided 587,000 troops between 1914–18. More recently, this figure has been put much higher – at 818,000, including 187,000 war workers in France. In spite of the colonial unrest this stimulated, and the virulent opposition to forced recruitment expressed by the new Governor-general of AOF, Joost van Vollenhoven, in 1917, French West Africa alone produced 56,000 new recruits in 1918. Furthermore, this was an achievement based in large part upon the active co-operation of the traditional indigenous elites in Senegal, French Guinea and French Sudan.[4] Indeed, it has been argued that one of the principal reasons behind the flight of several thousand Africans from Côte d'Ivoire and Upper Volta into the neighbouring British Gold Coast both during and after the First World War was the recognition that the French system of *commandant* administration had entirely co-opted local chiefs, making them enforcers of French demands. But, for all those Africans who fled, far more ended up in French military uniform.[5] Although the empire became fragmented after France's defeat in June 1940, once again the notion of colonies rallying to save the mother country resurfaced as a potent, if unreliable, symbol of imperial loyalty.[6]

In spite of the advances in military technology in the inter-war period, on the eve of the Second World War, French defence planners still viewed the empire in terms reminiscent of the earlier conflict. Although both French civil and military planning for imperial defence became increasingly sophisticated from 1936 onwards, it was none the less assumed that fighting men would constitute the empire's major contribution to European war. Little allowance was made for the possibility that metropolitan French troops might be required to make sacrifices to defend the empire, instead of empire troops arriving in droves to supplement the home commands. At the Paris military colleges and the newly established Centre for Higher Military Studies, 'imperial defence' scarcely featured on the curriculum for intending senior officers of the French armed services.[7] Echoes of the 1914–18 approach to imperial recruitment reverberated through Colonial and War Ministry planning in 1939–40. In February 1940, the Minister of Colonies, Georges Mandel, conjured an image of recruitment procedures based upon the concept of the 'nation of 100 million' *en marche*,

> In French Indo-China, large numbers of young men are leaving the countryside and coming to Saigon or Hanoi to offer their services, and Emperor Bao Dai [of Annam] is actively encouraging recruitment. In Togo and Cameroon, the *indigène* chiefs are organising *levées en masse* within their tribes and are sending [recruits] to Lomé, Yaoundé and Douala, asking that they should begin active service immediately. In A.O.F., several chiefs have sent a formal request to the Minister of Colonies that all young men above fifteen years of age 'be granted the honour to serve under the flag'.[8]

Across the empire, Algeria was first to experience the full impact of France's wartime manpower demands. Although there were limited indications of dissent when French mobilisation measures were extended in Algeria in September 1939, the fact that the call-up received support from both Ferhat Abbas and Dr Mohammed Bendjelloul, the leading supporters of assimilation among Algeria's Muslim elite *élus*, helped prevent any major incident.[9] On 28 May 1940, as the battle for France entered its decisive phase, the Algiers financial delegations – the principal administrative forum for Muslim *élu* representatives – expressed full confidence in a French victory. Six months earlier the delegations had rubber-stamped an onerous 1940 budget of which some 60 per cent was devoted to defence expenditure and recruitment costs.[10] In fact, between 1939 and June 1940 some 300,000 colonial conscripts were raised in French North Africa, 197,300 across AOF and 116,000 within the Indo-China federation. At the point when the armistice agreements were signed in June, a further 313,750 colonial troops had been scheduled for recruitment in 1940–41.[11]

Much as the First World War experience was writ large in Mandel's thinking in 1940, so too it had reinforced the bonds between a certain group of French professional soldiers and their colonial counterparts. Between the wars it became increasingly commonplace for junior career officers to spend several years serving within the empire, not with metropolitan units but with regiments of the French colonial armies in Africa, the French Levant or Indo-China. Many of General de Gaulle's future military subordinates within the Free French movement had a far more intimate knowledge of empire than the General himself. Algeria, for example, had long been regarded by the officer corps as a forcing ground for French commanders and a training school for the tacticians of France's colonial forces.[12] General Paul Legentilhomme, Governor of Djibouti in June 1940 and, later, Gaullist appointee to Madagascar in 1943, could boast over thirty years of colonial military service, most of it in Indo-China, where he had played a leading part in suppressing nationalist dissent after the Yen Bay mutiny in 1930. Another Free French colonial Governor, General Georges Catroux, had served in the empire for even longer than Legentilhomme. Following his admission to the Foreign Legion in 1900, Catroux also served extensively in North Africa and Indo-China and, like most of his fellow colonial officers, was profoundly influenced by contact with the apostle of French military colonialism, General Louis-Hubert Lyautey. For these men and the regiments they commanded, service in Europe during the First World War was a temporary interruption of their colonial careers.[13] Among their antagonists at Vichy, the range of colonial experience was equally pronounced. Appointed to the Vichy War Ministry in September 1940, General Charles Huntziger had served in Madagascar, Senegal and Tonkin before the First World War, and spent four years in the 1930s as land forces commander in the Levant. Marcel Peyrouton, who as Vichy Minister of the Interior in 1940–41 pioneered much of the legislation which gave the regime its authoritarian character, had entered the Ministry of Colonies *section Afrique* in 1910. His experience in suppressing nationalist dissent as Resident-general in Tunisia and then, briefly, in Morocco between 1933 and 1936 provided a fund of information to draw upon when extending police powers in Vichy France. General Alphonse Juin, armed forces commander in French North Africa from November 1941, was born in Bône, Algeria, and spent his entire youth in the Maghreb before entering a *zouaves* regiment in 1909. By 1939 Juin had accumulated thirty years of active service, most of it – excepting his time in the trenches – in North Africa. Even Philippe Pétain himself was not only hero of Verdun, but also the victor of the Moroccan Rif war in 1925–26.[14]

De Gaulle's military experience, though almost exclusively metropolitan, was no less significant. Promoted to lieutenant in 1914, he served with distinction within the 33e infantry regiment under, then Colonel, Pétain. A prisoner of war between 1916 and 1918, de Gaulle re-entered active service with the French expeditionary force in the Russo-Polish war of 1920–21. On this occasion his immediate commander was Maxime Weygand. In 1927 de Gaulle was confirmed as *aide-de-camp* to Pétain, who was by then vice-president of the Supreme War Council, Army Inspector-general and, indisputably, the pre-eminent soldier in France. De Gaulle spent the previous two years working closely with the Marshal in the development of army strategic planning. Pétain remained something of a patron to de Gaulle for much of the following decade.[15] With so many politicians of the Third Republic *hors de combat* after the dissolution of the National Assembly in July 1940, the upshot was that within the Free French movement and the Vichy establishment a disproportionately large number of empire specialists and revered military figures held major office between 1940 and 1944. Both the Spa hotels of Vichy, where the new regime's Ministries took up residence, and the Free French headquarters at Carlton Gardens in London could boast figures well versed in the application and military practices of colonial rule. These were individuals well suited to leadership in an undeclared and intermittent French colonial civil war.

The disappointments of inter-war reform

If the memories of the imperial contribution to the previous war were largely positive, the inter-war empire produced few innovations to inspire liberal French imperialists. Marred by major revolts in Morocco, Syria and Indo-China, and punctuated by growing nationalist unrest across the French North African Maghreb, the inter-war period was conspicuous for the near-total failure of plans for colonial reform in Afrique Française du Nord (French North Africa, AFN) and the French Levant. This was particularly ironic given that so many enthusiastic imperial lobbyists within the Parti Colonial of the early 1900s anticipated that victory in 1918 and the attendant destruction of the Ottoman empire would confirm France's new-found status as both Mediterranean and Middle Eastern power. Georges Leygues was one such. The leading French Minister of Marine in the 1920s and early 1930s and an erstwhile leader of a group of Senators devoted to extending French power in the Arab world, Leygues had confidently anticipated in 1915 that the new French empire would have two Muslim poles – Morocco in the west and Syria in the east. In each case, the French civilising mission would be pursued to the utmost.[16] Taking an even broader view, there were numerous skilled officials within the Ministry of Colonies who saw further justification in *Islam noir* – the African Islam of much of French West Africa – for a French claim to be the true protector of the Muslim world. In 1919 these French colonial 'scholar-administrators' looked forward to a French effort to refashion much of Muslim Africa and the Middle East in a Gallic image.[17]

Certainly, in the inter-war period French colonial policy was still notionally guided by the idea of closer assimilation. Buoyed by anticipated increases in colonial living standards, black African territories were expected to become more overtly French, whether this were manifested in the further construction of boulevards, *patisseries* and Catholic churches in colonial cities or in the spread of French literacy within remote administrative *cercles*. The exceptions to this rule were the North African protectorates of Morocco and Tunisia and the mandated Territories of Syria and Lebanon, where international treaties bound the French either to preserve indigenous dynastic rule or to prepare the territories for eventual self-government. As for less favoured regions of the empire, in some utopian future, France's colonial subjects were to cast off the trappings of African or Asian ethnicity to become fully fledged overseas French citizens – culturally acclimatised to French rule, devoted to France and eventually granted full political rights as reward. But even in French West Africa, where the most established French colony – Senegal – was considered the model for assimilationist doctrine in francophone black Africa (and where the famous 1916 Blaise Daigne law conferred citizenship upon established residents of Senegal's original four communes), the *indigène* elite that had acquired full French citizenship and voting rights numbered no more than 90,000 in 1938.[18] For all the rhetoric of assimilation and eventual parity between metropole and colony, the empire was still governed by decree, rather than by ordinary parliamentary statute.

Even Algeria, closest in constitutional form to the mother country, lived under a curious mixture of French law, decree legislation and Islamic practice. The confusion of French legislation regarding land tenure across the Maghreb provides an obvious example of this. Between 1881 and 1914, repeated efforts were made to avoid a repetition in Tunisia or Morocco of the chaos evident in Second Empire legislation regarding property ownership and tenancy terms in Algeria. But, in practice, neither in Morocco nor in Tunisia was settlement policy more enlightened or effective. French land policies were always guided by the attempt to suppress customary Islamic law in favour of French civil law, in which the principle of individual ownership of land was paramount. Since land holding across North Africa was traditionally family and kin-based, the Muslim population was bound to lose out. Hence, while French colonisation in Tunisia fell far below that of Algeria, by 1908 almost 50 per cent of the agricultural belt in the immediate hinterland of Tunis was owned by only sixty-eight individuals.[19]

While the Paris Peace Conference was still in session in 1919, the first batch of inter-war colonial electoral reforms – eponymously named after the reappointed Governor-general of Algeria, Célestin Jonnart – were put before Parliament by Georges Clemenceau's government. There, the proposals were watered down beyond recognition. Based upon what would become the staple of French reformist offerings, an extension of citizenship and voting rights to the tiny minority among the colonial population – in this case, Algerians – deemed to have sufficient independent means, property and French educational qualifications to qualify as évolués, Jonnart's reforms were faithful to the assimilationist ideal. To profit from reform, whether through emancipation or improved economic opportunity, it was first necessary to become demonstrably French. For native Algerians this required the abandonment of one's status as a Muslim through renunciation of the so-called *statut personnel*.[20] Only after this act of apostasy could Algerians acquire the French citizenship necessary to be allowed voting rights for the non-Muslim electoral college in Algiers which largely determined the complexion of Algeria's Consultative Assembly. But, since this electoral college had an in-built majority favouring the European settler population, to a devout Muslim the whole business was a singular waste of time. In one respect, culturally based assimilationist reforms were commendably colour-blind. But, in effect, they still served to emphasise French superiority, albeit culturally rather than racially defined. Neither of Algeria's two electoral colleges, nor the Consultative Assembly they elected, exercised much real authority in a country where the centralised administration of the Paris-appointed Algiers Governor-general ruled almost as a law unto itself.

In their final form, the abortive Jonnart reforms were timid. Their application was always restricted to Algeria. This requirement for separate packages of reform for individual overseas territories mirrored the diversity in French colonial administration and the differing Ministries to which colonial Governors reported. Typically, the primacy of the Foreign and Interior Ministries in controlling French North Africa and the Levantine mandates was justified in three ways: firstly, by reference to French respect for the pre-existing indigenous political systems in the Moroccan and Tunisian protectorates; secondly, by pointing to the terms under which France held its Type A mandates in Syria and Lebanon; and, finally, by emphasis upon the uniquely integrated nature of French local government within Algeria, based as it was upon a modified form of the French departmental system.[21] An inter-ministerial Commission on Muslim Affairs created in 1911 to rationalise French administration in North Africa had made little impact. A purely consultative body, its advice was easily ignored. More promising was the North African Conference, set up on the initiative of General Lyautey in 1920. Not yet the legendary figure that he became after the publication of André Maurois's classic biography in 1931, Lyautey was unable to give his plan for regular co-ordinatory meetings between the Governors of the three Maghreb territories much clear purpose. The first such conference, held in Algiers in February 1923, was impaired by its vague agenda and the obvious uninterest of Raymond Poincaré's government in Paris.[22] At much the same time, in Syria, the French Mandatory Commission under General Gouraud saw its plans for administrative rationalisation and financial reform undermined by lack of funding from Paris. The paucity of funds was indicative of the limited parliamentary interest in France's new Levantine interests.[23] Far from meeting their mandatory responsibilities, Gouraud and his successors spent a large part of their time and money on internal security measures, most notably in the southern Jebel Druze region during and after the Syrian revolt of 1925–27. For all these disappointments, French politicians of left and right showed remarkable consistency in their recourse to the incantations of 'assimilation' and 'association', regardless of the limited steps undertaken between the wars to give tangible form to these ideas.

When France fell, Algeria was represented in the French National Assembly by three Senators and ten Deputies. Algeria had sent six Deputies to Paris in the first years of the Third Republic between 1871–75 before the famous Plichon amendment reduced this figure to three on the grounds that there were insufficient French electors resident in Algeria to justify such representation. In 1881 Jules Ferry restored the number of Deputies for Algeria to six. After heightened French settlement following the First World War, colon representation was again increased to nine Deputies in 1927. In 1936 Algiers acquired an additional Deputy, bringing the total figure to ten.[24] The Algerian contingent was the largest among the colonial representatives in the Parliaments of inter-war France. But this was evidence of the power of the settler community rather than of a French commitment to introduce genuine democracy to the entire population of Algeria. Muslim influence was largely confined to the *djemâas* – or municipal councils – and to the higher tier of Conseils-Généraux at regional level. Only at these levels of administration were Muslim Algerian subjects able to vote and participate without renouncing their adherence to Islamic law. The unitary authority of the Governor-general's office in Algiers, Algeria's ability to raise and disburse its own budget, and the supposed innovation of mixed communes, wherein the Muslim population was allowed a limited role in local administration, were administrative foundations left largely intact by both the Vichy and the Gaullist administrations in Algiers. Much the same applied in the North

African protectorates. In Tunisia, Muslim Arabs served in local and regional administration through the system of Caïds' councils and regional committees. But here, too, the closer to national administration and substantial political debate, the less the Arab influence. In Morocco, though the sultanate retained more real authority than Tunisia's beylical administration, there was even less diffusion of rights and responsibilities among the country's Muslim population.[25]

A full twenty years after the rash of immediate post-First World War colonial reforms, in February 1940 Georges Mandel repeated the tired arguments of the assimilationist school in reference to the customs unions then being put in place across the bulk of French Africa and the Indo-China federation:

> British and French attitudes in the face of colonial resource problems offer fresh proof of the clear difference between the viewpoints of the two countries. French policy in respect of its North African territories has always been based upon assimilation. No other policy was compatible with the close organic unity that France has sought to achieve between the metropole and overseas France.[26]

Putting aside the manifest disparity between limited constitutional reform and the reality of arbitrary French control, the involvement of several Ministries in colonial government made for greater financial, military and political complexity within the administration of empire in Paris. Frequently, this resulted in individual colonial Governors ploughing distinct furrows with minimal consideration of the empire as a unified whole. Within the Corps of Colonial Administrators, established to administer sub-Saharan French Africa and staffed in large part by graduates of the Ecole Coloniale, the inter-war period represented an inglorious interlude between the pioneer administrators of the *belle époque* and the many innovative reformers of the post-1945 period. In 1931, Robert Delavignette, perhaps the pre-eminent Corps official of his age, lamented that French administrators in black Africa seemed apathetic and unresponsive to local needs. The historian, future Governor and one-time Corps member, Hubert Deschamps, also remembered the inter-war years as an era of colonial lassitude.[27] Across French Africa, colonial governments nominally wedded to the assimilationist ideal seemed moribund, reluctant to learn from the experience of other colonial powers and crippled by lack of energy, shortage of funds or a combination of the two. Hence, in July 1929, one finds the Minister of Colonies, André Maginot – remembered far more for his support of fixed frontier defences than for his achievements as a colonial advocate – bemoaning the insularity of French overseas administration.

> It is clear from the evidence that it is essential, in the interests of French

> colonisation alone, to take a closer interest in the administrative, economic and social evolution of different countries, whether independent or subject to a colonial power, which share common frontiers and developing relationships with our overseas possessions.[28]

One note of encouragement was that 1936–39 witnessed a marked increase in applicants to the Ecole Nationale de la France d'Outre-mer, with 420 applicants in 1939 alone. Inevitably, many of this new generation of future administrators first entered colonial service in Vichyite colonies. Indeed, under the aegis of Robert Delavignette, the Ecole's wartime director, the Vichy period saw further increases in Ecole Coloniale recruitment.[29]

In the North African context, during the 1930s the Quai d'Orsay became increasingly uncomfortable at the lack of uniformity in French overseas administration. In February 1935 this sentiment led the Foreign Minister, Pierre Etienne Flandin, to establish the Haut Comité Méditerranéen, an advisory committee with a specialist secretariat directed by the Maghreb expert, Charles-André Julien. Both Flandin and Julien agreed that French rule across the Maghreb and the Levant was inconsistent and diffuse. The Foreign and Interior Ministries too often competed for limited funding for the overseas territories in their charge. This was partially remedied by the referral of the annual budgets for the three North African territories to a single *rapporteur* within the Chamber of Deputies Finance Commission. Still, the high degree of autonomy conceded to the Residents General in Morocco and Tunisia, and to the Governor-general in Algeria, meant in practice that each could pursue Arab policies at variance with one another. In March 1937 the Haut Comité Méditerranéen submitted a damning report on the hierarchy of French administration in North Africa and the Levant. It suggested that Georges Leygues's famous lamentation in 1911 – that France had no clear policy towards its Arab Muslim territories – remained as valid as ever.[30]

In administrative terms, French North Africa was less than the sum of its parts. Morocco, Algeria and Tunisia were administratively disjointed. Though the Haut Comité Méditerranéen merely encouraged uniformity of practice, it was soon regarded by several Ministries within Paris as an agency committed to greater centralisation. This stirred memories of the failed experiment with a Ministry of Overseas France. Established as part of Edouard Daladier's second Ministry in February 1934, this department was buried within weeks of its creation. The service Ministries in particular were unwilling to see their military powers within the Mediterranean territories curtailed by a separate supervisory body. Hence the military opposition to a High Commission for French North Africa, an idea also floated in the early 1930s.[31]

In fact, the French colonial establishment had little to fear from the Haut Comité Méditerranéen. The committee increasingly confined itself to the task of combating the appeal of nationalism within France's Arab territories, and its agenda was ultimately determined by the Prime Minister's Office at the Hôtel Matignon. At its first session in 1935, for example, the committee ranged over possible restrictions upon press freedom in Algeria, measures to outlaw union membership among public servants in Tunisia, and increased surveillance of indigène students in French and North African universities. This role of surveillance and intelligence analysis was strengthened in February 1936 when the committee acquired a permanent secretariat, whose principal task was the preparation of monthly assessments of local conditions and popular mood across the Maghreb and Levant.[32]

The further frustration of reform, 1936–39

At much the same time as the Haut Comité Méditerranéen was taking on a new role as a quasi-intelligence agency, colonial reform acquired unprecedented importance within inter-war French politics. In 1936–37 Léon Blum's first Popular Front administration put forward an array of proposals, ranging from limited constitutional concessions in French North Africa to the correction of the worst abuses in French colonial rule across French West Africa, Madagascar and Indo-China. Child labour was to be prohibited, minimum wage regulations for colonial workers were to be either introduced or, for the first time, properly enforced and a colonial *code du travail* was to be instituted.[33] In AOF, where legislation dating from 1925 covering minimum wage levels had never before been upheld, the Governor-general, Jules-Marcel de Coppet, recognised that, in Dakar at least, labour unrest had become more sophisticated. Across sub-Saharan French Africa the dominant feature of the labour market was the *prestation* system of forced labour utilised by colonial administrations to provide African workers for European planters and public works projects.[34] Whereas, hitherto, absconding had been the favoured means to avoid forced labour or unbearable working conditions, from 1936 recourse to strike action revealed that black workers were fast developing a common appreciation of their basic rights and their collective strength.[35] But though de Coppet implemented measures to regulate industrial disputes, and to limit forced labour in conformity with the terms of the Geneva convention, a far more sustained programme of colonial reform and investment was required if the nature of French colonial rule in West Africa was to be fundamentally altered. In Madagascar similar importance was attached to the abolition of forced labour for public works projects and to reform of *indigénat* legislation covering land tenure. But here, too, nationalists from within the Merina community of Madagascar's central plateaus remained unconvinced of French willingness to match promises with deeds.[36] This scepticism was justifiable. Referring to the more humanistic, although still assimilationist, colonial ideals of the French Socialist Party, Blum's Minister of Colonies, Marius Moutet, informed the French Chamber of Deputies on 15 December 1936, 'For us [Socialists], colonisation refers to the development of colonial populations through improvements in their material, social, economic, intellectual and cultural life.'[37] In practice, constrained by domestic opposition and a lack of substantial funding, the rhetorical flourishes of Popular Front Ministers were not matched by any comprehensive programme of long-term reform in black Africa.

The extension of the earlier Jonnart reforms for Algeria, refashioned by Minister of State Maurice Viollette, in December 1936, aroused intense right-wing opposition in France. Viollette could not have been surprised. As a Senator, in 1931 he sponsored the creation of an Algerian Consultative Committee made up of Muslim representatives from the three departments of Algeria. The committee was supposed to advise the Ministry of the Interior regarding those reforms of most interest to the local Muslim population. In 1935 Viollette felt compelled to disown his creation. The committee had become a sham, its membership strictly controlled by the Algiers government. But Viollette's reformist ideas remained essentially conservative. As in 1931, his plans for Algeria under the Popular Front rested upon the cultivation of a pro-French indigenous elite, intended to become the cornerstone of support for French colonial rule.[38]

To be fair, this approach was not as anachronistic as it perhaps now appears. In 1936 the leading representative of *évolué* opinion in Algeria, Ferhat Abbas, professed his admiration for French republican ideals, famously stating, 'La France, c'est moi.' Later in the same year, a more or less loyalist Muslim Congress gathered together a number of Maghreb organisations. Faithful to Ferhat Abbas, the congress proclaimed 'its attachment pure and simple to France'. The most notable absentee from the Muslim Congress was Ahmed Messali Hadj's Etoile Nord-Africaine (ENA), a party founded in 1926 by North Africans then resident in France. Though it occasionally professed pan-Arab and communist ideas, the ENA was dominated by an inner core of Algerians, mostly from the mountainous interior of the Grand Kabylie. When the Blum government dissolved the ENA in January 1937, it resurfaced in April as the Parti Populaire Algérien (PPA). The PPA was soon established as the main voice of secular nationalism in Algeria, though the party was still based in France, with its head office at Nanterre.[39] The point to note here is that the French government refused to consider the PPA the true voice of Muslim Algeria.

The wish to develop co-operation with a loyal Muslim elite also informed the schemes of Viollette's Popular Front colleague, the Foreign Ministry Under-secretary, Pierre Viénot. He, too, put forward a series of limited reforms based upon extended autonomy in Tunisia and Morocco. Viénot was capably assisted in this by the new secretariat of the Haut Comité Méditerranéen.[40] Viénot was also charged with the negotiation of independence treaties for the Levant mandates of Syria and Lebanon. Critically, both of the resultant treaties were to come into effect only after a three-year probationary period. As with the Blum-Viollette project, so with Viénot's plans. The measures fell foul of French Senate opposition and settler protest, and were soon undermined by the financial crisis that engulfed the Popular Front coalition.[41]

Ironically, the Popular Front government eventually agreed to severe colonial repression in Indo-China, Morocco, Algeria and Tunisia – the very territories upon which reform plans were concentrated. During February and March 1937 the Moroccan Action Committee (Comité d'Action Marocaine) and the Indo-Chinese Congress (Congrès Indochinois) were dissolved. Six months later, Messali Hadj was arrested. In Tunisia, where Arab protest and strike action culminated in the shooting dead of nineteen demonstrators at Metlaoui on 4 March 1937, the main nationalist party, Habib Bourguiba's New Constitution Party (Néo-Destour) was eventually outlawed by Edouard Daladier's new government in April 1938.[42] Having raised expectations of reform within the empire, the Popular Front was hoist with the petard of parliamentary obstructionism. To make matters worse, there was precious little enthusiasm for colonial reform within the French Radical Party, which by mid-1937 had supplanted the Socialists as the dominant partner within the governing coalition. In November 1938, the PPA did not dare put forward candidates for municipal elections in Algeria, held under the auspices of Daladier's Radical-led administration. When war broke out in 1939, most of the measures enacted to quell colonial dissent in 1937–38 were still in force. Again the Algerian case is instructive. By October 1939 the PPA had been dissolved by decree, its newspaper, *El Ouma*, was banned in France and twenty-seven of its leaders, including Messali Hadj, were re-arrested. It is sad to reflect that the extension of authoritarian powers across various colonies in the early months of the war often built upon measures already enacted in the preceding Popular Front period of 1936–38.

For all its failure, the Popular Front's original 1936 plans marked a rare official attempt to place colonial reform near the heart of a governmental programme. With hindsight, it seems apparent that little was fundamentally changed across the French empire. Election-rigging and administrative collusion with settler interest groups remained commonplace. Both survived the war to reach their apogée in the selective application of the 1947 Statute for Algeria, with disastrous long-term consequences for the legitimacy of French rule in North Africa. As Pierre Nora noted in the last days of the Algerian war, 'the history of Algeria cannot be written according to its laws: its history is the manner in which the French of Algeria have got round them.'[43]

Had they succeeded, the Popular Front's proposed electoral reforms would have done little to temper settler dominance in colonial elections. Even with the limited extension of Algerian representation in the French Chamber of Deputies in March 1936, the twenty Deputies who sat in the Chamber – ten from Algeria, the others from Cochin China, Senegal, Réunion and the French West Indies – were largely ineffective in focusing French parliamentary attention upon imperial concerns.[44] Some of the colonies involved elected Senators and Deputies, others only the latter. Furthermore, whereas in Senegal *indigènes* could vote, in Algeria they could not. All too often, inter-war colonial elections became corrupt parodies of their French equivalents. Most of the empire, including the North African protectorates, the mandated Territories, most of the Indo-Chinese Federation and all of francophone black Africa beyond Senegal, played no part in these proceedings. These territories had yet to qualify for any metropolitan representation at all. Since the 1870s numerous French politicians had warned that if the entire empire were to be accorded even limited voting rights, colonial Deputies might swamp the French Assembly.[45] If these inconsistencies may be explained by reference to the differing historical paths of French colonisation, it is none the less difficult to see much coherence within the Third Republic's system of overseas representation in Parliament. As it stood, French colonial representation in the National Assembly served as a sop to the republican traditions of the French left, but did little to diminish the opposition to substantial colonial reform prevalent within the two main parties of the French right, the Alliance Démocratique and the Fédération Républicaine.

Although Marius Moutet was an energetic and effective publicist, and although the advent of the Front Populaire produced great anticipation among North African nationalists in particular, within France itself the failure of colonial reform did not provoke national debate. The Socialist left and French anarchist and Trotskyist groups made only marginal progress in achieving a popular identification of the Popular Front's anti-fascism with a generic anti-colonialism.[46] The Paris press all but ignored the widening repression in Indo-China and North Africa during 1937–38. According to Charles-Robert Ageron, the increasing militancy among colonial nationalists in both areas was largely unknown to the wider public in France.[47] This was to store up dangers for the future. Frustrated by the general stagnation of colonial reform, by 1937 most of the key post-war nationalist parties of French North Africa, Syria and Indo-China had already taken shape. Though seemingly at opposite ends of the political spectrum, in Algeria, the Ulemas associations of Muslim clerics and Messali Hadj's communist-inspired PPA were both proponents of an explicitly anti-French Algerian national identity by the late 1930s. Originally moderate in tone, in Tunisia, Bourguiba's Néo-Destour maintained a distinctive vision of Tunisia's national interest. But it was among the Vietnamese in Tonkin in northern Indo-China that the most impressive nationalist organisations took root in the shape of the Vietnam National Party (VNQDD) and, from 1930 onwards, the Indo-Chinese Communist Party. Both were nourished by a futile cycle of French censorship and repression imposed both before and after the 1930 Yen Bay mutiny, itself an act of sedition organised by the VNQDD.[48]

Popular imperialism and colonial development

After 1918, as before it, the call to empire failed to stir the French public as it did the British patriot. During the 1920s the old Parti Colonial deputies and lobbyists – reorganised in February 1921 into the Maritime and Colonial League (Ligue Maritime et Coloniale) – met little success in their avowed intention to educate the French public into the benefits of empire. Reduced to crass exaggeration of both its membership strength and of the circulation of its monthly journal, *Mer et Colonies*, the League was consistently frustrated in its efforts to persuade the Paris press to record events within French colonies. The 1930s heralded wider press coverage, notably in the weekly colonial supplement published by *Le Temps*, and the decade closed with a series of propagandist films produced in 1938–39 to celebrate the vitality of the empire. In the two years before the war, French film-makers produced seventeen films with a colonial theme. With rousing titles, such as *Légions d'honneur*, *Face au destin* and *Trois de Saint-Cyr*, most of these glorified imperial pioneers, the bravery of military conquest and the benefits of the French civilising mission. But it remains at best doubtful that empire had seized the popular imagination in France.[49] The magnificent Colonial Exhibition staged across the sweeping parkland of Vincennes in eastern Paris in 1931 was certainly a commercial success. But as an instrument of French colonial propaganda it proved less impressive. The 33 million tickets sold revealed a tremendous French appetite for the exoticism that the exhibition promoted rather than mass conversion to popular imperialism.[50] The 1931 exhibition, and a later French colonial showcase at the 1937 World Fair in Paris, were certainly designed to project an image of French imperial greatness – *la France des cinq continents*. Indeed, at the 1931 celebrations, Minister of Colonies Paul Reynaud affirmed that empire underpinned the French claim to world power.[51] Still, a genuine comparison with the British imperial outlook is hard to make. The French public were less conditioned to believe that the glory of France rested upon keeping the empire intact.

In February 1931, an exasperated former Prime Minister, André Tardieu, implored his electors to see beyond local and national concerns and develop a properly imperialist vision commensurate with the tremendous physical extent of the French empire. But with a mighty eastern neighbour only temporarily laid low after 1918, the French public could hardly be expected to subordinate European concerns to a newly discovered pride in imperial achievement. Not surprisingly, then, it is in the context of Franco-German relations that one finds some of the most ambitious projects for colonial development – the *mise en valeur* of black Africa in particular. Inspired by ideas of European integration as the optimum basis for a lasting Franco-German peace, politicians and colonialists as diverse as the Radical Party elders, Albert Sarraut and Joseph Caillaux, and enthusiasts for fascist planning such as Marcel Déat and Georges Valois, all saw colonial co-operation with Germany as fundamental to European prosperity and detente. In practice, their ideas of a *Eurafrique* economic federation petered out soon after Hitler came to power in 1933.[52] But it perhaps bears emphasis that many of the inter-war schemes for colonial development postulated closer ties between French colonies and a European economic community of some sort, and that the leading protagonists of such ideas were adamant that Germany could not be excluded from this process. During the Second World War, shades of *Eurafrique* were to be found in René Pleven's submissions to the Brazzaville conference in 1944 and, later, in the terms of the Treaty of Rome in 1957.[53]

Backed by the authority of his impressive career as both colonial administrator and Minister of Colonies, Albert Sarraut gave the clearest expression to the hopes of those inter-war imperialists who foresaw that France and its colonies might achieve economic self-sufficiency if only colonial development were accorded the priority it deserved in governmental planning. Sarraut published two influential books advocating comprehensive schemes for colonial development: *La Mise en valeur des colonies* (1923) and *Grandeur et servitude coloniale* (1931).[54] But he was driven to campaign in print for a systematic *mise en valeur* of the empire because the colonial development plans he put before Parliament while Minister of Colonies in the early 1920s had always been rejected, primarily on grounds of cost.[55] The other major excuse for the lack of investment in remote colonies was the depth of public ignorance about them. For the French Pacific territories and French Oceania – a series of island outposts which included Tahiti, the Windward and Wallis islands north-east of Fiji, in addition to several tiny islets such as Futuna – the physical isolation of these colonies always impeded any sustained effort to bring administrative cohesion or long-term investment to them. In the 1939 budget of Tahiti, for example, the native population were required to pay a twenty-five franc road tax though the island had no road system to speak of. In those Pacific territories, such as New Caledonia, with a large Melanesian population, French colonial administration remained unashamedly discriminatory, even preventing the free movement of resident Melanesians around the island.[56] Although a rising proportion of French public funds was channelled into infrastructural projects in sub-Saharan Africa in the fifteen years before the First World War, as the work of Jacques Marseille has indicated, the empire was integral only to certain sectors of the French economy in the inter-war period. Numerous French industries came to rely upon closed imperial markets. Outmoded production methods and the artificially high value of the franc before the devaluation of September 1936 left several companies desperate for empire custom as price competition within Europe intensified.[57]

During the inter-war period investment in black Africa and Indo-China increased fourfold, spurred by increasing interest among private investors in the four years after the establishment of the 'franc Poincaré' in 1926. In 1938 the empire accounted for 27 per cent of total French overseas trade. Once the war began, the Ministry of Colonies attempted to maintain effective price controls over primary export products within the empire, taking a base figure of goods prices in August 1939 as the norm. Mandel was prepared to lobby the Ministry of Finance in an effort to persuade the French Treasury to intervene on an *ad hoc* basis in order to preserve price stability.[58] The Minister further insisted that this model of a closed imperial trading bloc could easily be extended to cover the French and British empires in unison. Together, British and French Africa could then control world markets in vegetable oils, hardwoods and cocoa.[59] By 1940 some 45 per cent of

French overseas investment went to empire projects. These figures, revealed in an official inquiry into the economic importance of the empire conducted by the Vichy authorities in 1943, confirmed that empire trade had become the 'lifebuoy' of uncompetitive French industry.[60]

But, these points notwithstanding, the inter-war years were cloven in two by the impact of depression. From 1932, Paris governments found themselves with far less money to spend on colonial development. It was increasingly difficult for the French Treasury to act as ultimate guarantor of monetary stability within individual colonies, particularly as inflationary pressure had tended to increase over the course of the 1920s. In Morocco, for example, where the French Treasury was theoretically bound to maintain the solvency of the cherifan administration, there was only one French state loan issue during the 1930s to compare with four between 1914 to 1928. Algeria's economy stagnated in the early 1930s under the weight of crippling budgetary deficits which were eliminated only in 1937.[61] Another lasting effect of the depression was to increase the economic dependence of individual colonies upon the home market in France. North African wine and minerals, Indo-Chinese rice, West African cocoa, Equatorial African timber and Madagascan graphite – all were staple export commodities whose contribution to colonial economies was essentially determined by France's import requirements.[62] By the late 1930s, the empire's continuing economic importance was more a reflection of lost French markets elsewhere than of the inherent vitality of imperial trade. As Jacques Marseille concludes, 'The so-called *mise en valeur* remained a dead letter. The [bilateral] trade economy, the low level of industrialisation, and the limited scope of private investment all led to the perpetuation and to the sclerosis of colonial economic structures.'[63]

Imperial defence on the eve of war

It seems, then, that French perceptions of the economic benefits of empire were out of step with the more disappointing reality. A final sideways glance at empire defence reveals a similar picture. Most French imperial defence expenditure was devoted to French North Africa, owing to its large standing Armée d'Afrique garrison, an expansion of regional air defence and the rising maintenance costs of crucial naval bases from Casablanca to Bizerta. By July 1934 the construction of additional frontier defences and port facilities within French North Africa was included within the metropolitan defence budget disbursed among the three service Ministries. Other colonies received no such funding.[64] Even so, from 1936, French North Africa faced possible invasion or bombardment. The French General Staff recognised that war might well begin around the margins of the western Mediterranean. Following Mussolini's victory in the Abyssinian war, Franco-Italian relations deteriorated as the Rome government tied itself to Germany and staked a claim to an expanded North African empire of its own. General Francisco Franco's rebellion in Spain worsened the French strategic position in western Europe, the Mediterranean and on the disputed Franco-Spanish frontier in Morocco. Any Franco-Italian naval contest in the Mediterranean basin was sure to turn upon the defence of maritime communications between North Africa and the fleet bases and military assembly points at Toulon and Marseilles. In March 1937, the French Chief of Naval Staff, and future Vichy Deputy Premier, Admiral Jean-François Darlan, made this plain:

> The conquest of Ethiopia, the reinforcement of [Italian] military organisation in Libya, [Italian] political disruption in the Levant, in Tunisia and across North Africa, and Italian penetration in the Balearic islands and nationalist Spain ... are variously aspects of a policy intended to form a barrage between France on the one hand, its colonies and its sources of overseas supply on the other.[65]

Though Darlan's warning made good sense, the French defence budget was so tightly stretched by the requirements of metropolitan defence that the funding necessary to guarantee French imperial security was never forthcoming. Fearing the disruption of Mediterranean shipping and unable to send meaningful reinforcements to the Maghreb, successive governments sought increases in the production of strategic raw materials within the North African territories, hoping to make the region self-sufficient in the opening phase of a European war.[66]

Outside the Mediterranean, persistent funding crises inevitably dictated the shape of French imperial defence planning in sub-Saharan Africa, French Indo-China and France's island possessions. Throughout 1935, the Minister of Colonies, Louis Rollin, lobbied hard for parliamentary approval of a special colonial defence credit. This was eventually set at 281 million francs to be spent over nine years.[67] The expenditure was designed to improve the defensive infrastructure within individual colonies. It was largely assigned to improvements in port defences, the construction of new airfields and the expansion of munition reserves. The intention was to bring strategic coherence to the allocation of defence resources to individual colonies. In practice, as tension in Europe increased, it became harder to spare existing equipment or troops for colonial defence projects.[68] In Indo-China, for example, in early 1937 the Ministry of Colonies had been considering a reduction in the military service term for locally raised forces from three to two years. This would have released trained personnel to work on capital projects within the Indo-China Federation. Unfortunately, the outbreak of the Sino-Japanese war in July forced a complete reversal of this scheme. The three-year service term remained and urgent instructions were issued for the reorganisation of the *garde indigène* into regular army-style companies trained for the tasks of frontier defence.[69] In 1938, Mandel begun urgent, and ultimately fruitless, efforts to strengthen Indo-China's defences through the disbursement of a 400 million franc defence loan. This was one of several belated initiatives to raise additional short-term funding for urgent defensive works in Indo-China and AOF.[70]

Once the war in Europe broke out in 1939, General Jules-Antoine Bührer, head of the military staff devoted to colonial defence – the Etat-Major Général des Colonies – devoted most attention to the preparation of transports, barracks and stores for the colonial forces scheduled to be moved to metropolitan France.[71] To a degree, this was all that Bührer could do. Theoretically in charge of defensive preparations within individual territories, in fact Bührer was at the mercy of those Ministries and committees within Paris which took a direct interest in colonial administration. As Bührer informed the Chief of the General Staff, General Maurice Gamelin,

> I have insisted *more than once* upon the fact that the Minister of Colonies, [is] responsible for the internal security of those territories placed under his administration, [is] responsible for these territories' preparations against external threats, and [is] charged with the implementation of the instructions of the Conseil Supérieur de la Défense Nationale regarding offensive operations to be mounted by those forces stationed within the colonies against certain territories on France's imperial frontiers. But the Minister does not possess any real means to perform this, since he is obliged in practice to seek the prior approval of the service Ministries. [They] are likely to satisfy his demands only after the requirements of the Metropole and French North Africa have been met.[72]

Despite Bührer's complaints, in September 1939 it was relatively easy to contemplate reductions in the Armée d'Afrique garrison across French Africa largely because Italy remained neutral.[73] There was little danger of any German venture into Africa over the winter of 1939–40. By contrast, Japan's gradual push into southern China and the Gulf of Tonkin between September 1938 and March 1939 left French Indo-China perilously exposed.[74] Throughout the late 1930s the French General Staff recognised that it could not spare the troops or ships necessary to create a viable deterrent force in French Indo-China. Still, the likelihood of a Japanese attack became truly menacing only following the French defeat in June 1940.

Taking the empire as a whole, during the early stages of the phoney war over the autumn and winter of 1939, Paul Reynaud's government found little to distract it from the German threat in Europe. The three Maghreb territories were certainly judged a vital interest, with the three Algerian departments representing the constitutional embodiment of 'overseas France'. But, despite their vocal settler communities, the North African territories lacked the political pulling power of Britain's white Dominions. Nor did the demography of French Africa compare with the vast population of British India. There was nothing of strategic value in Syria or Lebanon which held the attention like the Suez Canal. Furthermore, the empire lacked a defensible chain of maritime or airborne imperial communications which might have facilitated the task of protecting far-flung black African and Asian colonies.

But this last point may perhaps serve to illustrate the problems encountered in developing and defending France's inter-war empire. For the French had long appreciated the civil and military importance of improved inter-colonial communications. French generals from Charles Mangin to Maurice Gamelin were proponents of a tran-Saharan rail link which, quite apart from its economic benefits, would speed the overland transport of troops from Niger to Algeria. Until a railway line was in place, colonial troops faced a lorry journey which took an average of twelve days to complete.[75] Over the winter of 1933–34 the Ministry of Colonies and the newly autonomous Air Ministry argued over the costs arising from the creation of a Bureau Africain within the Air Ministry. This office was intended to promote civil aviation within French Africa, based upon the development of air routes between France and the Congo and Algeria and Oubangui-Chari. In April 1934 decree legislation was passed in an effort to codify the colonial organisation of the French air force – the Armée de l'Air.[76] As matters stood in the mid-1930s, however, French Africa remained a place for pioneer aviators. In September 1934 a National Air Day was even held across AOF and AEF, sponsored by regional branches of the French Colonial Aero Club. The popularity of this perhaps masked the extent to which French colonies still lacked a modern communications infrastructure. In March 1935, for example, the French air force commander in AEF requested authorisation to begin reconnaissance of suitable sites for airfields in Cameroon. In practice, his suggestion had to await the completion of a suitable air base to house the survey aircraft due to reconnoitre AEF as a whole.[77]

Aerial communications were a little more advanced in Indo-China. Soon after his appointment as Governor in 1917, Albert Sarraut took delivery of six Farman biplanes – the beginnings of the French military Service d'Aviation in Indo-China. By 1918 bases had been established in Tonkin and Cochin China and squadrons of four to eight aircraft were assigned to frontier surveillance tasks. In the late 1920s there was strong competition within the French aircraft industry, led by the airframe manufacturer Jacques Bréguet, to develop an air service route along the coast of Annam between Vinh and Nha Trang.[78] This provided the network of aerial communications for the six ageing Armée de l'Air squadrons in place by the time war broke out in 1939. Indo-China was also the location of perhaps the largest single feat of French military transport engineers – the Trans-Indochinese railway, which ran from Saigon to Hanoi and beyond.[79] But as it hugged the coast between the two cities, the railway was always dangerously exposed to any invader who arrived by sea.

The stuttering development of communications routes illustrates the weakness at the heart of French colonial development and imperial defence planning. For all the efforts to bring some sort of economic and strategic coherence to the empire, with France's limited financial, maritime and military resources it was impossible to generate wider imperial unity. The federations in French Africa and East Asia were a lesser alternative. Neither economically, politically nor strategically was there a unified empire. As the conference of French colonial Governors had admitted in November 1936, their effort to create an integrated imperial economy was still in its infancy. In November 1938, the Radical Party leader and French Premier, Edouard Daladier, had told his party congress in Marseilles to look upon France in imperial terms – metropole and empire together comprising a vast 'security zone' whose inviolability was sacrosanct. But on the eve of war the General Staff had yet to resolve upon a single, overarching empire defence system.[80] Taken as a whole, by 1939 the French empire was indefensible. After the fall of France, the situation was far worse. In July 1940 François Charles-Roux, Secretary-general in the Vichy Foreign Ministry, listed all those states with actual or potential claims upon French colonial territory. It made depressing reading, but is worth dwelling on here as a guide to the external threats of the war years. Beginning with Italy's expansionist ambitions in Tunisia, French Somaliland and Chad, and Mussolini's likely demand for special privileges in the French Levant, Charles-Roux moved on to Spanish demands for frontier revision in northern Morocco and a possible claim upon Oranie in western Algeria.[81] When Hitler judged it opportune, Germany was expected to reiterate calls for the restitution of its former colonies – Cameroon and Togoland. The German high command might also demand the use of ports and airfields in North and

West Africa if the need arose. By July 1940 Japan's penetration of Indo-China had already begun. In the western hemisphere, the United States had discouraged Brazil and Venezuela from demanding protecting powers over French Guiana. But Washington's commitment to the Monroe Doctrine of regional non-interference might yet be twisted into a justification for an American take-over in the French West Indies. With British encouragement, Turkey might intervene in Syria if that were the sole means to keep Axis forces out of the Middle East. Meanwhile, across the French empire as a whole, the British were bound to seek Allies wherever they could be found.[82] A new era of precarious French imperial survival had clearly started.

Notes

1 Marc Michel, 'Colonisation et défense nationale: le général Mangin et la Force Noire', *Guerres Mondiales et Conflits Contemporains*, 145 (1987), 27–44.

2 Michel, 'Colonisation et défense nationale'; Myron J. Echenberg, 'Paying the blood tax: military conscription in French West Africa, 1914–1929', *Revue Canadienne des Etudes Africaines*, 10: 2 (1975), 171–92.

3 ANCOM, Papiers Albert Sarraut, Carton 9/Dossier 'Garde Indigène', President of Garde Indigène Friendly Association to Senator Humbert, 18 May 1913.

4 Marc Michel, *L'Appel à l'Afrique. Contributions et réactions à l'effort de guerre en AOF (1914–1919)* (Paris, Publications de la Sorbonne, 1982), pp. 43–66, 100–16, 254–60; Charles John Balesi, *From Adversaries to Comrades in Arms. West Africans and the French Military, 1885–1918* (Waltham, Mass., Crossroads Press, 1979), pp. 57–78. William B. Cohen offers the 818,000 figure and suggests that total colonial losses amounted to nearly 70,000, see his *Rulers of Empire: the French Colonial Service in Africa* (Stanford, Cal., Stanford University Press, 1971), p. 109. This has been supported in a recent collection: Claude Carlier and Guy Pedroncini (eds), *Les Troupes Coloniales et la Grande Guerre* (Paris, Economica, 1997), p. 16.

5 A. I. Asiwaju, 'Migrations as revolt: the example of the Ivory Coast and the Upper Volta before 1945', *Journal of African History*, 17: 4 (1976), 577–94. Asiwaju estimates that over 12,000 crossed into the Gold Coast in 1916–17, and up to 80,000 did so in the late 1920s and early 1930s.

6 ANCOM, Affaires politiques, Carton 2299/D3, Centre des Hautes Etudes d'Administration Musulmane, rapport par Capitaine Fondacci, 'Les troupes noires', 18 June 1946; Fonds Alger, Série S, S1/D8, Anciens Combattants, 1940–1955.

7 Marc Michel, 'La puissance par l'empire: note sur la perception du facteur impérial dans l'élaboration de la défense nationale (1936–1938)', *Revue Française d'Histoire d'Outre-Mer*, 69 (1982), 37.

8 ANCOM, Papiers Georges Mandel, Carton 18/PA1/Dossier 4, Mandel article, 'La coopération franco-britannique dans les colonies', 22 February 1940.

9 Mahfoud Kaddache, 'L'opinion politique musulmane en Algérie et l'administration française (1939–1942)', *Revue d'Histoire de la Deuxième Guerre Mondiale*, 114 (1979), 96–7.

10 AN, F[60]/187/DA1, no. 608/SG, no. 51094, Governor-general Le Beau to Ministry of Interior, 28 May 1940; Conseil Supérieur de l'Algérie, extraordinary session, 23 November 1939.

11 SHAT, Carton 1P33/D2, EMA, 'Etude sur l'importance militaire des colonies', n.d. February 1941.

12 ANCOM, Aff. pol., C2116/D2, section Afrique, deuxième bureau, 'Note sur le statut de l'Algérie', n.d., May 1947.

13 The son of a General, Catroux spent three years as *aide de camp* to Governor Beau in Indo-China between 1903 and 1905 before returning to work under Lyautey in Morocco before the First World War. He served with the Tirailleurs Algériens on the western front in 1914–16 and was wounded and then taken prisoner during the battle of the Somme, see Henri Lerner, *Catroux* (Paris, Albin Michel, 1990), pp. 49–70.
14 Maréchal Alphonse Juin, *Mémoires*, I (Paris, Fayard, 1959); Matthieu Séguéla, *Pétain-Franco. Les Secrets d'une alliance* (Paris, Albin Michel, 1992), pp. 15–18.
15 Churchill Archive Centre, General Edward Spears papers, file SPRS/1/134/1, aide-mémoire on de Gaulle, n.d., 1940; Jean Lacouture, *De Gaulle. I The Rebel* (London, Collins, 1990), pp. 75–84.
16 St Antony's College, Nevill Barbour papers, Box IV/1, Group Sénatorial – défense des intérêts français à l'étranger, 'Rapport sur la Syrie et la Palestine', n.d., 1915.
17 See Christopher Harrison's discussion of the 'scholar-administrators', Marie-François Clozel, Maurice Delafosse and Paul Marty, in his *France and Islam in West Africa*, pp. 97–107.
18 Henri Brunschwig, 'De l'assimilation à la décolonisation', in Charles-Robert Ageron (ed.), *Les Chemins de la décolonisation de l'empire française, 1936–1956* (Paris, Editions du CNRS, 1986), pp. 49–51; Denise Bouche, 'Dakar pendant la deuxième guerre mondiale: problèmes de surpeuplement', *Revue Française d'Histoire d'Outre-Mer*, 65 (1978), 426.
19 Rhodes House Library, MSS Afr. s. 1252, Paul Singer report on land tenure in Algiers and Tunis, 1919, 20 May 1919.
20 Jacques Thobie *et al.*, *Histoire de la France coloniale, 1914–1990* (Paris, Armand Colin, 1990), p. 84.
21 ANCOM, Aff. pol., C920/D1, Haut Comité Méditerranéen, rapport no. 5, 'Le régime administratif en AFN', n.d. February 1937.
22 ANCOM, Aff. pol., C920/D1, Haut Comité Méditerranéen rapport, 'Le Haut Comité Méditerranéen et les organismes d'information musulmane', 15 February 1937; for the Lyautey legend see Thobie *et al.*, *Histoire de la France coloniale*, pp. 164–7.
23 ANCOM, Aff. pol., C2661/D4, premier bureau, 'Note sur l'exercice de mandat en Syrie', n.d., September 1922.
24 Jacques-W. Binoche-Guedra, 'La répresentation parlementaire coloniale (1871–1940)', *Revue Historique*, 280 (1988), 524–9.
25 AN, F^{60}/202, Haut Comité Méditerranéen, rapport no. 4, 'Les Assemblées élus en AFN', n.d., March 1937; ANCOM, Aff. pol., C920/D1, Haut Comité Méditerranéen, rapport no. 5, 'Le régime administratif en AFN', n.d., February 1937.
26 ANCOM, Papiers Georges Mandel, carton 18/PA1, dossier 4, Mandel article, 'La coopération franco-britannique dans les colonies', 22 February 1940.
27 Both cited in Cohen, *Rulers of Empire*, pp. 108 and 127.
28 ANCOM, Aff. pol., C2538D1, Politique coloniale étrangère, no. 315, André Maginot circular to governors-general, 20 July 1929.
29 Charles-Robert Ageron, *France coloniale ou parti colonial?* (Paris, Presses Universitaires de France, 1978), p. 261; Cohen, *Rulers of Empire*, pp. 143–5.
30 ANCOM, Aff. pol., C920/D1, Haut Comité Méditerranéen, rapport no. 1, 15 February 1937.
31 *Ibid.*
32 *Ibid.*
33 William B. Cohen, 'The colonial policy of the Popular Front', *French Historical Studies*, 7: 3 (1972), 368–93.
34 Cooper, *Decolonization and African Society*, p. 36.
35 Ibrahim Thioub, 'Economie coloniale et rénumération de la force de travail: le salaire de Manoeuvre à Dakar de 1930 à 1954', *Revue Française d'Histoire d'Outre-Mer*, 81 (1994), 437.
36 Philip M. Allen, *Madagascar. Conflicts of Authority in the Great Island* (Oxford, Westview Press, 1995), pp. 41–3.

37 Cited in Jean-Pierre Biondi, *Les Anticolonialistes (1881–1962)* (Paris, Laffont, 1992), p. 210.
38 Biondi, *Les Anticolonialistes*, pp. 210–15.
39 ANCOM, Aff. pol., C904/D6, bulletin de renseignements, no. 2, 'Le nationalisme algérien', 23 February 1946.
40 William A. Hoisington junior, 'France and Islam: the Haut Comité Méditerranéen and French North Africa', in George Joffé (ed.), *North Africa. Nation, State and Region* (London, Macmillan, 1993), pp. 79–81; ANCOM, Aff. pol., C 920/D1, Haut Comité Méditerranéen, rapport 1, 15 February 1937.
41 Martin Evans, 'Algeria and the liberation: hope and betrayal' in H. R. Kedward and Nancy Wood (eds), *The Liberation of France. Image and Event* (Oxford, Berg, 1995), pp. 257–9.
42 Biondi, *Les Anticolonialistes*, pp. 216–17; Benjamin Stora, *Nationalistes algériens et révolutionnaires français au temps du Front Populaire* (Paris, Editions l'Harmattan, 1987), pp. 70–6, 89–93.
43 Pierre Nora, *Les Français d'Algérie* (Paris, Julliard, 1961), p. 98, quoted in David Prochaska, *Making Algeria French. Colonialism in Bône, 1870–1920* (Cambridge, Cambridge University Press, 1990), p. 5.
44 There were 612 Deputies overall in 1936. There were 307 Senators, seven of whom represented colonial seats.
45 Binoche-Guedra, 'La répresentation parlementaire coloniale', 524–30.
46 Benjamin Stora, 'La gauche socialiste révolutionnaire, et la question du Maghreb au moment du Front Populaire (1935–1938)', *Revue Française d'Histoire d'Outre-Mer*, 70 (1983), 68–73.
47 Charles-Robert Ageron, 'La perception de la puissance française en 1938–1939: le mythe impérial', in René Girault and Robert Frank (eds), *La Puissance en Europe, 1938–1940* (Paris, Sorbonne, 1984), p. 234.
48 Raymond F. Betts, *France and Decolonisation, 1900–1960* (London, Macmillan, 1991), pp. 35–46; regarding early Vietnamese nationalism in general see David G. Marr, *Vietnamese Anticolonialism, 1885–1925* (Berkeley, University of California Press, 1971); William J. Duiker, *The Rise of Nationalism in Vietnam, 1900–1941* (Ithaca, N.Y., 1976); Ralph B. Smith, 'The development of opposition to French rule in southern Vietnam, 1880–1940', Past & Present, 54 (1972), 94–129.
49 Ageron discusses these ideas in *France coloniale ou parti colonial?*, pp. 250–67; for colonial films, see: Rémy Pithon, 'Opinions publiques et représentations culturelles face aux problèmes de la puissance. Le temoignage du cinéma français (1938–1939)', *Relations Internationales*, 33 (1983), 94–7.
50 Panivong Norindr, 'Representing Indochina: the French colonial fantasmatic and the Exposition Coloniale de Paris', *French Cultural Studies*, 6 (1995), 42–7; John Chipman, *French Power in Africa* (Oxford, Blackwell, 1989), pp. 68–70.
51 Martin Shipway, 'The Brazzaville Conference, 1944. Colonial and imperial planning in a wartime setting', M.Phil. thesis, Oxford, 1986, p. 8.
52 Charles-Robert Ageron, 'L'idée d'Eurafrique et le débat colonial franco-allemand de l'entre-deux-guerres', *Revue d'Histoire Moderne et Contemporaine*, 22 (1975), 455–65.
53 Chipman, *French Power in Africa*, pp. 82–3; ANCOM, Papiers Robert Delavignette, carton 3, Affaires politiques, 'Rapport de la Sous-commission de l'Intégration Métropole-Outre-mer', n.d., 1953.
54 Sarraut had been Governor of French Indo-China before the First World War and served as Minister of Colonies in 1920–24 and 1932–33.
55 Shipway, 'The Brazzaville Conference', 1944, pp. 8–13; John Kent, *The Internationalization of Colonialism. Britain, France and Black Africa, 1939–1956* (Oxford, Clarendon Press, 1992), pp. 6–8.
56 MAE, Guerre 1939–45, Fonds CNF Londres, vol. 86, 'Etablissements français d'Océanie', 23 October 1942; Ismet Kurtovitch, 'New Caledonia: the consequences of the Second World War' in Robert Aldrich and Isabelle Merle (eds), *France Abroad. Indochina, New Caledonia, Wallis and Futuna, Mayotte* (Sydney, Department of

Economic History Occasional Publications, University of Sydney, 1996), p. 34.

57 Jacques Marseille, 'Les relations commerciales entre la France et son empire colonial de 1880 à 1913', *Revue d'Histoire Moderne et Contemporaine*, 31: 2 (1984), 291–4, 305–7.

58 ANCOM, Papiers Georges Mandel, carton 18/PA1/D4, I/6, aide mémoire, 'Politique des prix en général', 15 March 1940.

59 ANCOM, Papiers Georges Mandel, carton 18/PA1/D4, Note pour le Ministre, 'Conférence franco-anglaise', n.d., 1940.

60 Jacques Marseille, 'L'investissement français dans l'empire colonial: l'enquête du gouvernement de Vichy (1943)', *Revue Historique*, 122 (1974), 409–32.

61 Jean-Claude Allain, 'Les emprunts d'état marocains avant 1939', in Ageron, *Chemins*, p. 133; AN, F60/187/DA2, Cabinet du Gouverneur Général, 'Situation économique et commericale de l'Algérie en 1938', n.d., 1939

62 Michel, 'La puissance par l'empire', 39.

63 Marseille, 'L'investissement français dans l'empire colonial', 432. Also cited in Kent, *The Internationalization of Colonialism*, p. 8.

64 SHAT, 2N246, no. 109/1, Louis Rollin to Pierre Laval, 22 January 1935.

65 SHM, Sous-Série 1BB2/Carton 32, Darlan correspondence, 20 March 1937, cited in Christine Levisse-Touzé, 'La préparation économique, industrielle et militaire de l'Afrique du Nord à la veille de la guerre', *Revue d'Histoire de la Deuxième Guerre Mondiale*, 142 (1986), 6.

66 Levisse-Touzé, 'La préparation économique', 1–6.

67 SHAT, 2N246/D2, Louis Rollin to Pierre Laval, 8 July 1935.

68 SHAT, 2N246, CCDC procès verbal, 8 June and 27 July 1937.

69 SHAT, 7N4194/D3, General Victor-Henri Schweisguth note, 22 July 1937; CCDC, 'Avis concernant les modifications à apporter à la constitution des forces auxiliaires des colonies', 29 July 1937.

70 John F. Laffey, 'French Far Eastern policy in the 1930s', Modern Asian Studies, 23: 1 (1989), 140; Bertrand Favreau, *Georges Mandel, ou la passion de la République, 1885–1944* (Paris, Fayard, 1996), pp. 331–2.

71 ANCOM, Aff. pol., C2616/D6, no. 116/EM Col., 'Note au sujet de l'organisation des dépôts de guerre et des camps de transition', 16 September 1939.

72 SHAT, 2N246/D2, no. 12/EM Col., General Bührer to Gamelin, 10 January 1939.

73 SHAT, 7N4194/D6, CCDC, séance, 11 February 1938; 2N24/Colonies, Billotte rapport, 'Mesures à prendre aux confins libyens de l'Afrique noire', 9 November 1937.

74 Laffey, 'French Far Eastern policy', 141–3.

75 Ageron, 'La perception de la puissance française', 232 and n. 20.

76 ANCOM, Aff. pol., C840/D3, Direction des services militaires, projet de loi, 21 November 1933; no. 103, Note pour la direction des services militaires, 5 April 1934.

77 ANCOM, Aff. pol., C840/D5, Ministry of Colonies to President of National Aeronautical Federation, 4 September 1934; C840/D2, no. 163, Repiquet, Commissaire, Cameroon, to Ministry of Colonies, 15 March 1935.

78 ANCOM, Aff. pol., C840/D3, service militaire, 'Note au sujet de l'aviation militaire aux colonies', 8 November 1918; C840/D2, note by Gaston Joseph, 10 April 1934.

79 SHAA, Archive Guy La Chambre, Carton Z14403/D1, EMAA-2 note, 8 February 1939; Betts, *France and Decolonisation*, pp. 11–12. Started in 1898, the railway was completed in 1936.

80 Ageron, 'La perception de la puissance française', 228–9.

81 For a concise assessment of Italy's claims see Romain Rainero, 'La politique fasciste à l'égard de l'Afrique du Nord: l'épée de l'Islam et la revendication sur la Tunisie', *Revue Française d'Histoire d'Outre-Mer*, 64: 237 (1977), 504–12.

82 MAE, Guerre 1939–45, Vichy, Série E, Vichy–Levant, vol. 1, Secrétaire Général, note, 24 July 1940.

PART II

Clashes of French empire in Africa 1940–41

CHAPTER TWO

Territories divided, June–December 1940

> the problem of rallying the territories of the empire was at the real heart of the drama which unfolded between the authorities of Vichy and those of Fighting France, until the day when all the empire territories had rallied to combat and could add their contribution to the deliverance of occupied metropolitan France from the enemy. [René Cassin[1]]

Colonial governments and the fall of France

The collapse of France's metropolitan forces during the second week of June 1940 was a calamity for the French empire. The scale of the Allied reverses and the speed with which German troops overran the Low Countries and northern France was a shocking testament to the power of *Blitzkrieg*. For those Frenchmen serving within the empire – and particularly for those Armée d'Afrique officers accustomed to service within France – the enormity and rapidity of the defeat were perhaps more devastating than the actual losses incurred. The intensity of the fighting in key sectors – at Sedan and elsewhere along the river Meuse – combined with reports that the greater part of the French metropolitan army was taken prisoner (at least 1,650,000 troops in all), were facts which spread only slowly to the colonies. In June, the overwhelming truth appeared to be that the old France was gone and that the Wehrmacht was in Paris. A large part of the French nation had apparently taken to the roads in flight. As if to symbolise the disarray, by 13 June Paul Reynaud's government had left by train for Tours, thence to Cangé and on to Bordeaux.

A central pillar of French imperial control was the acknowledged prowess of French soldiery. For all the efforts of colonial administrations to maintain a show of normality, that pillar had collapsed. The French supreme commander, General Maurice Gamelin, was made the scapegoat for the German breakthrough and was dismissed in disgrace at the height of the battle on 19 May. His replacement and erstwhile colleague, General Maxime Weygand, failed to hold his eponymously named defensive line along the Somme.[2] There was to be no repetition of the heroic battle of the Marne in September 1914. This time neither generals nor *poilus* could stop the onslaught. To Weygand and Pétain the idea of continuing the struggle from Africa seemed ridiculous. German might was irresistible and, as Weygand quipped, 'L'empire? Mais c'est l'enfantillage.'[3]

Though an elusive concept, there is no doubt that Gallic imperial 'prestige' had a strongly military flavour. It was a source of great pride to the French War Ministry staff that the three French North African territories, with a combined population of some 17 million by 1935, were capably policed during the 1930s by gendarmes, Compagnies Républicaines de Sécurité and an Armée d'Afrique averaging some 245,000 troops. The adjacent colonies of Spanish Morocco and Italian Libya required garrisons of 70,000 and over 100,000 to control populations of under a million. Britain's far smaller Middle Eastern garrisons were quietly overlooked. French defeat in Europe was bound to make the preservation of imperial control more difficult – especially in North Africa, where nationalist groups, though largely banned, were none the less entrenched. Weygand's army staff was alert to this danger. Insisting that throughout the Arab world only strength was respected, the General Staff's military intelligence bureau reminded Pétain's new government that, in French North Africa, popular insurrection tended to follow military setbacks. This was the case in the Algerian Grande Kabylie in 1871 and across Algeria's Aurès mountains and southern Tunisia in 1916–17. But whereas these revolts, and the Rif rebellion of 1925–26, were primarily rural and tribal, Muslim unrest was now likely to be party political, town-based and overtly nationalist. Harsh pacification measures in the preceding twenty years appeared to have stifled resistance within the French North African interior. The military intelligence planners concluded that the bustling coastal cities now posed the major problem in AFN: 'In effect, there are new infinitely dangerous ferments – nationalism, communism or antisemitism – which may produce serious urban agitation within a very short period. One may be sure that from now on riots are most likely to begin within the towns.'[4]

Paradoxically, it was not the fear of indigenous protest, but the exclusion of any transfer of France's overseas territory from the armistice terms with Germany and Italy that precipitated the rifts between those civil and military authorities anxious to fight on and those loyal to the new government of Marshal Philippe Pétain. The choices made by French colonial Governors between July and October

1940, rather than any popular upheaval or direct Axis intervention, split the empire asunder for the subsequent three years. Tunisia was a case in point. In Tunis, popular unease over the French defeat was fuelled by the intimidating shadow of neighbouring Italian Libya and the rapid arrival of Italian armistice commissioners in the capital. Nevertheless, Resident-general Marcel Peyrouton ensured that the protectorate remained obedient to Pétain. This was not an easy task. During July, inter-racial tension among French and Italian settlers erupted into street brawling, attacks on property and an Italian boycott of French Catholic church services.[5] Italian settlers in Tunis demanded union with Libya and Arab supporters of Tunisia's hitherto divided Destour party organised mass demonstrations in the major towns. But Peyrouton's announcement of severe military penalties for any public show of disloyalty ensured the restoration of order by the end of the month.[6] Impressed by this resolve, the Italian Armistice Commission even assisted French efforts to curb anti-French Italian radio broadcasts directed at the immigrant population of Tunis.[7] Morocco and Algeria followed the same pattern of limited unrest quickly contained by the threat of draconian punishment.[8]

Within the Levant states, High Commissioner Gabriel Puaux congratulated himself on his earlier suppression of political parties and the suspension of parliamentary government in Syria and Lebanon in 1939. This gave him greater freedom to hunt down Free French supporters, first within his civil administration, then within the French community as a whole.[9] Puaux's determination to suppress dissent between July and October 1940 was driven by his need to recover lost credibility. The High Commissioner and the Levant army commander, General Eugène Mittelhauser, dithered in the last ten days of June. They initially contacted Pétain, Weygand and the supreme commander in French North Africa, General Charles-Auguste Noguès, on 21 and 25 June over the possible continuation of resistance before studiously ignoring telegrams from Charles de Gaulle pleading for decisive action. On 28 June the British consul in Beirut relayed information for de Gaulle from the port's naval command indicating that a Free French 'rallying committee' was in place. But this group refused to commit itself until Mittelhauser made up his mind. Lacking clear evidence that French North Africa would fight on, the High Commission leadership in Damascus and Beirut precluded any unilateral action.[10] Though both Puaux and Mittelhauser ultimately declared for Pétain, their days in office were numbered. Further embarrassed by the high-profile escape from Syria to Palestine of a dissentient staff officer and future Free French hero, Colonel Edgard de Larminat, Mittelhauser was recalled to France and replaced by General Fougère, chief of staff of the Syrian paramilitary forces, the *troupes spéciales*. Meanwhile, Puaux's downfall followed inevitably once Pierre Laval took office as Prime Minister at Vichy in October. The Levant High Commissioner was replaced by General Henri Fernand Dentz in December 1940, the designated successor, Jean Chiappe, having been killed in an air crash in November. By this time, Puaux's monumental self-delusion regarding his supposed containment of the Syrian National Bloc was painfully clear to the Vichy administration in Damascus. This was made obvious by the July assassination of the National Bloc's main rival, the pro-British Syrian People's Party leader, Dr Abd al-Rahman Shahbander.[11]

In June 1940, the British government soon lost the initiative in persuading the French colonies to continue the fight. The Prime Minister, Winston Churchill, was quick to declare support for de Gaulle, and both men knew that the French were not totally without military means. Considerable land and air forces were shipped to North Africa in the latter half of June and the French fleet remained largely unscathed. But the authorities in French North and West Africa required tangible evidence of enduring British power before rejecting Pétain's authority. In London, this was taken to mean British military support, financial aid and commercial guarantees. Neither Resident-general and regional commander Noguès in Morocco nor Pétain's personal appointee, Pierre Boisson, first the Governor in Brazzaville and then Vichy High Commissioner in Dakar, was inclined to risk everything in a potentially futile heroic gesture.

On 17 June Noguès sent his personal liaison officer, Major Marius Guizol, to ascertain from Weygand whether the North African command was expected to ignore the armistice and fight on. Though he had conserved his reputation as a republican general following his appointment to Rabat in 1936, whether Noguès was serious or merely making a show of bravery for local consumption is open to question. Whatever the case, Weygand's ambiguous reply left Noguès with room for manoeuvre.[12] On 22 June – the day of the Franco-German armistice – in his capacity as supreme commander in French North Africa, Noguès summoned Governor Georges Le Beau of Algeria and Resident-general Peyrouton of Tunisia to the Rabat residency. All three men feared a punitive armistice, and Le Beau had suggested on 18 June that the French government should pursue the war from Algiers. None the less, the North African Governors were edging towards compliance with Pétain's wishes. In fact, in summoning Le Beau and Peyrouton, Noguès's prime objective was less to clarify the prospects for continued resistance than to measure the likelihood of civil disturbance and military insubordination within the North African territories. Armed with information from Weygand's representative, General Louis Koeltz, about the possible intentions of the Bordeaux government, both Noguès and Peyrouton warned Foreign Minister Paul Baudouin that any colonial cessions to Germany or Italy would be disastrous. They predicted Arab riots and a wholesale switch of settler allegiance to de Gaulle.[13] As the battle for France got under way and additional reinforcements from North Africa were called upon, Noguès warned that he would be ill equipped to combat a breakdown in civil order if his Armée d'Afrique reserves were more seriously depleted. Once it became clear that German forces were gaining the upper hand after they breached the French defensive line on the river Meuse in the last week of May, Noguès also began to doubt the loyalty of North African soldiers (there were then twelve Armée d'Afrique divisions fighting in the battle for France). He instigated extraordinary measures to isolate his troops from the local population, even refusing family visits. Crucially, Armée d'Afrique units were denied up-to-the-minute reports on events in France.[14]

On 22 June – the same day as his meeting with Le Beau and Peyrouton – Noguès discussed his problems with General Dillon, head of the British liaison mission sent to Morocco to encourage resistance. Noguès confided his fear that the new French Deputy Premier, Pierre Laval, might be ready to transfer French forces, including a large part of the fleet, to Axis control. Armed with this information, the British Admiralty hastened its plans to neutralise the French Mediterranean fleet.[15] The exclusion of any colonial transfers or major naval concessions within the Franco-Italian armistice scotched the idea that Laval might yet surrender all in an effort to ease the occupation terms in France. More than any other consideration, the relative moderation of this armistice kept French North Africa loyal to Pétain.[16] Denied firm German support, the Italian negotiators did not press their territorial claims in south-eastern France, eastern Tunisia, south eastern Algeria or French Somaliland. Instead, the armistice ordered the demilitarisation of these regions under the supervision of the newly established Italian Armistice Commission, based at Turin.[17]

The final breakdown of the Anglo-French alliance during the latter half of 1940 was played out on the African continent, in heavily defended French imperial territory of vital strategic importance to Allied communications. The continued exercise of imperial sovereignty in North and West Africa was central to the Vichy regime's self-image as a government which retained a measure of diplomatic and military independence despite its signature of armistice agreements with the Axis powers. The British government's fear that any such vestiges of independent foreign policy control existed entirely at German and Italian convenience made conflict over Vichy African territories highly likely, particularly after Churchill had formally recognised the Free French movement.

De Gaulle's *Appel* – his BBC radio broadcast on 18 June calling for continued French resistance against Germany – produced limited short-term results. Encouraged by Major-general Edward Louis Spears, soon to be head of the War Office liaison mission to the Free French headquarters, Churchill persuaded his Ministers individually to permit de Gaulle's broadcast in the first place. Neither Lord Halifax's Foreign Office, nor the newly created Cabinet Committee on Foreign (Allied) Resistance (CFR), chaired by the former Foreign Office Permanent Under-secretary, Sir Robert Vansittart, showed much enthusiasm for the *Appel*. As a result, de Gaulle was denied permission to make further broadcasts to France for several days after his preliminary calls to arms on 18 and 19 June.[18] Though seen as the first authoritative announcement of a Free French movement, the *Appel* provoked a limited response. Many French people were not in a position to hear the broadcast. Among those who did, it is not surprising that hopes faded when no further statement was forthcoming as France finally surrendered.[19] As de Gaulle admitted in his memoirs, he continued to seek the backing of more senior military figures – Generals Weygand, Mittelhauser and Noguès above all – before accepting that he should lead a Free French movement personally.[20] Even Admiral Emile Muselier, future head of the Free French naval forces, the Forces Navales Françaises Libres (FNFL), rallied to the British in Gibraltar on 28 June without concerting his action with de Gaulle. For the next eighteen months the two men found one another's company insufferable.[21]

When de Gaulle's sonorous voice first came across the air waves, the armistice agreements were not yet signed. In mid-June, those who hoped that a French government would fight on looked primarily to the clutch of Deputies and Ministers from the Bordeaux government that had sailed for Casablanca aboard the *Massilia* on 21 June. These included the former Premier, Edouard Daladier, and the Minister of Colonies, Georges Mandel. The Bordeaux government pledged to continue the struggle from North Africa, and Noguès briefly seemed willing to organise an insurgent army from the 270,000 troops under his command. But the politicians aboard the *Massilia* found that an armistice was concluded while they were at sea. Between 27 and 30 June Noguès confirmed the opinion he formed during the 22 June meetings: Pétain had to be supported. The *Massilia* politicians were detained on the ship while the first Vichy administration took shape. This decision mirrored the thinking of most Armée d'Afrique officers and NCOs. In their eyes it was essential for their units in North Africa, unexpectedly reprieved by the armistice, to be kept intact to assist Pétain's reconstruction of France. Hopeless defiance would jeopardise Pétain's government, provoke a complete occupation of France and, perhaps, generate a French political polarisation liable to result in civil war on the Spanish model. In short, the Armée d'Afrique was reverting to its traditional and primary purpose as a force for order.[22]

As civil government in France began to disintegrate in the closing weeks of the battle for France, so the French communities in Africa and the Middle East increasingly tuned in to British radio broadcasts to obtain information about events back home. These reports were directed by Jonathan Griffin and Emile Delavenay within the BBC's European Intelligence Department.[23] Independent of this, on 19 June de Gaulle made his first radio broadcast specifically intended to appeal to French Governors in Africa. He chose flattering imagery, beckoning 'the Africa of Clauzel, of Bugeaud, of Lyautey and of Noguès, to refuse the enemy's conditions'.[24] A forceful personality, de Gaulle was none the less a junior brigadier-general with only limited experience in government as Under-secretary at the War Ministry. His relatively lowly status, combined with his brusque precocity, did not make an appealing blend to the French authorities in North Africa, AOF or Syria – the three major points from which resistance might have been continued. Hence those best able to respond to the *Appel* were always more likely to respect Pétain, a revered figure whose impassioned plea for France to lay down its arms did not prefigure the later collaborationism of Vichy.

Only in those colonies where there was no proximate Axis threat were the administrators in charge likely to be more responsive to pressure from below. Two examples were the Pacific territory of New Caledonia and the North Atlantic islands of St Pierre and Miquelon, each of which was governed by an administrator who, by custom, consulted an elected advisory council. In New Caledonia and St Pierre, French naval vessels loyal to the armistice government were stationed in the islands, threatening to block Gaullist take-overs which were supported by members of the advisory councils. Similarly, in both cases, the local administrator – Georges Pelicier in Noumea and Gilbert de Bournat in St Pierre – refused to defy the Pétain government.[25] But whereas New Caledonia rallied to Free France in September 1940, St Pierre and Miquelon took a further sixteen months to do so. These ralliements were peaceful, although each colony faced a slight risk of recapture by Vichy naval expeditions mounted from Indo-China to Noumea, and from Martinique to St Pierre. In New Caledonia, the presence of the Australian cruiser HMAS *Adelaide* in Noumea harbour facilitated the early transfer of allegiance.[26] This naval theme also emerges in the French Caribbean, where the French West Indian territories of Martinique, Guadeloupe and French Guiana submitted to the military control of Admiral Georges Robert, commander of the French western Atlantic squadron based at Fort-de-France in Martinique. Robert's threat of force was sufficient to ensure that Martinique's Vichyite Governor, Yves Nicol, retained control in the face of a nascent pro-de Gaulle movement led by several of the island's local mayors and *conseillers-généraux*.[27] Similarly, the arrival of Robert's cruiser, *Jeanne d'Arc*, in Guadeloupe heralded a round-up of Gaullist sympathisers which intimidated the island into obedience.[28]

Colonial support for Free France: Indo-China

In spite of the prevailing conservatism within French colonial administration, during July and early August converts to the Free French cause emerged in a number of French territories, particularly in those where adventurous Coloniale officers unfamiliar with the stark reality of German strength were keen to fight on. In some cases this led to repression, in others support for de Gaulle was too diffuse to make much impact. The strongest among these early indications that a major colonial administration might turn to Free France came from Indo-China. Appointed in June 1939, the federation Governor, General Georges Catroux, was a somewhat unusual choice. Catroux had spent the bulk of his colonial career in North Africa, though he had served as *aide de camp* to Governor Paul Beau in Hanoi some thirty-five years earlier.[29] The new Governor arrived in Indo-China with instructions from Georges Mandel to undertake a modest development programme. But Mandel ordered Catroux to concentrate upon increasing Indo-China's supply of primary products and Annamite military recruits for France. In late 1939, the army commander in French Indo-China, General Maurice Martin, hastily assembled two infantry divisions – one destined for metropolitan France and one for Syria – as well as some 15,000 unskilled Indo-Chinese labourers intended to work in French factories. This left meagre land forces, backed by a derisory number of obsolete reconnaissance aircraft, to defend the federation itself.[30]

In the week before the collapse of France, the French position in the Far East was severely compromised, first by the conclusion of a humiliating non-aggression pact with Thailand, and then by the start of talks in Tokyo between the French ambassador, Charles-Arsène Henry, and the Deputy Foreign Minister, Tani Masayuki. On 20 June Henry conceded that a Japanese control commission under Lieutenant-general Nishihara Issaku could be dispatched to Tonkin to monitor the closure of Indo-China's northern frontier with Nationalist China.[31] Catroux also saw little alternative to this having been informed by René de Saint-Quentin, French ambassador to Washington, that the American government would furnish neither material aid nor strong diplomatic support if Catroux resisted Tokyo's demands. A French military mission to Washington sent earlier in June with instructions to purchase up to $2 million worth of military equipment made little headway, not least because President Roosevelt had just approved the continued sale of petroleum products, including high-octane fuel, to Japan.[32] Not surprisingly, the US administration offered no substantial assistance to the French authorities in Indo-China in 1940.[33] The one bright note was that the French settler community initially united around Catroux in support of a firm policy. This patriotic will to resist evaporated once news of Mers el-Kébir and of Washington's noncommittal attitude spread through the federation in early July. The French historian Pierre Lamant captured the settler mood:

> Counting neither on their British ally, too preoccupied elsewhere, nor on the United States, [which was] already hostile to the French presence in the [Indo-China] peninsula and which maintained an ambassador at Vichy until November 1942, the great majority [of settlers], backed by derisory military forces with outmoded and exhausted equipment, estimated that the sole solution was to close ranks and to hold fast for better or worse to the mother country ...[34]

Catroux estimated that a policy of unilateral concessions to Tokyo might forestall the more extreme military demands favoured by Japan's army commanders in southern China. Admiral Jean Decoux, commander of French naval forces in Indo-China, was more sceptical. A Pétain loyalist, and no lover of the Third Republic, Decoux none the less prided himself on his detached objectivity. At Admiral Darlan's suggestion, Decoux replaced Catroux as Governor on 20 July.[35] Though it was Decoux who kept Indo-China faithful to Pétain, he also liaised closely with Admiral Sir Percy Noble, commander of the British fleet's China station. On 28 June the two admirals conferred in Saigon over possible mutual support in the event of a Japanese attack. Though Noble promised no real support, a large part of his own forces having been recalled to the Mediterranean, he and Decoux concluded a 'gentlemen's agreement' under which neither British nor French vessels were to attack one another if Noble received orders to impose a naval blockade upon Indo-China. In the event, this was largely irrelevant. Most vessels sent to reprovision Indo-China were intercepted in the Indian Ocean by Royal Naval ships under Admiral Leatham's command at Trincomalee in Ceylon.[36]

Catroux misread Japanese intentions. With *de facto* control of Indo-China, the Japanese military command would be well placed to impose terms upon Chiang Kai-shek's Chinese Nationalist administration in Chungking. By permitting the transit of essential supplies to the Nationalists since the outbreak of the Sino-Japanese war in July 1937, the French authorities in Indo-China had forfeited any claim to generous treatment from the Japanese.[37] On 26 June the Japanese army command in Canton announced its intention to 'cut off by force' the transport of war materials through Tonkin to Chiang Kai-shek's forces. This directly contravened the agreement reached in the preceding week between Charles-Arsène Henry and Mitsumasa Yonai's outgoing Cabinet, in fulfilment of which Catroux announced a general closure of the frontiers of Indo-China. In mid-July, to back up its demand that Indo-China should sever all ties with China, the new Tokyo government headed by Prince Konoye confirmed its readiness to use over 100,000 troops locally available on the islands of Hainan and Formosa. Japan's China squadron was on alert off the Gulf of Tonkin.[38]

Immediately Decoux took over as Governor in Hanoi he informed the newly appointed Minister of Colonies, the Martiniquan Senator, Henry Lémery, that his capacity to negotiate was compromised by Catroux's earlier concessions. Decoux anticipated further Japanese encroachment on Indo-Chinese territory and government:

> My conclusion, after an examination of the situation, is that some very large concessions, even going beyond those that were demanded, were accorded to the Japanese [by Catroux] without any return in order to create a favourable atmosphere with a view to obtaining security guarantees. The facts prove that our concessions hitherto have only resulted in developing [the] Japanese appetite.[39]

Decoux dispatched this report upon receipt of a communication from Lémery which admitted that compromise with the Japanese was inevitable. Reduced to the fundamental task of maintaining French sovereignty, Decoux's policy was to be guided by 'empiricism' and 'circumstance'.[40] On 22 September Decoux conceded that the Japanese southern army would be permitted to maintain air bases in Tonkin, to garrison the main northern Indo-Chinese port of Haiphong, and to use the Tonkin–Yunnan railway for the transport of military supplies. Other than the Burma Road, the Yunnan railway was the principal supply route to the Chinese Nationalists. The importance of the rail link was further increased once the British government had acquiesced in the temporary closure of the Burma supply road on 17 July. With the Haiphong railway also brought under Japanese supervision, French Indo-China was effectively co-opted into Japan's strategy in

South East Asia. The facade of independent French colonial rule would be further exposed over the coming year.[41]

Catroux's decision to capitulate to the Japanese had provoked outrage within Pétain's government. Angered at Catroux's failure to consult him, Lémery's predecessor as Minister of Colonies, Albert Rivière, led the chorus of disapproval. The Council of Ministers agreed with Darlan's suggestion that Decoux should be instructed to take over. As John Dreifort has shown, this was sheer hypocrisy. Given the chaos of France in late June, Catroux was within his rights to act independently. Resistance to the Japanese was not a viable alternative. Furthermore, Foreign Minister Paul Baudouin, the head of the Ministry's Far East section, Jean Chauvel, and the Secretary-general, François Charles-Roux, had already formulated plans which conferred sweeping powers on any colonial administration unable to maintain regular contact with the metropolitan government. It seems, then, that the vitriol directed at Catroux stemmed less from his appeasement of Tokyo than from his concurrent willingness to explore continued co-operation with the British.[42] In Catroux's opinion the Vietnamese population appreciated the need to conciliate the Japanese army, whereas they were baffled by the French surrender to Germany. Catroux considered the armistice premature and, as such, unpardonable. Pétain's capitulation posed a greater threat to the long-term future of French rule in Indo-China than the temporary presence of Japanese monitors.[43] De Gaulle's *Appel* was widely heard among the settler communities in Hanoi, Haiphong and Saigon and, immediately after it, Catroux confirmed that he, too, was prepared to continue the struggle. The commander of the one major naval vessel in Indo-China, the ageing cruiser *Lamotte Picquet,* added that he was ready to sail to Singapore to open a dialogue with the British authorities.[44]

In spite of these early indications of support for de Gaulle, Catroux opposed a scheme to organise a Free French movement in southern Indo-China, where support for continued resistance was strongest. This proposal emanated from a delegation in Saigon representing the *Anciens Combattants* associations across Cochin China. Numerous serving officers in General Martin's Indo-Chinese command also indicated their readiness to fight on. Catroux appears to have taken fright at the implications of this. He rebuffed General Martin and warned that no action should be taken without the Governor's express approval. Catroux was convinced that any public indication that the colony was turning towards Britain would precipitate a Japanese invasion.[45]

When Catroux was replaced in late July, there was no concerted opposition to Decoux's declarations of support for Vichy. Unfortunately for those who advocated a Free French *ralliement* in Indo-China,

Catroux's initial capitulation to Japan provided a stick which Decoux employed whenever talk of a Gaullist alternative was heard. Whatever the case in Europe, Africa and the Middle East, in Indo-China Decoux could claim with some justification that, in the name of Vichy, he had mounted the more effective resistance to the demands of a hostile power. When Catroux left Indo-China to make his way to de Gaulle in London, he was easily discredited. By October 1940, in a dispatch that proved woefully misguided, Decoux reassured the new Minister of Colonies, Admiral Charles Platon, that even in Cochin China both the settler population and the *indigènes* required only 'discreet surveillance'.[46]

Colonial support for Free France: French Africa

If Catroux and Decoux could defend their action – or inaction – by reference to a pressing military threat, the same could not be said of the colonial administrations in sub-Saharan Africa. During the third week of June, while still in post as Governor of AEF in Brazzaville, Pierre Boisson seemed willing to support continued resistance against the Axis. His prerequisite was that French North Africa should fight on as well.[47] By the end of the month, Boisson's misgivings about support for Britain and de Gaulle had mushroomed in the absence of any indication that Noguès would oppose the armistice agreements. Some of Boisson's subordinates were less dispirited. Félix Eboué, the French Guyanese Governor of Chad, AEF's northernmost territory, showed undimmed enthusiasm for continued resistance. Fortified by the presence of the cruiser HMS *Dragon* in Douala harbour, Cameroon High Commissioner Richard Brunot was ready to begin detailed co-operation with the British colonial and military authorities in West Africa.[48] More important to de Gaulle and Churchill were the tentative indications of potential support from Léon Cayla, Governor-general of AOF, and Gabriel Puaux in the Levant. As with Boisson, the first priority for Cayla and Puaux was to see which way Noguès turned.[49]

In French West Africa and the Levant prominent figures within the civil and military administrations and the business communities of the major cities were reluctant to accept France's defeat. But it is impossible to speak of any functioning Gaullist movement as such. Sympathy for the British within Dakar, for example, was soon undermined when the French battleship *Richelieu* limped into the port, having been attacked by Royal Naval aircraft in conjunction with the Mers el-Kébir operation. Support for de Gaulle declined further when Boisson replaced Cayla as Governor-general in July 1940.[50] Indeed, Pétain's government planned a reprisal attack mounted from Dakar upon the British port of Freetown in Sierra Leone.[51] According to Pétain himself, early enthusiasm for de Gaulle among French colonial communities was easily explained away. Reluctance to bow to the armistice was patriotic but misguided: 'Poorly informed about the situation [in June 1940], they refused to admit that it was impossible for France to redress its fortunes within the imperial theatre, not having been permitted to do so during the campaign.'[52]

The will to resist among French colonial administrations also proved short-lived. British inability to lend substantial military assistance, the limited impact of de Gaulle's initial appeals for support and the apparent ease with which the parliamentarians of the Third Republic voted that regime out of existence to make way for the new government at Vichy – all seemed to emphasise the triumph of German power. On 2 July any lingering hopes that French North Africa might re-enter the war were dashed as the partial disarmament of the Armée d'Afrique got under way. The Vichy government was particularly anxious about this because only in North Africa was the indigenous population judged likely to oppose the armistice.[53] Within Algeria, Governor Le Beau warned the prefectural authorities and town mayors that demobilised North African troops repatriated from France required sensitive treatment. Families that had lost menfolk were to receive priority in matters of housing and limited welfare provision. In Morocco, too, demobilisation was handled with remarkable delicacy under the direction of a former Syrian High Commissioner, General Henri Gouraud.[54] After his hectic exchanges with Weygand and his fellow North African Governors in late June, Noguès calculated that his military reputation would be served better by maintaining an efficient armistice army on high alert than by risking everything in a foolhardy bid to help the British.[55] To make his compliance with the armistice agreements easier to swallow, Noguès planned to defend French rule in North Africa at all costs. In the short term, however, the French military priority in North Africa was to ensure that the demobilisation of troops proceeded without incident.

Far from preparing to re-enter the war, French military intelligence in Algiers was also preoccupied with demobilisation measures. On 13 July the intelligence staff concluded: 'The morale of the Army remains good on the whole. The return to civil life is the essential preoccupation of the great majority of reservists who now regard their work as being to help in the economic recovery of the country. The soldiers of North Africa have retained confidence in their leaders.'[56] While the naval forces in North Africa needed little incentive to serve Vichy after the attack on Oran, even the traditionally conservative French Marine was not monolithic in outlook. In the last ten days of June

1940, among naval ratings in Toulon, Dakar and Martinique, desertion and demands for immediate repatriation were so widespread that the local Marine commanders anticipated violent disorder.[57] In late July, most of the 10,000 or so French sailors who had been stranded in British ports since the armistice disembarked at Casablanca. Their repatriation to French territory was agreed following their refusal to rally to Muselier's emergent Free French navy. But, according to Admiral d'Harcourt, the naval commander in Morocco, most were equally unenthusiastic about Vichy. D'Harcourt bemoaned the fact that, having spent three weeks in Britain forced to drink tea instead of their usual wine ration, the sailors were interested only in drunken celebration and prompt demobilisation.[58]

As the French North African authorities began adapting to life under the armistice at the start of July, the idea of Free France still appeared heroic to some, ludicrous to others. Within days the Free French movement acquired a totally different complexion. The British attack on Admiral Marçel Gensoul's western Mediterranean squadron at Oran on 3 July gave real substance to the idea of Britain's betrayal of France. By association, de Gaulle became party to a supposedly unwarranted attack on loyal French ships which had left some 1,285 sailors dead, 977 of them killed aboard a single vessel, the battleship *Bretagne*. Not surprisingly, in the two years which followed, Vichy's anti-British propaganda had a pronounced naval flavour. Dunkirk, Mers el-Kébir and, later, the September 1940 assault on Dakar, formed a potent troika, not least to French colonial communities cut off from France by a British naval blockade.[59]

There is no doubt that Mers el-Kébir assisted Pétain's government in its efforts to curb colonial dissidence during July. Two days after the assault, Baudouin dispatched a circular to all French colonial administrations reporting on the bombardment. Ferocious in tone, the dispatch ended on an optimistic note. The British attack nullified those armistice clauses intended to prevent the French empire from re-entering the war in alliance with Britain. On the evening of 3 July, the Italians suspended their demands for the demilitarisation of French naval and air forces in North African and Levant ports. In practice, the German Armistice Commission followed suit. The empire was now at liberty to defend itself against all comers.[60] The presence on the Italian Armistice Commission of a known Francophile, the former director of the Italian Foreign Ministry, Leonardo Vitetti, was expected to result in further concessions to French interests in Africa.[61] On 6 July, the Italian Chief of Staff, Marshal Piétro Badoglio, was delighted by news that French bombers had launched a retaliatory raid against Gibraltar. Badoglio immediately instructed his Armistice Commission representatives in Clermont Ferrand to propose that Vichy air and naval forces in North Africa should join the Italians in further combined operations against Gibraltar and possibly Egypt. As bait, the Italians hinted that the French Mediterranean fleet would be allowed greater freedom of movement, including unlimited communication with Syria and Lebanon.[62]

Seen from Vichy, before Mers el-Kébir the colonial picture had been more gloomy. Unsure of the loyalty of colonial garrisons, and lacking the mobile forces necessary to reimpose order, the only course of action hitherto open to Pétain was to dispatch trusted placemen to take over administrations which had wavered in the preceding weeks. As we have seen, this accounted for Boisson's move from Brazzaville to the Governor's residence at Dakar on 29 June. Boisson regarded the attack at Oran as wholly immoral. By the time a Royal Navy task force arrived off Dakar in September, the new Governor-general identified entirely with the spirited defence of the port's naval shore batteries. Much the same could be said of Léon Cayla. Demoted from Dakar to the governorship of Madagascar, Cayla immediately set about ingratiating himself with Lémery's Ministry of Colonies by applying Vichy ordnances with particular vigour – the more so after the discovery of a pro-British 'plot' within the Tananarive administration during the first week of September.[63] In Madagascar Cayla replaced Jules-Marcel de Coppet, another Governor who showed less than exemplary loyalty to Pétain in June, and an official who, like Noguès in North Africa, was oringinally appointed by the Popular Front government in 1936. Much like Boisson, Cayla justified his change of heart by reference to the Mers el-Kébir attack. With records to hand of the telegraphic correspondence sent from Madagascar to the Ministry of Colonies imploring France to fight on, it was a straightforward task for Cayla's officials in Tananarive to pick out individuals likely to support de Gaulle.[64] After discussions with the Inspector of Police in the Madagascan capital, the new Governor set about dismantling *Anciens Combattants* committees which he considered the principal forum for opposition to Vichy. When news of the British naval blockade spread in early August, Cayla also found it easier to justify his position, and to close British consulates in the ports of Tamatave and Majunga.[65] In November 1940, the departing British consul at Majunga estimated that the Governor had completely crushed what remained of Free French support within Madagascar.[66]

Elsewhere, loyalty to Pétain's new regime was secured by a combination of changes in leadership, uncertainty within the colonial administrations and one-sided reports of British behaviour. In French Somaliland, a tiny pocket of territory adjacent to British and Italian colonies, the Commandant-supérieur, General Paul Legentilhomme, kept in close contact with his British neighbours. From August 1939, Legentilhomme worked with Major-general Arthur Chater, soon to be appointed Military Governor in British Somaliland, in order to plan joint operations against Italian East Africa.[67] In April 1940 the French and British agreed contingency plans for the evacuation from Somaliland of the indigenous population and European and Indian residents in the event of an Italian offensive in east Africa.[68] Contacts such as this persisted throughout the battle for France. Hours before de Gaulle's *Appel* on 18 June, Legentilhomme informed Chater: 'I remain with all my forces at the disposal of General Wavell. I shall never capitulate!' Archibald Wavell, the British Middle East commander, was keen to reciprocate by shipping several hundred Free French volunteers drawn from Syria, Cyprus and Alexandria to reinforce Legentilhomme in Djibouti.[69] Throughout July Legentilhomme assured the British East African command in Nairobi that he would never allow Italian forces into Djibouti. Though this was technically prohibited under the terms of the Tunis armistice convention, it was fast becoming a real possibility because of Legentilhomme's refusal to co-operate with the Italian Armistice Commission delegate, General Emmanuel Beraudo di Pralormo. In spite of his outward confidence, Legentilhomme doubted the loyalty of his 10,000 strong garrison.[70]

In fact, Legentilhomme was deeply unsure what to do. Weygand made his mind up for him. Angered by events in Djibouti, the President of the Turin Armistice Commission, General Piétro Pintor, threatened Weygand with the seizure of further French military equipment as a penalty for non-compliance with the armistice. In response, Weygand dispatched General Germain – an officer senior to Legentilhomme – to French Somaliland with orders to bring Legentilhomme into line. When Germain reached Djibouti on 18 July he received a 'glacial welcome'. Legentilhomme spoke openly of defying Vichy. Once Pintor heard of this, he insisted that Pétain's government should appoint Germain as replacement for both Legentilhomme and the civil Governor of French Somaliland, Hubert Deschamps. On 23 July the Vichy government complied, vesting full civil and military power in Germain and appointing General Aymé as his deputy in succession to Legentilhomme.[71] Now thoroughly isolated, Legentilhomme effectively allowed French Somaliland to declare for Pétain before he quit the colony to join the Free French movement.

Free French successes in AEF

Throughout July Pétain's government brought several wavering colonial administrations into line. In sub-Saharan Africa, the one card the British had left to play was their ability to resupply French colonies by land and sea. It was thus possible to guarantee the economic future of territories within AOF and AEF which declared for de Gaulle.[72] In the month after Mers el-Kébir, three French African colonies looked most promising to the Colonial Office and Vansittart's Committee on Foreign (Allied) Resistance as potential dissident territories.[73] Ironically, these assessments were made with little reference to the Free French in London. Not yet organised into a coherent executive authority, de Gaulle's followers lacked the status of a full government in exile. As a result, the Free French were not represented on the Vansittart Committee. This added to the isolation felt by the early Gaullist supporters overseas.[74]

Eboué in Chad and Brunot in Cameroon maintained contact with the British via local consuls and representatives of Sir Bernard Bourdillon's colonial administration in Nigeria. During meetings held in April and May 1940, Georges Mandel and Malcolm MacDonald laid the foundations of the later co-operation.[75] Brunot even publicised his intention to work with the British, issuing a decree which confirmed his power to do so. On 7 July Churchill's War Cabinet authorised Bourdillon to pursue these contacts and to extend them to AOF territories contiguous with British West African colonies. One promising territory was Dahomey. The colony was heavily reliant upon communications and trade with Nigeria, and there were a series of pro-Gaullist demonstrations in June directed by business leaders in the capital, Porto-Novo.[76] Britain accounted for 65 per cent of Dahomey's export trade. But since the Dahomey administration was quick to suppress public dissent, the French Côte d'Ivoire under Governor Horace Croccichia appeared the most likely convert.

Since the armistice, a steady influx of Côte d'Ivoire troops serving within the Tirailleurs Sénégalais crossed into the neighbouring Gold Coast, some to join British forces, others to escape military service altogether.[77] On 25 June, in the capital, Abidjan, an *Anciens Combattants* committee consisting of French officers and former Tirailleurs issued a proclamation urging continued resistance. Between 24 June and 12 July a British liaison mission from Accra remained in Abidjan in an attempt to boost the Governor's resolve to defy orders from Dakar. The mission pressed Croccichia hard to side with Britain. On 29 July the Vansittart Committee issued urgent instructions for the transport of a three-man Free French mission to the Côte d'Ivoire to work upon Croccichia and, eventually, Boisson.[78] At this point, Croccichia announced his intention to follow Boisson in recognising Pétain's authority. The British liaison missions in the Côte d'Ivoire and in Dahomey were promptly expelled.[79] There was one last glimmer of hope from the Côte d'Ivoire when on 20 July the colony's garrison commander intimated his wish to march his entire force into the Gold Coast. Fearful of reprisal action authorised by Boisson, and perhaps still hopeful that Croccichia might turn, the Colonial Office issued urgent instructions to Sir Arnold Hodson, Governor at Accra, to dissuade the French troops from moving.[80]

In the last week of July, the Vichy government recovered the upper hand across AOF. Pétain sent three of Darlan's most trusted naval commanders – now among the most vigorous Anglophobes within the Vichy administration – to French Africa. French naval representatives took a leading role in reminding colonial administrators that dissent would be punishable by military tribunal as an act of treason. Henceforth, Vichy threatened to treat serving Free French forces as *franc-tireurs*. On 20 July, Admiral Jean Abrial, a hero in France after his direction of the French evacuation from Dunkirk, was named Governor-general of Algeria, replacing Governor Le Beau, who had reached retirement age. Within weeks, Admiral Jean-Pierre Esteva, French naval commander in French North Africa, also took a political post, replacing Marcel Peyrouton as Resident-general in Tunis. Admiral Jean de Laborde was appointed supreme commander of all forces in AOF.[81] Vice-admiral Charles Platon, soon to be made Minister of Colonies, spent much of late July and early August trying to enforce Pétain's will in both AOF and AEF.[82] Platon's visits to Brunot in Cameroon and Governor Georges-Pierre Masson in Gabon left the two French officials thoroughly intimidated and confused. Platon then secured the transfer to Gabon of General Marcel Têtu, formerly Armée de l'Air commander in French North Africa, to bolster the Vichy presence still further.[83] With Decoux in charge in Hanoi, Admiral Robert the de facto ruler in the French West Indies, and Admiral Platon so firm over AEF, there is some substance to the idea that Vichy and its empire was coming under the sway of Vichy's naval staff.[84] Evidence of increased Vichy resolve produced the first major division between the Vansittart committee and the Colonial Office. The former advised a British take-over of the Cameroon administration as a 'decisive step' expected to encourage other French colonies to rally to Free France. But the Colonial Office was convinced that the 'psychological moment' for this had passed. The British Chiefs of Staff warned on 8 July that any military intervention should be sanctioned immediately or not at all. But the service Ministries did not have ready forces available for such action.[85]

Though the French land forces commander in Brazzaville had requested British military support on 24 June, to repeat his request now would constitute an open act of rebellion. Direct British intervention was more likely to turn other French colonies against de Gaulle, especially as Boisson in Dakar now toed the Vichy line.[86]

The progressive extension of Pétain's control in July has made the *ralliement* of Chad, the French Congo, Oubangui-Chari and Cameroon in the last week of August appear all the more audacious. But it bears emphasis that these declarations for Free France were palace revolutions, not popular uprisings. In Chad, for example, the fall of France was neither publicised nor widely discussed. Local departmental chiefs reported that anxiety for the future was largely confined to the white population.[87] Lacking active popular support, the success of the first Free Frenchmen in Africa stemmed from the fact that this handful of individuals decapitated Vichyite administration so neatly. In Chad there was no one to remove. In the capital, Fort Lamy, the Governor, Félix Eboué, simply made his change of allegiance public. Throughout July, Eboué and his deputy administrator, Henri Laurentie, liaised with Governor Bourdillon's administration in Lagos to establish how Chad might be supplied and defended once it declared for de Gaulle. Eboué was also reasonably certain of the loyalty of his regional military commanders, Lieutenant-colonel Marchand (a nephew of the Fashoda general) and a newly arrived Corsican, Commandant Colonna d'Ornano.[88]

Italy's entry into the war transformed Chad's strategic importance. Hitherto the colony was viewed as inhospitable and inaccessible – the northern backwater of AEF. It had been visited only once by an AEF Governor-general throughout the inter-war period.[89] From June 1940, Chad acquired new significance as the only French African territory below the Sahara which bordered hostile territory. But Chad was also highly vulnerable. It was landlocked below Italian Libya, and was reliant on overland supplies from British Nigeria. Finally, the colony soon became vital to the transit of American aircraft and equipment from Takoradi in the Gold Coast, via Nigeria, Chad and Sudan, to the British Middle Eastern command in Cairo.[90]

According to the headquarters of Vichy's African military administration in Algiers, Chad turned to de Gaulle for three reasons. Demoralisation over the armistice was fuelled by a second consideration: the absence of any direct communication until mid-July between Vichy and Eboué's government in Fort Lamy. Finally, the colonial garrison was strongly influenced by a group of Corsican officers, Colonna d'Ornano among them, who anticipated that their island home might be ceded to Italy. The Corsicans were most persuasive, arguing that if the Italians were allowed to take Corsica, they were sure to seize Chad as well. The Vichy calculation that Chad was turned by a cabal of discontented administrators and military officers informed the Ministry of Colonies decision that the territory should be immediately recaptured. It had already been agreed on 6 August that Eboué should be replaced by a pro-Vichy Governor, Jean-Victor Chazelas, but the decree giving effect to this was still unsigned when the colony rallied to de Gaulle.[91] On 28 August Boisson was instructed to assemble a force to enter the colony from Zinder in southern Niger. General Aubert, the senior ranking officer in the Niger–Chad region, was assigned to head this expedition. It was to be supported by an assortment of military aircraft gathered from the Armée de l'Air squadrons at Thiès in Senegal and at Bamako and Gao in French Sudan. Later the same day, Boisson ordered the immediate arrest and trial by military tribunal of known Gaullist sympathisers within all the territories of AOF.[92] Though under threat of Vichy attack, in the short term, Eboué was relatively safe. Chad was exceedingly remote – over 2,000 km from Dakar or Algiers – and its administration remained intact. At the start of the war it took colonial officials an average of sixty to seventy days to complete the journey to Fort Lamy by land and sea from Bordeaux. To reach the colony by air was still considered a *performance sportive* worthy of national press coverage.[93] By contrast, Eboué's supporters in Chad could reasonably expect some assistance from General George Giffard's British West African command forces in Nigeria, or even from the British forces fighting the Italians in East Africa.

Precisely because they were less remote from other French colonial garrisons, in Brazzaville and Douala the Free French were more exposed. In late July, British consular officials in Léopoldville and neighbouring Brazzaville reported the existence of an organised Free French committee in the French Congolese capital. With Churchill's assent, de Gaulle assembled a liaison mission at Carlton Gardens to be sent to Equatorial Africa. The main figures within this were René Pleven, Claude Hettier de Boislambert and Captain Philippe de Hauteclocque (who had assumed his famous alias of 'Major Leclerc'). In Léopoldville, the London mission rendezvoused with Colonel Edgard de Larminat, formerly a senior Coloniale staff officer to Legentilhomme in Djibouti, who had travelled to Equatorial Africa from Syria. The colonel had already made a name for himself in the Levant owing to his escape from Damascus after his clash with General Mittelhauser over support for Free France. De Larminat further enraged Mittlehauser by encouraging French military defections to the British in Palestine. Impressed by his leadership qualities, de Gaulle assigned de Larminat to be Free French Governor of AEF once the *ralliement* of Brazzaville was achieved.[94]

The successful conversion of Chad, Cameroon and the French

Congo between 26 and 28 August was followed a day later by a declaration for de Gaulle by Governor Pierre de Saint Mart in Oubangui-Chari. This was approved during a peaceful – though heated – meeting of officials in the capital, Bangui. As a consequence, virtually the whole of AEF was in Free French hands by September.[95] Only Gabon, always the runt of the AEF confederation, remained loyal to Vichy. This was largely because Governor Masson, having been cajoled into temporary obedience by Platon, was again prevented from rallying by the Bishop of Libreville and naval officers faithful to Pétain.[96] Overwhelmed by the pressure exerted by both sides, Masson committed suicide on 16 November. Among these AEF conversions, only in Cameroon was there anything like a military operation. But even this involved no more than thirty individuals. De Larminat later maintained that the British West African command denied him the use of Senegalese and Côte d'Ivoire troops based in the Gold Coast. But, according to General Giffard, these soldiers refused to participate in the Cameroon operation. As a result, the Gaullist 'expedition' to Douala on 26 August consisted of a small landing party led by Leclerc and de Boislambert. During the night of 26–7 August, the two men first persuaded the port garrison to support them, then packed their converts aboard a train to the capital, Yaoundé. In the French Congo there was even less of a struggle. Learning of the events in Douala, General Husson, the recently appointed Governor-general in Brazzaville, simply fled across the river to Léopoldville, leaving de Larminat to take over by crossing the Congo in the opposite direction.[97]

Though the undoubted bravery of Leclerc, de Boislambert, de Larminat and their daring Coloniale followers soon became rooted in Gaullist folklore, the conversion of AEF territories was driven by their precarious economic position.[98] The British and de Gaulle's Carlton Gardens advisers were well aware of this. The itinerant officials from Bourdillon's Nigerian administration, such as Theo Hoskyns-Abrahall, who visited Cameroon, Gabon and Brazzaville, and Theodore Adams and L. C. Giles, who worked closely with Eboué and Laurentie in Chad, all emphasised that fear of economic collapse was central to the incipient Free French movements in each colony.[99] Across AEF, local resisters also passed information regarding settler opinion direct to the few remaining British consular officials. This was especially valuable in Cameroon where High Commissioner Brunot wavered throughout late July, leaving the British increasingly reliant upon the local Gaullist network directed by a civil engineer who directed the colony's railway network, M. Mauclère.[100] With a total population of some 2,380,000, there were only 3,106 European residents registered in Cameroon in 1940. Among these Europeans, some 1,100 were planters and their dependants, while the administration employed a further 633 French staff. Most of the settler population were in some way dependent upon the 300 French businesses in the colony, the overwhelming majority of which were concerned with the export of four staple Cameroon products: timber, palm oil, bananas and cocoa. Before the armistice, the principal recipients of these goods were metropolitan France, Germany and the Netherlands. Since these markets were disrupted by the French defeat, from June 1940 Cameroon relied upon British Nigeria as an economic lifeline.[101]

Within Douala, Cameroon Africans had long been employed both by European trading companies and by the *cadre local indigène* of French administration. Other Doualas controlled cocoa and palm planations of their own. Among these *indigènes*, alarm at the possible collapse of export revenue prompted calls in early August for Brunot to make amends with the British authorities in Nigeria in recognition of the 'interdependence' of the two colonies.[102] Similarly, the threat of economic collapse in Cameroon quickly undermined Vichy efforts to persuade the settler community to remain loyal. Instead, the economic agreement arrived at between the British envoys and the Association of West African Merchants in Cameroon, which included provision for the shipment of goods by sea and from storage sites along Nigeria's river Benue, was pivotal to the settlers' readiness to accept a Free French alternative.[103] The animosities prevalent between settlers and administrators in Cameroon by 1940 were nicely captured by Major J. G. C. Allen, a Spears Mission liaison officer attached to AEF:

> Many of the officials were immersed in a welter of paper and a popular tradition among the planters was that their efforts were concentrated solely on self-advancement, to which red tape and paper were the surest roads. The planters were themselves chiefly interested in obtaining the highest prices for their produce and many of them considered that the primary function of government was to provide them with virtually unlimited quantities of native labour to work for them at totally inadequate wages. Thus, as in many British colonies where the same circumstances arise, the rock on which these two elements split was the native labour question and, since the government insisted and rightly refused to coerce the natives to labour for private ends and the planters refused to offer an economic rate of wages, these two factors became irrevocably estranged.[104]

The Vichy government was also aware of the escalating tension between European planters and officials in Cameroon. On 1 August, Vichy's Inspector-general of Colonies, Huet, met a hostile reception in Douala, having been sent by Henry Lémery to reassure Brunot that the Vichy government would take urgent steps to resume trade. Huet was convinced that Brunot could not convince the settler community of this. He was equally certain that it was pointless trying to appeal direct to the indigenous population, which had long regarded the French mandate as oppressive. Unable to coax the French community into loyalty, upon Huet's return the Vichy government began threatening naval reprisals from Dakar in the event that Cameroon rallied to Free France.[105] Without openly admitting it, the Foreign and Colonial Ministries in Vichy expected Cameroon to turn against Pétain weeks before Leclerc arrived. The irony was that, within two months of his arrival, Leclerc was, in turn, convinced that unless the British government could immediately ship out the colony's banana crop and replenish local banks with a sterling reserve the Free French, too, would be quickly ousted.[106]

The story was much the same in neighbouring colonies. As has been noted above, Chad was landlocked and was threatened by invasion from Italian Libya. The Gabon economy was dependent upon the export of a single staple – bastard mahogany, a favoured timber for the manufacture of quality laminates. By August, Britain offered the only market for this.[107] Even the far larger territory of French Congo was of little use if Brazzaville ceased to function as a working port. Throughout AEF as a whole, it is no surprise to find that local chambers of commerce played at least as prominent a role in the early pressure for conversion to Free France as the serving officials and *Anciens Combattants*, upon whom attention has more often been focused.

Vichy reaction to Free French success in Africa

Once news of the *ralliements* in AEF came through, the Secretariat of Marine took the initiative in seeking Armistice Commission approval for the limited reinforcement of several key French imperial outposts. In addition, Darlan's naval staff formulated revised plans for the recapture of AEF by means of an expedition sent from Dakar. This idea was put to the German Armistice Commission immediately after the events in Fort Lamy, Douala and Brazzaville. In mid-September, a Vichy naval squadron – Force Y – left Casablanca for Dakar from where it was to lead combined operations against French Equatorial Africa. Force Y was intercepted by the British ships heading south to attack Dakar under Operation Menace in the third week of September.[108] Given their leading role in the Anglo-French colonial confrontations across Africa and the Middle East, it is no surprise that from September 1940 the French naval staff played the dominant role in Vichy's imperial defence planning, supplanting the authority of the inter-service Supreme Council of National Defence (Conseil Supérieur de la

Défense Nationale).[109] Marine planners took the lead in arguing for modification of the armistice restrictions to allow the fleet to resume operations in defence of the empire.

The planned attack on land-locked Chad was the exception to the more general rule that the Vichy navy took the principal responsibility for planning operations against Free French territory. Boisson knew that an attack upon Chad would require careful planning and a transfer of land forces within AOF that would take several weeks to arrange. He duly argued for a postponement of the Vichy scheme to retake Fort Lamy. Aware that a military campaign was impossible during the rainy season, Boisson preferred a combination of political and economic pressure and promises of lenient treatment in order to win over the Chad administration.[110] From mid-October, Boisson was supported by General Weygand, whom Pétain had just appointed Delegate-general for French Africa. Still a revered figure in spite of his role in the June defeat, Weygand was expected to restore colonial loyalty to Pétain. He arrived in Algiers in mid-October with a large military staff clearly designed to pursue a task that was always as much political as military, one of their early responsibilities being to reorganise police powers across French North Africa. Weygand's *deuxième bureau* military intelligence staff under Commandants Navarre and Coue, immediately began monitoring political conditions across French North and West Africa.[111] While still Minister of National Defence in August 1940, Weygand helped direct the planning for the recapture of Chad. With the agreement of the German and Italian Armistice Commissions at Wiesbaden and Turin, all demobilisation within AOF was suspended, the transport of additional Senegalese troops from North to West Africa was arranged and further transport aircraft were dispatched to Dakar.[112] Once in his new post at Algiers, Weygand was supposed to ensure that no other African territories rallied to Free France. He was also to refine the existing plans for the recapture of AEF. In the event, he concentrated on the former task to the virtual exclusion of the latter. In mid-November, for example, Weygand recommended that Platon should support Boisson's efforts to improve the defensive position within AOF. Only when this was achieved would an assault on Chad become a feasible proposition.[113]

Though the Vichy government and its colonial lieutenants were intent upon crushing Free French rule in Equatorial Africa, between September and December 1940 the administrations of French North and West Africa attached greater priority to preventing any further colonial declarations for de Gaulle. During the autumn, Weygand, Boisson, War Minister Charles Huntziger and a host of specialist military missions toured French North Africa and AOF to bolster support for Pétain among settler communities and individual colonial garrisons. One such military mission was sent to North Africa by the Naval Secretariat at Vichy. The mission chief, du Jonchay, reported in mid-October that the majority of serving French personnel in all three services across AFN still sympathised with de Gaulle. A handful of pilots in Morocco had, for example, attempted to steal aircraft in order to fly to Gibraltar to enlist in de Gaulle's forces. But active support for the Free French was by then largely confined to Casablanca and Tunis, where the local Jewish communities and the city police forces were singled out as especially unreliable.[114] Having conducted a similar tour of North Africa in early December, Weygand advised Huntziger to provide additional magistrates to clear the backlog of officers, pilots and community leaders awaiting trial by military tribunal for attempted 'dissidence'.[115] Concern about dissent within the large Jewish population in Algeria was by late 1940 reflected in a more systematic application of Vichy's developing body of antisemitic legislation. In the country's principal cities, Governor Abrial enforced the *Statut des Juifs*, which itself built upon the repeal of the so-called Crémieux decree which had previously guaranteed rights of citizenship to the Jewish population of French North Africa.[116]

In Syria and Lebanon, too, news of events in AEF and the outcome of the battle of Britain rekindled dissent within the officer corps of the Levant army. This was also stimulated by the expansion of the Italian Armistice Commission in Beirut. The French authorities in Damascus expected the Italians to cultivate links with the Turkish and Iraqi governments, and with local Syrian nationalists, in order to undermine the French position and so advance Mussolini's imperial ambitions in the Middle East.[117] For their part, the Italian monitors warned the Armistice Commission executive in Turin that plans were well under way for a Free French *coup* directed by a group of unnamed junior French officers. This was a reasonably accurate forecast. In London, both Carlton Gardens and the Vansittart Committee were eager to support a Syria *coup*, but both agreed that an effective leader had to be found. Unfortunately, the obvious choice, de Larminat, was by now preoccupied in AEF. The other dissident with extensive Levant experience, General Catroux, was not yet fully reconciled to serving the Free French cause under de Gaulle. In the absence of a viable plan, the British service chiefs ruled out any speculative or ill co-ordinated action. In late September Catroux was appointed head of the Free French mission in Cairo with a view to an eventual take-over in the Levant. At this stage, Catroux seemed to be more a British creature than an enthusiastic Gaullist. Wary of Catroux, de Gaulle also knew of the Italians' closer scrutiny of potential dissent in the Levant. He was alerted to it by his representative in Malta, a Foreign Legion officer formerly based in Tunisia, Commandant Robert. But de Gaulle was anyway consumed with the imminent attack on Dakar. He was not in a position to challenge British military reluctance to take action in Syria and Lebanon.[118]

Though complacent about the passivity of the Arab and Druze population, High Commissioner Gabriel Puaux was anxious to stamp upon dissidence among the governing French elite in Damascus and Beirut. His credit with the Vichy administration remained perilously low following his uncertain performance in June. As a result of an unsuccessful Free French attempt to bribe the head of the Levant Sûreté Générale, Puaux's administration discovered that Gaullist plans for a *coup* were well advanced.[119] On 12 September Puaux instructed General Fougère to organise a military inquiry intended to root out those officers thought to be responsible for the dissemination of Gaullist propaganda among individual garrisons.[120] The inquiry team, led by two of Fougère's trusted staff deputies, Lieutenant-colonel Lasserre and Captain Mordant, confirmed within a week that the Italian suspicions were well founded. Alarmed at the number of military reports indicating widespread disaffection in the Levant, on 20 September Baudouin instructed Puaux to undertake a more thorough administrative purge, adding that Darlan intended to send a vessel to Beirut to repatriate all those whom Puaux identified as 'undesirables'. Puaux, it seemed, was inclined to be cautious and forgiving, traits which were read in Vichy as further affirmation of his limited commitment to the Pétainist cause. Reinforced by the arrival of a Colonel Bourget, sent from Vichy to inject backbone into Puaux's investigations, in late September the military inquiry team made their first arrests. Two senior administrative officers, two Beirut financiers and two junior officers were detained on suspicion of involvement in a plot to depose the High Commissioner.[121] This caused dismay within the foreign affairs commissariat at Carlton Gardens. The Commissariat was never kept fully abreast of the *coup* plans.[122] Ironically, as we have seen, it was not the Free French plotters who removed Puaux, but rather Pierre Laval. In the wake of the attack on Dakar in late September, Laval was determined that all colonial Governors should prove demonstrable loyalty to Vichy. Puaux had failed the test.

While administrative dissent in the Levant centred on a small military cabal, in AOF it became apparent that, across several colonies with administrative *cercles* bordering British West African territory, local officials and village heads allowed the continuation of trade and transmigration to neighbouring British colonies. Stimulated by the attack on Dakar, and pressed to act more severely by Platon, during October

1940 Boisson began a more thorough purge of his colonial administration. Officials were encouraged to monitor any settlers known to have left-wing sympathies. A number of British residents were interned. Governors and district administrators who failed to pursue these tasks with sufficient vigour faced penalties ranging from temporary suspension to indefinite imprisonment.[123] Following another tour of inspection in November, Weygand instructed Boisson to increase police surveillance in the principal towns of AOF. The intelligence services in Dakar were also reorganised following Weygand's visit. The local Sûreté Générale office was expanded and a new intelligence-gathering agency – the Bureau de Centralisation de Renseignements – was set up. Henceforth, the Sûreté kept up-to-date lists of suspects, including Jewish residents, known Communist Party and Socialist Party supporters and 'all those whose intrigues appear, whether under foreign influence or otherwise, to seek to break the loyalty of Frenchmen to the head of state and to undermine the work of national recovery'.[124] This work was encouraged by the principal German agent in Dakar, a Dr Klaubé, formerly the director of Lufthansa traffic at Bathurst in the Gambia, who had built up an intelligence network of his own in neighbouring Senegal.[125] Clearly, the shock of the Anglo-Free French assault on Dakar was instrumental in transforming the nature of Boisson's regime. As in Syria and Lebanon, the extension of military and police powers across AOF during late 1940 precluded the development of an effective Gaullist opposition.

From Indo-China, through the Levant to AOF it was obvious by October 1940 that the tide of Free French dissent had been stemmed, if only temporarily. De Gaulle's inability to take Dakar and the greater self-assurance among Vichy's remaining colonial governments marked the beginning of a new phase in the struggle for the French empire. Over the winter of 1940–41 the nature of this contest was shaped by three new factors. Most important was Vichy's shift towards collaboration with the Axis powers, heralded by Pétain's meeting with Hitler at Montoire on 24 October 1940. This immediately increased the strategic importance of French African territories, since it became more probable that the Vichy regime would offer colonial concessions in order to ease Axis impositions upon metropolitan France. Owing to this threat of greater Axis penetration of the French empire, the treatment of Vichyite territories and colonial officials became a source of dispute between Britain and the United States. By 1941 this second problem had coalesced into a three-sided argument between Free France, Britain and its Dominions, and the US government. Were Vichy colonies to be coaxed into changing sides with the promise of British protection and Anglo-American trade, or were they to remain subject to blockade and hostile propaganda? This question hinged upon the third new factor in the French colonial equation – General Weygand, now installed in Algiers as Delegate-general for Vichy Africa. The effort to turn General Weygand formed part of a wider Anglo-American attempt to undermine the Vichy empire by more subtle means than Britain's previously straightforward support for pro-de Gaulle dissidents. This confronted Free France with a dilemma. How could de Gaulle and his followers determine British and US policy towards the Vichy empire whilst Free French supporters in these colonies were laid low and Gaullist forces could not liberate these territories alone? These problems form the subject of the next chapter.

Notes

1 Cassin, *Les Hommes partis de rien*, p. 185.

2 For a succinct discussion of the French collapse see Martin S. Alexander, 'The Fall of France, 1940', *Journal of Strategic Studies*, 13: 1 (1990), 10–44.

3 Thobie *et al.*, *Histoire de la France coloniale*, p. 314.

4 MAE, Série E, Vichy Levant, vol. 1, EMA-2, 'Note sur les dangers intérieurs de l'Afrique du Nord', n.d., August 1940. The fear of a linkage between nationalist unrest and Muslim antisemitism was shared by Noguès's administration in Rabat, see Michel Abitbol, *The Jews of North Africa during the Second World War* (Detroit, Wayne State University Press, 1989), p. 42.

5 SHAT, 2P12/D2, no. 16140/BCR, General Blanc to War Ministry, 6 August 1940.

6 MAE, Série P, Vichy Tunisie, vol. 12, Esteva to affaires étrangères, 3 September 1940.

7 Romain H. Rainero, *La Commission Italienne d'Armistice avec la France. Les rapports entre la France de Vichy et l'Italie de Mussolini* (Paris, SHAT, 1995), doc. 12, pp. 418–20.

8 MAE, Série M, Vichy Maroc, vol. 1, EMA-2, 'Etat d'esprit du personnel', 9 October 1940.

9 MAE, Papiers 1940, Papiers Paul Baudouin, vol. 9, Puaux to Baudouin, 24 September 1940. Puaux insisted in his memoirs that his actions in 1940 were dictated by the tenuous French hold upon Syria and Lebanon, see Gabriel Puaux, *Deux Années au Levant. Souvenirs de Syrie et du Liban* (Paris, Plon, 1952), pp. 201–3.

10 Churchill College archive, Cambridge, Spears papers, SPRS/1/134/2, Message from Chef de Service de Renseignements, Marine, 28 June 1940; Aviel Roshwald, *Estranged Bedfellows. Britain and France in the Middle East during the Second World War* (Oxford, Oxford University Press), 1990), pp. 13–16.

11 Maroun Bou Assi, 'La crise libanaise de 1941, ou, La bataille du Levant', in Charles-Robert Ageron, *Les Chemins de la décolonisation française, 1936–1956* (Paris, Editions du CNRS, 1986), pp. 308–10; Salma Mardam Bey, *La Syrie et la France. Bilan d'une équivoque (1939–1945)* (Paris, Editions l'Harmattan, 1994), pp. 39–45.

12 William A. Hoisington, *The Casablanca Connection. French Colonial Policy, 1936–1943* (Chapel Hill, University of North Carolina Press, 1984), pp. 165–77; regarding French North Africa's capacity to fight on, see Albert Merglen, 'La France pouvait continuer la guerre en Afrique Française du Nord en 1940', *Revue d'Histoire Diplomatique*, 106 (1992), 99–119.

13 MAE, Vichy Tunisie, vol. 1, Peyrouton to Affaires étrangères, 23 June 1940; Hoisington, *The Casablanca Connection*, pp. 172–3; Abitbol, *The Jews of North Africa*, pp. 47–8.

14 ANCOM, Fonds Département Alger, S1/D8, EMA, note de service, June 1940;

Anthony Clayton, *France, Soldiers and Africa* (London, Brassey's, 1988), pp. 122–4.

15 PRO, CAB 101/95, report by G. M. S. Stitt, 'The French fleet and Oran', n.d.

16 Pierre Queuille, 'Le décisif armistice franco-italien, 23–24 Juin 1940', *Revue d'Histoire Diplomatique*, 90 (1976), 100–111.

17 MAE, Vichy Levant, vol. 1, 'Texte italien de la convention d'armistice', 24 June 1940; Rainero, *La Commission Italienne d'Armistice*, pp. 47–50.

18 Churchill College archive, Spears papers, SPRS/1/134/1, Spears to Churchill and Eden, 20 June 1940; François Kersaudy, *Churchill and De Gaulle* (London, Collins, 1981), pp. 77–80.

19 St Antony's College, Middle East Centre archive, Spears papers, box IX/file 1, Manuscript extracts – relations with de Gaulle, n.d.

20 Charles de Gaulle, *Mémoires de Guerre. L'Appel, 1940–1942* (Paris, Plon, 1954), pp. 78–80.

21 SHM, Sous-série C, FNFL, Carton TTC 1, text of Muselier lecture, 1 May 1941.

22 PRO, WO 208/52, Redman mission to Ismay, 18 June 1940; Jean Daladier (ed.), *Edouard Daladier. Prison Journal, 1940–1945* (Boulder, Colo., and Oxford, Westview Press, 1995), pp. 1–2; Clayton, *France, Soldiers and Africa*, p. 128.

23 Martyn Cornick, 'The BBC and the propaganda war against occupied France: the work of Emile Delaveney and the European Intelligence Department', *French History*, 8: 3 (1994), 316–20.

24 De Gaulle, *L'Appel*, p. 79.

25 The two ships in question were the gunboat *Dumont d'Urville*, stationed at Noumea in New Caledonia, and the sloop *Ville d'Ys*, based at St Pierre.

26 Kim Munholland, 'The trials of the Free French in New Caledonia, 1940–1942', *French Historical Studies*, 14 (1986), pp. 549–52; Douglas G. Anglin, *The St Pierre and Miquelon Affaire of 1941. A Study in Diplomacy in the North Atlantic Triangle* (Toronto, Toronto University Press, 1966), pp. 17–19. The most detailed file regarding the events at Noumea was a 170 page report prepared by the head of the mining service in New Caledonia, see SHM, Archives FNFL, carton TTC 47, EM de Gaulle, 'Rapport de m. Mesple, chef du service des mines de la Nouvelle Caledonie', 5 October 1941; W. J. Hudson and H. J. W. Stokes (eds), *Documents on Australian Foreign Policy, 1937–49*, IV, *July 1940–June 1941* (Canberra, Australian Government Publishing Service, 1980), docs 92, 93, 118, 150.

27 Richard D. E. Burton, '"Nos journées de juin": the historical significance of the liberation of Martinique (June 1943)', in Kedward and Wood, *The Liberation of France*, p. 227.

28 PRO, CO 968/86/6, tel. 782, Brazzaville consulate to FO, 12 May 1942.

29 Lerner, *Catroux*, pp. 52–4.

30 Lerner, *Catroux*, pp. 133–35; Claude Hesse d'Alzon, 'L'évolution des conceptions stratégiques du commandement français en Indochine entre 1940 et 1945', *Revue d'Histoire de la Deuxième Guerre Mondiale*, 138 (1985), 6.

31 MAE, Série E, Vichy–Asie, vol. 261, Henry to affaires étrangères, 21 June 1940.

32 John E. Dreifort, 'Japan's advance into Indochina, 1940: the French response', *Journal of Southeast Asian Studies*, 13 (1982), 279–81; MAE, CNF Londres, Indochine, vol. 70, CN des affaires étrangères, 'L'invasion Japonaise en Indochine', 21 August 1942.

33 Julian G. Hurstfield, *America and the French Nation, 1939–1945* (Chapel Hill, University of North Carolina Press, 1986), pp. 20–1.

34 Pierre L. Lamant, 'La révolution nationale dans l'Indochine de l'Amiral Decoux', *Revue d'Histoire de la Deuxième Guerre Mondiale*, 138 (1985), 22.

35 Decoux, A la Barre de l'Indochine, pp. 69–70; Lamant, 'La Révolution nationale', 23; regarding Catroux's talks with the Japanese see Hata Ikuhiko, 'The army's move into northern Indochina', in James William Morley (ed.), *The Fateful Choice. Japan's Advance into South East Asia, 1939–1941* (New York, Columbia University Press, 1980), pp. 162–8.

36 Decoux, *A la Barre de l'Indochine*, pp. 41–6.

37 John E. Dreifort, 'France, the powers and the Far Eastern crisis, 1937–1939', *Histo-*

rian, 39 (1977), 733–53; Laffey, 'French Far Eastern policy', 135–40.

38 MAE, CNF Londres, Indochine, vol. 70, press extracts, 6–10 August 1940.

39 MAE, Vichy–Asie, vol. 261, no. 666, Decoux to Colonies, Vichy, 23 July 1940.

40 Communication quoted in Decoux, *A la Barre de l'Indochine*, p. 57.

41 MAE, CNF Londres, Indochine, vol. 70, direction des affaires politiques, note, 25 July 1941; Kiyoko Kurusu Nitz, 'Japanese military policy towards French Indochina during the Second World War: the road to the Meigo Sakusen (9 March 1945)', *Journal of Southeast Asian Studies*, 14 (1983), 331; John Pritchard, 'Winston Churchill, the military and imperial defence in East Asia', in Saki Dockrill (ed.), *From Pearl Harbor to Hiroshima. The Second World War in Asia and the Pacific, 1941–45* (London, Macmillan, 1994), pp. 36–7.

42 Dreifort, 'Japan's advance into Indochina', 282–4.

43 Lerner, *Catroux*, p. 137.

44 MAE, CNF Londres Indochine, vol. 70, FFL, 'Rapport du Sous-lieutenant Renault', n.d., 1941.

45 MAE, CNF Londres, Indochine, vol. 70, Commissariat national des affaires étrangères, 'L'invasion japonaise en Indochine', 21 August 1942; Dreifort, 'Japan's advance into Indochina', 284–5.

46 MAE, Vichy–Asie, vol. 255, Decoux to Platon, 23 October 1940. Many attributed Lémery's rapid dismissal from the Ministry of Colonies to his Martiniquan origin and his alleged links with Freemasonry.

47 PRO, WO 208/53, Consul, Dakar, to CO, 18 June 1940.

48 Kent, *Internationalization of Colonialism*, pp. 30–2; Rhodes House, MSS Afr. s. 1334(10), T. C. Hoskyns-Abrahall, 'Mission to the Free French, July 1940'.

49 Thobie et al., *Histoire de la France coloniale*, p. 315.

50 St Antony's, spears Papers, Spears IX/1, Manuscript – relations with de Gaulle, fo. 70.

51 Robert O. Paxton, *Vichy France. Old Guard and New Order, 1940–1944* (London, Barrie and Jenkins, 1972), pp. 56–7.

52 SHAT, 1P89/D2, 'Instruction de mission, M. le Général Weygand', 5 October 1940.

53 *Ibid.*

54 ANCOM, Fonds Département d'Alger, S1/D8, Le Beau to Prefects, Sub-prefects and Mayors, 2 July 1940; SHAT, 1P208/D3, EM-Section de Chiffre, n.1, 'Troupes de Maroc', 17 September 1940.

55 SHAT, 1P89/D1, Noguès, 'Instruction relative au Commandement en Chef de l'Afrique du Nord', 17 July 1940.

56 SHAT, 1P89/D2, EMA-2, rapport no. 516/2, 13 July 1940.

57 Hervé Coutau-Bégarie and Claude Huan, *Darlan* (Paris, Fayard, 1989), p. 299.

58 SHM, Fonds Amiral Sacaze, GG2/142, EMM-1, Forces Maritimes d'Atlantique Sud et d'Afrique, 'Discipline des marins évacués d'Angleterre', 31 July 1940.

59 Philippe Masson, *La Marine française et la guerre, 1939–1945* (Paris, Tallandier, 1991), pp. 142–65; Cornick, 'The BBC and the propaganda war', 317. The attack on Dakar is dealt with more fully in chapter three.

60 MAE, Vichy-Levant, vol. 1, Baudouin circular tel., 5 July 1940.

61 MAE, Vichy-Levant, vol. 1, Politique général, note, 5 July 1940; Rainero, *La Commission Italienne d'Armistice*, p. 62.

62 MAE, Vichy-Levant, vol. 1, 'Note au sujet des travails de la CIA', 6 July 1940.

63 SHAT, 1P34/D6, EM-Colonies, aide mémoire, Madagascar, 1 October 1940.

64 *Ibid.*

65 MAE, Vichy-Afrique, vol. 99, nos 756 and 890, Cayla to Lémery, 1 and 30 August 1940.

66 PRO, ADM 199/1277, Lord Harlech, Pretoria, to DO, 19 November 1940.

67 LHCMA, Papers of Major-general A. Chater, Box VIII, file 3/1/6, Chater to Legentilhomme, 24 August 1939.

68 ANCOM, Aff. pol. C 2536/D3, no. 2566, Conseiller d'Etat, Colonies, to Clauson, CO Under-secretary, 20 April 1940.

69 PRO, CO 323/1791/31, Wavell to WO, 12 July 1940.

70 Rainero, *La Commission Italienne d'Armistice*, p. 88; LHCMA, Chater papers, file 3/1/6, Legentilhomme to Chater, 18 June and 26 July 1940; Lacouture, *The Rebel*, pp. 270–1.
71 Rainero, *La Commission Italienne d'Armistice*, pp. 88–9.
72 PRO, CO 323/1791/34, CO tel. to West African Governors, 13 July 1940.
73 Vansittart was appointed deputy to Hugh Dalton, the chief of Britain's new subversive warfare organisation, the Special Operations Executive; see David Stafford, *Britain and European Resistance, 1940–1945* (London, Macmillan, 1980), p. 26.
74 Jean-Paul Cointet, 'Les relations entre de Gaulle et le gouvernement britannique durant la seconde guerre mondiale', *Revue Historique*, 268: 2 (1982), 432–3.
75 Rhodes House, MSS Afr. s. 1334(10), T. C. Hoskyns-Abrahall, 'Mission to the Free French, July 1940'; MSS Afr. s. 1085. L. C. Giles, 'First British contacts with Eboué (1940)', 30 October 1967; ANCOM, Aff. pol., C2536/D3, Mandel circular, 18 May 1940.
76 Sylvian C. Anignikin, 'Les facteurs historiques de la décolonisation au Dahomey (1936–1956)', in Ageron, *Chemins*, p. 508.
77 PRO, WO 208/53, Vice-consul, Douala, to CO, 24 June 1940; WP (40)258, Lord Lloyd memo, 'French Equatorial and West Africa', 11 July 1940.
78 PRO, WO 208/52, Hodson, Gold Coast, to Lord Lloyd, 8 July 1940; Churchill College archive, Spears papers, SPRS/1/136/1, Vansittart note for Halifax, 29 July 1940. The proposed Free French mission consisted of Captain Claude Hettier de Boislambert, Commandant Leclair and René Pleven.
79 Catherine Akpo-Vaché, *L'AOF et le seconde guerre mondiale. La Vie politique (septembre 1939–octobre 1945)* (Paris, Editions CNRS/Karthala, 1996), pp. 28–36.
80 PRO, WO 208/52, 13076/4/40, Lord Lloyd to Hodson, 20 July 1940.
81 Hervé Coutau-Bégarie and Claude Huan, *Lettres et notes de l'Amiral Darlan* (Paris, Economica, 1992), doc. 118, Darlan to Pétain, 21 August 1940.
82 PRO, CO 323/1791/34, CFR, thirty-third meeting, 22 July 1940; Jérôme Ollandet, *Brazzaville, capitale de la France Libre. Histoire de la résistance française en Afrique (1940–1944)* (Brazzaville, Editions de la Savane, 1980), pp. 38–9.
83 Rhodes House, MSS Afr. s. 1334(10), T. C. Hoskyns-Abrahall, 'Mission to the Free French, July 1940'; SHAT, 4P12/D1, France Libre communiqué, 10 November 1940.
84 This idea was proposed by Philippe Masson, see *La Marine française*, p. 295.
85 PRO, WO 208/52, COS(40)536, COS sub-comm. meeting, 8 July 1940.
86 PRO, CO 323/1791/34, J. S. Bennett memo., 26 July 1940.
87 Bernard Lanné, 'Le Tchad pendant la guerre (1939–1945)', in Ageron, Chemins, pp. 441–2.
88 PRO, CO 323/1791/34, Lord Lloyd memo., 'French Equatorial and West Africa', 11 July 1940; Kent, *Internationalization of Colonialism*, pp. 34–5; Brian Weinstein, *Eboué* (London, Oxford University Press, 1972), chapter 8. Regarding contacts between Bourdillon's Nigeria administration, Henri Laurentie and Eboué in Chad and Governor Brunot in Cameroon, see Robert D. Pearce, *Sir Bernard Bourdillon. The Biography of a Twentieth-century Colonialist* (Oxford, Kensall Press, 1987), pp. 285–96.
89 Lanné, 'Tchad pendant la guerre', pp. 439–40.
90 Deborah Wing Ray, 'The Takoradi route: Roosevelt's prewar venture beyond the western hemisphere', *Journal of American History*, 2 (1965), 340–58.
91 SHAT, 1P89/D2, Délégation Générale, Afrique Française, 'Etude sur la marche à suivre pour réduire la dissidence en AEF', 16 October 1940.
92 SHAT, 1P34/D6, EM-Colonies, aide mémoire, 23 September 1940; Lanné, 'Tchad pendant la guerre', p. 442.
93 Lanné, 'Tchad pendant la guerre', p. 439.
94 PRO, CO 323/1787/1, WP(40)195, Lord Lloyd memo., 'The Colonial Empire', 26 September 1940; Lacouture, *The Rebel*, pp. 271–2.
95 SHAT, 4P12/D5, Pierre de Saint Mart report, 'Ralliement de l'Oubangui-Chari', 15 August 1941.

96 SHAT, 2P12/D3, de Larminat tel., 22 September 1940; Jean-Louis Crémieux-Brilhac, *La France Libre. De l'Appel du 18 juin à la Libération* (Paris, Gallimard, 1996), p. 115.
97 PRO, WO 106/2156, Giffard to VCIGS, WO, 22 August 1940; Kent, *Internationalization of Colonialism*, p. 35, n. 16.
98 James L. Giblin, 'A colonial state in crisis: Vichy administration in French West Africa', *Africana Journal*, 5 (1994), 332; Gloria E. Maguire, *Anglo-American Relations with the Free French* (London, Macmillan, 1995), pp. 115–16.
99 Rhodes House, MSS Afr. s. 1334(10), T. C. Hoskyns-Abrahall, 'Mission to the Free French, July 1940'; MSS Afr. s. 1085. L. C. Giles, 'First British contacts with Eboué (1940)', 30 October 1967; Kent, *Internationalization of Colonialism*, pp. 32–5.
100 PRO, WO 208/52, WP(40)299, WO note on 'Situation, French Colonies in West Africa', 4 August 1940; Pearce, *Bourdillon*, p. 289.
101 MAE, Vichy-Afrique, vol. 98, Colonies Vichy, Inspection Générale des Travaux Publics, rapport no. 4, 28 November 1940.
102 MAE, Vichy-Afrique, vol. 98, direction politique, Afrique, Note pour le Ministre, 18 August 1940; Jonathan Derrick, 'The "Germanophone" elite of Douala under the French mandate', *Journal of African History*, 21 (1980), 258–61.
103 Churchill College archive, Spears papers, SPRS/1/136/1, Notes on AOF/AEF, n.d., August 1940.
104 PRO, WO 202/73, Major J. G. C. Allen report, 3 September 1942.
105 MAE, Vichy-Afrique, vol. 98, Colonies, Direction des Affaires Politiques to Baudouin, 8 August 1940; PRO, WO 106/2156, Giffard to WO, 15 August 1940.
106 SHM, Sous-série C, FNFL, TTC 1, Leclerc letter to Muselier, 8 October 1940.
107 Rhodes House, MSS Afr. s. 1334(10), T. C. Hoskyns-Abrahall, 'Mission to the Free French, July 1940'.
108 Coutou-Bégarie and Huan, *Lettres et notes de l'Amiral Darlan*, no. 120, Darlan to Amiral le Luc, 29 August 1940; no. 124, 'Note sur le comportement de l'Amiral Bourragué', 23 September 1940.
109 Coutau-Bégarie and Huan, *Darlan*, p. 340; Ronald Chalmers Hood III, *Royal Republicans. The French Naval Dynasties between the World Wars* (Baton Rouge, University of Louisiana Press, 1985), p. 175.
110 Akpo-Vaché, *L'AOF et le seconde guerre mondiale*, p. 38.
111 SHAT, 1P89/D1, Délégué Général, Alger, Journal de Marche, 1940–42.
112 SHAT, 1P34/D4, no. 4404/DSA, Weygand, note for General von Stulpnagel, Wiesbaden, 28 August 1940.
113 SHAT, 1P89/D2, Cabinet Militaire du Weygand, rapport no. 146, 10 November 1940.
114 MAE, Vichy-Maroc, vol. 1, no. 727, EM-2, Maroc, 'Etat d'esprit du personnel', 9 October 1940; Mission du Jonchay, AFN, rapport, 18 October 1940.
115 MAE, Vichy-Maroc, vol. 1, no. 478, Weygand to Huntziger, 5 December 1940.
116 Abitbol, *The Jews of North Africa*, pp. 59–64. The Crémieux decree was abrogated on 7 October 1940. The *Statut des Juifs* was introduced to North Africa in two stages under the Alibert law of 3 October 1940 and the more severe Vallat law of 2 June 1941. Both were most thoroughly applied in Algeria.
117 Roshwald, *Estranged Bedfellows*, pp. 24–7.
118 PRO, WO 106/2156, Commandant Robert to de Gaulle, 7 September 1940; Roshwald, *Estranged Bedfellows*, pp. 26–9.
119 Roshwald, *Estranged Bedfellows*, pp. 31–4.
120 MAE, Papiers 1940, Papiers Baudouin, 9, no. 457, Charles Rochat to Puaux, 4 September 1940; no. 1114, Puaux to Baudouin, 13 September 1940.
121 MAE, Papiers Baudouin, 9, no. 492, Baudouin to Puaux, 20 September 1940; no. 1240, Puaux to Baudouin, 27 September 1940; Roshwald, *Estranged Bedfellows*, pp. 32–5.
122 MAE, Londres CNF, vol. 39, Affaires étrangères memo., 14 October 1940.
123 Akpo-Vaché, *L'AOF et le seconde guerre mondiale*, pp. 36, 54–60.
124 Quote from Boisson papers, cited in Akpo-Vaché, *L'AOF*, p. 61.
125 MAE, Papiers Maurice Dejean, vol. 25, Dejean memo., 28 April 1941.

CHAPTER THREE

The empire between the Axis and the Allies, 1940–41

I have an Armistice Army. What can I do with that?' [General Maxime Weygand, 4 February 1941[1]]

Uneasy coexistence: Vichy and Free French territories in Africa

During August 1940 Churchill's government confirmed its support for Free France. Following an agreement reached with the Prime Minister on 7 August, de Gaulle was officially permitted to recruit armed forces under Free French jurisdiction. Technically, as de Gaulle's only qualified legal adviser, René Cassin, was quite prepared to admit, the British based their support upon the general personally.[2] René Pleven, who along with Cassin was largely responsible for the first drafts of the 7 August accord, stressed the importance of a legal document which could provide a juridical basis for the recruitment of Free French volunteers then in Britain, and for their payment by the British government.[3] Prior to this, de Gaulle's only source of finance was the 100,000 francs entrusted to him in early June by Paul Reynaud from the French government's emergency funds.[4] The Free French movement was still embryonic, most of its early supporters were little known in France, Britain or overseas, and de Gaulle was clearly the linchpin of the entire venture. Taking advantage of the Allied Forces Act, the British agreed on 22 August that, for the foreseeable future, Free French servicemen would be supplied and paid for by monthly advances from the British Treasury.[5] The same Treasury coffers were made available to ensure the buoyancy of any colonies which rallied to de Gaulle. In practice, this meant that Free French territories could value their currencies against an agreed sterling rate, while the actual value of the colonial francs in circulation would be generally safeguarded thanks to Britain's promise to purchase unsold export produce. By late 1940 the banks of Free French Africa relied upon the assurance of regular sterling transactions within individual colonies to assure their liquidity.[6]

By contrast, from July 1940 Vichy colonies in Africa were subjected to an increasingly stringent British naval blockade. It was imposed above all upon French North Africa and the Indian Ocean territories of Madagascar, Réunion and French Somaliland, which depended upon the slim chance of long-haul convoys evading detection by Royal Naval patrols.[7] As so little Vichy traffic reached the Indian Ocean, Indo-China was also severely affected, even though it was deliberately excluded from direct blockade for fear of the likely Japanese reaction. In short, where applied with vigour, the British blockade was a real threat to the Vichy empire. As Pétain admitted in October, the revitalisation of economic activity within loyal African colonies largely depended upon how much maritime tonnage could get through the blockade on a monthly basis. Since Vichy France was now an imperial rather than a continental power, this was a battle that had to be fought if the regime was to be anything more than a puppet state.[8] Pétain's military staff agreed. The empire was now the principal counterweight to Vichy weakness within Europe. Possession of colonies afforded Vichy 'a world-wide role in certain respects independent of her [German] victor'. Any loss of colonial territory would allow Germany and Italy to make greater demands upon metropolitan France. The armistice agreements almost represented implicit agreement to that effect.[9]

On 4 September, Admiral Henri Duplat, president of the French delegation to the Italian Armistice Commission in Turin, explained the French dilemma to his Italian hosts:

> Without colonial trade, France is doomed to famine and social unrest consequent upon unemployment. How can we protect this [maritime] traffic against British cruisers without warship escorts backed by further important forces? ... It would be dangerous to think that the near total interruption of maritime traffic and of commerical relations with the colonies, when added to [existing] British pressure, will not one day lead, in North Africa and in the empire as a whole, to a dissident movement against which no resistance will be feasible, whatever the French government's engagements to the contrary.[10]

Aware that the blockade was becoming the principal focus of Vichy's anti-British propaganda, and keen to lessen the popular identification of Free France with the solitary figure of de Gaulle, on 4 August Churchill backed the creation of an Empire Defence Council to serve as an executive arm of the Free French movement in all matters affecting Gaullist territory.[11] In practice, a full nine-member Empire

Defence Council was not formally established until 27 October and, once in operation, it was tightly controlled by de Gaulle. Since so many of its members – among them, Félix Eboué, Georges Catroux, Edgard de Larminat, Philippe Leclerc, Emile Muselier and Henri Sautot – were either in post as governors or on active military service, it was virtually impossible for the Empire Defence Council to meet as a group. Furthermore, in November 1940, de Gaulle created an almost parallel authority – the High Commission for Free French Africa. It was not clear how administrative responsibilities were to be shared between Eboué, newly appointed Governor-general of AEF, and General de Larminat, the first High Commissioner. The one point beyond doubt was that both men were expected to put Gaullist Africa's contribution to the war above any considerations of long-term reform within Free French territory.[12] Hence the Empire Defence Council was entrusted with the general prosecution of the Free French war effort and was assigned jurisdiction over all contacts between foreign governments and Free France. These measures seemed to herald a more aggressive Anglo-Free French policy in black Africa. This did not long survive the successful *ralliements* of late August.

Writing in mid-November 1940, the British Colonial Secretary, Lord Lloyd, concluded that the recent spate of Free French successes in Africa was at an end. French North and West Africa were expected to remain 'solidly pro-Vichy'. The British Chiefs of Staff concurred, noting that the political, economic and familial links between Mediterranean (now Vichy) France and the *colons* of Algeria and Tunisia had already generated a manifest community of interest between the two. Furthermore, the danger of compromising the British position in Palestine, Egypt or Iraq if an unsuccessful attempt were made to sponsor revolt in Syria effectively ruled out any such plans.[13] Though Churchill backed the idea of a Free French Empire Defence Council in theory, once the council was established in October the Foreign Office dismissed it as a rubber-stamp authority likely to add to de Gaulle's autocratic power. Under Lord Halifax, the Foreign Office was always a restraint upon Churchill's enthusiasm for Free France. Halifax thought it incumbent upon his department to explore any possible opportunities for detente with Vichy, especially given the mounting indications of serious rivalry between the increasingly collaborationist Pierre Laval and Paul Baudouin's vaguely Anglophile followers, based upon a nucleus of Quai d'Orsay officials.[14] For their part, the British service chiefs – Admiralty representatives above all – judged the anti-Vichy blockade an expensive and avoidable commitment whose maintenance owed more to the tenacity of Hugh Dalton, the Minister of Economic Warfare, than to any sound strategic thinking.[15]

The British blockade of Vichy Africa did not yield immediate results. In the last quarter of 1940, as Delegate-general for Vichy Africa, Weygand achieved considerable success in consolidating loyalty to Pétain among subordinate colonial officials. Most administrations across AOF were now effectively controlled by loyal military personnel after purges of known Gaullist sympathisers between August and November. Though he admitted that there was little real Anglophobia among the administrative elite in Algeria and Morocco, Weygand referred with growing confidence to genuine political cohesion among the rulers of North Africa and AOF. What dissent remained was to be eradicated by further *épuration*. In order to preempt disloyalty among the indigenous population, Weygand sought to re-establish the military prestige of French colonial authority. Henceforth, the ceremonial and policing duties of the Armée d'Afrique and the colonial garrisons of North and West Africa became closely intertwined.[16] Weygand's speeches typically blended Vichy propaganda with choice words regarding patriotic obligation and the military prowess of French colonial soldiery. His report to Pétain on his tour of AOF in late October captured this well:

> In all the towns I visited I spoke at length to officers, administrators and often to local notaries. I made sure they understood the course of events in France, without omitting the failings of our British Allies. I made it clear from this that our return to war twenty-one years after the Victory was due to the Anglo-Saxons who toyed with us in denying the guarantees they had promised during the negotiation of the Treaty of Versailles, and who had only taken their own interests into account when the time came to decide their fate. I stigmatised the conduct of the traitors who have taken up arms against their country. Finally, I concluded that only discipline and unity around the flag, held high and firm by Marshal Pétain, would protect our country against any eventuality that may arise in the current difficult circumstances – and this is our duty. My listeners followed my words closely, with obvious approval. Everywhere I was greeted by declarations of loyalty and readiness to defend the soil of the Empire against any attack, no matter where it might come from.[17]

The apparent success of Weygand's policies in Africa was not lost on the British service chiefs. It was equally clear to them that British attacks on other, more remote parts of the French empire were also out of the question. For instance, once he put a stop to the wave of post-armistice desertions from the ships under his command, Admiral Robert's naval garrison took a firm grip upon the French West Indies. In order to ensure Robert's neutrality, the US government effectively sanctioned this state of affairs. During a conference of the Organisation of American Republics in Havana in July 1940, the US delegation steered through a resolution affirming the inviolability of European imperial possessions in the western hemisphere. This was a clear signal to the Axis powers to keep out of the Vichyite French West Indies as well as the British and Dutch colonies in the Caribbean. Article 1 of the Havana convention affirmed that any transfer of national authority within these European colonies would justify the intervention of one or several of the American republics to prevent any permanent change of sovereignty. Though the Foreign Office welcomed the Havana statement, the US warning was judged equally applicable to Britain, lest Churchill was tempted to advance de Gaulle's cause at Admiral Robert's expense.[18]

Elsewhere, the prospects for Anglo-Free French military intervention were similarly bleak. There were no troops readily available to mount an invasion of Madagascar or a swift occupation of Djibouti. Having fled to join de Gaulle in London, General Paul Legentilhomme, the former Somaliland Governor, warned that if pressure on Vichy territory was to consist solely of a British-led blockade, colonial hostility to Free France was bound to increase.[19] But there were no ready alternatives available. Indo-China was another case in point. By January 1941 the Free French Empire Defence Council admitted that it was unlikely to possess the military means to effect a change of regime in Indo-China for years to come. Even propaganda or subversion was ruled out in the short term for fear of unleashing a complete Japanese military occupation of the federation.[20] Furthermore, in Free French eyes, the British will to resist seemed weakest in South East Asia. One indicator of this was that, at the behest of the Japanese, in July Churchill had agreed to the temporary closure of the Burma supply road to the Chinese Nationalists.

Setting the seal on the *status quo* across French Africa, on 26 November, General Giffard urged the War Office to oppose any Free French operations liable to involve his own forces in clashes with AOF troops. At worst, this might lead to Vichy occupation of exposed British colonies such as Sierra Leone or the Gambia. Whatever the case, the Takoradi-to-Cairo Middle East reinforcement route would be needlessly endangered.[21] This string of African air bases and landing sites was an essential lifeline to General Wavell's Middle East command, and the volume of equipment dispatched increased considerably during the course of 1941.[22] The new caution evident in British policy owed much to this general re-evaluation of strategic priorities. But what changed the political picture across the French empire most dramatically was the failure of the Anglo-Free French attack on Dakar between 23 and 25 September 1940.

The attack on Dakar and the seizure of Gabon

With Operation Menace (the codename for the Dakar assault), de Gaulle became openly complicit in British attempts to destroy what remained of Vichy's overseas armed forces. Henceforth, Vichy portrayed him as both traitor and fratricidal murderer of his compatriots. The assault on Dakar was an embarrassing reverse for the Free French. Within Whitehall, the failure of the British naval assault was soon ascribed to inadequate preparation, Free French security lapses, coastal fog and the natural inaccessability of Dakar harbour. Nevertheless, the ferocity of the Vichy defence came as a rude shock. The Dakar garrison was stronger than at any point since September 1939. The port's defences had recently been reinforced by the unscheduled arrival of the Toulon naval squadron – Force Y – which was originally designated to lead the recapture of AEF. It included three fast cruisers, *Gloire*, *Georges Leygues* and *Montcalm*. Frustrated in his attempt to reach Brazzaville, the squadron commander, Vice-admiral Jean Bourragué, was anxious to redeem himself through his actions at Dakar.[23] In co-operation with Admiral Lacroix, the naval garrison commander, Bourragué successfully frustrated British attempts to target the Vichy ships in port. Ironically, the Cabinet Defence Committee was prepared to cancel Operation Menace as soon as intelligence of the arrival of Bourragué's cruisers came through. The situation was further complicated by the knowledge that a substantial part of the Polish and Belgian state gold reserves, originally intended for shipment to Canada, had been redirected to Senegal. De Gaulle and the British task force commander, Vice-admiral John Cunningham, persuaded the Defence Committee to proceed.[24] Immediately after Menace, the Chiefs of Staff made plain that they rued this decision:

> The reason which led us to undertake Operation 'Menace' was the belief that there was a fair chance of de Gaulle being welcomed in French West Africa or at least establishing himself there with little or no opposition. Since it is now evident that this belief was unfounded, our efforts should be to restore the status quo as soon as possible and [to] avoid further hostilities with the French in North West Africa, including the bombing of Gibraltar.[25]

Having sailed with the British task force to Dakar, de Gaulle then secured onward passage to AEF. Before he returned from Africa to London in late November, he, too, had ample time to mull over the humiliation of Menace. The capture of Gabon in November did little to compensate for the earlier failure at Dakar. Admiral Muselier warned that the British Admiralty was now determined to avoid any joint operations in support of the Free French. The lack of enthusiasm in London for the Gaullist assault on Libreville, capital of Gabon, confirmed this.[26] Indeed, there was little to celebrate about the conversion of the colony. The two columns of Free French forces which entered Gabon in the first week of October were held up by skirmishes around Lambaréné and Mitzac at the end of the month.[27] With little sign of any spontaneous support for the Gaullist invaders, the colonial capital and the Vichy sloop *Bougainville*, at anchor in Libreville harbour, were bombed by way of inducement. The tragic suicide of Governor Masson found a less spectacular echo in the general fear among the settler population in Libreville that assocation with Gaullism meant indefinite exile from France. Furthermore, an embarrassing, if undisclosed, number of the Tirailleurs that participated in the assault on the town took advantage of the resultant confusion to change into civilian clothing and abscond.[28]

Taken together, the failure of Operation Menace and the ambiguous victory in Gabon were profoundly discouraging. De Gaulle duly confirmed to General Spears that he had no immediate plans to take the offensive in AOF. Dissuaded by General Giffard and Governor Sir Bernard Bourdillon, de Gaulle shelved proposals to attack either Dahomey or Niger from Nigerian territory. He also abandoned a similar tentative scheme to march into French Guinea from Sierra Leone in the face of British hostility to the idea. Neither the Chiefs of Staff nor de Gaulle's supporters at Carlton Gardens possessed solid evidence to confirm that the Vichyite administration in Konakri would be willing to defy Governor-general Boisson. The Vansittart Committee settled matters. The CFR refused to sanction any Gaullist attacks mounted from British territory upon Vichy-controlled colonies. The Colonial Office and the Admiralty took the same view.[29] Instead, throughout early 1941, Free French troops in AEF were increasingly directed towards Chad and the developing British-led campaign against Italian Libya.[30]

Though French naval gunners keen to avenge the losses of Mers el-Kébir directed the greater part of the fighting at Dakar in September, the abject failure of Free French efforts to parley with the AOF administration proved that many French personnel considered Pétain's Vichy a cause worth fighting for. Boisson submitted an ebullient report to Admiral Platon on the defence of Dakar: 'The success of the [Vichy] French forces was complete. Niether by surprise, nor by intimidation, nor by violence did the enemy manage to undermine the determination of our defence ... Success was due to the cohesion, the absolute accord and the team spirit which governed the measures taken at all levels of the [military] hierarchy.'[31] Admiral Bourragué perhaps offered a more honest assessment when he reported his first impressions of Dakar to Darlan. According to Bourragué, the city's administration and commercial sector teemed with Gaullists. Army and air force officers feared wholesale desertions and the Pétainist navy was thoroughly detested.[32] Dakar was certainly bustling with a fast-expanding population of some 165,000. Many of these Dakar residents – both African and French – had been in the city for less than a generation. Inadequate water supplies, the constant threat of epidemics and severe overcrowding in the poorest Médina district, to the north of the port, added to the impression of a city on the brink of some sort of crisis, social or political.[33] Boisson lent further credence to Bourragué's estimate by arresting the city mayor, the director of the Ecole Normale and the president of the Dakar Chamber of Commerce during the British attack.[34]

Whether Boisson or Bourragué was closer to the mark, once the British task force arrived, any latent military opposition to Vichy authority evaporated. AOF Governors and Free French intelligence reports from West Africa indicated that Operation Menace transformed opinion among the French settler community.[35] The obvious question is why? Aside from Boisson's intensive propaganda drive, the most convincing explanation derives from the economic and strategic position in West Africa. Prior to the French collapse, a fragile symbiosis characterised relations between British West Africa and French West Africa. In a major war, British territories stood to profit from the French military presence in the region but in more normal times France's land-locked territories in AOF and AEF depended upon transit rights across British territory for their economic survival. By October 1940 the British Treasury had intervened decisively in Free French AEF by stabilising the AEF franc at 175.6 to £1.[36] Further economic support consolidated the loyalty of Free French Africa. In the Cameroon, for instance, in response to Leclerc's increasingly desperate pleas, the British government provided sterling advances to cover the import of essential fuel and foodstuffs, and reiterated its pledge to purchase the colony's annual crop output as soon as shipping became available to collect it.[37] With lingering hopes that similar financial support might encourage AOF territories to turn to de Gaulle, the British government contemplated excluding French West Africa from the list of French territories placed under British blockade once Pétain's government moved to Vichy in July 1940. In practice, however, the Royal Navy South Atlantic command was under instructions to curtail maritime traffic to AOF.[38] Though this muddle in British blockade policy originated in the lack of sufficient ships to enforce it properly, Churchill's government remained unsure about how best to deal with the Vichy empire after Operation Menace. Two questions remained unanswered.

Firstly, would economic pressure upon Vichy territories serve any useful purpose? The solution to this puzzle rested upon the second question – were there individuals within the Vichy government and individual colonial administrations who might yet be persuaded to change sides? With hindsight, it is clear that in late 1940 and early 1941 there were not. The irony is that in this same brief period the British pursued a series of semi-official contacts with Pétain, Baudouin, Huntziger and eventually Weygand, all of which proved worthless.[39]

Anxious lest French merchant shipping should fall into British hands, throughout August and early September 1940 the German Armistice Commission rejected Vichy requests for a relaxation in the restrictions imposed upon French convoy traffic.[40] More importantly, after Mers el-Kébir, Darlan's Secretariat of Marine repeatedly sought German and Italian permission to protect commercial traffic to the empire with naval vessels that were re-released for active service in response to the Oran bombardment.[41] Until the assault on Dakar the Wiesbaden armistice commissioners remained intransigent. It was only as Hitler studied incoming reports of the fighting at Dakar that he confirmed his willingness to support the Vichy empire against Anglo-Gaullist attack. Within days, the Wiesbaden Commission put forward plans to reinforce Vichy Africa in readiness for a conflict with Britain and Free France.[42] The Dakar authorities were fully aware that a spirited defence offered the best prospect of German concessions. Already faced with commodity shortages and a mounting weight of export produce rotting away for want of shipping, Boisson's administration appreciated that a show of resolve in the face of British pressure was likely to result in a local relaxation of armistice restrictions. Put simply, what defined the Vichy faith in AOF was the perception that French interests were best served by keeping the empire safe from outsiders. Though inherently xenophobic, this outlook was nourished by the belief that de Gaulle was ultimately beholden to the British government – itself the cause of rising economic misery across French West Africa. It is well to remember that the defenders of Dakar had one eye on the easing of the pressure of blockade.

For all de Gaulle's efforts to portray Free French AEF as a major strategic asset, the British remained largely unconvinced. From the British Admiralty perspective, AOF was far more crucial. Dakar was the most important French imperial port, particularly as Britain's Mediterranean contingency planning acknowledged a potential need to abandon the British position within that sea, albeit temporarily, in order to meet the Japanese threat.[43] By contrast, in no circumstances was control of the South Atlantic to be relinquished, although the volume of British West African trade was curtailed in order to release vessels for the shipment of war material.[44] From Dakar, British sea communications via the Cape of Good Hope could be threatened, potentially isolating South Africa and the Australasian Dominions. The South African and Australian governments were fully alive to this danger. The South African Premier, Jan Christian Smuts, emphasised repeatedly that he expected Britain to take matters in hand.[45] Britain's own West African deep-water port, Freetown in Sierra Leone, was within reach of Dakar by land, air or sea expedition. After the Mers el-Kébir attack, the possibility of sustained French reprisal attacks against Malta and Gibraltar added to the importance of Freetown to the British South Atlantic naval command.[46] In 1940 the port did not possess a large garrison, a resident fleet or fixed anti-aircraft defences, though it was vital as a convoy assembly point. The focus of British strategic interest in West Africa during the last six months of 1940 was thus weighted towards Vichy-controlled Senegal, Dakar in particular. From March 1938, French naval planners shared these appreciations of the relative importance of Dakar and Freetown to both successful imperial defence and the maintenance of Atlantic communications.[47] A week after the events at Oran, Darlan's immediate naval deputy, Admiral Jean de Laborde, arrived in Dakar to assess the prospects for a combined land and sea assault upon Freetown. The more sanguine AOF army commander, General Barrau, was hard pressed to discourage the admiral's enthusiasm for an attack.[48]

De Gaulle expected the conversion of Dakar to produce a wholesale change of allegiance among the subordinate Governors of AOF. But, lacking reliable intelligence, neither the general nor his advisers studied this in much detail. Instead, Carlton Gardens appeared more inspired by the possibility that success at Dakar would enable de Gaulle to persuade the British to back an operation against the Levant.[49] The irony was that, while the failure of Operation Menace inspired a new caution in Anglo-Free French policy in Africa, it also revitalised Vichy plans to regain control in AEF. On 30 August the Italian supreme command notified the French War Ministry that, in the absence of any further British attacks on Vichy territory, it planned to revoke the armistice concessions made in July. The Italians even contemplated reducing the Armée d'Afrique in French North Africa from its 120,000 global figure to a mere 30,000. Darlan reacted with horror, warning of an immediate breakdown of civil order in North Africa if the threat were carried out.[50] Ten days before Menace, on 12 September, Admiral Duplat advised Darlan that the Italian and German governments were becoming impatient with Free French success in Africa. If Vichy failed to restore its authority, the Axis governments reserved the right to take matters into their own hands. Furthermore, even if Vichy intended to act, it would have to obtain Armistice Commission approval on a case-by-case basis.[51] This was a dire warning indeed. But, just as the welcome relaxations of armistice provisions brought about by Mers el-Kébir were being questioned by the armistice commissioners, the Dakar assault reversed the process. Pétain's military commanders found their limited freedom of manoeuvre restored.

The Vichy fleet derived most benefit from the additional concessions granted after Operation Menace. As a result, two key changes were made, both of which added substance to Vichy imperial defence planning. Firstly, more Vichy warships were released to protect empire convoy traffic and so break the British blockade. Secondly, additional vessels were made available to protect colonial ports against further Anglo-Gaullist attack. The German Armistice Commission authorised the Secretariat of Marine to combine those warships stationed in Morocco and French West Africa into *forces coloniales océaniques*. These units were granted wider powers to use force against the Royal Navy and British merchant shipping in French African waters. In parallel with this relaxation of control, the Italian Armistice Commission indicated that the French warships in Algeria, Tunisia and Lebanon, plus a specified contingent of the Toulon-based fleet, could reinforce French imperial defences in the event of renewed British or Free French assaults. From this point on, Toulon became the appointed centre of a Force de Haute Mer, commanded by Admiral de Laborde. In conception, de Laborde's ships were regarded as a rapid reaction force intended to deter British attacks on French-controlled ports or vital communications. This force included almost a quarter of the entire Vichy French navy. The Armistice Commissions were prepared to release the munitions for this Toulon fleet, known as the Groupe Strasbourg, provided that a larger quota of the French navy as a whole was removed from active service.[52]

Early collaborationism in the Vichy empire

On 11 October 1940 Pétain made a speech accepting the requirement for limited Franco-German collaboration. In Marc Ferro's memorable phrase, Pétain's statement was thrown like a message in a bottle to drift towards the German Reich.[53] Hitler had good reason to respond. The events at Dakar illustrated Vichy's capacity for imperial defence in an otherwise disappointing six weeks for Germany. The battle of Britain was clearly lost by September and Hitler's meeting with General Francisco Franco at Hendaye on 23 October was not a success. It was quite impossible for Hitler to marry closer collaboration with

Vichy alongside Franco's demands for territorial concessions in North West Africa – in French Morocco and Algeria's western Oranie region above all. Though a Spanish alliance remained a far greater prize than Vichy goodwill, Franco's price was always too high. After his meeting with the Caudillo on 23 October – discussions which Hitler famously likened to having teeth pulled – the Führer was unexpectedly receptive to Pétain when the two leaders met at Montoire a day later.[54] Since Franco was unlikely to enter the war while Britain remained undefeated, a more pugnacious Vichy North Africa offered greater short-term rewards to Hitler as he attempted to undermine the British position in the Mediterranean basin.

In late October, Laval and General Huntziger capitalised upon the 'spirit of Montoire' by pursuing further talks with the German Armistice Commission over permissible reinforcement of French North Africa and the Levant, the two regions where the Axis powers were most chary of substantial concessions.[55] Hitler disappointed Mussolini by indicating his support for Vichy's effort to defend its African possessions.[56] In consequence, the Wiesbaden commissioners proved more flexible than their Italian counterparts. Neither Berlin nor Vichy kept the Rome government fully informed of the diplomatic exchanges which preceded Montoire. Though the original armistice agreements made Italy the senior supervisory power across French North Africa, in this region at least, Axis policy was becoming discordant. General von Stulpnagel, the president of the German Armistice Commission at Wiesbaden, was now willing to allow tacit naval and aircraft reinforcement of French North Africa provided that the Italians were not told of it *a priori*. By contrast, the Italian armistice controllers in North Africa tried unsuccessfully to recalculate the global figure for the Armée d'Afrique by including air force and naval units in a reduced overall force strength of 100,000 men. It was hardly in Italy's interest to see Vichy made stronger in North Africa when Mussolini clearly harboured grand designs upon Maghreb territory.[57]

Darlan followed up Huntziger's approaches to Wiesbaden with requests for the further release of mothballed ships and aircraft in order to resume the planning of operations against AEF.[58] During November, the Vichy government debated two alternative War Ministry proposals for the reconquest of Gaullist territory. The first built on earlier schemes to coax AEF settlers and officials back to the Vichy side through a combination of vigorous propaganda and threats of legal punishment. This was to be backed up by an assault force under General Falvy, based at Niamey, capital of Niger. Though Falvy's troops were unlikely to be used in practice, they might prove a sufficiently intimidating presence to secure a change of loyalties in AEF. The second proposal also exploited this Niger assault force, strengthened by the redeployment of several Armée de l'Air squadrons from North Africa to AOF air bases. This scheme, however, envisaged actual military operations, beginning with an invasion of Chad supported by air raids against Fort Lamy and Free French military installations in the colony. Though it promised swifter results, this latter plan of attack was ruled out because it was expected to result in an Anglo-Vichy conflict.[59] It seemed probable that the British would resist any assault on Chad, as the colony formed the southern flank of Wavell's campaign in Libya. The British were also expected to intervene in order both to keep the Takoradi route in operation and to deter Vichy attacks elsewhere. As Minister of Colonies Platon admitted, *le facteur anglais* was decisive because Vichy could not risk outright British hostility. But, in one sense, it did not much matter whether actual operations took place. An ulterior motive of Vichy's offensive planning was to intimidate any potential Gaullist dissidents within AOF. If it appeared that Vichy confidently anticipated the recapture of Free French territories, there would be less chance of colonies within AOF turning to de Gaulle.[60]

Overland attacks traversing the vast interior of AEF stood little chance of success without the backing of seaborne assaults on the principal ports of the Congo, the Cameroon and Gabon. On 23 November Darlan informed Weygand that it was impracticable to redeploy vessels from Vichy's Mediterranean fleet to AOF. Though the German and Italian armistice commissioners might warm to the idea if the British consolidated their early successes in North Africa, the French fleet was bound to be isolated once it reached AEF. Unless Freetown were first 'neutralised', the British South Atlantic command could either intercept or impede French warships once they left the protection of Dakar. The venture was simply too dangerous for a navy with severely limited resources to contemplate.[61] The experience of Bourragué's cruiser squadron in September proved Darlan's point. Those ships that succeeded in sailing beyond Dakar were forced to abandon their onward passage to AEF because the British intercepted the refuelling vessels that were vital if any of Bourragué's cruisers were to make it back to Vichy African ports.[62] Fuel shortages, rather than any inadequacies of equipment or personnel, also undermined the proposed land and air operations directed from AOF. Though the German naval command delighted in the possibility of Vichy planes wreaking havoc upon Freetown and Takoradi, in fact, these ports, while certainly soft targets, could be subjected only to intense short-term bombing.[63]

Taking these reservations into account, in early December the Secretariat of Marine formulated definitive instructions regarding attacks on British or Gaullist colonial territory. As long as British hostility towards the Vichy empire fluctuated, colonial commands were to maintain a permanently 'menacing attitude'. But operations were strictly confined to reprisal actions, and were sanctioned only in the event of direct attacks on AOF, convoy seizures or any other acts of overt Anglo-Free French aggression. By confining action to reprisals against British or Free French attack it was also easier to guarantee the continued loyalty of the troops involved. The Vichy War Ministry doubted that the troops available in AOF would remain loyal if ordered to undertake gruelling route marches or long-term operations.[64] Moreover, Pétain's service chiefs preferred limited aerial bombardment of British colonial ports as the optimum means of reprisal, since it carried less chance of an immediate British declaration of war. So long as AOF remained unmolested, and coastal traffic between Dakar, the Côte d'Ivoire and Dahomey continued without great interruption, Vichy would not sanction any military venture against AEF or British West Africa.[65]

For all the talk of offensive planning, Vichy policy remained cautious. Although General Walther Warlimont, head of the Wehrmacht Operations Staff, twice visited Paris to discuss operations against AEF, Laval's pleasure at this German support was offset by the Vichy government's more sober analysis of the practical impediments to a major offensive.[66] Though it originated in Vichy's Secretariat of Marine, this studied ambiguity was nowhere better illustrated than in the actions of Pierre Boisson in Dakar. Boisson complied selectively with the armistice accords. He persuaded his fellow Governors across AOF to observe the armistice terms in spirit if not in detail. In early August 1940 Boisson dispatched the Inspector-general of Colonies, Boulmer, on a tour of French Sudan, upper Côte d'Ivoire and Niger, the object being to reinforce Vichy authority at ground level.[67] Boisson then utilised the danger of British and Free French incursion to secure German and Italian acquiescence in the maintenance of 33,000 Vichy French troops in West Africa.[68] In early November, General von Stulpnagel notified his French counterpart, General Noyen, that the Wehrmacht command approved Vichy's request to raise a mobile army group in AOF. This force corresponded to a reinforced infantry regiment in size. The Wiesbaden authorities set no limits upon the use of this force. Previously, the armistice commissioners insisted that the naval reinforcement of Dakar should be monitored by a German Naval Control Commission which arrived in the port on 22 September 1940. The German high command even authorised the disbursement of metropolitan stocks of war material to set up the army group, should

Noguès be unable to send the necessary equipment from North Africa. Stulpnagel also indicated German approval for the constitution of a fourth AOF bomber group comprised of recently purchased Glenn Martin aircraft to be released from North Africa and, if necessary, metropolitan France. Backed by an additional two groups of troop transport aircraft, these measures were still more threatening in their obvious offensive potential.[69]

Despite these reinforcements, French effectives across AOF were kept below the pre-armistice position. The cuts were accomplished by releasing the bulk of those conscripted under the 1939 and 1940 recruitments.[70] This, however, leaves the Tirailleur and other African forces which had served in France, Syria and East Africa entirely out of the reckoning. After September 1940 there thus remained a professional army core within French West Africa. By late October the War Office Directorate of Intelligence estimated that there were ten active companies within Dakar and a further fourteen companies of Tirailleurs, ten of which were motorised, across Senegal.[71] Skilled regular units dominated the standing imperial forces of the Armée d'Afrique and La Coloniale. These were the troops allocated a combatant role within the pre-war imperial defence planning of the supreme command and its subordinate imperial wing, the Etat-Major Général des Colonies.[72]

French ground forces were complemented by a strong Armée de l'Air presence, much of it composed of aircraft hastily returned to Noguès's command from metropolitan France in June 1940. By the end of 1940 the Vichy authorities in French North and West Africa could call upon 1,500 trained pilots, with adequate ground staff to maintain over 700 aircraft then still available to them. Many aircraft were obsolete, but by December 1940 American Glenn Martin bombers and Curtiss fighters, all purchased since 1939, were deployed in AOF. In addition, two squadrons of French Cebire 298 torpedo bombers were stationed in Dakar from November to deter any naval bombardment by static vessels. Boisson's commanders were in an excellent position to repel all attackers, provided that their fuel did not run out.[73]

Free French retrenchment and British support

Aware of Vichy's stronger hand, during November and December 1940 the Foreign Office, Spears mission representatives in London and Brazzaville and the British West African Governors' conference worked to reconcile the Free French to a more patient conversion of individual colonies within AOF. This was easily achieved once de Gaulle left Brazzaville for London on 17 November. Churchill, Eden and Spears were better placed to rein the general in, at least until the Dakar failure receded from memory. Meanwhile, in Brazzaville itself, de Larminat, newly appointed High Commissioner for Free French Africa, opposed further military ventures in the short term. According to US intelligence, supplied to the British military attaché in Washington in January 1941, if Boisson ignored the armistice terms completely, French West Africa could raise up to 400,000 native troops.[74] Hitherto, both Boisson and the Vichy Ministries of Colonies and War had chosen to manipulate the armistice terms rather than challenge them outright. If Gaullist supporters continued to act like loose cannon in West Africa, this might change. De Larminat agreed that the wisest course of action was to establish more reliable contacts with Gaullist supporters in AOF. To avoid any repetition of the events at Dakar, there would be no military intervention until local conditions were so ripe 'as virtually to amount to [an] invitation to [the] Free French to co-operate'.[75] In pursuit of de Larminat's policy, Free French liaison commissions were established in Lagos and Freetown. These soon became the focal points of propaganda, the reception of new volunteers from AOF, and intelligence-gathering in Senegal and Côte d'Ivoire. In fact, the movement of refugees and volunteers from Vichyite territory into British West African colonies had by then slowed to a trickle.

Until the invasion of Syria in June 1941, the nucleus of Free French supporters in Africa faced mounting strain. There were few qualified personnel to conduct administration and insufficient troops to form powerful colonial garrisons.[76] The Free French military effort, at this stage largely conducted by seasoned Coloniale and Foreign Legion troops serving under Leclerc's command, was confined to sporadic attacks upon Italian forces in the Fezzan. The skill of long Saharan marches and the romance of outnumbered units achieving against-the-odds victories, such as the famous seizure of the Kufra oasis in March 1941, helped generate a specifically Gaullist military tradition of tremendous propaganda potential. But, overall, Free French forces were still too small to make a strategic impact. Even the victory at Bir Hakeim deep in the Libyan desert won by the mixed troops of General Pierre Koenig's first Free French Brigade during May–June 1942 must be seen in this light. The Gaullist veneration of Koenig's forces, and the evocation of Verdun implicit in reports of Free French troops refusing to give ground, marked a bold assertion of the military significance of Free France after the frustrations of the previous year.[77]

Having lost impetus in Africa over the winter of 1940–41, the Free French movement increasingly depended upon the continued assurance of Churchill's personal support in order to survive. In the first week of 1941, the British government again promised to co-operate with the Free French Empire Defence Council in planning combined overseas operations, and in the maintenance of political and economic stability within Gaullist territories. For the immediate future, the latter took priority. Confirming this steady evolution of Free France into a quasi-government-in-exile, in mid-January 1941, Carlton Gardens issued the first *Journal Officiel de la France Libre*. On 21 January the British government and the Empire Defence Council agreed terms for the purchase of the 1941 export crops from AEF, the Cameroon above all. In addition to buying AEF bananas, cocoa, hardwoods and palm and groundnut oils, the British also brought the Free French empire within the privileged circle of the sterling area.[78] In March the Treasury further codified arrangements covering sterling payments for Free French colonial produce and the rates of exchange between sterling and Free French African francs. On behalf of the Empire Defence Council, on 21 March, de Gaulle signed up to a Treasury agreement which made British cash advances available for Free French military expenditure. By contrast, the agreement stipulated that civil expenditure in individual Gaullist colonies was to be met from locally raised budgets. Although there was no agreed 'spending round' as such, in practice, each month the Carlton Gardens administration lobbied the Treasury for funds in a manner not dissimilar to that of individual Whitehall departments.[79]

The French National Committee was not officially established until 24 September 1941. But, throughout the year, Churchill allowed the legal distinctions between the Free French movement and a properly constituted legal authority to become further blurred. De Gaulle's ability to visit loyal colonies, and the Free French role in the planning of operations against the Vichy Levant, helped speed this process along. By December 1941, AEF even received consignments of US equipment provided under Lend Lease arrangements, ostensibly made with the British government, but, in fact, knowingly channelled to those Gaullist colonies whose strategic importance was expected to increase over time.[80]

On 28 January 1941, from Dakar, Pierre Boisson indicated his willingness to exchange prisoners-of-war with the British authorities in West Africa. Two days later Colonel Gilbaud, army commander in the Zinder region of Niger, held the first of a series of meetings with a British liaison officer from General Giffard's staff. It was in Zinder that Vichy operations against Chad were planned from September 1940. Though Gilbaud was replaced in March 1941, by this point Sir Bernard Bourdillon had pursued earlier Colonial Office instructions to develop unofficial links with neighbouring Vichyite administrations. These contacts were strictly hidden from the Free French in Brazzaville. This surreptitious detente helped establish a more or less stable period of Anglo-Vichy coexistence in Africa.[81] As the battle of the Atlantic gathered momentum during 1941, the Admiralty's reluctance to 'waste' ships on blockades of Vichy ports increased. Furthermore, having watched the post-Menace reinforcement of AOF with mounting alarm in October and November 1940, by the turn of the year, both Bourdillon and General Giffard felt confident that Boisson intended to use his additional forces to repel all comers rather than to attack British or Free French territory.[82] Though the alleged British carnage at Dakar became a favourite theme of Vichy propaganda within AOF (a number of highly evocative posters depicting hundreds of black and white graves were in circulation by 1941), in fact, Vichy casualties during Operation Menace were slight: fourteen dead and thirty-three wounded.[83] Boisson appeared content to exploit the political capital arising from the September attack, rather than approving detailed plans to avenge it.

Contacts with General Weygand

During early 1941 the prospect of an immediate clash between Vichy AOF and Gaullist AEF receded. Furthermore, the most worrying indications of Vichy empire collaborationism came from North Africa and the Levant. Free French efforts to persuade the British and, to a lesser degree, the US administration, to respond to this were much weakened by the pervasive uncertainty regarding General Weygand's intentions. Neither de Gaulle's supporters in London, nor General Spears's liaison mission, attached much weight to reports of Weygand's growing resistance to Axis demands. Spears insisted that the US State Department, principal centre of a growing Weygand fan club, should not vest any hopes in the general, or in his ability to sway Pétain,

> From the day that the Paul Reynaud Government collapsed and I flew General de Gaulle from Bordeaux to England, I have maintained *a.* that France, which was about to be cut off from the outside world and would be subjected to the strongest anti-British pressure, could only be kept morally on our side if there were Frenchmen fighting the common enemy; *b.* that Pétain and Weygand, who had imposed an Armistice on France and refused to fight in Africa, would never call on France to take up arms again. To do so would have been to proclaim to the world that they had made a fatal mistake when they had chosen to give up the fight. How could they ask a France they had disarmed to renew the struggle minus the weapons they had told her to hand over to the enemy?[84]

Maurice Dejean agreed. Before the war Dejean headed the French press service at the Berlin embassy. From February 1941 he acted as senior foreign policy adviser to René Pleven before assuming full control of the foreign affairs commissariat (with a total staff of only thirty-four in 1941) within the Carlton Gardens administration later in the year.[85] In Dejean's view, Weygand was timorous. He was much fatigued by the responsibility placed upon him since the battle for France. Though not a committed Vichyite, the general consistently maintained that Britain's self-interested betrayal of France had brought about the June 1940 defeat. This was not a man about to defy Pétain.[86]

There was ample evidence to support Dejean's pessimism. Between December 1940 and May 1941, German influence in French North Africa increased markedly. After Wehrmacht forces arrived in Sicily in January 1941, German armistice commissioners took an increasing interest in the export capacity of French North Africa. To the British, the threat was obvious. As General Ismay reminded Churchill in mid-February, 'The importance of Casablanca as a point on the Vichy blockade running system is a good reason for the German desire to take over the [Armistice] Commission. They would want to control the blockade running, and, in particular, to ensure that an undue proportion of the traffic is not diverted for the benefit of General Weygand.'[87] By early May there was a fully operational Armistice Control Commission for North Africa headquartered at Casablanca. This brought the total figure of German and Italian monitors in French North Africa to 652. The German representatives concentrated primarily upon reorganising the export of Moroccan and Algerian strategic raw materials to suit the needs of the Nazi war economy. But the German commissioners also mounted a closer surveillance of Armée de l'Air installations and ensured that the Armée d'Afrique remained an ill-equipped force confined to a policing role.[88]

Under the cover of armistice supervision, German espionage activity mushroomed. Although forced to wear civilian clothes, and closely scrutinised by Noguès and his police forces, the presence of armistice commissioners in Morocco remained profoundly worrying. Ironically, although Noguès deeply resented the Germans in his midst, this did not preclude efficient co-operation between control commissioners and the local gendarmerie, who together monitored the activities of local Gaullists.[89] But most important was the marked increase in the scale and strategic importance of raw material supplies sent to Germany from Maghreb ports. Between 1941 to 1942, for example, 37.5 per cent of French North African phosphate exports were sent direct to the Reich.[90]

Though Weygand did not openly defy the Armistice Commissions, he was never reconciled to their presence. In March 1941 he recognised that the German Control Commission in place in Morocco was conducting a systematic audit of French North Africa's raw material capacity. This was co-ordinated by an *Abwehr* intelligence officer serving in the press attaché's office at the German consulate in Tangiers. Weygand was outraged. He reminded Pétain that the armistice was not a final peace treaty; the Germans were still the enemy, and they had now initiated a surreptitious take-over of the North African empire.[91] As Weygand refused to collaborate openly, the increases in North African supplies to Germany took place under Darlan's broad supervision. The admiral directed the creation of an inter-departmental North African Economic Affairs Committee. This helped arrange the fulfilment of the May protocols with the German high command, discussed below. Though he clearly resented it, Weygand did little to oppose the committee's work.[92]

The British were sceptical of the good intentions of the Vichy military. But the slim chance that Weygand might change sides was too tempting to ignore. The future of French North Africa was vital to Britain's Mediterranean position. It held greater strategic significance within British war planning than any other region of the French empire from sub-Saharan Africa, through the Syrian Levant to the collapsing French position in Indo-China. British hesitancy regarding Weygand was compounded by the information received from Pierre Dupuy. Formerly the Canadian chargé d'affaires in Paris, in November 1940 Dupuy began a series of visits to Vichy as representative of the Ottawa government, and unofficial intermediary for the British. Until Canada finally severed relations with Vichy in mid-1942, Dupuy consistently exaggerated the prospects of a more favourable Vichy imperial policy. But he also warned that Pétain might, *in extremis*, bargain colonial bases with the Axis powers in order to secure more lenient treatment for France. Uncertainty continued in the two months after Montoire between Paul Baudouin's resignation as Foreign Minister on 28 October and Pierre Laval's abrupt dismissal as Vice-Premier on 13 December 1940. In this brief interlude, the British and Free French found it hard to measure Laval's influence. Nevertheless, the danger to Anglo-Gaullist imperial interests seemed obvious.[93] In consequence, both Churchill and, later, Anthony Eden, who succeeded Lord Halifax as British Foreign Secretary on 22 December 1940, were prepared to test the water further. As is well known, this resulted in numerous secret Anglo-Vichy exchanges between October and December 1940. Though Weygand was the focal point of them, the principal French intermediaries were Professor Louis Rougier of the University of Besançon and the appropriately-named Colonel Mittelman, who worked in conjunction with Catroux's staff in Cairo. After the war, the so-called 'Rougier mission' became a *cause célèbre*. In a series of post-war books and court actions, Rougier maintained that he concluded a formal arrangement with Churchill, Halifax, and senior Foreign Office officials, including Sir William Strang. The essence of this 'deal' was Pétain's supposed agreement after the Montoire meeting to work surreptitiously for an Allied victory, notably by keeping the Axis out of the Vichy empire.[94] Rougier had much to be aggrieved about. He was officially stripped of his university post in 1949 in punishment for his Vichy activities. Recent releases of Lord Strang's papers at Cambridge make it plain that Rougier did not conclude a formal pact. But on 25 October 1940 Churchill, Halifax and Strang agreed that the professor should approach Weygand with the proposal to organise a 'sphere of resistance' in French North Africa.[95]

On 9 January 1941 these discussions produced the British offer of a six-division force to support the Armée d'Afrique once Weygand re-entered the war on Britain's side. To prove its goodwill, on 5 January the British government issued a communiqué which formally recognised the sovereignty of the Free French Empire Defence Council – but over existing Gaullist territories only. The clear implication was that Vichy authority would be respected elsewhere. René Pleven correctly surmised that this qualified statement was designed to appeal to Weygand.[96] A fortnight later, on 22 January 1941, Dupuy relayed further messages to the Vichy War Ministry, approved at the highest level by Churchill, the Chief of the Imperial General Staff, Field Marshal Sir John Dill, and Dill's eventual successor, General Sir Alan Brooke. Dupuy was by now convinced that Pétain was playing a subtle double game based upon conserving Vichy neutrality and keeping the empire intact. In fact, Weygand had strung the British along.[97] He knew that the British could not lend enough material support to preclude a Germano-Italian descent upon French North Africa. Furthermore, Weygand was keenly aware of the material weakness of the Armée d'Afrique. In the light of this, the assurance of decisive British military support for French North Africa was an absolute prerequisite which London simply could not satisfy. While Dupuy was in the process of relaying Churchill's messages to Vichy, on 22 January Pétain cautioned Weygand that British military successes in Libya would produce increased Axis pressure for the use of base facilities in Tunisia. If this took place, the protectorate might become ungovernable. This seems to have been an indirect warning to Weygand not to identify with the British cause in North Africa. If so, it was quite unnecessary. Weygand recognised that direct contact with the British would only increase his political difficulties in North Africa. He had made this perfectly clear to Rougier in early December and to Colonel Mittelman in Algiers over the Christmas period, so undermining the entire idea of a viable, secret Britain–Vichy pact.[98] As to the economic future of the Maghreb, this was better assured by developing contacts with Roosevelt's North African envoy, the itinerant consul, Robert Murphy, who was in North Africa to supervise delivery of US aid convoys, rather than by pleading with Churchill to end Britain's blockade. As Dejean predicted, contacts with Weygand were doomed to fail.

Anglo-American confusion over Weygand and his subordinate North African Governors was understandable. Throughout 1941, the situation in the French Maghreb typified all the ambiguities of Vichy's imperial defence policy. On the one hand, Weygand supervised the implementation of Vichy policies with vigour and, in the case of antisemitic legislation, with obvious enthusiasm.[99] On the other hand, between July and September 1941, Weygand first took over as Governor of Algeria from the fanatically anti-British Admiral Jean-Marie Abrial and then promoted two future heroes of French Liberation, General Alphonse Juin and General Jean de Lattre de Tassigny, to the senior commands in Morocco and Tunisia. In November Juin assumed command of the entire Armée d'Afrique in succession to Weygand himself.[100] In due course, these generals joined the Allied cause without condemning their erstwhile chief. Similarly, when he appeared before a High Court tribunal in February 1946, Weygand's Chief of Staff, Colonel (later General) de Perier, insisted that Weygand's actions successfully protected the French empire against Axis incursion. Perier maintained that Weygand never intended to seek a confrontation with the Free French.[101]

Even de Gaulle was sufficiently tempted by the prospect of North Africa being turned to reconsider opening a channel of communication with Weygand. In February 1941 de Gaulle told Spears of his hopes that not only Weygand, but also the Toulon fleet commander, Admiral Jean de Laborde, might yet agree to form a Free French triumvirate with the general. Aware that, at the time, de Laborde was the most popular naval figure within Vichy France and its empire, Gaullist envoys established a secret liaison with de Laborde by way of his Spanish sister-in-law. The ideal scenario was that the Toulon fleet should sail to join a rallying Weygand in North Africa, securing the Maghreb in the process, and leaving the German government with no option but to occupy the southern zone. Admirals Abrial in Algeria and Esteva in Tunisia would be bound to recognise either Weygand or de Laborde. De Gaulle would thus be left in joint control of a united empire and Pétain's rule would be totally discredited in France.[102]

Collaborationism in the Mediterranean and the Levant

In the event, the British and Free French contacts with Weygand were soon undermined by increased Vichy collaborationism. As expected, most of the concessions made to the German government involved colonial territory. The increased threat of an actively hostile Vichy empire resulted in the attack on Syria in June 1941, the first major Anglo-Free French land operations of the war. Yet this did not improve relations between Whitehall and Carlton Gardens. Before 1941 there was little prospect of a serious breach between Britain and Free France. The weakness and dependence of the latter effectively ruled this out. Carlton Gardens personnel relied upon the good offices of the BBC to make themselves heard in France. The British Political Warfare Executive and the expanding Special Operations Executive (SOE) maintained a tight grip upon propaganda to France and upon the early contacts with the fledgling resistance movements in the country. De Gaulle's supporters even required British approval to secure passage to Free French colonies. The discipline induced by this one-sided relationship was shattered only when the future of the French Levant became a pressing issue.[103]

The increased naval tension between Vichy and British naval forces in the Mediterranean also contributed to the launch of the attack on Syria and Lebanon. During the lull in Anglo-Vichy tension in early 1941, the British relaxed their naval blockade of Vichy Africa.[104] This came to an abrupt end. On 30 March 1941, Vichy coastal convoy K42, consisting of four merchant ships escorted by the destroyer *Simoun*, was intercepted on its route between Casablanca and Oran by six Royal Naval ships lying off Nemours, Algeria. In reponse, Vichy coastal batteries fired upon the British ships. A bombardment by aircraft from Tafaraoui, near Oran, followed later in the day. The twin outcomes of this otherwise inconclusive engagement were, on the one hand, to confirm British disenchantment with Weygand and, on the other, to stimulate further rearmament of the Vichy navy. Tense stand-offs between British patrols and Vichy convoys again became commonplace. From May 1941 all convoy traffic between Vichy France and AOF was accompanied by armed escort, Darlan having compiled a persuasive 'inventory' of all unprovoked British attacks to date. On 29 May the RAF conducted an air raid against the Tunisian port of Sfax, the first of several British bombardments of Axis shipping in Tunisian ports which left a trail of French casualties.[105]

In the immediate aftermath of the Nemours convoy incident, the Vichy government approved German use of Levant facilities and French war material in support of Prime Minister Rashid Ali al-

Ghailani's anti-British *coup* in Iraq. With the approval of the Levant High Commissioner, General Henri Fernand Dentz, the Italian armistice commissioners in Beirut, under General Fedele di Giorgis, assisted in these transit arrangements.[106] This was an early example of implementation of the May protocols agreed in Paris between Darlan, his personal adviser, the Minister of State, Henri Moysset, and General Walther Warlimont. Under the terms of these agreements the French government confirmed arrangements to deliver almost 2,000 trucks to the Africa Corps. In addition, German U-boats were given theoretical permission to refuel in Dakar harbour (a promise never actually fulfilled). From the German perspective, Darlan demanded a small price for an arrangement which set the seal upon future Vichy collaborationism. It was particularly easy for the Germans to make naval concessions, since these simply increased the likelihood of Vichy conflict with Britain in defence of individual French colonies and empire trade.[107] Darlan duly secured German assent to the rearmament of the battleship *Provence*, and the seaplane carrier *Commandant Teste*. In addition, the battleship Jean Bart was re-equipped as a 'floating battery' in Casablanca harbour and French construction of seven torpedo boats and six destroyers was allowed to proceed.[108]

Darlan subsequently reneged on part II of the May protocols, which covered German use of Bizerta as a supply route for the Africa Corps. This reflected his disappointment at Hitler's continuing refusal to treat Vichy as a potential ally against Britain. It did not indicate a turn away from imperial collaborationism *per se*. Similarly, it was the German government that dropped its request for Dakar facilities, anticipating that the Anglo-American reaction would offset the advantages of access to the port.[109] Darlan's treatment of the Italians was quite different. In the months following the May protocols, the Italian Armistice Commission team in French North Africa found little echo of Vichy's more ready collaboration with Germany. In October 1941, General Biagini and the North African Armistice Commission head, Admiral Farina, persuaded Admiral Ollive, fleet commander at Mers el-Kébir, to conduct aerial reconnaissance sorties of British Gibraltar. But Ollive and General Juin agreed that the French pilots involved should act 'blind', reporting nothing of significance to the Italians, regardless of what they actually saw. Juin insisted that collaboration should be kept to a strict minimum to avoid any possibility of compromising the neutrality of French forces in the developing North African campaign.[110]

While Darlan's negotiations with General Warlimont were under way in Paris, in mid-May 1941 de Gaulle was among fervent supporters in Brazzaville. This proved to be a handicap. Far removed from the circuit of British policy-making towards Vichy France, de Gaulle was none the less surrounded by keen supporters. De Larminat caught the bumptious, sometimes intoxicating, mood of the Free French capital, 'Perched on our coconut palms in Central Africa, we flung impudent defiance at Hitler and Vichy.'[111] Nourished by this atmosphere, the more de Gaulle learnt about unfolding British plans regarding Syria and, to a lesser extent, Djibouti, the more he became infuriated. Afraid that Free French requirements in the Middle East would be overlooked, on 12 May de Gaulle informed René Pleven that he planned to recall General Catroux from Cairo to Brazzaville. De Gaulle wished to offer Catroux some other, less sensitive post. In the interim, de Gaulle wished to establish Gaston Palewski and General Legentilhomme with the British Middle East command to act respectively as Free French civil and military representatives. He expected these appointees to stiffen his position, their mission being to ensure a prominent Free French role in any operations in the Levant or against French Somaliland. The ever diplomatic Catroux was not suited to this task. As de Gaulle concluded. 'The more the English [*sic*] neglect us, the more this will cool French opinion [towards us], and the more Vichy will collaborate.'[112] In the event, these personnel changes were not fully carried out.

But de Gaulle's intentions were clear. Wary of Catroux's senior position and lengthy colonial experience, de Gaulle was determined to confine him to a junior role. Catroux's political caution and natural aristocratic reserve facilitated de Gaulle's task. A damaging contest between de Gaulle and the one Free French general of really eminent rank seemed imminent. Churchill helped prevent it. In mid-February, he warned the British Chiefs of Staff not to allow their preference for Catroux's mild manner and proven military record to cloud their judgment: 'I consider de Gaulle a bigger man than Catroux. Indeed I find him very remarkable having regard to the heartbreaking difficulties of his position. His authority should be respected by Catroux, and it is the only Free French authority recognised by His Majesty's Government.'[113] This statement gives the lie to any notion that the British government was prepared to dispense with de Gaulle in the months preceding the invasion of Syria. Instead, the Levant campaign and its aftermath transformed the atmosphere of Anglo-Gaullist relations. If the failure of the attack on Dakar precipitated a re-evaluation of strategic priorities in Whitehall, Carlton Gardens and Vichy, the Syrian campaign marked a more fundamental shift in the political relationship between the Free French empire and its principal external backer. Events in the Levant created tensions between Free France and the Anglo-Saxon powers which lasted the course of the Second World War and beyond it. Furthermore, the Anglo-Gaullist contest in the Middle East helped determine the more fitful extension of Free French imperial control after 1941. In an effort to place this in proper context, the discussion of Syria and Lebanon which follows will consider the wartime period as a whole.

Notes

1 PRO, WO 106/2156, Notes on Weygand, 4 February 1941.
2 Cassin, *Les Hommes partis de rien*, pp. 212–13.
3 NAC, Ottawa, MG 32/A2, Papers of Georges P. Vanier, vol. 14/6, Pleven speech, Chatham House, 19 March 1942.
4 Jean-Baptiste Duroselle, 'Une création *ex nihilo*: le Ministère des Affaires étrangères du Général de Gaulle (1940–1942)', *Relations Internationales*, 31 (1982), 316.
5 Jean-Paul Cointet, 'Les relations entre de Gaulle et le gouvernement britannique', 432–4, 442.
6 PRO, CO 323/1791/38, William Strang record of FO meeting, 6 September 1940.
7 SHAT, 1P34/D6, EM-Colonies, aide mémoire, Madagascar, 1 October 1940. The Pondicherry enclave had already declared for de Gaulle.
8 SHAT, 1P89/D2, Pétain, 'Instruction de mission pour M. le Général Weygand', 5 October 1940; SHM, Fonds Amiral Sacaze, GG2/142, Forces Maritimes Françaises, (FMF-3), memo, 8 September 1940.
9 SHAT, 1P33/D2, EMA, 'Etude sur l'importance militaire des colonies', n.d., February 1941.
10 Rainero, *La Commission Italienne d'Armistice*, doc. 13, p. 422.
11 PRO, CO 323/1791/38, Strang to William Somerville-Smith, 25 September 1940.
12 Duroselle, 'Une création *ex nihilo*', 319; Elikia M'Bokolo, 'French colonial policy in equatorial Africa in the 1940s and 1950s', in Gifford and Louis, *Transfer of Power*, pp. 176–7.
13 PRO, CO 323/1787/1, WP(R)(40)204, Lord Lloyd memo., 'The colonial empire', 16 November 1940; WO 208/53, WO notes on COS(40)704(JP), 5 September 1940.
14 François Charles-Roux, *Cinq mois tragiques aux affaires étrangères (21 mai–1 novembre 1940)* (Paris, Plon, 1949), pp. 182–3.
15 R. T. Thomas, *Britain and Vichy. The Dilemma of Anglo-French Relations, 1940–1942* (London, Macmillan, 1979), pp. 58, 66–9, 73.
16 SHAT, 1P89/D2, Weygand to Laval, 29 September 1940; no. 146/CAB, Weygand report to Pétain, 10 November 1940.
17 SHAT, 1P89/D2, no. 146/CAB, Weygand to Pétain, 10 November 1940.
18 Robert Dallek, *Franklin D. Roosevelt and American Foreign Policy, 1932–1945* (Oxford, Oxford University Press, 1979), p. 235; *Documents on Canadian External Relations*, II, 8, doc. 658, enclosure II, 21 June 1940.
19 Churchill College archive, Lord Lloyd papers, file GLLD 21/6, Legentilhomme letter to Lord Lloyd, 3 December 1940.
20 MAE, CNF Londres, vol. 70/Indochine, Affaires extérieures, 'Mémorandum relatif à la situation en Indochine', 20 January 1941.
21 PRO, CAB 80/19, COS(40754(JP), JPS note, 16 September 1940; CO 323/1791/42, Giffard to WO, 26 November 1940.
22 St Antony's College archive, Spears II/5, Spears memo., 27 May 1941.
23 Coutau-Bégarie and Huan, *Lettres et notes de l'Amiral Darlan*, no. 120, Darlan to Amiral le Luc, 29 August 1940; no. 124, 'Note sur le comportement de l'Amiral Bourragué', 23 September 1940. Darlan was furious at Bourragué's failure to reach AEF.
24 PRO, CAB 69/1, DO(40), thirty-second meeting, 25 September 1940; de Gaulle, *L'Appel*, pp. 109–11.

25 PRO, CAB 80/19, COS(40)781, COS memo., 27 September 1940.
26 SHM, TTC 1, Muselier record of meeting at Admiralty, 18 October 1940.
27 SHAT, 4P12/D1, France Libre communiqué, 10 November 1940.
28 SHM, TTC 47/D1, no. 3921, Vichy intercept, 'Rapport de l'administrateur adjoint des colonies, Marcel Saint-Plancet: Le Gabon et la dissidence', 4 June 1941; Churchill College archive, Spears papers, SPRS/1/136/1, Spears mission, 'Operations in Gaboon', n.d. November 1940.
29 PRO, CAB 80/19, COS(40)781, COS memo., 27 September 1940; CO 323/1791/61, CFR(40)92, 'Projected operations against Dahomey or the Niger', 18 November 1940; CO 323/1791/46, CFR meeting, 4 November 1940.
30 PRO, CO 323/1791/63, J. K. Lloyd minute, 10 December 1940.
31 SHAT, 1P34/D4, no. 2290, Boisson report, 30 September 1940.
32 SHM, Fonds Sacaze, GG2/142, Bourragué report to Darlan, 16 September 1940.
33 Bouche, 'Dakar pendant la deuxième guerre mondiale', 424–6.
34 Giblin, 'Colonial state in crisis', 330–1.
35 Akpo-Vaché, *L'AOF et la seconde guerre mondiale*, p. 41; Giblin, 'Colonial state in crisis', 328–9.
36 Kent, *Internationalization of Colonialism*, pp. 13–26; PRO, CO 323/1781/1, WP(R)(40)204, Lord Lloyd memo., 16 November 1940.
37 SHM. TTC 1, Leclerc to Muselier, 8 October 1940.
38 PRO, T 160/1100/F17006/03, M.E.W. memo., 'French West Africa', 20 August 1940.
39 These contacts are analysed in Thomas, *Britain and Vichy*, pp. 69–87.
40 SHAT, 1P34/D6, no. 2405, Huntziger to General Stulpnagel, 19 August 1940; no. 506, Weygand to Lémery, Colonies, 27 August 1940.
41 SHM, TTA 35/Dossier FMF-5, Direction des Affaires Politiques, 21 July 1940.
42 Paxton, *Vichy France*, pp. 69–73.
43 PRO, ADM 205/168, First Sea Lord memo., 30 September 1940.
44 PRO, T 160/1100/F17006/03, M.E.W. memo., 'French West Africa', 20 August 1940.
45 PRO, CAB 80/19, COS(40)793, 'Operation Menace', annex 1, 30 September 1940.
46 PRO, ADM 1/19180, Admiralty to flag officers, Force H, 12 July 1940; PRO, CO 323/1791/57, tel. to Dominion High Commissioners, 11 November 1940.
47 SHAT, 2N246/D3, EMA-3, 'Défense des colonies', Ministère de la Marine, SEG, Bulletin du Haut Commandement, 14 March 1938.
48 Akpo-Vaché, *L'AOF et la seconde guerre mondiale*, p. 40.
49 PRO, WO 106/2156, Spears mission tel., de Gaulle to Muselier, 19 September 1940.
50 SHAT, 2P12/D2, no. 4406/DSA, Weygand to Duplat, 31 August 1940; no. 519191/DSA, Darlan to Duplat, 9 September 1940.
51 SHAT, 2P12/D1, no. 570/P, Duplat to Darlan, 12 September 1940.
52 Coutou-Bégarie and Huan, *Lettres et notes de l'Amiral Darlan*, nos 130–1, Darlan to Laborde, and 'FMF Ordre du jour', both 24 September 1940; SHM, TTA 102, FMF-3, 'La Marine depuis l'armistice', 17 March 1941; Masson, *La Marine française et la guerre*, pp. 225–7.
53 Marc Ferro, *Pétain* (Paris, Fayard, 1987), p. 178.
54 Paul Preston, 'Franco and Hitler: the myth of Hendaye 1940', *Contemporary European History*, 1: 1 (1992), 1–16; François Delpha, *Montoire. Les Premiers Jours de la collaboration* (Paris, Albin Michel, 1996), pp. 128–84; Ferro, *Pétain*, pp. 184–91; Paxton, *Vichy France*, pp. 74–6.
55 Rainero, *La Commission Italienne d'Armistice*, docs. 14 and 15, pp. 424–9.
56 Paxton, *Vichy France*, pp. 76–80. Hitler made this comment at a meeting with Mussolini in Florence on 28 October.
57 SHM, Série TT, Guerre 1939–1945, TTA 2/Cabinet Militaire, no. 138, Darlan to Weygand, 7 November 1940; SHAT, 1 P34/D1, Jean Bergeret to Weygand, 3 December 1940; Darlan to Huntziger, 13 December 1940.
58 SHM, Série TT, Guerre 1939–1945, TTA 2/Cabinet Militaire, Darlan to Weygand, 7 November 1940.
59 SHAT, 1P34/D5, EMA, 'Reconquête des territoires dissidents', 1 May 1941.
60 SHAT, 2P12/D3, no. 1292/EM-COL, Platon, 'Instruction sur l'action à mener vis-à-

vis de la dissidence en AOF et AEF', 20 November 1940.

61 SHAT, 2P12/D1, FMF-3, no. 2536, Darlan to Weygand, 23 November 1940.

62 SHM, Fonds Sacaze, GG2/142, no. 51, Bourragué to Darlan, 16 September 1940.

63 PRO, CAB 69/1, DO(40), thirty-sixth meeting, 22 October 1940.

64 MAE, Papiers Maurice Dejean, vol. 25, Direction des affaires politiques, 'Dernières informations concernant l'Afrique française', 30 June 1941.

65 SHM, TTA 102/FMF-3, Etude no. 8, 'Represailles éventuelles contre la Gambie et la Sierra Leone', 8 December 1940.

66 Paxton, *Vichy France*, pp. 83–5, 96.

67 PRO, PREM 3/254/1, JIS report on French African colonies, 30 August 1940.

68 This figure had increased to 100,000 by 1942, see Clayton, *France, Soldiers and Africa*, p. 129.

69 SHAT, 1P55/D5, Groupes Coloniales, Stulpnagel to General Noyen (President of French Delegation to Wiesbaden Armistice Commission), 13 July 1940. Regarding German monitoring at Dakar, see Kent, *Internationalization of Colonialism*, p. 41.

70 Michael Crowder, 'The 1939–45 war and West Africa' in J. F. Ade Ajayi and M. Crowder (eds), *History of West Africa*, II (London, Longman, 1974), p. 599.

71 WO 208/2851, DMI Report 3(a), 'Notes on Senegal', 26 October 1940.

72 SHAT, 2N246/D2, Troisième Section, Minister of Colonies, Louis Rollin to Pierre Laval, 8 July 1935, *Journal Officiel*, 2 July 1938; SHAT, 7N4194/D1, Comité Consultatif de la Défense des Colonies, procès verbal, 8 June 1937.

73 ANCOM, Aff. pol., C2616/D6, Air Minister, Guy La Chambre, to Commandants de l'Air, AOF and AEF, 17 February 1940; SHAA, Carton Z14403/D1, Guy La Chambre memo., 'Afrique du Nord et Empire', 7 February 1939.

74 PRO, WO 208/53, Military Attaché, Washington, to WO, 30 January 1941.

75 PRO, CO 323/1791/61, Spears mission, Brazzaville, to WO, 10 December 1940.

76 PRO, CO 323/1791/43, Sir Arnold Hodson to CO, 26 November 1940; CO 323/1791/38, Spears to Ismay, 9 November 1940.

77 Clayton, *France, Soldiers and Africa*, p. 135; Crémieux-Brilhac, *France Libre*, pp. 352–68.

78 SHM, TTC 1/Renseignements 1941, memo., 'Free allies in Britain – economic resources', 26 December 1941.

79 MAE, CNF Londres, vol. 191, no. 2735, De Gaulle message, 24 March 1941; see Gloria Maguire's excellent chapter on financial links in her *Anglo-American Relations with the Free French*, especially pp. 116–18.

80 Cointet, 'Les relations entre de Gaulle et le gouvernement britannique', 434–5.

81 PRO, CO 968/30/3, R. L. Speaight to J. S. Bennett, 30 January 1941; WO 208/53, DMO summary, 'Demi-official contacts with the Vichy French', 21 February 1941.

82 PRO, CO 323/1791/42, Bourdillon tels. to CO, 22, 24 and 26 November 1940.

83 SHAT, 1P34/D6, EM-Colonies, aide mémoire, col. 5, entry for 26 September 1940.

84 St Antony's College archive, Spears II/5, Spears memo., 27 May 1941.

85 Duroselle, 'Une création *ex nihilo*', 322–3.

86 MAE, Archives Privées, Papiers Maurice Dejean, vol. 25, Dejean memo., 'La situation politique en France et le problème de l'Afrique du Nord', 26 April 1941.

87 PRO, PREM 3/317/3, Ismay to Churchill, 13 February 1941.

88 MAE, Papiers Maurice Dejean, vol. 25, Dejean memo., 26 April 1941.

89 SHAT, 2P12/D2, 'Note sur l'activité de la Commission Allemande de Contrôle', 19 February–15 March 1941; Churchill College archive, miscellaneous files: HARS 2, Theodor Harris memoir, 'Adventures in Morocco', 8 October 1942; Paxton, *Vichy France*, pp. 114, 302.

90 Christine Levisse-Touzé, 'L'Afrique du nord pendant la seconde guerre mondiale', *Relations Internationales*, 77 (1994), 12–13.

91 PRO, ADM 223/298, NID Section 12, orange summary volumes, 'Vichy France', 24 September 1945; SHAT, 1P89/D4, no. 66/CAB, Weygand to Pétain, 26 March 1941.

92 SHM, TTA 2, no. 94/Cabinet ordinaire, Darlan to Ministry of National Economy, 3 December 1941; regarding Darlan's efforts to extend collaboration in Vichy Africa, see Paxton, *Vichy France*, pp. 113–15.

93 Thomas, *Britain and Vichy*, pp. 74–81. Regarding Laval's removal and brief period under arrest, see Paxton, *Vichy France*, pp. 92–5.
94 Robert Paxton exposed the contradictions of Vichy's supposed 'double game', see *Vichy France*, part I.
95 Churchill College archive, Lord Strang papers, file STRN 2/13, E. W. Young, FO memo., 15 June 1964.
96 NAC, Ottawa, Vanier papers, vol. 14/6, Pleven speech, Chatham House, 19 March 1942.
97 NAC, Ottawa, Vanier papers, vol. 13/27, Dupuy letter to O. D. Skelton, 22 January 1941; Thomas, *Britain and Vichy*, pp. 83–7.
98 SHM, Fonds Sacaze, GG2 142, no. 2228/DSA/5, Pétain to Weygand, 22 January 1941; Churchill College archive, Strang papers, file STRN 2/13, E. W. Young, FO memo., 15 June 1964.
99 SHAT, 1P89/D2, no. 146/CAB, Weygand to Pétain, 10 November 1940.
100 SHAT, 1P89/D1, Délégation Générale, Alger, *Journal de Marche*, 1940–42.
101 SHAT, 1P89/D1, de Perier, deposition to High Court of Justice, 1 February 1946.
102 Churchill College archive, Spears papers, SPRS/1/134/3, Spears note for Churchill, 26 August 1940; SPRS/1/137/2, Spears note on Weygand, n.d., February 1941.
103 Cointet, 'Les relations entre de Gaulle et le gouvernement britannique', 435–8.
104 By March the British had seized 108 French ships *en route* to Vichy colonies, see MAE, Londres CNF, vol. 299, 'Analyse de FO tel. 361', 14 March 1941.
105 SHM, GG2 142, no. 16,615, General Paul Doyen, to General Vogl, 6 April 1941; TTA 102, FMF-3, 'Protection des convois entre Dakar et Gibraltar', 1 May 1941; SHAT, 1P89/D1, Weygand, Journal de Marche, 29 May 1941.
106 Rainero, *La Commission Italienne d'Armistice*, pp. 149–50.
107 *Documents on German Foreign Policy*, series D, vol. XII, docs 421, 559; Paxton, *Vichy France*, pp. 117–21. Warlimont's talks opened at the German embassy on 20 May. Protocols were signed on 28 May 1941.
108 SHM, TTA 29/FMF-1, Darlan to de Laborde, 24 May 1941.
109 Paxton, *Vichy France*, pp. 120–2.
110 SHAT, 1P218, no. 1359/FMS, Ollive, C-in-C Forces Maritimes du Sud, to Darlan, 28 October 1941; no. 1291/EMA, Juin to Colonel de Saint Didier, 11 July 1942.
111 Quoted in Lacouture, *The Rebel*, p. 281.
112 MAE, CNF Londres, vol. 191, de Gaulle, Brazzaville, to Pleven, 12 May 1941.
113 PRO, WO 216/123, Churchill to Wavell, 14 February 1941.

PART III

The second wave of Free French empire 1941–45

CHAPTER FOUR

The empire goes to war: the Syrian campaign and Free French administration in the Levant, 1941–45

> In war, there are problems that one can evade only so long as the enemy does not raise them. The Levant problem was one such. [Georges Catroux[1]]

France and the Levant

Premier Raymond Poincaré first officially confirmed French ambitions in Syria in 1912. These aspirations were soon fulfilled. During the First World War, as First Secretary in the French embassy in London, François Georges-Picot helped direct the Franco-British negotiations designed both to exploit the Arab revolt against Ottoman Turkey and to delineate respective spheres of French and British influence in the post-war Middle East. Throughout these talks, France maintained a primordial interest in Syria, as well as a direct claim to act as protector of the Maronite Christians of Lebanon, and a subsidiary interest in northern Palestine. Only with regard to the latter objective was French Middle Eastern policy frustrated. The diplomatic basis of the inter-war French mandates over Syria and Lebanon was thus established well before Turkey's ultimate defeat.[2]

In two other key respects, the lineaments of France's Levant policy were set during the early years of French mandate administration, provision for which was made at the Conference of Allied Powers at San Remo in April 1920. Firstly, as Syria was thought to require a French whip hand, especially after the enforced deposition of King Faisal ibn al-Husain in 1920, it was inevitable that France's mandatory government would be military in character. The severity of the Syrian revolt against French rule between 1925–27, and the protracted pacification measures which followed it, added to the military's grip upon the Beirut High Commission. During 1927, for example, the French Levant command took the initiative in establishing a Druze tribal presence just south of the Syria–Transjordan boundary in order to justify a slight extension of French sovereign control in the strategically important Yarmouk valley. Strong military influence compounded the French inclination to administer Syria and Lebanon according to the associationist tenets of Marshal Lyautey's Moroccan residency, hitherto the outstanding example of effective indirect rule by French soldier-administrators. Trying to adapt Lyautey's precepts of subtle French control in Morocco to the more volatile and disparate politics of the Levant gave rise to a second tenet of colonial administration in the Levant mandates. In an effort to curb their military commitments and prevent united opposition to French authority, successive High Commissioners sought to divide the Arab and Christian elites of the Levant, and to cultivate the loyalties of those minority groups in Syria and Lebanon judged most likely to fear Arab Muslim domination more than French political control.[3]

With the style of French governance in the Levant mandates set in the 1920s, there was little modification in approach over the succeeding twenty years. The one critical advance was the negotiation of Franco-Syrian and Franco-Lebanese independence treaties in fulfilment of France's mandate obligations in 1936. But these treaties were placed in limbo on the eve of the war, along with a more general suspension of parliamentary government in Damascus and Beirut. Since these measures were justified as short-term exigencies in 1939, the overriding political question in the wartime Levant was when, and in what circumstances, France would recognise the independence of Syria and Lebanon. In this respect, Vichy administration and Free French administration shared much in common in that each sought to evade France's implicit obligation to quit the Middle East. Meanwhile, within Syria in particular, internal nationalist pressure and the external influence of de Gaulle's supposed Allies increased as the war proceeded.

Background to the 1941 invasion

Though Gabriel Puaux brought the French Levant into line with Vichy in July 1940, it was no secret that the High Commissioner had previously worked well with the British in Palestine. This had been matched by General Eugène Mittelhauser's co-operation with General Archibald Wavell's Middle East command. Neither Wavell nor Godfrey Havard, the British consul-general in Beirut, expected their erstwhile French partners to change their spots completely. Since Britain had far more pressing worries in late 1940, Wavell's advice to let sleeping dogs lie in the French Middle East was more or less followed by the

British government. Although Churchill refused to consider any relaxation of the British economic boycott of the Levant territories, there was little enthusiasm for active confrontation.[4] Unwilling to side with the British, Puaux was equally reluctant to act against them. Like most of the Levant army officer corps, Puaux was vehemently hostile to General di Giorgis's Italian armistice commissioners in Beirut, fearing that the disarmament of his forces would fatally compromise French authority. Puaux's equivocal reaction to the abortive Free French *coup* in September 1940 indicated that the High Commissioner lacked enthusiasm for Vichy's more aggressive self-defence against Britain and Free France.[5] Furthermore, it became obvious following General Fougère's more spirited purge in autumn 1940 that the Free French movement in the Levant was neither centrally directed nor well funded.[6]

Once Puaux was replaced by General Henri Fernand Dentz in December 1940, Anglo-Vichy relations in the Middle East deteriorated rapidly. Laval made it plain at the funeral ceremony for Puaux's intended replacement, the former Paris chief of police, Jean Chiappe, that he had personally selected Chiappe for the Beirut post. This was a strong indication of the likely direction of French policy in the Levant.[7] Dentz was assigned more sweeping powers than his predecessor. He not only took on the job of High Commissioner but became regional military commander as well. Though clearly not the creature of Laval that Jean Chiappe appears to have been, Dentz believed fervently in Pétain and the cause of Vichy's National Revolution. Within weeks of taking office, the new High Commissioner had accelerated the repatriation of over a hundred known Gaullist sympathisers for trial by Vichy military tribunal.[8]

Dentz's arrival almost coincided with General Catroux's move from London to Cairo.[9] After their first official encounter at Fort Lamy airfield on 18 October 1940, Catroux tactfully dropped his earlier reservations about de Gaulle's leadership. This was not to last.[10] In broadcasts on 14 and 28 November, Catroux announced that his task was to direct the Free French movement in the Middle East, the ultimate objective being the conversion of the Levant states. In Cairo, on 27 November, Catroux discussed the prospects for the conversion of Syria with General Wavell, Air Chief Marshal Longmore and the British ambassador to Egypt, Sir Miles Lampson. Catroux estimated that only 'a gross betrayal' by Vichy or a direct threat of Axis incursion would induce the Levant army to abandon Pétain.[11] With no immediate prospect of British support for an invasion, Catroux devoted himself to propaganda and direct appeals to the leaders of the Levant army. He was much assisted in this by Baron Louis de Benoist, president of the Free French committee within Egypt and a highly effective propagandist.[12] Nevertheless, Catroux made virtually no impact upon the civil and military leadership in Syria and Lebanon. Nor could he persuade General Wavell of the merits of a Levant invasion. In January 1941 Dentz played host to a German Foreign Ministry envoy, Werner Otto von Hentig, sent to assess how the Levant territories might best serve the Axis cause. In response, Catroux abandoned his tentative efforts to open a dialogue with Dentz, an action which had never been approved by de Gaulle or Carlton Gardens anyway.[13]

The Vichy authorities in Beirut maintained a heightened alert throughout General Dentz's first months in office in early 1941. From late February commercial life in the major towns of Syria was periodically interrupted by nationalist strikes, demonstrations and riots. These constituted a direct challenge to French authority, Dentz having prohibited all unapproved public assemblies on 6 January. But it was not until 12 March that the administration began a thorough crackdown upon strikes and nationalist dissent.[14] In Lebanon and Syria, moderate Maronite and Arab leaders exploited these incidents to secure Dentz's agreement to the formation of Consultative Assemblies in Beirut and Damascus, capitalising upon Dentz's fear that von Hentig would return to stir up Arab protest as a pretext for the imposition of German political control across the Levant.[15] In Beirut, for example, the National Bloc leader, Emile Eddé, was replaced in early April as head of a distinctly malleable government by an equally pliable Maronite Christian, Alfred Naccache.[16]

The leadership changes that so concerned Dentz and the representatives of the Maronite and Sunni Muslim elites in Lebanon and Syria had little bearing upon general Arab opinion. Rather, the immediate catalyst of popular discontent was the increasing severity of Syria's wheat crisis. While the British blockade remained, periodic Syrian bread shortages were bound to recur.[17] Dentz became increasingly reliant upon the Levant native levies to maintain order. Following the 1940 defeat, the French Levant army was gradually reduced from three full divisions to a single enlarged division. Most French military equipment was either repatriated in conformity with armistice obligations or hidden from the Italian Control Commission in designated sites across the Levant. From October 1940 the Italians also assumed responsibility for all the strategic war reserves of the Levant army, including its fuel.[18]

In Syria and Lebanon French imperial policing was traditionally conducted by the French-officered *troupes spéciales*. Derived from the Légion d'Orient, created in 1916 to oppose Ottoman rule, the *troupes spéciales* were instrumental in suppressing nationalist dissent from

1920 onwards. To that end, *troupes spéciales* recruits were carefully selected along ethnic lines. This helped ensure the loyalty of individual units and was designed to maintain a balance between those local elites that played a major part in the commercial and political life of the Levant and those tribes and communities that were largely excluded from the national politics of Syria and Lebanon. Once a particular community, whether it were Sunni Muslim, Shi ite Alawi or Maronite Christian, gained a stronger foothold in urban politics, its representation within the *troupes spéciales* was correspondingly diminished. By the time of the Anglo-Free French invasion, this meant in practice that Sunni Arabs were proportionately under-represented within the *troupes spéciales*. Since the Arab nationalist resurgence in Syria was led by representatives of the Sunni community, this trend continued throughout the period of Gaullist administration.[19]

In early 1941 the Free French lacked reliable intelligence about the situation in Damascus, Aleppo and Beirut. By contrast, Vichy intelligence regarding Free French and British designs on the Levant was generally of good quality. An important source of information was the naval staff of Admiral René Godfroy, whose eastern Mediterranean cruiser squadron – Force X – had been interned in Alexandria harbour since the 1940 armistice. Godfroy was well informed about British intentions. He was close to the British Middle East command centre at Cairo, privy to the comings and goings of the British Mediterranean Fleet, and on excellent terms with the fleet commander, Admiral Andrew Cunningham. He also received frequent visits from Sir Miles Lampson and, later, the Minister of State, Oliver Lyttelton, both of whom added their weight to Cunningham's efforts to persuade Godfroy to join the British. Lampson and General Wavell were never protagonists of an attack on Syria. Indeed, during the spring of 1941, they became increasingly concerned about the knock-on effects of Britain's blockade of the Levant upon the economies of Palestine and Transjordan.[20] Little surprise, then, that on 3 April Godfroy sent Vichy a crucial early warning. He reported that de Gaulle was awaited in Cairo, where he was expected to direct Free French efforts to rally Lebanon and Syria.[21]

In fact, de Gaulle was deeply humiliated by his experiences in Cairo during early April. Wavell was reluctant to discuss matters with him and, adding fat to the fire, seemed quite prepared to negotiate a settlement with the Vichyite Governor, Pierre Nouailhetas, in Djibouti without consulting the Free French. This in spite of de Gaulle's apparently cordial exchanges in March with General Platt, head of Britain's East African command, and the earlier redeployment to East Africa of the core component of the Free French infantry under General Legentilhomme.[22] Though these troops – later reorganised into the First Free French Division – participated in operations against the Italians in nearby Eritrea, neither de Gaulle, Catroux nor Legentilhomme could induce the British commanders to back any assault upon French Somaliland.[23] The British Chiefs of Staff regarded the wider strategic position in East Africa as the critical factor. Until Platt's command could be easily reinforced, and the Italians were evicted from the region, Somaliland was to be left alone.[24]

Operation Exporter and its aftermath

Both the Free French and the British claimed that Vichy complicity in Axis support of Rashid Ali al-Ghailani's Iraqi revolt justified the Anglo-Gaullist atack on Syria on 8 June. This was somewhat misleading. Dentz's administration certainly acquiesced in Italian contacts with the Iraqis and facilitated German supplies to the rebel forces. But by 30 May the Baghdad *coup* had been suppressed; Rashid Ali had fled to Germany via neutral Turkey. Still, the British could legitimately argue that the whole episode confirmed that the existence of a potentially hostile Levant so close to Palestine and Egypt was intolerable. British service chiefs estimated that Hitler still hankered after Soviet and Allied oil reserves in the Caucusus and Middle East. While Syria remained in Vichy hands, it would always present an easy point of access for any German invasion intended to seize these oilfields. Evicting Dentz from the Levant would strike a blow at German strategic plans at relatively little cost to the overall British war effort in the Middle East.[25]

A further consideration was the heightened tension between the British and Vichy authorities in the Middle East following General Catroux's unsuccessful proclamation on 14 May calling for the Levant army to mount a military uprising.[26] Though it produced little immediate result, on 29 May twenty-nine French officers and five squadrons of *troupes spéciales*, led by a senior cavalry commander, Lieutenant-Colonel Robert Collet, did cross the Syria–Palestine frontier. This was seen by both sides as the likely trigger to a mass defection. Collet was a much celebrated French military figure in Syria. His impressive command of the Tcherkess (Circassian) *troupes spéciales* forces along the southern Syrian frontier led to comparisons with Lawrence of Arabia, and Dentz clearly feared that, were Collet's defection to pass unpunished, the remaining native troop units would become dangerously unreliable.[27] Catroux met Collet secretly on 21 May. As a result, he anticipated that Collet could induce his entire 18,000-strong force to follow him. Though Collet did not manage this feat, his warning that Dentz was determined to resist any invasion helped persuade Catroux that the only remaining option was a major land invasion involving Free French and British empire forces.[28] The likelihood that the Levant army would mount some resistance also added to Churchill's enthusiasm for an unequivocal British guarantee regarding Syrian and Lebanese independence. Without securing de Gaulle's prior approval, Catroux acceded to this on 24 May, referring explicitly to Britain's guarantee in his own announcement regarding Free French respect for the eventual independence of the Levant states.[29] It was crucial to Syrian and Arab opinion generally that British forces could be portrayed as liberators. Churchill and the Foreign Office warned Spears to tailor his sympathy for Free France to the wider requirements of Britain's Middle Eastern policy in all his dealings with Catroux.[30]

The British empire and Free French columns that invaded the French Levant from Palestine and Transjordan on 8 June fell under the overall command of General Sir Henry Maitland Wilson. He still hoped that the defending Vichy forces might quickly surrender and change allegiance. Wilson instructed his field commanders accordingly: 'It was considered that, whilst a proportion of the Vichy troops were old soldiers and would fight doggedly from their sense of honour if ordered to do so, they would seize upon any reasonable excuse to give themselves up should the opportunity be offered. Accordingly methods of "peaceful penetration" were to be tried in the first instance.' Free French and French-speaking British officers were attached to individual invading columns in the expectation that they would be called upon to parley with the defending forces. Nowhere did this succeed.[31] As at Dakar, so in Syria. Wilson was thoroughly misguided about the ferocity of Vichy resistance. Pétain immediately made a radio broadcast relayed to the Vichy radio stations in Beirut and Damascus in which he affirmed his government's decision to defend the Levant territories. A day later the first naval engagements of the campaign occurred off Beirut. From that point on, the re-supply of the defending Vichy garrison by sea became extremely dangerous.[32] Though aircraft were flown into Beirut from French North Africa and a battalion of troops departed from Marseilles on 1 July, adequate reinforcement was impossible without the use of a battleship convoy to protect Vichy troopships. Darlan toyed with the idea of using the bulk of the Toulon fleet as convoy escort but abandoned the idea once General Huntziger stressed the risk of all-out war with Britain.[33]

With little prospect of reinforcement, even though the Vichy garrison was served by eleven well stocked ammunition depots, the minimal mechanised equipment and limited fuel supplies left to Dentz's troops put them in a desperate position.[34] Though Algerian and Tirailleur Sénégalais units put up particularly strong resistance, in southern Syria at least, Collet's earlier defection, and the understandable reluctance of Tcherkess and Druze forces to fight one another, helped ensure a rapid Allied advance.[35] On 10 June Vichy military intelligence concluded that, while the British justified their invasion by reference to the recent Iraqi *coup*, their operations were clearly intended to secure the northern perimeter of Britain's Middle Eastern position. In addition, if the British secured the Levant, they might yet induce neutral Turkey to enter the war. In all, Huntziger's intelligence staff recognised that the British sought a broad strategic advantage, with only secondary consideration of the claims of the Free French.[36] Certainly the behaviour of British empire forces in Syria did little to suggest that either Indian Army units or Major-general J. D. Lavarrack's Australian troops were briefed to prepare the country for a Gaullist administration. Although highly effective in combat, indiscipline within the two Australian divisions caused serious embarrassment to British negotiators and those Free French political officers endeavouring – with minimal success – to persuade the Vichy garrison to back de Gaulle.[37]

Free French administration

Throughout the Syrian campaign in June–July, Churchill and the Chiefs of Staff together maintained that in no circumstances could the installation of a Free French administration be allowed to interfere with Britain's Middle Eastern strategic requirements. This outlook informed the British approach to the negotiation of the Syrian armistice at Acre on 14 July. In the short term, the British preferred to risk Free French anger rather 'than to be faced with widespread Arab disaffection which might constitute a serious military commitment'.[38] As the Levant was occupied by British land forces, the War Office bore primary responsibility for the cost of the occupation administration. But since the Levant states were not considered enemy territory, they did not fall under the jurisdiction of the Standing Inter-departmental Committee on the Administration of Occupied Territories chaired by the Financial Secretary to the War Office, Sir Richard Law. As a result, a special Occupied Territories (Syria) Committee was established under Law's direction. By 14 July this new committee had agreed that the best solution for Syria was a Free French administration with full executive powers. British financial and political experts were to be attached to this, primarily to ensure that War Office funds were being wisely spent. Essentially, this proposal met Free French demands. In the event, Law's new committee abandoned its proposals in the face of Oliver Lyttelton's insistence that the Spears liaison mission should be accorded wider powers to act as 'the pivot of the administration of Syria'.[39] Knowing that Churchill backed Lyttelton, and that he wanted the new Syria Committee disbanded, Sir Richard Law and his fellow committee members immediately gave way. Hence, in spite of sensible Treasury and War Office proposals to the contrary, the scene was set for the contest between the expanded Spears mission and Catroux's administration.[40]

In October 1941 Spears was formally appointed British Minister of State in Beirut. Two months later, the rising influence of his Levant mission was underlined by its transfer from War Office to Foreign Office jurisdiction. From mid-December 1941, the Spears mission reported direct to the Foreign Office French Department. This brought it into line with the liaison missions to other governments-in-exile in London.[41] Spears was ruthless in exploiting divisions within Catroux's government in order to increase his own power. He also promoted Syrian and Lebanese nationalism both out of conviction and as a means to undercut French authority. From 1942 onwards, this policy of divide and rule was the mainstay of Spears's regional influence.[42] But it was inherently unstable. The Syrian National Bloc and Lebanese nationalists led by Bishara al-Khoury, for so long hampered by their own factionalism, were quick to capitalise upon signs of division between Free France and Britain. Increasingly, the nationalist tail wagged the Spears mission dog.

This process was further complicated by the rival Arab dynastic claims upon Syria. The Syrian National Bloc leader, Shukri al-Quwatli, tended to favour the Saudi dynasty of Ibn Saud. Three of his senior colleagues had temporarily fled into exile in July 1940 following the assassination of their rival, the Syrian People's Party leader, Dr Abd al'Rahman Shahbandar, who had been a supporter of the Jordanian Hashemite dynasty of Amir Abdullah. Finally, nationalist opponents of both Quwatli and Shahbandar often gravitated towards the rival Hashemite rulers of Iraq. In all cases, the Arab royal houses envisaged various schemes for a re-partition of the Middle East, built upon the assimilation of Levant territory into a 'Greater Syria' under their influence or direction.[43] Apart from their shared belief that French rule was intolerable, one feature common to the Syrian nationalist groups and their external Arab backers was their expectation that the other powers might be enlisted to hasten the process of French withdrawal.[44]

In the first months of his administration, Catroux suffered as a result of the British calculation that he was fundamentally a weak leader ultimately beholden to de Gaulle. This image was undoubtedly strengthened by the formidable and often intimidating presence of Madame Catroux. More important, Catroux never developed an effective working relationship with his key political adviser, the Secretary-general to the Levant *délégation générale*, Paul Lépissier.[45] Lépissier was at least a dedicated supporter of Free France. Others within Catroux's *délégation générale* were less enthusiastic. Two diplomats recently arrived from the Vichy embassy in Ankara, Jean Baelen and Jean-Marc Boegner, quickly rose to prominence within Catroux's private office, his *cabinet civil*.[46] After their appointment in 1941, Baelen and Boegner, if not actively spying for Vichy, were certainly at cross-purposes with their Free French political masters. The picture of a factionalised and ineffectual French administration came into sharper relief in November 1943. By this point it was obvious that the French administration in Beirut was deeply divided in its response to Lebanese nationalists who were now fortified by the legitimacy of victory in freely held elections. On 11 November Catroux's successor, Jean Helleu, ordered the detention of the entire Lebanese government. In an amazing lapse, Helleu failed to warn the Free French executive in Algiers, the Beirut Minister-Counsellor, Yves Chataigneau, or the local military commands of his decision.[47] The presence of unreconstructed Pétainists within the Beirut administration continued well into 1944. General Paul Beynet, appointed Delegate-general in February 1944, brought with him as Secretary-general a Monsieur Binoche who had served as Pierre-Etienne Flandin's *chef de cabinet* at Vichy before moving to Tunis to serve on Admiral Esteva's staff. During 1941, Beynet had himself served on Weygand's staff in North Africa before joining the Vichy delegation to the German Armistice Commission in Wiesbaden in July of that year.[48]

In the early days of Free French administration in the Levant, de Gaulle was less concerned about Catroux's subordinate personnel than about the Delegate-general himself. De Gaulle was constantly nervous lest Catroux's conciliatory approach should result in unauthorised agreements with the British or the Syrian and Lebanese nationalists. Much as de Gaulle attacked Catroux for his alleged failure to overcome the hesitancy of Wavell's Middle East command in the spring, so too he blamed him for the growth of British military and political influence in post-armistice Syria.[49] But de Gaulle was certainly in no hurry to reaffirm the validity of the treaties of independence negotiated with Syria and Lebanon in 1936. As a result, Catroux's early administration was understandably tentative.[50]

To contend with Spears, Catroux had to make some sense of the contradictions of British policy towards the Levant. Unfortunately for

Catroux, as A. B. Gaunson has shown, it was impossible for the Free French to accept the British position:

> Syria was to be independent but the French must retain privileges which were anathema to the Syrians; France was to keep some presence in the Levant, but she must give the Syrians an independence which they would use to evict France; and Britain had no imperial ambitions, but then again she did, for she must sponsor a Franco-Syrian deal in such a way as to satisfy Arab leaders in her own Muslim empire.[51]

Spears exploited this ambiguity in British policy in order to appear all things to all men. To the nationalists, he was broadly conciliatory; to the French, he displayed increasing intolerance. In consequence, the Spears mission quickly developed into a multi-faceted shadow authority at a time when, according to de Gaulle, Catroux was supposed to be establishing a solid administrative framework for Free French rule.

De Gaulle was reluctant to admit the extent of division within the Free French administration over how best to restore French standing in the Levant. On the one hand, following the Acre armistice in July, Maurice Dejean, then the principal foreign policy adviser within Carlton Gardens, maintained that the unratified 1936 treaties of independence should serve as the model for Catroux's policy. These treaties at least guaranteed the French a privileged position within the Levant that the Syrian and Lebanese nationalist parties were unlikely to tolerate for much longer. Furthermore, implementation of the treaties was originally blocked in 1937 thanks to a Senate vote orchestrated by Vichy's influential Washington ambassador, Gaston Henri-Haye. In revitalising the 1936 treaties, the Free French would simultaneously re-establish constitutional continuity with the Third Republic and confirm that, unlike Vichy, de Gaulle had no place for old imperial reactionaries like Henri-Haye.[52] The problem was that, seen from an Arab perspective, there was little difference between de Gaulle's views and those of the reactionaries Dejean pilloried.

De Gaulle always subordinated Levant state independence to the greater needs of Free France. Syria and Lebanon were vital to the Free French as a source of manpower, economic resources and, above all, political clout. Nothing could be allowed to compromise these prior requirements until France was liberated and French power restored. In consequence, de Gaulle ruled out any meaningful concessions for the foreseeable future. He was supported in this by his military entourage in London, Cairo and Brazzaville. De Larminat, in particular, shared the general's outrage at Britain's evident willingness to allow the bulk of the Levant army to be repatriated to France, taking the contents of their bank balances with them. Free French recruiters were denied unrestricted access to the detained Vichy troops awaiting shipment.[53] Although de Larminat secured the transfer of the Levant army's 155 mm Howitzers and 75 mm field guns to Free French forces in AEF, at least one historian has interpreted Britain's generosity to Vichyite POWs as affirmation of a British plot to perpetuate Free French regional weakness by denying fresh military resources to de Gaulle. So long as Britain held more rifles than de Gaulle in Syria and Lebanon, Free France could not exercise unfettered control in the Levant.[54]

As Middle Eastern commanders, neither General Wavell nor his successor, General Claude Auchinleck, spared much time or sympathy for Gaullist demands. Their attitude reflected the wider strategic concerns that dominated British thinking about the Levant. Only days before the 1941 invasion began, the British service chiefs and the Foreign Office Eastern department were still debating whether or not to invite Turkey to participate in joint operations, with Turkish forces sweeping southwards to ocupy northern Syria. This suggests that British policy was less premeditated than de Gaulle and his followers tended to assume. The Levant operations were hastily put together as Churchill's government was engaged in a precarious balancing act in the Near East. Anxious to conciliate wider Arab opinion, and required to prove Britain's regional dominance in order to induce the Turks to remain at least benevolent neutrals, the British government approached Levant problems from a broad regional perspective. In consequence, Turkey, Iraq, Transjordan and Egypt figured almost as large as Syria and Lebanon in British thinking. Since Turkey had territorial claims to large tracts of northern Syria, including the city of Aleppo, it was virtually impossible simultaneously to please Syrians, Lebanese, Turks and Arabs within the British Middle East.[55] The relatively parochial interests of the Free French came even lower down this list of priorities.

It was hardly surprising that in holding camps in Palestine and Lebanon Vichyite officers were allowed to intimidate many Levent army prisoners who appeared ready to change sides. By September, from a total of 3,716 Vichyite POWs transferred to Palestine, only 1,098 of Dentz's troops chose to remain in the Middle East under Catroux's command. Nearly all of the Levant army officers and NCOs remained faithful to Vichy.[56] Only Dentz and a clutch of his senior commanders were kept in British captivity as hostages pending the release of some 500 British prisoners shipped out from Beirut in the early stages of the campaign.[57] Humiliations such as this added to de Gaulle's confrontational attitude over Levant affairs. It manifested itself both in ferocious arguments with Churchill, Eden and the Cairo Minister of State, Oliver Lyttelton, and in the general's stubborn reluctance to contemplate bold administrative reform in Beirut. As usual, Catroux got caught in the cross-fire. De Gaulle railed against the new Delegate-general for acquiescing in the repatriation of Vichy troops. De Gaulle predicted a dire outcome: 'these [armistice] conditions will result in bringing back to North and West Africa troops war-seasoned at our expense and warmed with the flame of battle and which we shall find against us in Chad or even in Syria as soon as Hitler gives [the] order to Darlan'.[58]

De Gaulle never accepted Dejean's claims that French administration could be wound up before war's end, and that Franco-British unity was vital to the longer-term security of the Middle East. Instead, de Gaulle closed his mind to all thought of reform within weeks of signing the July accords with Lyttelton that modified the original Acre armistice agreement.[59] De Gaulle had a string of valid grievances when he first took issue with the British government, Spears and Lyttelton in late July. His complaints all derived from the fact that the British commander, General Wilson, exceeded his authority in negotiating an armistice with Dentz which took precious little account of the Free French and which denied them access to demobilised Vichy troops.[60] But de Gaulle's blunt impertinence, combined with his threat to withdraw all military co-operation, evoked a wave of antipathy across Whitehall which was exceeded only by Spears's dramatic conversion from chief protagonist to arch-antagonist of Free France.[61] While the Lyttelton–de Gaulle accords marked a short-term triumph for the French general, their adverse impact upon official British attitudes to Free France totally undermined de Gaulle's achievement.[62] Barely was the ink dry on the de Gaulle–Lyttelton agreements before Churchill set himself against a generous interpretation of the vague provision for French 'pre-eminence' within the Levant states which was theoretically to be included within the final treaty arrangements with Syria and Lebanon.[63] Political unrest across the Levant continued throughout July and August 1941, exacerbated by the command rivalries between British and Free French forces on the ground. With the Free French increasingly ostracised in London, it became impossible to co-ordinate Levant policy effectively. Meanwhile, in Syria, the process of clearing out Dentz's forces and the remaining traces of Vichy administration proved painfully slow. With a heavily armed local population, an insufficient number of loyal Gaullists to supplant the outgoing Vichy authorities and the pervasive British uncertainty over how best to ensure their own regional security requirements, dissent was inevitable.[64]

Catroux needed to make a show of action in the first months of Free French administration, if only to keep the lid upon wider nationalist demands. On 27 September, he took the plunge. Keen to be rid of the Syrian government of Kheled al-Azm, which, according to Spears, Dentz had appointed in April 1941 largely at the behest of the Italian Armistice Commission, Catroux selected another compliant, but unpopular, figure, Sheikh al-Hasani Taj ed-Din, to serve as President of the Syrian Republic.[65] Catroux also proclaimed provisional Syrian independence, the implementation of which was to await the outcome of the war. The popular response to this was understandably cool.[66] Undaunted, two months later, on 26 November 1941, Catroux named Alfred Naccache President of the Lebanese Republic and again proclaimed theoretical Lebanese independence under actual French tutelage.[67] Neither the Lebanese population, the French National Committee or the Spears mission showed any enthusiasm for Catroux's supposedly bold initiative. So long as the Free French authorities, without the constitutional legitimacy of a properly constructed government, insisted upon ruling the Levant as if in perpetuity, there was no reason for either Syrian or Lebanese nationalists to accord them much respect, particularly as it was abundantly clear that the British military still held the whip hand across the region as a whole.[68]

Contested authority in Syria and Lebanon

De Gaulle's sensitivity to the perceived shortcomings of his imperial deputies was sharpened by the developing rivalry between the authorities in Brazzaville and Fort Lamy as alternative administrative centres for AEF. Immediately after the seizure of Gabon in mid-November 1940, de Gaulle had appointed de Larminat to a new post of High Commissioner for Free French Africa – a deliberate emulation of Weygand's similar title under Vichy. Félix Eboué was appointed Governor-general of AEF while Leclerc passed on the governorship of the Cameroons to Pierre Cournarie. This allowed Leclerc to take office as Governor at Fort Lamy in Chad.[69] Brazzaville was clearly the established administrative heart of the AEF federation. But during 1941 Chad acquired far greater strategic importance, enhanced by the performance of Leclerc's Free French troops in the North African campaign.[70] General Serres, nominal Commander-in-Chief of AEF, played little part in these operations, and Leclerc was deeply suspicious of Serres's Brazzaville colleague, General Adolphe Sicé. De Gaulle's relationship with de Larminat was also strained by arguments over the administration of AEF. Meanwhile, in Cameroon, settler hostility to Gaullist authority almost brought the local economy to a standstill in the autumn.[71] Hence, by December 1941, in the Levant and AEF, the two major centres of Gaullist authority, French colonial administration appeared divided and ineffective.[72]

To make matters worse, once captured, Syria and Lebanon proved something of an economic liability to the Free French and their British paymasters. Although the British government brought the Levant states under the umbrella of Treasury support for Free French territories, in practice the British had little use for the foodstuffs, textiles and tobacco that were staples of the Syrian export trade. A more pressing concern was the acute shortage of fuel oils and foodstuffs within Syria in particular. In the short term, the arrival of the British worsened Syria's food crisis as the reopening of the export trade with Palestine led to general increases in foodstuff prices for Syrian consumers.[73] But British eagerness to remove the trade barriers and price controls maintained by the previous administration effectively obliged Spears's representatives to maintain the provision of adequate grain deliveries.[74] During the first year of British military occupation, some 80,000 tons of wheat and flour were shipped into Lebanon for general distribution. By January 1943, this figure had risen to 171,695 tons, a total still judged insufficient by the Foreign Office Eastern department.[75] In May 1942 the Syrian Wheat Office (Office des Céréales Panifiables) was established in readiness for the local harvest under the aegis of the Spears mission. Since this was a solid indication of where real power lay, de Gaulle was deeply antagonised by it. The Wheat Office was packed with over sixty Spears mission functionaries, and, to add insult to injury, Spears utilised the negotiations over wheat distribution to ingratiate himself further with a number of Syrian and Lebanese nationalist figures.[76] But the Free French alternative was patently absurd. In November 1941 Catroux suggested that the established organisation of the British Middle Eastern Supply Centre at Cairo might be bypassed. Free French empire products could then be shipped directly between Africa and the Levant. In fact, there was neither the volume of products nor sufficient ships to make this viable.[77]

After admitting the Levant to the sterling area on 15 September 1941, over the winter of 1941–42 the British Treasury made regular sterling payments to the military administration in the Levant.[78] Furthermore, though the French National Committee tried to conceal the fact, the Treasury supported the monthly expenditure of the Free French security administration. This influx of capital was only marginally offset by increases in British purchases of Syrian export produce, even though attempts were made to purchase the entire export stock of Syrian wool.[79] With shortages of essential commodities an entrenched problem, and with an occupation force attempting to make purchases in sterling as well as local Free French francs, price inflation quickly worsened. The Treasury was not much inclined to curb the money supply by encouraging the local population to invest their savings in British-backed banks. Moreover, since the Free French consistently submitted monthly expenditure requests for Syria which far exceeded their pre-invasion predictions, British Treasury officials exploited Syria and Lebanon's inclusion within the sterling area as a pretext to lecture Catroux on proper fiscal management.[80] Catroux was advised to increase taxation, and to improve standards of collection, as a means to curb the inflationary pressure within the Levant economies.[81] On 10 March 1943 Catroux and Spears agreed a series of stringent financial penalties to induce the Syrian government to cut its outstanding deficit. This was hardly calculated to increase the popularity of Free French rule. By March 1942, the severity of the economic position undermined the beneficial effects of Catroux's relaxation of martial law in readiness for elections in both Lebanon and Syria.[82] The general population was more interested in the outbreak of serious food riots in Damascus on 20 March. This followed the government's reduction in the allotted bread ration. With seven demonstrators killed, over thirty gendarmes injured, and further rioting over the subsequent week, Catroux again declared an *état de siège*.[83]

Improved foodstuff distribution was clearly vital to the preservation of political control. So the ability to control the delivery of emergency wheat supplies to the Levant provided the British with a sure means to exert influence upon the Free French administration in Beirut.[84] Britain's Middle Eastern command also considered this a strategic imperative. In March 1942, General Wilson warned that a combination of high inflation and a poor harvest would undermine residual Syrian respect for French authority. So long as commodity prices continued to spiral, Levant farmers and merchants were bound to keep hoarding grain. If Free French troops were employed to requisition these supplies, the Syrian National Bloc would cry French oppression. As a result, British foodstuff shipments were the principal safety valve for the rumbling political discontent that Catroux was powerless to resolve. Until elections were held and nationalist administrations properly installed in Beirut and Damascus, Catroux could not hope to carry the population with vague promises of jobs and food aid.[85]

Levant politics had reached an impasse. The Syrian and Lebanese nationalist leaders were on course to achieve clear victories at the ballot box. The Free French were not only reluctant to proceed with free elections, they were ill prepared to cope with their outcome once held. At a Foreign Office meeting in October 1942, Maurice Dejean committed the Beirut administration to announce the dates for elections before the end of the year. But, in the new year, René Pleven maintained that the French National Committee had yet to finalise electoral arrangements with Catroux – a weak excuse which prompted Eden to intervene personally when Catroux stopped over in London on 12 January 1943.[86] Upon his return to the Levant, Catroux duly called for elections, only to find his position severely compromised by the death in office of President Taj ed-Din, previously a key instrument of French influence upon Syrian politics.[87] Elections eventually took place in July and September 1943. The low turn-outs in both Syria and Lebanon (well under 50 per cent in both cases) confirmed that nationalist politics remained the preserve of urban and landed elites in both countries. The greater part of the population was still preoccupied with the hardships induced by the war, price inflation and foodstuff shortages above all.[88]

Although Catroux worked hard to accommodate Wilson and Spears in matters of foodstuff distribution and the control of local labour, these issues remained divisive.[89] But Franco-British tension stemmed primarily from disputed military control and the sluggish pace of French reform.[90] The French National Committee estimated that British policy in Syria and Lebanon was governed by political to the exclusion of military influences. The British government maintained that the exact reverse was true.[91] In early September 1942 de Gaulle informed the British government that he intended to take over military command in the Levant states within a fortnight. This amounted to a renunciation of the Lyttelton–de Gaulle agreements, which stipulated that the Levant states came under British military authority because they fell within the Middle East theatre of operations. Churchill was dismissive of de Gaulle's threat to assume unilateral control and was himself becoming more intransigent.[92] Since Free French reluctance to concede the principle of full independence for the Levant states threatened to undermine the local security position, it could no longer be tolerated.[93]

Anxious to reverse the drift towards Anglo-Gaullist confrontation, on 11 September 1942, at Catroux's behest, Alfred Naccache lectured the American special envoy, Wendell Wilkie, on the popularity of the French among the Lebanon's Christian population. This was one of several rather pathetic attempts to dent the rising confidence of the Spears mission and the British military administration in the Levant. In fact, Wilkie caused de Gaulle considerable embarrassment by suggesting to Naccache that the Americans might persuade the British to quit the Levant states, provided, of course, that the provisional independence of both Syria and Lebanon were first assured.[94] Secretary of State Cordell Hull later took up this point. During a meeting in Washington in March 1943, he warned Eden against any exclusive arrangements with de Gaulle liable to perpetuate French political control.[95] Over subsequent months, it became clearer still that the State Department favoured outright Syrian and Lebanese independence unfettered by special French privileges.[96]

British military planners were also increasingly intolerant of the French hegemony in the Levant implicit in the terms of the Lyttelton–de Gaulle accords. In May 1943 the Free French tried to undermine Spears's hold upon the Syrian Wheat Office by packing it with Gaullist appointees. It was further suggested that Syria and Lebanon should be admitted to the franc bloc of Gaullist colonies, a measure likely to result in the collapse of the Wheat Office and the restoration of differential price controls. In Beirut, Admiral Philippe Auboyneau, head of the FNFL, proposed that all Levant ports should come under his direct control, effectively placing them outside the remit of Britain's Middle East command.[97] These proposals provoked an angry response. On 13 May, the Middle Eastern War Council, responsible for Britain's long-term strategic planning in the region, suggested that the French presence in the Levant was wholly irreconcilable with British plans to conciliate moderate Arab opinion prior to a possible re-partition of Palestine. The council also discussed possible support for a Greater Syria, a scheme based upon a federation of Syria, Lebanon, Transjordan and northern Palestine. Regardless of long-term British preferences, the French administration was judged too weak to cope with major internal disorder without the assistance of British occupation forces. Once British troops withdrew, the result would be a local instability liable to spill over into Palestine.[98]

Free French control in crisis

In an effort to arrest the decline in Franco-British relations, in July 1943 René Massigli, newly appointed as the FCNL Commissar of Foreign Affairs, agreed to work with Eden to restore co-operation in the Levant. This was a meagre silver lining in an otherwise cloudy sky.[99] Throughout 1943–45, the Free French suspected that Britain intended either to usurp French imperial rule directly, or to evict the French from Syria in order to curry Arab favour and so facilitate the creation of some form of pro-British Arab federation encompassing Syria. By the end of the war, this suspicion had become official dogma: 'The British stuck to their line of conduct: eviction of the French from all key positions in Syria. There is no détente evident in Franco-British relations.' So ended a typical weekly report from French military intelligence in Damascus submitted on 16 July 1945.[100] Convinced of

British designs upon the Levant, from 1941, the Free French Delegates-General, Georges Catroux, Jean Helleu and Paul Beynet, all pursued certain common tactics in an effort to break the unity of the Lebanese and Syrian oppostion to French rule, and to strengthen the hand of the French security forces in a crude show of muscle. Within Beirut, the French General Delegation reverted to the inter-war practice of setting Maronite Christians against Sunni Muslims, primarily by raising the spectre of pan-Arabism to intimidate the former. If the Maronite community could be made to acquiesce in French imperial control, the Lebanese Parliament was unlikely to vote the two-thirds majority necessary for any amendments to the country's existing constitution.[101] The desperate ferocity of the French reaction to the outcome of the Lebanese elections in late 1943 revealed the bankruptcy of such tactics. Unwilling to accept the verdict of the ballot box, Jean Helleu arrested the Lebanese Cabinet on 11 November. Lebanon threatened to descend into violence.[102]

The British reacted immediately. Though Macmillan learnt from Massigli in Algiers that Helleu had acted without the clear approval of the French Committee of National Liberation, on 14 November de Gaulle threatened to withdraw all French officials and troops from the Levant if the British proceeded with plans to reimpose order through a declaration of martial law.[103] De Gaulle's bluff was called. Though the British deadline for the release of the Lebanese Ministers was twice extended, the prospect of British occupation forces assuming full political and military control in Lebanon was too great a risk for the FCNL to take. With the release of the Lebanese Ministers on 23 November, further French concessions were urgently required. As Helleu was irredeemably discredited, this was a task that fell to Catroux.[104]

After the disastrous French mismanagement of the elections, it was little wonder that by the end of 1943 Syrian and Lebanese nationalists were utterly exasperated with the continuation of Gaullist administration in the Levant. Catroux returned to the region with instructions from Algiers to clear up the mess left by Helleu. The string of concessions to the Damascus and Beirut governments that followed in late December 1943 suggested that the FCNL was prepared to concede only the bare minimum in an effort to keep French authority intact. Between January and June 1944 over twenty protocols were signed between the French and the Levant governments. These turned upon the transfer to sovereign control of various executive authorities as well as customs administration and the lucrative state tobacco monopoly.[105] Still the French wielded ultimate power from Beirut. This was confirmed by the appointment of General Beynet as at once regional commander and new Delegate-general in February 1944.

Beynet retained control over the deployment and recruitment of both the civil and paramilitary police and the *troupes spéciales*.[106] This was clearly the most potent symbol of continued French mastery. Logically, transfer of the *troupes spéciales* to unilateral Syrian control was fundamental to national independence and was publicly recognised as such by Catroux in December 1943.[107] As the principal arms supplier to the *troupes*, Britain inevitably became immersed in the worsening dispute over Syria's security forces during 1944–45.

At a meeting with Britain's Levant commander, General Julius Holmes, and the Minister of State, Richard Casey, on 15 March 1944, the Syrian President, Shukri al-Quwatli, proposed that the *troupes spéciales* should be transferred to Allied control and placed at the disposal of Britain's Middle East command. Conscious that these forces would form the core of a future Syrian national army, Quwatli had made this suggestion on a number of occasions since December 1943. The President and the Syrian Prime Minister, Saadullah Jabri, freely admitted that the great merit of this gesture would be to prevent French use of the *troupes* for imperial policing tasks.[108] After six months of intermittent talks over the transfer of the *troupes* to Syrian authority, in June 1944 French negotiators suspended further discussions. By this point, the Syrian government was thoroughly exasperated. Meanwhile, within the FCNL in Algiers, there remained a deep current of resentment at Britain's firm reaction to the November 1943 Lebanese crisis. Massigli suggested that Britain's earlier threat of intervention in Lebanon had encouraged the Syrian and Lebanese governments to press their demands with indecent haste.[109] He was convinced that since the Levant governments could not possibly afford to maintain professional armed forces, they must have received secret pledges of British financial support. Not surprisingly, Massigli identified Spears as the prime suspect, though this was immediately repudiated in London.[110] Spears was typically ebullient:

> Massigli is evidently completely ignorant of the state of feeling here. In the main towns student demonstrators have been offering themselves for enlistment and federations of merchants and others have offered to provide the necessary finance while it has been suggested that all officials should sacrifice part of their salaries for this purpose. I am impressed by the suggestion that at my instigation the people of the Levant are prepared to tax themselves and turn themselves into soldiers but I have no such power. In this, as in so many other matters about which Massigli has complained of my alleged interference, [the] French are up against [a] strong and perfectly spontaneous manifestation of local sentiment.[111]

Beyond the symbolic importance of the transfer of local security responsibilities, the *troupes spéciales* dispute turned on French insistence that the Syrian gendarmerie could not cope with civil disturbances. As long as the FCNL retained civil authority in the Levant, French representatives were determined to keep possession of a supplementary military force to uphold order. To the Syrian and British counter-charge that the gendarmerie could manage if it were properly armed with British automatic weapons, along the lines of the Palestine police, French representatives suggested that this would produce a general insurrection.[112] The dispute had become a circular one. General Beynet's new administration equated jursidiction over local armed forces with the prevention of immediate civil breakdown. Furthermore, the parallel refusal of the French to loosen their grip upon the principal internal security agency, the Beirut Sûreté Générale, was compounded by the abiding suspicion that the British Security Mission, which worked alongside the Sûreté in gathering intelligence, was actually intended to undercut French authority.[113] Conversely, the Syrian and Lebanese governments feared that, without national armies of their own, the Levant states would be unable to resist French demands for treaty revision, military facilities, exlusive alliance arrangements and even the installation of overtly pro-French puppet regimes in Damascus and Beirut. Much to Foreign Office annoyance, until Syria and Lebanon had their own national armies, nationalists in both countries were expected to look upon a British military presence as a short-term guarantee of French restraint.[114]

In fact, neither the FCNL nor the General Delegation in Beirut was willing to begin meaningful negotiations over the Levant armed forces before the war was over. In late July 1944, Massigli and Eden tried to agree terms for the re-equipment of the Syrian gendarmerie with sufficient rifles and small arms to enable them to police disorder effectively. But Beynet and his regional commander, General Humblot, still maintained that any paramilitary security tasks were better undertaken by the 24,000 *troupes spéciales* under direct French control.[115] Contrary to Spears's advice, the British Cabinet agreed that it would mark a dangerous Middle Eastern precedent to permit Syria and Lebanon to assume complete control over all security forces without cast-iron guarantees of French treaty rights. The US State Department and their new Damascus envoy, George Wadsworth, were generally more supportive of the Syrian case. For his part, Churchill was little concerned if the negotiations over the *troupes spéciales* made painfully slow progress.[116]

Without agreement over the control of the *troupes spéciales* and the Sûreté Générale, it was impossible to proceed with wider negotiation regarding the implementation of the treaties of independence. The

Syrian and Lebanese governments remained convinced that, if they retreated over the *troupes* and the Sûreté, the French would insist upon broader privileges as part of any final treaty arrangement. In December 1944, Georges Bidault, Foreign Minister in the newly designated Paris provisional government, publicly affirmed his intention to implement earlier FCNL promises of full independence. But in Damascus and Beirut he was simply not believed.[117] This was particularly unfortunate since Bidault needed some indication of support from the Levant governments and the British in order to strengthen his hand with de Gaulle. Though Bidault shared de Gaulle's wish to conserve special privileges for France within the Levant states, the Foreign Minister was determined to work in harmony with Britain and the United States.[118] In fact, the depth of Lebanese and, especially, Syrian antipathy to all things French was now so endemic that dialogue was becoming impossible.[119]

From 1944, perhaps the surest evidence of the depth of Syrian opposition to Gaullist administration was the readiness of the Damascus government to 'soft-pedal' on Syria's irredentist claims to the 'Four Cazas' of Hermel, Baalbek, Rashaya and Hasbaya. These regions were assigned to Lebanon following the eviction of King Faizal in August 1920.[120] Many Lebanese, notably within the Maronite community, challenged the long-standing Syrian claim that these territories were denied to Syria on political and strategic grounds. Since the Cazas question inevitably raised the spectre of religious conflict between Muslims and Christians, Quwatli's willingness to let the question lie fallow confirmed his short-term commitment to sustain a solid Syrian–Lebanese front against French rule. Furthermore, numerous Lebanese Sunni Muslims seemed reconciled in practice to the permanent partition of Syria and Lebanon.[121] In July 1944, Brigadier Clayton, head of Britain's Middle East intelligence centre in Cairo, explained the significance of the Syrian government's attitude:

> They wish to place their relations with Lebanon on the friendliest possible footing. Although at heart they do not believe in Lebanese independence and some at least of them have an ineradicable suspicion of the good faith of the Christian Arabs, they realise that for the present the particularist feeling of Lebanon must be respected, since any violent attempt to assimilate Lebanon to Syria would drive the Christians back into the arms of France.[122]

As the war in Europe neared its close in early 1945, at least four problems were entwined in the final settlement of Syrian and Lebanese independence. First and foremost was the increasing intractability of the Levant governments and the Paris authorities.

Bidault's apparent inability to moderate de Gaulle's insistence upon extensive French treaty rights compounded the problem.[123] Secondly, in the absence of mutual trust, French efforts to retain special treaty privileges regarding such matters as base facilities, French educational provision, commercial interests and local taxation within Lebanon were readily interpreted as evidence of a secret plot to sustain French imperial control. This problem was itself linked with the post-war status of Lebanon. If, as was widely expected, Syria laid claim to Lebanese territory, France might, in turn, intervene in the guise of protector of Lebanon. Throughout 1945, the French government raised the spectre of Syrian irredentism and Lebanon's possible assimilation into an Arab-dominated federation in an effort to cultivate support for France among the Maronite community.[124] A third issue of more pressing concern was the continued French jurisdiction over Levant security forces. To the Syrians, the *troupes spéciales* formed part of the so-called Common Interests (*Intérêts Communs*). As such, they should have been transferred to sovereign control under the terms of the agreements Catroux had negotiated on 22 December 1943, in the immediate aftermath of the Lebanese crisis.[125] Without a final agreement over the *troupes spéciales*, fears of a French-inspired *coup* and subsequent repression ebbed and flowed according to the wider progress of independence talks. Finally, as Churchill's government increasingly turned its attention to post-war planning across the Middle East, British determination to contain the Levant problem – and to avoid being characterised as French lackeys by other Arab states – added to the desperation of the French to preserve some vestiges of their own Middle Eastern power. But so long as the 28,000 troops of General Holmes's Ninth Army remained within the Levant, the British still retained ultimate military supremacy.[126] Hardly surprising that, in February 1945, de Gaulle informed a Paris press conference that the Levant problem could have been settled but for the unwelcome intervention of 'outsiders'. All would have been well 'si nous étions restés en tête à tête'.[127]

On 5 April 1945, at a meeting of Ministers attended by General Beynet and the Quai d'Orsay Secretary-general, Jean Chauvel, de Gaulle again ruled out any *a priori* transfer of the *troupes spéciales*. As expected, he argued that this would deny French negotiators the trump card necessary to secure base facilities for France in any eventual treaty. It was also at this meeting that the decision was taken to dispatch three colonial battalions to Lebanon.[128] On 6 May 1945 the French cruiser *Montcalm* arrived in Beirut with 850 Tirailleurs Sénégalais intended to relieve part of the French Levant garrison. Though the newly arrived troops were thus supposed to replace, rather than reinforce, standing French forces, Syrian and Lebanese fears of an imminent French crackdown quickly intensified following Beynet's return to Beirut from talks in Paris on 12 May. In the intervening week, in an ironic echo of events across the Mediterranean at Sétif in eastern Algeria, French settlers and officials in Beirut used the occasion of the VE celebrations to taunt the local population and parade French supremacy. The volatility of the local position, and the symbolic importance of the rivalry between the French-led *troupes spéciales* and the Syrian gendarmerie, was captured by a British staff mission report from Beirut covering the period 8–10 May:

> Troupes Spéciales personnel beat up a soldier from 16 Arab B[attalio]n Palestine Regiment at a Hama *v.* Lattakia football match. They mistook his shouts of 'goal' for oppobrious remarks about General de Gaulle. The crowd intervened, attempting to lynch the *Troupes Spéciales*, but the police [gendarmerie] prevented this by taking them into protective custody. The crowd then proceeded to the Sûreté aux Armées where they tore down the French flag and ceremoniously destroyed and evacuated on it. The *Troupes Spéciales* were later released.[129]

In more serious disorders across Syria, British troops were forced to intervene – an affirmation that the British still set the boundaries of permissible French action within the Middle East. On 17 May another French cruiser, *Jeanne d'Arc*, arrived in Beirut with a further battalion of 600 North African *zouaves*.[130] Two days later, violent demonstrations against the continued French presence began in Damascus. From 20 May, major disturbances were reported in Aleppo, Homs and Hama. French troops deployed mortars and heavy weapons to suppress the dissent. On 29 May Humblot's replacement as local commander, General Fernand Oliva-Roget, unleashed a murderous French bombardment of Damascus by artillery and aircraft. According to US figures, it caused 641 civilian deaths.[131] Bidault, the one Minister likely to have challenged this recourse to force, was far removed from events, since he led the French delegation to the San Francisco conference, in session between 25 April and 30 June. Hence the Foreign Minister was poorly placed to curb the escalating violence in a mandate territory notionally under Quai d'Orsay authority.[132] However, the Syrian Prime Minister, Faris al-Khouri – also present at the San Francisco conference – showed no inclination to work with Bidault. Instead, he approached Britain's representative, the Dominions Secretary, Lord Cranborne, from whom he sought assurances that Britain would not acquiesce in the perpetuation of French rule in Damascus.[133]

Having first attempted to consult President Truman, on 31 May, Churchill and Eden sanctioned the immediate deployment of the 31st

Indian Armoured Division across Damascus in order to keep the local population and the French military apart. Initially, the French headquarters in Damascus refused to acknowledge the right of General Sir Bernard Paget's Middle East command to interject British forces. General Oliva-Roget made little initial effort to comply with the British cease-fire order that accompanied the first deployment of Indian troops. Though de Gaulle was furious at British intervention, he did not possess the means to resist it. To the last, the contrast between nominal French political control and actual British arbitral power in the Levant determined the outcome of Gaullist policy. After order was restored in the first weeks of June, the British Ninth Army took a more prominent role in the policing of Syrian cities and designated tribal areas over the summer and autumn of 1945.[134]

On 13 December 1945, Foreign Secretary Ernest Bevin informed the British Cabinet that an Anglo-French common evacuation agreement had been reached covering the withdrawal of forces from the Levant states. Pending the conclusion of a final evacuation schedule negotiated in Beirut with Generals Beynet and de Larminat, French forces were to be reduced and regrouped within Lebanon.[135] The implementation of this agreement was hampered by the abiding Syrian and Lebanese suspicion that France might yet contravene its evacuation pledges. The French negotiators were expected to cling to local military control on the pretext that local French interests required protection, that France was best placed to maintain regional collective security, or that the Damascus and Beirut governments were too unstable to be left without external military protection.[136] Though the full independence of the Levant states was now imminent and the strategic importance of the Middle East was fast being transformed by the developing Cold War, the final stages of French involvement in Syria and Lebanon were still governed by a confrontational outlook shaped during the years of Free French administration. By the time the last French soldiers evacuated Beirut in August 1946, few bridges between Paris and the Levant governments had been rebuilt.[137]

Notes

1 Catroux, *Dans la Bataille de la Méditerranée*, p. 104.
2 F. W. Brecher, 'French policy toward the Levant, 1914–18', *Middle Eastern Studies*, 29: 4 (1993), 642–6.
3 V. M. Amadouny, 'The formation of the Transjordan–Syria boundary, 1915–32', *Middle Eastern Studies*, 31: 3 (1995), 537; Edmund Burke III, 'A comparative view of French native policy in Morocco and Syria, 1912–1925', *Middle Eastern Studies*, 9: 2 (1973), 175–86; Philip S. Khoury, 'Factionalism among Syrian nationalists during the French mandate', *International Journal of Middle East Studies*, 13 (1981), 441–56.

4 Roshwald, *Estranged Bedfellows*, pp. 16–21.
5 Roshwald, *Estranged Bedfellows*, pp. 39–40.
6 MAE, CNF Londres, vol. 39, Informant's report, Damascus, 14 October 1940.
7 MAE, CNF Londres, vol. 39, 'Note chronologique et politique sur les événements de Syrie', 30 March 1941. On 27 November 1940 Jean Chiappe's aircraft was shot down by the RAF, north of Bizerta, while he was *en route* to his Levant posting.
8 Churchill College archive, Spears papers, SPRS/1/137/2, Spears to Cadogan, 17 February 1941.
9 Lerner, *Catroux*, pp. 156–7.
10 PRO, CIGS papers, WO 216/123, Wavell to WO, 11 February 1941.
11 PRO, WO 106/2156, COS committee note, 27 November 1940.
12 SHAT, 3P102/D8, EMA-2, 'Mouvement de Gaulliste en Proche-orient', 21 December 1940.
13 Lerner, *Catroux*, pp. 170–7; for a full analysis of von Hentig's visit see Roshwald, *Estranged Bedfellows*, pp. 48–53.
14 MAE, CNF Londres, vol. 39, 'Note chronologique et politique sur les événements de Syrie', 30 March 1941.
15 MAE, CNF Londres, vol. 39, Délégation générale, FFL, Levant, 'Chronologie des événements politiques au Liban', n.d., 1943.
16 A. B. Gaunson, *The Anglo-French Clash in Lebanon and Syria, 1940–1945* (London, Macmillan, 1987), pp. 27–8; Roshwald, *Estranged Bedfellows*, p. 59.
17 Philip S. Khoury, *Syria and the French mandate. The Politics of Arab Nationalism, 1920–1945* (Princeton, N.J., Princeton University Press, 1987) p. 591; Roshwald, *Estranged Bedfellows*, pp. 53–4.
18 SHAT, 1P233/D1, no. 200/ES, CIA, Turin, note, 9 October 1940.
19 N. E. Bou-Nacklie, 'Les troupes spéciales: religious and ethnic recruitment, 1916–1946', *International Journal of Middle East Studies*, 25 (1993), 645–60.
20 St Antony's College archive, Papers of the first Baron Killearn, 1941 Diary, entries for 15 April and 5 May 1941.
21 SHAT, 1P33/D1, EM-COL, Note d'information no. 115, 3 April 1941.
22 Churchill College archive, Spears papers, SPRS/1/137/1, D/RLM/2, Le Mesurier to Spears, 20 May 1941; De Gaulle, *L'Appel*, pp. 153–7.
23 Catroux, *Dans la Bataille*, pp. 96–101.
24 PRO, WO 106/2156, COS committee note, 27 November 1940.
25 Rainero, *La Commission Italienne d'Armistice*, p. 150; N. E. Bou-Nacklie, 'The 1941 invasion of Syria and Lebanon: the role of the local paramilitary', *Middle Eastern Studies*, 30: 3 (1994), 515.
26 For the text see Catroux, *Dans la Bataille*, pp. 123–4.
27 For Collet's, and the *troupes spéciales*', pivotal role in 1941 see Bou-Nacklie, 'The 1941 invasion of Syria and Lebanon', 512–16.
28 Roshwald, *Estranged Bedfellows*, p. 68; St Antony's College archive, SPRS II/5, Spears memo. on interview with Collet, n.d., 1941.
29 Martin L. Mickelson, 'Another Fashoda: the Anglo-Free French conflict over the Levant, May-September 1941', *Revue Française d'Histoire d'Outre-mer*, 63 (1976), 77–8.
30 PRO, PREM 3/422/8, FO tel. to Lyttelton, and Churchill minute, 14 July 1941.
31 PRO, WO 32/10168, Syrian campaign report, 8 June–11 July 1941.
32 SHAT, 1P12/D1, Secrétariat d'Etat, Marine, synthèse, 1–10 Juin 1941.
33 Masson, *La Marine française et la guerre*, pp. 321–5. On Darlan's parallel attempts to negotiate with the British see Coutau-Bégarie and Huan, *Darlan*, pp. 428–31.
34 PRO, WO 201/848, Notes on French troops in Syria, March–June 1941, 'Syria defences', n.d., March 1941.
35 Rainero, *La Commission Italienne d'Armistice*, p. 150; Bou-Nacklie, 'The 1941 invasion of Syria and Lebanon', 519–21.
36 SHAT, 1P12/D2, EMA-2, Bulletin d'information, 10 June 1941.
37 PRO, WO 202/35, Notes of Spears mission conference, 27 July 1941; Churchill College archive, Spears papers, SPRS/1/137/1, Spears notes on report by Captain Masse,

6 July 1941. Australian troops were variously accused of looting and theft, destruction of a vital Air France wireless station, and mutilation of dead French troops.

38 PRO, WO 32/9800, WO first meeting regarding Syrian administration, 3 July 1941.

39 PRO, WO 32/9800, Standing Interdepartmental committee, seventh meeting, 9 July 1941; Occupied Territories (Syria) Committee, second meeting, 14 July 1941.

40 PRO, WO 32/9800, Churchill minute to Spears, 15 July 1941.

41 St Antony's College archive, SPRS II/I/Correspondence, Spears to Lyttelton, 18 October 1941; Cointet, 'Les relations entre de Gaulle et le gouvernement britannique', 447.

42 Catroux, *Dans la Bataille*, pp. 197–8.

43 Yossi Olmert, 'A false dilemma? Syria and Lebanon's independence during the mandatory period', *Middle Eastern Studies*, 32: 3 (1996), 43–8; Y. Porath, 'Abdallah's Greater Syria programme', *Middle Eastern Studies*, 20: 2 (1984), 180–5.

44 Olmert, 'A false dilemma?', 60–3.

45 SHAT, 3P102/D8, EMA-2, 'Syrie–Liban. Politique générale', 13 August 1941; St Antony's College archive, SPRS IC/2, no. 192, Spears to General Wilson, 16 September 1941; Roshwald, *Estranged Bedfellows*, pp. 122–3.

46 Catroux claimed that both men went astray only after his departure from the Levant, see Catroux, *Dans la Bataille*, pp. 204–5.

47 Gaunson, *Anglo-French Clash*, p. 125; Crémieux-Brilhac, *La France Libre*, pp. 653–4.

48 PRO, FO 371/40299, E826/23/89, Spears to FO, 4 February 1944; Maxime Weygand, *Memoirs. Recalled to Service*, English trans. (London, Heinemann, 1952), p. 305.

49 St Antony's College archive, Killearn papers, 1941 Diary, entry for 14 May 1941; Spears papers, SPRS I/1941 Diary, entry for 20 July 1941.

50 Churchill College archive, Spears papers, SPRS/1/137/1, Spears notes on report by Captain Masse, 6 July 1941.

51 Quoted from Gaunson, *Anglo-French Clash*, p. 78.

52 MAE, CNF Londres, vol. 39, Dejean memo., 16 July 1941.

53 PRO, WO 201/950, Commission of Control, progress return, 9 August 1941.

54 Mickelson, 'Another Fashoda', 80–1; PRO, WO 201/950, Commission of Control, progress return, 18 August 1941.

55 These problems were apparent after the fall of France, see PRO, CAB 66/9, WP(40)251, Eden memo, 'Situation in Syria', 28 June 1940; Yossi Olmert, 'Britain, Turkey and the Levant question during the Second World War', *Middle Eastern Studies*, 23 (1987), 444–8.

56 PRO, WO201/931, Committee no. 8 to Commission of Control, 5 August 1941, WO 201/904, Committee no. 8 final report, n.d., September 1941; St Antony's College archive, SPRS IA/Pre-armistice tels., no. I/472, de Gaulle to Churchill, 13 June 1941.

57 PRO, WO 201/908, Major-general Chrystall to General de Verdillac, 8 July 1941.

58 St Antony's College archive, SPRS, IA/Pre-armistice tels., de Gaulle to Catroux, 15 July 1941.

59 MAE, CNF Londres, vol. 39, Aff. pol. memo., 5 July 1941; Kersaudy, *Churchill and de Gaulle*, pp. 141–9.

60 St Antony's College archive, SPRS I/1941 Diary, entry for 17 July 1941.

61 St Antony's College archive, SPRS I/1941 Diary, entry for 20 July 1941.

62 St Antony's College archive, SPRS I/1941 Diary, entry for 17 July 1941; Mickelson, 'Another Fashoda', 87–9.

63 PRO, PREM 3/120/6, Churchill parliamentary statement, 9 July 1941; Eden memo. for Churchill, 22 September 1941; Churchill–de Gaulle conversation, 30 September 1942.

64 St Antony's College archive, SPRS I/Syrian Committee files, tel. 2252, Spears to Somerville Smith, 17 July 1941.

65 PRO, FO 371/35206, E3569/507/89, Spears 'Report on leading personalities in Syria', 8 June 1943.

66 Bey, *La Syrie et la France*, pp. 67–70.
67 MAE, CNF Londres, vol. 39, Délégation générale, FFL, Levant, 'Chronologie des événements politiques au Liban', n.d., 1943.
68 St Antony's College archive, SPRS IC/tels. 1941–42, no. 3588, Spears message, via Lampson, to FO, 15 November 1941.
69 PRO, WO 106/2156, Free France circular tel., 17 November 1940.
70 PRO, WO 202/26A, Lieutenant-Colonel Le Mesurier to Colonel Archdale, 24 September 1941.
71 PRO, WO 202/26A, Lieutenant-Colonel Le Mesurier to Sicé, 4 September 1941; note 5, 'Current policy of the High Commission', n.d., October 1941.
72 Churchill College archive, Spears papers, SPRS/1/137/1, Lieutenant-Colonel Le Mesurier to Major R. K. Knox, 13 December 1941.
73 SHAT, 3P102/D8, EMA-2, 'Syrie–Liban. Politique générale', 13 August 1941.
74 PRO, WO 202/35, Record of meeting at Spears's residence, 29 September 1941.
75 St Antony's College archive, SPRS II/4, Spears memo., 14 April 1954; PRO, FO 371/35199, Eastern Department, Wheat Plan purchase statistics, 6 January 1943.
76 Gaunson, *Anglo-French Clash*, pp. 88–91, 155.
77 PRO, WO 202/38, tel. 109, Lyttelton to Spears, 14 December 1941.
78 St Antony's College archive, SPRS I/Syrian Committee files, tel. 2988, FO to Lampson, 22 August 1941.
79 PRO, FO 892/121, tel. 353, Treasury memo to Lyttelton, 20 January 1942; tel. 461, Eastern Department to Lyttelton, 26 January 1942.
80 St Antony's College archive, SPRS I/Syrian Committee tels., no. 354, Treasury to John Rosa, 20 January 1942. By January 1942 the Treasury's average monthly payments for Catroux's military expenditure alone were some £1.6 million.
81 Churchill College archive, Spears papers, SPRS/1/137/26, Bank of England memo. for Spears, 'Inflation in Syria', 24 February 1942.
82 PRO, FO 660/35, no. 198, Spears to Eastern Department, 19 March 1943, E2151/27/89, Spears to Eden, 1 April 1943.
83 PRO, FO 371/35199, E1624/159/89, Spears to Eastern Department, 20 March 1943; FO 660/35, Spears to Eastern Department, 22 March 1943.
84 PRO, CAB 66/44, WP(43)572, Treasury memo, 'Middle Eastern cereal prices', 17 December 1943; Aviel Roshwald, 'The Spears mission in the Levant', *Historical Journal*, 29 (1986), 901–3.
85 St Antony's College archive, SPRS IB/K7, tels. 707 and 209, Spears to FO, 7 and 8 March 1942.
86 PRO, FO 371/35174, E56/27/89, Spears to Eastern Department, 3 January 1943; E273/27/89, Sir Maurice Peterson record of interview with Catroux, 9 January 1943.
87 PRO, FO 371/35174, E615/27/89, Spears mission, weekly political summary, no. 43, 12 February 1943.
88 Olmert, 'A false dilemma?', 50–5.
89 PRO, WO202/38, Spears to Lyttelton, 21 November 1941.
90 PRO, WO 202/35, Notes of meeting between Wilson and Catroux, 17 January 1942; record of meeting with Minister of State, Cairo, 25 February 1942.
91 PRO, CAB 81/90, JIC(42) eleventh meeting, 31 March 1942.
92 PRO, PREM 3/120/6, Prime Minister's conversation with de Gaulle, 30 September 1942.
93 PRO, WO 202/103, Henry Hopkinson, Cairo, memo, 'Outline of propositions which FNC should be required to accept', n.d., September 1942.
94 St Antony's College archive, SPRS I/I, Diary, entries for 3 and 11 September 1942. Wilkie had been Republican nominee in the 1940 presidential elections.
95 PRO, FO 371/35167, E1852/12/89, Lord Halifax to FO, 23 March 1943.
96 PRO, FO 371/35167, E6791/12/89, Halifax to Eden, 3 November 1943.
97 PRO, CAB 121/131, MOS 79, Cairo Minister of State to Churchill, 29 May 1943.
98 PRO, CAB 66/37, WP(43)247, Edward Bridges' summary, 'Resolutions of the Middle Eastern War Council – political situation in the Middle East', 17 June 1943.
99 PRO, FO 660/35, Z8042/6504/69, Eden–Massigli conversation, 19 July 1943.

100 SHAT, 4H360/D2, CSTL, EMA-2, rapport no. 1946/2S, 16 July 1945; Roshwald, *Estranged Bedfellows*, pp. 171–4, 193–5.
101 PRO, WO 201/1007, MEHQ to Brigadier Hatton, Ninth Army, 27 June 1943.
102 The November 1943 crisis is recounted in detail in Roshwald, *Estranged Bedfellows*, chapter 8; Gaunson, *Anglo-French Clash*, chapter 7; Khoury, *Syria and the French mandate*, pp. 614–15; Lerner, *Catroux*, pp. 252–6.
103 PRO, CAB 122/810, no. 7839, Eden to Halifax, 14 November 1943.
104 PRO, CAB 122/810, no. 7931, Macmillan to Eden, Cairo, 19 November 1943.
105 PRO, FO 371/40299, E98/23/89, Spears mission, weekly political summary, no. 90, 5 January 1944.
106 Gaunson, *Anglo-French Clash*, p. 145.
107 PRO, WO 201/1007, Ninth Army HQ memo, 'Handing over of the *troupes spéciales*', n.d., February 1945; *DDF*, 1944, II, nos. 98, 191.
108 PRO, WO 201/987, Conversations with Syrian President and Prime Minister, 15 March 1944.
109 PRO, FO 371/40110, E24/20/88, Spears to Eastern Department, 28 December 1943.
110 PRO, FO 371/40310, E612/217/89, Duff Cooper to Eden, 26 January 1944.
111 PRO, FO 371/40310, E656/217/89, Spears to Eastern Department, 28 January 1944.
112 PRO, WO 201/987, Conversations with Syrian President and Prime Minister, 15 March 1944.
113 PRO, FO 371/40310, E343/217/89, A. J. Kellar to R. M. A. Hankey, 13 January 1944; Roshwald, *Estranged Bedfellows*, pp. 172–3.
114 PRO, FO 371/40308, E4292/59/89, Beirut Chancery, report, 'The situation in Damascus', n.d., July 1944.
115 PRO, FO 371/40315, E4541/217/89, Spears memo, 18 July 1944, E4592/217/89, FO minutes, 31 July 1944.
116 PRO, FO 371/40310, E749/217/89, Churchill minute for Spears, 17 February 1944, E1458/217/89, Eden to Duff Cooper, 9 March 1944; James A. Melki, 'Syria and the State Department, 1937–41', *Middle Eastern Studies*, 33: 1 (1997), 97–9.
117 PRO, FO 371/40307, E7465, Spears mission, weekly political summary, no. 138, 6 December 1944, E7501/23/89, R. M. A. Hankey conversation with Lebanese *chargé*, Khoury, 30 November 1944.
118 Jean-Rémy Bézias, 'Georges Bidault et le Levant: l'introuvable politique arabe (1945–1946)', *Revue d'Histoire Moderne et Contemporaine*, 42: 4 (1995), 611–12.
119 PRO, FO 371/45556, E8/8/89, Shone to Eastern Department, 30 December 1944.
120 PRO, FO 371/40307, E7799/23/89, Spears, final Beirut dispatch, 21 December 1944.
121 PRO, FO 371/40110, Spears mission to Eden, enclosure, 'The boundaries of the Lebanon', 17 February 1944; Khoury, *Syria and the French Mandate*, p. 613.
122 PRO, FO 371/40308, E4292/59/89, Beirut Chancery, report, 'The situation in Damascus', n.d., July 1944.
123 Bézias, 'Georges Bidault et le Levant', 612–15.
124 SHAT, 4H360, CSTL, EMA-2, rapport no. 2450/2S, 5 October 1945.
125 PRO, FO 371/45556, E320/8/89, Colonel Furlonge, record of conversation with Syrian President, 23 December 1944.
126 PRO, FO 371/45556, E276/8/89, Duff Cooper to Eden and reply, 11 and 26 January 1945; WO 201/1031, ADC 810, C-in-C Middle East to WO, 30 April 1945.
127 PRO, FO 371/45559, E1001/8/89, Duff Cooper to Eden, 11 February 1945.
128 Bézias, 'Georges Bidault et le Levant', 313–14.
129 PRO, WO 201/1004, HQ Ninth Army/British Staff Mission, Beirut, daily summaries, n.d., May 1945.
130 PRO, WO 201/1007, Ninth Army HQ report, n.d., 1945; FO 371/455580, E5800/8/89, Colonel Atkinson to Eastern Department, 23 June 1945.
131 SHAT, 4H360/D1, CSTL, EMA-2, no. 1591/2S, 1 June 1945; Roshwald, *Estranged Bedfellows*, pp. 198–204; Melki, 'Syria and the State Department', 100.
132 Bézias, 'Georges Bidault et le Levant', 614–16.
133 PRO, CO 968/162/4, Note on Lord Cranborne conversations, 15 May 1945.
134 PRO, WO 201/1031, HQ Ninth Army, 'Notes on withdrawal of British troops from

Levant states', 19 July 1945, ME Cmmd to NORLEVANT, 24 November 1945.

135 PRO, FO 371/45587, C9903/8/G, Extract from Cabinet conclusions, 63(45), 13 December 1945; E9971/8/89, Duff Cooper, Paris, to FO, 19 December 1945.

136 PRO, FO 371/45587, E9911/8/89, Young, Beirut, record of conversation with Lebanese Foreign Minister, 18 December 1945.

137 For summaries of the evacuation talks see Roshwald, *Estranged Bedfellows*, pp. 213–21; Bézias, 'Georges Bidault et le Levant', 617–21.

CHAPTER FIVE

Empire as diplomatic incident: St Pierre and Miquelon and the Madagascar invasion, 1942

> After [the] way Vichy has connived in Indo-China we are put doubly on our guard in regard to Madagascar and after such warning it would be unpardonable to be caught napping. [Jan Christian Smuts to Churchill, 12 February 1942[1]]

The French imperial position in 1942

The unhappy Free French experience in Syria and Lebanon indicated that, where Gaullist interests clashed with Allied strategic and political requirements, French imperial control was liable to be thrown into crisis. A similar pattern would emerge in French Indo-China once de Gaulle's supporters set about the task of resurrecting French authority from 1944 onwards. In 1942, however, French North Africa was the obvious focal point of Gaullist and Allied concern. This was a very different proposition. The French Maghreb was the one region where a direct confrontation between Anglo-American, Vichy and Axis forces remained likely. It was also the most prized territory of the Vichy empire, the best defended and the most rigorously controlled.

After the loss of Syria and Lebanon, the pace of Vichy empire collaboration quickened. In December 1940 the Secretariat of Marine operations division had imposed a blanket ban upon assaults against British or Free French African territory, other than in response to a prior attack. In the week following the Syrian armistice on 14 July 1941, Darlan's naval staff reconsidered this decision. Since it fell to the French Marine to transport any troops designated for operations against Free French Equatorial Africa or British West Africa, the navy had an effective veto over military action. Though a comprehensive scheme to reinforce Vichy territories in Africa was duly relayed to Wiesbaden and Turin on 22 July 1941, Darlan's admirals again precluded any operations in the short term. Neither in North or West

Africa was there any serious military response to Vichy's reverses in the Levant.[2] Instead, the Vichy service Ministries redoubled their pressure upon the Axis Armistice Commissions to release further aircraft and fuel stocks for the protection of AOF and French North Africa.[3] Furthermore, in an effort to cut down desertions and so raise the long-term combat effectiveness of Tirailleur units across AOF, on 31 July Admiral Platon permitted long-service units to stand down pending the introduction of additional specialist forces. The War Ministry and Platon's Ministry of Colonies agreed that only by rapid improvements in the terms and conditions of service for native troops could a credible Coloniale force be maintained.[4] De Gaulle was less inclined to restraint. On 27 August he formally offered the use of AEF ports and air bases to the United States in the event that America joined the war against the Axis. If the Americans ever wished to take up this offer, they would first have to neutralise Dakar.[5]

Some months later, on 11 November 1941, the Secretariat of Marine naval planning division conceded that the British maritime blockade of Vichy Africa might yet prove as effective as direct military intervention:

> The English, in trying to isolate France and its colonies, well appreciate that, so long as seaborne traffic is cut off from the metropole, French colonies – most of which cannot survive on their own – will be driven towards the English-speaking powers to find [trade] outlets and necessary provisions. The loyalty [of colonies] will not stretch to a total sacrifice of their interests.[6]

In the previous month, the German Armistice Commission decreed a unilateral extension of its inspection rights across North Africa. This came only days after Rommel's forces in Libya began taking delivery of the 1,100 lorries promised them as part of the May protocols.[7] Henceforth, Vichy Tunisia was inextricably linked with the fate of the Axis forces in North Africa. German and Italian use of Tunisian ports, refuelling facilities and communications routes in 1941 led inevitably to the Axis take-over of the country's infrastructure in November 1942, and so to the Tunisian campaign that ensued between December 1942 and May 1943.

Weygand's recall from Algeria in mid-November 1941 threatened to open the flood gates to the limited collaborationism already under way in North Africa. On 14 August 1941, Hermann Goering had warned Laval's official delegate in Paris, the former *Matin* journalist, Fernand de Brinon, that he considered Weygand an impediment to effective collaboration. On 25 September Hitler and the German high command jointly demanded Weygand's removal from North Africa. Otto Abetz was instructed to pursue this matter with Darlan and his Secretary-general, Jacques Benoist-Méchin.[8] Weygand's subsequent dismissal, Darlan's complicity in it, and the greater degree of collaboration which it heralded, all confirmed the Free French analysis of the deteriorating situation at Vichy.[9] But the French National Committee reaped little immediate reward from Weygand's departure. Admittedly, the State Department took note that Weygand's off-the-record pledges to oppose further empire collaboration were instrumental in his downfall.[10] As a result, on 19 November 1941, State Department officials notified the British Admiralty that two Vichy supply ships carrying US foodstuff supplies for Morocco had left New York four days earlier. With Weygand ousted, these vessels were now considered legitimate targets for British interception.[11] But this early promise of a firmer American line towards Vichyite territories soon faded. Instead, evidence of de Gaulle's diminishing standing with the English-speaking powers emerged during November and December 1941 as Free French proposals regarding the Djibouti enclave fell on deaf ears in London.

Throughout the latter half of 1941, the British Admiralty flatly refused to allocate significant time or resources to either a naval blockade or a seaborne assault against French Somaliland. In September, the Free French were forced to withdraw the one aircraft they kept available in East Africa to make leaflet drops upon Djibouti port. Hitherto, this had proved the most effective means of spreading Gaullist propaganda within the colony.[12] On 13 November de Gaulle abandoned his claim to participate directly in any negotiations with the Vichy French administration in Djibouti. By this stage, the British fleet commander, the First Sea Lord, Admiral Sir Dudley Pound, had made the Admiralty's view still clearer: the Royal Navy was in no mood to risk unnecessary clashes with Vichy units in pursuit of marginal imperial gains for Free France. The underlying message was simple. The British service chiefs were no longer prepared to help extend the Gaullist empire if any substantial risk of outright Vichy hostility were involved. Weygand's dismissal only added to this caution.[13]

The exclusion of the Free French left the way open for Britain's Middle East command to arrange a settlement in French Somaliland. The surrendering Vichyite authorities were to be guaranteed repatriation under an interim British military administration, provided that neither port installations nor the vital Djibouti-to-Addis Ababa railway were destroyed.[14] These terms were agreed in outline on 19 July 1941 during discussions in Cairo between de Gaulle, Oliver Lyttelton and General Wavell. But in November the British government dropped its previous insistence that the colony must acknowledge Free French authority as part of any surrender deal.[15] De Gaulle was left with an implicit understanding only; Free French officials would probably be allowed into Djibouti, but only at the convenience of General Platt's East Africa command. If the British found this transfer of power inconvenient, de Gaulle's supporters were not to be admitted at all. This ignored de Gaulle's repeated attempts to settle the terms of a Free French take-over prior to any decisive British action.[16] In a rare burst of anger, Catroux later condemned Britain's readiness to bargain with Pierre Nouailhetas, the Vichy Governor in Djibouti, in order to secure unrestricted access to the port and its rail link. According to Catroux, Carlton Gardens inevitably read this as damning evidence of the limited British commitment to Free France.[17] In fact, the Djibouti problem simply confirmed that, in the wider strategic context of British operations, the Free French were small fry indeed. Ironically, the outbreak of war with Japan, and the consequent redeployment of the British vessels previously assigned to maintain the Djibouti blockade, prolonged the colony's agonies for a further twelve months.

In 1942 Djibouti was a minor unresolved problem for de Gaulle. The major colonial prizes of French North and West Africa, both still firmly under Vichy control, were far more critical. The other major colonial federation – French Indo-China – receded further beyond Free French grasp once Japan's advance through South East Asia gathered momentum at the start of the year. Though the success of General Eisenhower's North African landings under Operation Torch in early November 1942 brought about a rapid disintegration of Vichy authority across French Africa as a whole, it is well to remember that for most of the preceding twelve months the French National Committee was more deeply immersed in Levant affairs than in planning for a liberated Maghreb. The Gaullists were systematically excluded from Anglo-American preparations for Torch. A key question to be examined in this chapter is whether this was an effect or a cause of the rising tension between the French National Committee and the British government in particular. In so far as both London and Washington saw less reason to trust the Gaullists, two other colonial episodes confirmed this tendency in Allied policies towards Free France during 1942. The year began with a simmering inter-Allied row over the peaceful 'liberation' of the tiny islets of St Pierre and Miquelon, just south of Newfoundland, on Christmas Eve 1941. This action was directed by a Free French naval squadron under Admiral Emile Muselier, Chief of Staff to the FNFL. The year ended with an uneasy compromise between Carlton Gardens and the British government over Free French admission to Madagascar, the island having been captured by British empire forces in a two-stage invasion between May and September 1942. It is to these two events that we now turn.

The St Pierre and Miquelon affair

Long after the dissolution of the first French empire in North America, St Pierre and Miquelon's fishing community – the only all-white French colony – remained faithful to France. This loyalty was, in turn, respected in Paris, not least because possession of the islands offered privileged access to the cod reserves of the Grand Banks. Admiral Muselier's successful intervention at St Pierre and Miquelon in December 1941 became a *cause célèbre*, providing a focal point for Anglo-American suspicion of de Gaulle's leadership.[18] Muselier converted St Pierre with three corvettes recently assigned to the FNFL by the Royal Canadian Navy to assist in convoy escorts in the North West Atlantic. Their brief diversion to St Pierre looked like a striking success. No one was killed during the course of Muselier's take-over, and the islanders were released from an increasingly oppressive Vichyite administration. But Muselier's intervention – the plans for which were exhaustively debated in London, Ottawa and Washington over the preceding three weeks – provoked official Anglo-American criticism at variance with the widespread popularity of this minor *coup* in the United States, Britain and Canada.

Over the preceding eighteen months, St Pierre and Miquelon remained under the firm hand of the islands' pro-Vichy administrator, Gilbert de Bournat. Support for Free France, centred upon St Pierre's *Anciens Combattants* association, peaked in October 1940 when a plebiscite was organised in favour of Free France.[19] But once the seasonal population of Breton trawlermen agreed to sail back to metropolitan France before the winter set in, the islands' politics quietened.[20] Furthermore, from July 1940, the St Pierre and Miquelon economy was buoyed up by Canadian and US government assistance. Canadian–US financial support and generous export purchase arrangements ensured the *de facto* neutrality of de Bournat's administration.[21] In their own small way, St Pierre and Miquelon were thus integrated into the wider US policy of sustained diplomatic contact with Vichy combined with measured economic assistance to the Vichy empire. This was supposed to limit Vichy collaboration and to loosen French imperial ties with Pétain's regime. The Canadians, too, maintained diplomatic relations with Vichy. But, for William Lyon Mackenzie King's government in Ottawa, it formed part of a more subtle balancing act. Ottawa's contact with Vichy facilitated Britain's surreptitious discussions with Pétain's government and postponed a divisive row between English and French Canadians over the status of the competing French authorities. In Quebec province, residual sympathy for Pétain narrowly outweighed support for de Gaulle. Numerous French

Canadians considered the British naval blockade of France and Vichy Africa unnecessarily vindictive.[22] The United States and Canada had good reason to tolerate the incongruous status of St Pierre and Miquelon as a Vichy satellite on the near horizon of the North American continent.

In July 1940 the Organisation of American States convened in Havana to discuss the regional consequences of Germany's recent European victories. Here, the US government insisted that it would intervene to prevent any hostile seizures of the European colonial possessions in the western hemisphere, a statement obviously relevant to St Pierre and Miquelon.[23] The islands were theoretically subordinate to the Vichyite administration controlled by Admiral Georges Robert in the French West Indies. If pressed, Robert might dispatch a cruiser from his western Atlantic squadron to keep St Pierre in Vichy hands. But to the United States, Canada and the Newfoundland Commission of Government a short-wave radio transmitting station on St Pierre posed a more serious threat. The one substantial collaborationist measure open to de Bournat was to transmit intelligence and meteorological information to Vichy pertinent to the local movements of North Atlantic convoys. Quiet diplomacy seemed the best means to keep de Bournat from such folly.

The Canadian historian Douglas Anglin has produced an unsurpassed study of the immediate origins and diplomatic context of the St Pierre and Miquelon take-over. The US and British governments criticised the take-over on several grounds, but their anger turned on de Gaulle's secret instruction of 17 December ordering Muselier to seize St Pierre. The general thus contravened an earlier promise not to act unilaterally.[24] Colonial *ralliements* were fundamental to the Gaullist self-image as the legitimate heirs of French republicanism. As such, the French National Committee was committed to 'liberate' St Pierre and Miquelon at the first opportunity. In this case, de Gaulle's instruction to Muselier was also a pre-emptive strike. The Canadian government planned to send a supervisory team to St Pierre to ensure that the island radio station could not transmit any intelligence to Vichy likely to be of assistance to Germany in the intensifying U-boat war off Newfoundland and Nova Scotia. De Gaulle feared that the installation of these Canadian monitors formed part of a deal under which de Bournat's administration would be protected. As in French Somaliland, an easy picking might be kept from Free France.[25] According to the English-speaking powers, Muselier's take-over needlessly exposed the Vichy authorities to additional pressure from the Axis Armistice Commissions. A sensible and patiently organised Canadian solution was destroyed.[26]

The US State Department over-reacted in its criticism of the St Pierre events, seeing in de Gaulle's actions the confirmation of a deep-seated plot to undermine the foundations of American policy towards France. Secretary of State Cordell Hull's European Division advisers such as Adolf Berle and the division chief, Ray Atherton, also suspected that the British and Canadians were privy to Muselier's change of plan. Like Roosevelt, Cordell Hull disliked de Gaulle's manner, distrusted his political ambition and considered Free France an inchoate organisation ultimately beholden to the general's personal whims. The St Pierre take-over compounded these prejudices. In consequence, the dispute over the St Pierre and Miquelon *coup* derived from State Department suspicion that de Gaulle had exploited a minor imperial gain in order to strike at the heart of US policy. There were several facets to this. Firstly, the ink was scarcely dry upon a fresh agreement concluded on 17 December between the US navy representative, Admiral Horne, and Admiral Robert in Martinique. It reaffirmed the non-belligerency of the French West Indies naval squadron and kept the French Caribbean free of significant Axis influence.[27] Since de Bournat reported to Robert, the St Pierre occupation threatened to rekindle a controversy over the status of French western hemisphere colonies which the Americans thought they had resolved.[28]

Cordell Hull and the State Department legal adviser, Green Hackworth, further concluded that Muselier's action contravened the Havana convention. Sovereign authority had changed hands within a western hemisphere colony without the prior approval of the United States or the South American republics, something which also called the Monroe Doctrine into question.[29] But in the eyes of Canadian, American and British public opinion, St Pierre had merely abandoned Vichy and opted for a pro-Allied French regime. The Free French also had a mandate to remain. On 26 December a plebiscite held across St Pierre and Miquelon registered overwhelming support for the *ralliement* among the all-male electorate. Though the vote was marred by the simplistic and emotive phraseology used on the ballot slips – a high proportion of which were deliberately spoiled – the islands' menfolk clearly embraced Gaullist rule.[30]

The final element of the State Department's position was perhaps the most crucial. According to Cordell Hull, de Gaulle deceived Washington, probably with Canadian and British complicity, in order to undermine the prospects for US dialogue with Vichy over French North Africa. The take-over proved that the French National Committee was a sectarian, politicised organisation more concerned with the eventual triumph of Gaullism in France than with winning the war in co-operation with its notional Allies.[31] Cordell Hull's tirade exposed the deeply rooted mistrust of Free France which had flourished in Washington over the preceding eighteen months.

The French National Committee tackled these State Department criticisms head-on. De Gaulle condemned the US ratification of the neutrality and non-interference accord arranged in Martinique in the week before the St Pierre *coup*.[32] The Robert–Horne agreement built upon an earlier agreement concluded in 1940 affirming the *de facto* neutrality of the French Antillies. As a result, apart from general surveillance of the region, the US government only imposed a partial blockade of the French West Indian territories during late 1940 and 1941. This enabled Robert to maintain Caribbean regimes which, during 1941, became increasingly oppressive; devoted, above all, to the preservation of white French and Creole interests. In response to later Free French criticism of US support for Vichyite repression in the French West Indies, voiced most strongly by Félix Eboué, himself a native of French Guiana, Under-secretary of State Sumner Welles retorted that 'the great majority of the islanders [of Martinique] were illiterate negroes who had no views one way or the other'.[33] The Gaullist opposition which took shape in the French West Indies in the following year was thus denied much effective assistance from Free France. The liberations achieved by Guadeloupe, French Guiana and Martinique between March and June 1943 were accomplished largely by organised protest in the three capitals: Pointe à Pitre, Cayenne and Fort-de-France.[34]

According to de Gaulle, such American efforts to neutralise the French empire piece by piece drove him to act over St Pierre and Miquelon.[35] Roosevelt felt that the Free French should respect the US requirement of stability in the western hemisphere. To the French National Committee, the exact reverse applied. In an official communiqué to Adrien Tixier, the Free French representative in Washington, de Gaulle noted, 'It is, in fact, impossible for it [the French National Committee] to subscribe to any arrangement tending to neutralise the French empire piecemeal, to sow seeds of discord therein and to deprive the French nation of the means still available to it for taking an active part in the common struggle and victory.'[36]

As to the supposed linkage between the Gaullist take-over in St Pierre and increased Axis pressure upon Vichy, the May protocols had indicated that the German Armistice Commission could make unprecedented demands upon Pétain's government at any point. The removal of General Paul Doyen as principal French delegate to Wiesbaden in July 1941 initiated a closer relationship between Darlan and the German military. The fulfilment and further expansion of the May protocol provisions became increasingly probable as Erwin Rommel's

North African campaign developed in late 1941. Indeed, Weygand's replacement as land forces commander in French North Africa, General Alphonse Juin, visited Berlin in the week prior to the St Pierre take-over to discuss the implications of a German military retreat from Libya into Tunisia.[37] Although Darlan claimed that the German authorities suggested that Muselier's *coup* proved the need for Axis forces to protect French Morocco, no such troop movements took place.[38] It was frankly ridiculous to imagine that the German high command would delay operational planning in North Africa until the Free French offered fresh justification for renewed pressure upon Vichy.

In spite of lasting acrimony over the St Pierre and Miquelon affair, between February and April 1942 the US government made important concessions to the Free French movement. But Washington still preferred to deal with individual Gaullist colonies rather than direct with the French National Committee. The resultant confusion was nowhere more obvious than in the French Pacific territories, centred upon New Caledonia and Tahiti. US forces collaborated uneasily with the Free French authorities in Noumea, capital of New Caledonia, after Adrien Tixier initialled a military co-operation agreement in Washington on 15 January 1942. Pursuant to this accord, on 26 February Sumner Welles confirmed formal US recognition of sovereign Gaullist control over the French Pacific islands. He even suggested that this formed part of a wider policy of recognition of the Free French empire.[39] But, on the ground, Admiral Georges Thierry d'Argenlieu, Free French High Commissioner for the Pacific territories, was not made privy to US strategic planning in the Pacific theatre.[40] This led him into confrontation with Major-general Alexander Patch, commander of the US garrison force which arrived in New Caledonia on 12 March in fulfilment of the January agreement. The US and British Chiefs of Staff agreed that it was essential for Patch to retain a free hand to bring New Caledonia into line with broader Allied operational requirements in the Pacific. He was authorised to 'circumscribe' the Gaullist administration if necessary. De Gaulle's cavalier approach to St Pierre added to American suspicions of d'Argenlieu. This was an unfortunate complication since the new High Commissioner – a former Carmelite monk whose religious fervour complemented his political inflexibility – was hard enough to deal with anyway.[41] Always uneasy about the introduction of US forces to New Caledonia, d'Argenlieu was sensitive to any slight upon his authority. He was deeply unpopular with the New Caledonians, not least by comparison with his predecessor as Governor in Noumea, Henri Sautot. The byzantine power struggle that ensued between d'Argenlieu, Sautot and a local Gaullist rival, Michel Vergès, exasperated Patch. To the Americans, it was yet further evidence that Gaullist colonial politics were dominated by petty squabbling and political in-fighting – all to the detriment of an efficient war effort.[42]

As the bizarre drama in New Caledonia unfolded over the spring with a finale involving the kidnap of Sautot by d'Argenlieu's staff on 5 May, American representatives were none the less appointed to the Gaullist administrations in AEF and Syria.[43] In mid-April 1942, Pierre Laval's return to power at Vichy set the seal upon grudging US co-operation with Free French colonies, including St Pierre and the Pacific territories. Even though the State Department continued to obstruct Gaullist involvement in US dealings with the French West Indies, it was now only a matter of time before US and Canadian diplomatic representation in Vichy came to an end.[44] The Vichy collaborationists accomplished what de Gaulle could not, ensuring that Free France could administer St Pierre and Miquelon without Allied interference.

As a diplomatic incident, the St Pierre and Miquelon affair withered on the vine in the early months of 1942. But there was no inter-Allied agreement with de Gaulle over the islands, beyond general acceptance that the territory should remain under sovereign French control. In short, the dispute over St Pierre and Miquelon was not settled.

The whole business underscored the US government's reservations about Free France. Throughout 1941 the Roosevelt administration justified its disdain for de Gaulle as the by-product of its attempts to encourage Vichy's resistance to Axis demands while ensuring that the Vichy empire kept out of the war.[45] Reaction to Muselier's take-over indicated that the State Department's French policy drew upon emotive snap judgements as well as rational diplomacy. The St Pierre and Miquelon dispute had lasting implications for US–Free French relations. It became part of the received wisdom within Roosevelt's government which informed the agreements in French North Africa with Admiral Darlan and General Giraud after the launch of Operation Torch in November 1942.[46] De Gaulle could not be trusted because he placed Free French interests – readily equated with his personal ascendancy – above Allied strategic requirements. Conversely, St Pierre entered Gaullist folklore as a tangible proof of the general's tenacity and vision in the face of English-speaking prejudice against him. The tactics of 24 December 1941 were repeated several times over as the war progressed.[47]

Background to the invasion of Madagascar

During 1942, de Gaulle grew increasingly bitter over his inability to verify details of Allied planning for a descent on Morocco and Algeria.

The proposed occupation of Vichyite Madagascar also contributed to this inter-Allied friction, and actually took up more French National Committee time than discussion of French North Africa. Much like Indo-China, the Vichy government concluded that Madagascar was indefensible against a first-class power. Although the Vichyite Governor, Paul Annet, instructed Madagascar's defending garrison to resist the British empire forces that invaded the island on 5 May 1942, the subsequent two-stage campaign was something of a foregone conclusion.[48] This made the loss of the island a little easier for Vichy to stomach – and to dismiss. Furthermore, the events in Madagascar were quickly eclipsed by the German sweep into unoccupied France after the success of the Allied North African landings in early November. It is worth recalling that, as Operation Torch began, the Free French were still digesting the humiliation of exclusion from Madagascar. In both the North African and the Madagascan cases, the English-speaking powers took little interest in the reconstruction of the French empire in a Gaullist image. Ranged together, the British invasion of Madagascar and the American-led operations in Morocco and Algeria placed the credibility of the Free French movement – and the independence of its empire – in doubt. As such, the crisis generated by the Madagascar problem merits further discussion.

Japan's relentless southward advance during the spring of 1942 transformed Madagascar's role within British strategic planning for the defence of the Indian Ocean. A week after the Pearl Harbor attack, de Gaulle proposed a Free French assault on Majunga, the principal port on Madagascar's western coast, requesting the British to provide naval transport and air cover for the initial landing. By this time, the Chiefs of Staff Joint Planning Committee had twice objected to French National Committee plans to seize the tiny Vichy-controlled island of Réunion, to the north of Madagascar.[49] On 13 December 1941, three days before de Gaulle suggested his Majunga scheme, Churchill noted that control of the Mozambique Channel was imperative to Britain and South Africa alike. Hoping to coax Roosevelt into a quick decision, the Prime Minister envisaged a joint Anglo-US approach to either Vichy or Algiers, advocating the amicable transfer of Madagascar's ports to British control.[50]

In the early months of 1942 the British government rejected further Free French proposals for a joint invasion of the island. The British loss of Singapore in mid-February 1942, the consequent retreat of the British Far Eastern fleet to Colombo in Ceylon and the increased Japanese threat to the western Indian Ocean made Madagascar pivotal to the security of communications to the Colombo base. The island was also an obvious shield to Britain's African dependencies from

Cape Town to Mombasa. The collapse of the British position in South East Asia hastened the Whitehall decision, reached in March, to attack Diego Suarez, the principal port of Madagascar. Situated on the north-west coast of the island, Diego Suarez offered an excellent deep-water anchorage and a secure bridgehead from which operations into the interior of Madagascar could be mounted at British convenience.

Free French involvement was precluded from the outset. Churchill, the British Chiefs of Staff and the Foreign Office were equally determined, not only to exclude Free French forces from the invasion, but also to prevent the French National Committee from learning the details of operational plans. This uncompromising position was the result of three considerations. Firstly, it was generally agreed that Carlton Gardens would deliberately leak rumours of an imminent attack on Madagascar in order to undermine Vichy's claim to supremacy in French Africa. Sensitive British military planning would be threatened, all for the sake of a marginal Gaullist propaganda victory.[51] Secondly, the scheme for a Royal Navy assault on a far-flung French African port armed with shore batteries obviously stirred memories of the humiliating failure at Dakar in September 1940.[52] For the service chiefs, one lesson derived from Dakar was that both they and Churchill were duped by faulty Free French intelligence suggesting that the defending garrison would rally to de Gaulle with little fuss. The same mistake was not to be repeated at Diego Suarez. Finally, neither the British, still less the Americans, saw any reason for generosity towards Carlton Gardens in early 1942. While the British government did not take the St Pierre and Miquelon business to heart to the same extent as the US State Department, relations between Britain and the Free French administrations in Syria and Lebanon were increasingly sour. In crude terms, the British government planned to use Madagascar as a lever both to extract concessions from de Gaulle over the Levant and to assuage the inevitable Free French anger over exclusion from Torch.

The British War Cabinet's decision to occupy Madagascar clashed with US efforts to reach local agreements with Vichyite colonial Governors.[53] From 1941 the Vichy government relied upon US trade to ensure the re-supply of Madagascar. But this commercial traffic was fast diminishing because Roosevelt was reluctant to contravene the British naval blockade of Vichy's black African territories.[54] This confusion in Anglo-American objectives was compounded by British and Free French ignorance of the true state of opinion among the French military and civilian population across Madagascar. The British had instituted a blockade of Madagascar on 29 July 1940 after Annet's predecessor, Governor Léon Cayla, confirmed his loyalty to Vichy by arresting the few known supporters of Free France in and around the capital, Tananarive. It was the single most effective blockade of any Vichy colony.[55] By 1942 the economic hardships it produced were biting hard among the French planter community and Madagascar's town populations. By the time of the invasion, Madagscar's export trade was only 22 per cent of its pre-war level. Popular sympathy for de Gaulle was evidently growing as the blockade gradually strangled the island's staple agricultural and mining industries.[56]

The British hoped that, by stemming the flow of Vichy propaganda and offering immediate repatriation to those colonial officials unwilling to join de Gaulle, Annet's administration would crumble once an invasion began. But at the start of 1942, an invasion of Madagascar seemed rash, particularly as Governor Annet, a close colleague of Pierre Boisson in Dakar, shared the latter's devout loyalty to Pétain. The Colonial Office suggested that, unless they could plead *force majeure*, the French administrative elite in Madagascar would remain loyal to Annet. Until reports to the contrary were received from the SOE personnel working within Tananarive and Réunion, the Foreign and Colonial Offices feared that the Madagascar garrison would remain loyal to Vichy for fear of a British plot to annex the island.[57] The Free French commissariat of foreign affairs conceded that the naval forces in Madagascar were profoundly Vichyite and Anglophobic. With this in mind, from February 1942 SOE operatives in Madagascar tried unsuccessfully to bribe the commander of the naval garrison, a Commandant Maerton, into abandoning Vichy.[58] The British invasion planners considered the 8,000-strong Coloniale garrison of French, Senegalese and Malgache troops less of a problem. In the event, these forces considerably slowed the British penetration into the interior of Madagascar.

By the time the Madagascar invasion scheme came before the British Cabinet in early March, Churchill was determined to exclude the Free French until the operation was successfully completed.[59] From Washington, Lord Halifax warned that, in conversation with Admiral Leahy, Darlan had indicated that he might request US assistance if he learnt of any Japanese designs on Madagascar. But under no circumstances would the Vichy government tolerate Allied use of Free French forces to defend the island.[60] At various points, Pétain, Darlan and Annet all insisted that the French garrison would resist any Japanese incursion in Madagascar.[61] In London, these promises counted for nothing. The British use of force was still conditioned by the fear of a possible Vichy accommodation with Japan rather than by any firm evidence of French–Japanese collusion in Madagascar. The fall of Singapore made a pre-emptive strike against Madagascar worth while.

The passage through the Indian Ocean of a convoy of troops destined to garrison Colombo provided the opportunity for a British-led assault.

In March 1942, de Gaulle responded sensibly but ineffectively to his exclusion from Britain's Madagascar planning by turning to the Allied leader most directly affected by the situation in Madagascar, General Jan Smuts, Prime Minister of South Africa. In December 1941 de Gaulle appointed Colonel Zinovi Pechkoff as his representative in Pretoria. Pechkoff enjoyed frequent access not only to Smuts but also to the South African External Affairs department and Britain's High Commissioner, Lord Harlech. In late February de Gaulle also instructed General Adolphe Sicé, then Free French High Commissioner in Brazzaville, to put the case for a French-led operation directly to Smuts.[62] Sicé was at least able to move freely by air, unlike his colleagues in London, whose access to British air transport was periodically withheld during 1941 and 1942 to maintain Churchill's grip upon de Gaulle's imperial peregrinations.[63]

In Pretoria, Colonel Pechkoff diminished the force of his argument by over-stressing his case. Smuts and South Africa's Chief of General Staff, Sir Pierre van Ryneveld, appreciated the strategic significance of Madagascar. Durban might be needed as a principal fleet base should Japan's advance enable it to dominate the Bay of Bengal.[64] Lord Harlech also kept Smuts abreast of all British planning regarding the island and SOE reports from Madagascar and Réunion were made available to the South African government.[65] Fully apprised of British objectives, Smuts was immune to Pechkoff's lobbying. Conversely, Smuts certainly influenced Churchill's view of Madagascar. In February 1942 he condemned British plans to request the US government to pre-empt any hostile incursion into Madagascar by concluding a trade accord with Vichy. The Americans were, at the time, negotiating increased purchases of fuel oils, groundnut oil, phosphates, cotton and rubber from Vichy African territories. A similar arrangement covering Madagascar would allow the US exclusive purchase rights of Madagascan mica, graphite and animal hides.[66] But Smuts insisted that the supposed advantage of drawing Madagascar into America's commercial orbit would be more than offset by the concomitant loss of Britain's freedom of action. He summarised his fears in a letter to Churchill on 12 February, 'I look upon Madagascar as the key to the safety of the Indian Ocean and it may play the same important part in endangering our security there that Indo-China has played in Vichy and Japanese hands. All our communications with our various war fronts and the empire in the East may be involved.'[67] The Committee on Foreign (Allied) Resistance, the Ministry of Economic Warfare, the Foreign Office and Churchill himself were all persuaded by this. The commercial discussions with Washington over Madagascar were shelved.[68]

On 28 March General Sicé proposed a variant of de Gaulle's original Free French invasion plan to Smuts. Two to three Free French battalions drawn from African commands were to land at Majunga, moving inland and then northward to assault both Tananarive and Diego Suarez by ground attack. But, as Smuts recognised, with no modern aircraft and little shipping of their own, de Gaulle's troops were bound to remain dependent upon British backing. In any event, the issue was academic. On 24 March Churchill informed Smuts that a British invasion force (Force F) under the command of Major-general Sturges and Rear-admiral E. N. Syfret, himself a South African, had departed for Madagascar.[69] More important, Churchill persuaded Smuts to string Free French representatives along in order to keep Pechkoff and Sicé off the scent of the actual invasion plan.[70]

The Madagascar take-over

The landings at Diego Suarez commenced on 5 May. The attack went well and the port was soon made secure.[71] Such was the success of the surprise assault that Darlan ordered an immediate reorganisation of the command structure in both French North Africa and French West Africa to facilitate a more flexible response when confronted with an unforeseen attack.[72] Though the Vichy government issued a stern protest, no retaliation followed comparable to the bombardment of Gibraltar after Mers el-Kébir. In March 1942 Roosevelt agreed to Churchill's request for a symbolic US naval contribution to the British Home Fleet. This sent a powerful warning to Vichy, reinforced when Roosevelt personally informed the new Laval government of the British landings in Madagascar.[73]

Once Diego Suarez was taken, the British government confronted the problem of what to do next. It faced two main problems. Firstly, the bulk of the attacking force was urgently required to proceed by convoy to garrison Colombo.[74] Any British advance into the heart of Madagascar would require fresh troops, probably drawn from elsewhere in the East African command. Secondly, there was no agreed policy regarding the treatment of Annet's administration in Tananarive, itself little affected by the landings several hundred miles to the north. Admiral Syfret's offer of terms to the Governor of Diego Suarez, accepted on 8 May, was decidedly ambiguous. Nothing was said precluding eventual Free French involvement in the occupation. But none of the British proclamations referred explicitly to de Gaulle's movement. Instead, the British stated their intention to 'ensure that

Diego Suarez remains French and under the administration of the French authorities'.[75]

The bewildering nature of the Vichy response to the May attack added to British indecision. French defence of Madagascar was built on the assumption that, given the immensity of the island, hostile landings would be difficult to prevent.[76] Owing to the poor quality of interior communications, any British march on the capital was bound to be slow. This offered the chance for French attacks on British communications, protracted negotiation and possible retreat and resistance in the southern highlands between Antsirabe and Fiarantsoa, the major towns south of the capital. Major-general William Dimoline, the commander of the British East African Brigade which spearheaded the eventual southward advance, conceded that the retreating Vichy troops displayed great ingenuity in blocking the advance of his motorised columns.[77]

Annet sowed further doubt among the invasion commanders by feigning willingness to reach a *modus vivendi* with the British garrison at Diego Suarez. Syfret and Sturges reacted warmly to Annet's approaches. The resultant exchanges dragged on for three months. They were conducted via the unlikely combination of Annet's *aide de camp*, Captain Fauché, who also headed the Governor's military intelligence section, and Leslie Barnett, British representative of the Vacuum Oil Company of South Africa in Tananarive, who was approached by Fauché's staff.[78] Churchill's Cabinet chose to ignore that its field commanders were negotiating with Annet's Vichyite administration. On 14 May the government announced that, owing to 'overriding political considerations', the Free French would play a role in Madagascar – eventually.[79] If not quite left out in the cold, the French National Committee was still nowhere near the hearth.

It made sense to both the British War Office and the Admiralty to remain deliberately imprecise. Neither department wanted to invest further effort in a lengthy conquest of the entire island when control of its principal port appeared sufficient to protect the Mozambique Channel. The British service chiefs insisted that, while it might be stated in London that the Free French would administer the island, British commanders in Madagascar should not admit this. Anthony Eden was appalled. He reminded Churchill on 18 May of the numerous examples of previous Vichy hostility. The Foreign Secretary pointed out that when the Diego Suarez assault began, Laval's government even appealed to Tokyo for assistance.[80]

Churchill disliked the dialogue with Annet's administration, but he approved it on grounds of economy alone. Hence, from May to September 1942, the British pursued a dual policy of talks with Annet and preparations for an eventual march southward from Diego Suarez. The Free French executive was once more ignored. This was the clearest proof yet that the French National Committee relied entirely upon British support in order to secure those colonial territories beyond the reach of the Free French armed forces. In Madagascar, the sad fact was that, as in Indo-China, French Somaliland and AOF, once the limited enthusiasm for Free France among colonial bureaucrats and settlers was stymied by an official crackdown in 1940, the British military authorities had little incentive to work closely with Carlton Gardens.

In Diego Suarez, what had started as an impressive assault, compensation for the failure of the attack on Dakar in September 1940, now threatened to end in shabby deal-making. In late May Churchill instructed Syfret to keep a channel open to the Governor in Tananarive.[81] So the unofficial negotiations between Fauché and Barnett continued much as before. These exchanges quickly stalled. The British contested Annet's right to continue receiving orders from Vichy and his continued control of the island's policing and commerce. On 28 May, Smuts again acted decisively by proposing a conference in Pretoria to discuss future policy in Madagascar. This enabled him to review matters with Generals Platt and Sturges and their political officer, Brigadier M. S. Lush. Prior to the Pretoria meeting, Smuts stressed that control of Diego Suarez could not in fact secure South Africa. The ports of Majunga and Tamatave might still be used as bases for forays by Japanese submarines. It was thus Smuts, strongly backed by Eden in London, who prompted the decision, reached at Pretoria in June, to attack these two ports and then move inland against Tananarive once the rainy season lifted in the autumn.[82] It remained to persuade the British service chiefs that the necessary reinforcements could be found.[83]

On the night of 30 May a Japanese midget submarine attacked HMS *Ramillies*, at anchor in Diego Suarez. Although *Ramillies* limped safely back to Durban, the incident confirmed Smuts's warning.[84] Although the Pretoria conference recommended an advance on Majunga and Tamatave in September or October, this did not mark the abandonment of talks with Annet. On 21 June, Smuts and Platt agreed to continue discussions with the Governor. Their sole proviso was that Annet should transmit official proposals, as opposed to the purely unofficial *démarches* made hitherto.[85] This marked an uneasy compromise between the War Office wish to continue talks in any form in the hope that Annet's administration might come over to the British cause, and the Foreign Office view that the adverse impact of negotiations upon Anglo-Free French relations should preclude them entirely.[86]

At the suggestion of the Committee on Foreign (Allied) Resistance, on 20 July the US State Department tied American offers of increased trade with Madagascar to the progress of British discussions with Annet.[87] In the event, while talks continued until late August they never reached the level of official discussions. Annet excused his reluctance to reach any agreement by suggesting that the presence of German Armistice Commission representatives in Vichy prevented him from obtaining official and frank instructions. SOE's Durban station warned that its operatives in Tananarive were convinced that Annet was deluding Sturges and Syfret in an effort to prevent a British march on the capital.[88] As Eden feared, the damage to relations with Carlton Gardens was done. Although the Foreign Secretary reassured de Gaulle that he would be guaranteed a part in the government of Madagascar, the British still calculated that the islanders opposed the Free French cause. De Gaulle commented that it was a contradiction in terms to keep the Free French out on the grounds that they were still detested, while maintaining that a Gaullist Governor would eventually be installed.[89] Still suffering from an earlier bout of malaria, de Gaulle none the less planned for his assumption of authority in Tananarive. Assuming that British estimates of loyalty to Vichy across Madagascar were true, it was essential that de Gaulle's nominee as head of government, his commander in the Levant, General Paul Legentilhomme, should arrive with at least a bare-bones Free French administrative team. But it was difficult to prepare this government-in-waiting because the British did not intend to inform the French National Committee of the timetable for 'Operation Streamline Jane' – the attacks on Majunga, Tamatave and Tananarive – until 10 September, the day the action began. Churchill also refused to lift the earlier restriction on transport facilities for Free French leaders. Still working on de Gaulle's behalf in Pretoria, Colonel Pechkoff could not assess the situation in Madagascar, as General Platt denied him permission to visit the island.[90]

The British seizure of complete control across Madagascar took just under a month to complete. Reports on these further British advances by General Parisot, chief French delegate to the Italian Armistice Commission in Turin, indicated that Annet's forces were caught off guard.[91] The delay between the capture of the ports and the final entry into Tananarive was occasioned by the destruction of roads by the retreating Vichy troops. Annet instructed the garrison to fight on, though he left the capital with his family on 18 September. Captain Fauché was left to sign the final armistice on 6 November.[92] Once it was clear that British forces would soon have full control of Madagascar, Smuts pressed Churchill for concessions to de Gaulle. On 26

September the South African Premier warned that the French National Committee regarded the transfer of authority in Madagascar as the acid test of British good faith. Eden admitted that this applied not just to Madagascar but to the Levant states and, above all, to French North Africa, where the planning of the Anglo-American landings was now in its final stages.[93] In August the British Cabinet agreed that a swift hand-over of Madagascar to de Gaulle 'would soften the blow of not being let in on "Torch"'.[94] Yet this never became official policy. De Gaulle told Smuts that he felt Churchill was simply punishing him in Madagascar for the continued frictions over the correct interpretation of the July 1941 Lyttelton–de Gaulle agreements regarding Syria's future administration. Eden warned Churchill on 22 September 1942 that the British had indeed pledged to cede control in Madagascar once the Free French made a firm commitment to hold free and fair elections in the Levant states. Supported by advice from his private secretary, Desmond Morton, Churchill chose to overlook this after an exceptionally bruising meeting with de Gaulle on 30 September.[95]

There were more substantial reasons for Churchill's continued prevarication. Far from sharing the Cabinet's view that control of Madagascar would make the Free French more compliant, on 29 August the British Chiefs of Staff suggested that it would add to the determination of the Vichyite authorities in French North Africa to resist the Torch landings.[96] On 6 October the Committee on Foreign (Allied) Resistance discussed an extended term of British military administration in Madagascar once Tananarive fell. Major-general Lord Rennell, Platt's chief political officer within the East Africa command, was designated to take charge of that administration in September. He advised the War Office that only a sustained period of British rule would keep the settler population passive. This irritated the Foreign Office, which would be 'heirs to the problem' once a Gaullist civil administration was established. A delayed transfer of authority could only worsen Anglo-Gaullist relations.[97]

The dispute with the Free French over political control in the Levant states increased Churchill's reluctance to allow Legentilhomme to take up office in Tananarive. The Prime Minister's reticence was tactical. It hastened French National Committee efforts, directed by Maurice Dejean, the Commissioner of Foreign Affairs, to formulate a workable power-sharing agreement in Syria and Lebanon.[98] But the Torch landings were of far greater importance than either the Levant or Madagascar. If Gaullists were let into Madagascar prematurely, there was a remote possibility that the Vichyite administrations in Algeria and Morocco might resist Allied landings more fiercely.[99]

Advice from the Committee on Foreign (Allied) Resistance, the War Office and the Foreign Office regarding the likely consequences within North Africa of a transfer of power in Madagascar thus assumed critical importance.

In late September 1942 General Platt and the War Office planning directorate sought Cabinet approval for a three to six-month extension of British military administration in Madagascar.[100] As usual, it fell to Eden to take the opposing line. On 22 September, he reminded Churchill that generosity to de Gaulle over Madagascar might reconcile the general to non-involvement in Torch. But Eden conceded that the experience of Syria and Lebanon could be held to disprove this.[101] Later the same day, Churchill replied, 'It is quite possible that as a result of "Torch" we may be in relation with a French anti-German organisation very much wider in its basis than that presided over by de Gaulle. It would be wise to keep options in our hands as long as possible.'[102] The Prime Minister had a point. Although the commander of land forces in North Africa, General Alphonse Juin, would soon establish himself as a leading Gaullist, Juin was the exception, not the rule. It is hard to imagine that Admiral Darlan would have issued his 10 November instruction to French forces in Morocco, Algeria and Tunisia to co-operate with the Allied landings had de Gaulle been fully involved alongside Eisenhower, Roosevelt and Churchill in the launch of Torch.[103] On 6 November, only two days before the first Torch landings, Darlan issued a radio message urging continued military resistance to British forces in Madagascar.[104] His rapid conversion was undoubtedly encouraged by the low profile imposed upon de Gaulle by the British over the preceding three months.

Although immediately before Torch the British government closed ranks against concessions to de Gaulle in London, Grafftey-Smith, the British consul in Tananarive, worked hard to develop a more conciliatory occupation policy in Madagascar itself. True to the Foreign Office's greater sympathy for the Free French, from early October, Grafftey-Smith tried to build administrative ties with any local organisation prepared to endorse Legentilhomme. The new consul was soon disappointed:

> No such organisation existed. I found instead a number of separate and mutually hostile groups, none of which could claim any official association with General de Gaulle ... The first group to claim our interest was led by a hotel chef and a doctor, who profitably combined the activities of a V.D. clinic with discriminatory pimping. They claimed to have 350 supporters and I rashly asked for a list of names. They proceeded to canvass the town, taking the name of the British military administration in vain, collecting signatures. Their most cogent argument with hesitants

was that, unless people enough clamoured for a Fighting French administration, the British would never relinquish Madagascar.[105]

This was not what the Foreign Office hoped for. The delay in ceding control to Legentilhomme chimed perfectly with Vichy propaganda which warned that Britain intended to keep Madagascar to help compensate for its loss of territory in the Far East.[106] Almost six months after the initial Diego Suarez landings it appeared that the War Office and the military commanders on the ground had indeed got it right: French settlers in Madagascar had little enthusiasm for the Allied cause. Although no longer 'pro-Vichy', the local elite certainly remained 'anti-de Gaulle'.[107] As de Gaulle feared, Anglo-American co-operation with Darlan added to the cynicism and confusion evident among the French of Tananarive. To de Gaulle, the only remedy was the immediate installation of Legentilhomme.

The installation of Free French administration in Madagascar

Once the French National Committee formally acquiesced in the Allied collaboration with the Algiers authorities, the British reconsidered the distribution of their Madagascan *largesse*. After meeting de Gaulle on 8 November, Churchill and Eden resurrected the plans for an immediate transfer of authority to a Free French administration which, while able to raise its own land forces in Madagascar, would remain a part of Platt's East African command. There was little else at issue between the Foreign Office negotiating team, led by the principal clerk of the French department, Ronald Speaight, and the Gaullist delegation headed by René Pleven.[108] So why was it a further nine weeks before Legentilhomme arrived in Madagascar?

Both Grafftey-Smith and the interim military administration in Tananarive, now led by Major-general Smallwood, GOC Islands Area, were anxious to see a Gaullist administration in place. This made obvious sense. French National Committee suspicions of any delay were magnified by the enduring inability of the British authorities in Tananarive to build close ties with the settler population. A 'provisional committee' established by the infamous chef and doctor, and intended to act as a shadow Free French administration, held no official authority at all. Carlton Gardens never sanctioned its existence.[109] Clearly, life for Smallwood and Grafftey-Smith was not easy. It was unlikely to improve so long as the duration of British sovereignty remained subject to question.

The ostensible British explanation for the delayed hand-over of authority was prosaic. While a vessel was quickly made available to transport an unrepentant Annet to detention in Durban, allegedly, there were neither aircraft nor ships available to conduct Legentilhomme first to Cairo and thence to Madagascar.[110] This reflected the wider British problem of maintaining essential supplies to the island, let alone of fulfilling the Allied promise of a swift restoration of maritime trade adequate to secure the loyalty of the indigenous population. This was further hampered by the French National Committee's understandable reluctance to participate in a Madagascan supply board prior to Legentilhomme's installation as head of government.[111]

De Gaulle suspected that the British might renege on their promises. His fears grew in response to American enthusiasm for co-operation with Darlan and General Henri Giraud in Algiers. Furthermore, de Gaulle had leadership problems closer to home. Admiral Muselier, whom de Gaulle had ousted as head of the FNFL in March 1942, redoubled his criticism of the general's autocratic style of leadership from December onwards. It was unsurprising that de Gaulle's antagonist of early 1942 was now eager to join forces with Giraud, the new antagonist of 1943.[112] Free French worries that the Allies might abandon de Gaulle in favour of a less truculent figure were also nourished by the ambivalent outcome of the Djibouti blockade. In October 1942 Governor Nouailhetas was recalled to Vichy, never to return. He was replaced by the garrison commander, General Truffert, who recognised that the colony faced imminent starvation. By late November, it was obvious that the Vichyite garrison was nearing capitulation. On 28 December a surrender accord was duly signed in a railway carriage at Chébelé station. It ceded interim control of French Somaliland to the British East African command.[113]

Although the Free French delegate in East Africa, Ludovic Chancel, participated in the final stages of transfer talks during November and December, the British government authorised General Platt to conclude or delay a take-over at Djibouti as he thought fit. This angered Carlton Gardens staff, since it was obvious that the French Somaliland garrison was by now thoroughly infiltrated by the Gaullist underground in Djibouti. The local Gaullist leader, Bernard Cothier, even organised a 'soldiers' soviet' which met regularly in the Djibouti branch of the Banque d'Indochine, and his followers sabotaged much of the military equipment remaining to Truffert's forces.[114] On 28 November, a substantial part of the Djibouti garrison under Truffert's immediate subordinate, Colonel Raynal, defected to the British by marching into Zeila, administrative heart of British Somaliland. General Truffert was obviously complicit in this. He even had Raynal's coat and *kepi* sent on to him a week later![115] Together, Cothier and

Raynal ensured that Truffert acquiesced in British demands. The British showed little appreciation of this hard work. Might they show the same lack of good grace over Madagascar, a far more important prize?

In fact, the British government did not link its policies regarding the transfer of authority in Djibouti and Madagascar. Within the Foreign Office, on 19 and 20 November, Ronald Speaight and William Strang reminded Eden that the French department wished to hurry the implementation of a Madagascar agreement in order to prove British fidelity to de Gaulle and so consolidate the influence of the French National Committee in North Africa.[116] In the following week, de Gaulle pleaded with Eden to make good the British pledges over Madagascar. Speed was of the essence lest the serving French officials in Tananarive declared for Darlan's transformed administration in Algiers.[117] On 2 December Strang gave René Pleven a draft transfer agreement amended by General Platt and Lord Rennell to clarify the sole responsibility of the East African command for Allied strategy affecting Madagascar.[118] This last obstacle to a formal agreement was under review as the Free French pulled off another daring island *coup* – on 29 November the Vichy-controlled island of Réunion was captured by a skeleton force aboard the FFS *Léopard* and a Gaullist Governor installed.[119]

Legentilhomme eventually flew from Cairo to Nairobi on 16 December. The *Léopard* ferried him on to Tamatave. On 7 January 1943 he disembarked, bearing the cumbersome title 'High Commissioner of French Possessions in the Indian Ocean'. British military administration immediately lapsed, though both military and civil liaison officers remained in Tananarive. The immediate transfer of power was facilitated by Legentilhomme's public affirmation that there would be neither witch hunts nor reprisals against those who had served the Annet regime. During his four months as High Commissioner, Legentilhomme worked with mixed success to increase Madagascar's production of strategic raw materials, notably graphite, metal ores and animal hides. Provision of these materials marked the island's major contribution to the Allied war effort from then on. Legentilhomme stated his wish to revive the achievements of France's greatest proconsul in Madagascar, General Joseph Galliéni, who had governed the colony between 1896 and 1905. Legentilhomme's emulation of Galliéni's *politique des races* required a decentralised administrative system built around co-operation with local Merina and other tribal elites. This made little constructive impact upon a country crippled by the wartime collapse of exports, price inflation and often chronic rice shortages.[120] Legentilhomme's successor, Pierre de Saint-Mart, appointed to the redesignated post of Governor in May 1943, quickly proved his merits as an experienced civil administrator. But since the FCNL refused to concede greater autonomy to post-war Madagascar, much of the Governor's work counted for little.[121] Saint-Mart also increased exports of strategic raw materials to add to Allied war production. Madagascar made a greater contribution to this process once vessels from the small Free French merchant fleet began serving the island.[122] For the Malagasy, this meant the continuation of forced labour exactions and foodstuff requisitioning. Economically at least, Gaullist administration imposed unprecedented demands, whereas Annet's regime had been powerless in the face of the collapse in trade due to blockade. In sum, Madagascar's new French rulers did little to diminish the appeal of an emergent Malagasy nationalism which drew upon the fierce independence of the Merina people and which found full expression in the Democratic Movement for Malagasy Renewal (MRDM) founded in 1946.[123] Luckily for Free France, the nationalist insurrection which erupted across Madagascar in late March 1947 was not presaged during the closing stages of the Second World War.

Certain conclusions may be drawn from the Anglo-Gaullist dispute over Madagascar. There is no doubt that a hostile presence in Madagascar became intolerable to the British government after the devastating loss of Singapore. If the Vichy regime conceded the use of Madagascar to the Japanese, Allied control of the western Indian Ocean would have been jeopardised as surely as the British empire in South East Asia was endangered by the French capitulation in Indo-China. In the event, the invasion of Madagascar was conducted without direct Free French support. When the attack began, the French National Committee was still ignorant of British operational plans. De Gaulle read into this a British attempt to keep Carlton Gardens subservient, and perhaps a more sinister plot to destroy French imperial rule in Madagascar. To the Free French, the Madagascar operations were a missed opportunity for decisive action by their forces to reassert Gaullist authority after the humiliation of the British-directed take-over in Syria and Lebanon in July 1941. To Pierre Laval's incumbent government in Vichy, Britain's seizure of the island provided another bitter proof of Albion's treachery.

British motives were not as malevolent as de Gaulle supposed. This does not, however, exonerate Churchill's government, which used the future installation of a Gaullist Governor in Tananarive as a bargaining chip. The chip was played whenever de Gaulle dissented over British policy towards French North Africa or the Levant. This made the interim British administration of Madagascar stuttering and vacillatory. Caught up in the squabbles between Britain and the Free French movement – and, more personally, between Churchill and de Gaulle – the Madagascar story, like the St Pierre and Miquelon affair before it, was an object lesson in the limitations of notional co-operation between two distrustful and intransigent Allies.

In the absence of any strong local reaction, French or Malagasy, to the assumption of Free French control in Tananarive, it is tempting to conclude that the months of confusion between May and December 1942 stemmed solely from the British governmental use of Madagascar as both carrot and stick in its dealings with de Gaulle. Once Churchill began withholding concessions over Madagascar in order to strengthen his hand with Carlton Gardens, little consideration was given to the effect this would have in Madagascar itself. With a greater vested interest in the security of the western Indian Ocean, Smuts was the greatest Free French advocate throughout. But he, too, recognised that de Gaulle ultimately had little alternative but to live with the meanderings of British policy towards Madagascar. While the limited Free French capacity for independent strategic initiative was made manifest by the Madagascar episode, the experience also confirmed the British viewpoint, adhered to consistently until the liberation of France, that the French empire would not fight as one in the Allied cause unless a unified provisional French government-in-exile was first established.[124] In that sense, the Free French movement suffered no lasting harm from its limited role throughout the Madagascar take-over.

Notes

1 PRO, PREM 3/265/2.
2 SHM, TTA 102/FMF-3, Etude 18, 'Opportunité d'une opération de débarquement à Bathurst', 28 July 1941; SHAT, 1P34/D1, Huntziger to Darlan, 16 October 1941.
3 SHAT, 1P34/D1, no. 01166/EMAA, General Bergeret to Darlan, 16 August 1941.
4 SHAT, 1P34/D4, Platon to Secretariat of Marine, 31 July 1941.
5 SHM, TTA 39/FMF correspondence, FMF-2, 'Note: Convoitises étrangères sur l'empire colonial français', 3 September 1941.
6 SHM, TTA 102/FMF-3, Etude no. 20, 'Conséquences de l'évolution de l'attitude britannique', 11 November 1941.
7 SHAT, 1P89/D4, Note for Weygand, 'Relevé des récents abandons de nos droits consentis aux Commissions de Contrôle en AFN', 15 October 1941.
8 SHAT, Fonds Privées, Papiers du Maréchal Juin, 1K496/Papiers du Général Raymond Pédron, copy of Darlan report to Pétain, 8 November 1941.
9 Paxton, *Vichy France*, pp. 125–7.
10 Weygand informed Robert Murphy in early October that Gaullist territories in Africa would be left alone and that Axis forces would be kept out of Morocco and AOF, see PRO, FO 892/117, tel. 4682, Halifax to FO, 14 October 1941.
11 PRO, FO 892/117, tel. 6948, Halifax to FO, 19 November 1941. The ships in question, *Ile de Normantier* and *Ile d'Ouessant*, were making for Casablanca.
12 PRO, ADM 199/1277, Admiralty DNI correspondence with Naval Intelligence, Cape Town, 29 July 1941; PRO, AIR 40/1870, Air HQ, East Africa, to RAF Middle East, 17 September 1941. The aircraft – a Blenheim medium bomber – was sent to

Damascus to help train Free French volunteer pilots.

13 PRO, ADM 199/1281, COS committee, 371st meeting, 29 October 1941.

14 MAE, CNF Londres, vol. 88, CNF memo, 13 November 1941.

15 MAE, CNF Londres, vol. 88, CNF memo, 6 June 1942.

16 Churchill archive, Spears papers, SPRS/1/137/2, Z10377/675/G, FO memo., 'Jibuti', 22 December 1941; SPRS II/4, Record of Churchill–de Gaulle meeting, 12 September 1941; PRO, ADM 199/1281, C-in-C Middle East to Platt, 29 November 1941.

17 Catroux, *Dans la Bataille*, p. 100.

18 Three excellent works on St Pierre are Anglin, *The St Pierre and Miquelon Affaire of 1941*; William A. Christian, *Divided Island. Faction and Unity on St Pierre* (Cambridge, Mass., Harvard University Press, 1969); David B. Woolner, 'Storm in the North Atlantic. The St Pierre and Miquelon Affair of 1941' (MA thesis, Montreal McGill, 1990). See also Martin Thomas, 'Deferring to Vichy in the western hemisphere: the St Pierre and Miquelon affair of 1941', *International History Review*, 19: 4 (1997), 000–00.

19 PRO, FO 892/34, Memo. by Archibald Bartlett, 10 September 1940; Crémieux-Brilhac, *La France Libre*, p. 279.

20 PRO, FO 892/34, Newfoundland government to DO, 24 September 1940.

21 NAC, MG 26, Mackenzie King papers, Series J4, vol. 400, reel H-1558, Memo. for O. D. Skelton, 17 August 1940.

22 J. F. Hilliker, 'The Canadian government and the Free French: perceptions and constraints, 1940–44', *International History Review*, 2: 1 (1980), 88–92; Paul M. Couture, 'The Vichy–Free French propaganda war in Quebec, 1940 to 1942', *Canadian Historical Association Historical Papers* (1978), 200–2.

23 David R. Murray (ed.), *Documents on Canadian External Relations* (Department of External Affairs, Ottawa, 1976), Part II, vol. 8, doc. 658, enclosure II, External Affairs memo., 21 June 1940.

24 Anglin, *St Pierre and Miquelon Affaire.*

25 De Gaulle, *L'Appel*, pp. 192–4 at 192.

26 The official US, Canadian and British governmental responses to the 24 December *coup* are detailed in *FRUS*, Conferences at Washington, 1941–42, and Casablanca, 1943, section D, St Pierre and Miquelon, pp. 377–87.

27 External affairs memo., 8 January 1942, NAC, RG 25, vol. 2938, file 2984–40–C; *The Memoirs of Cordell Hull* (London, Macmillan, 1948), II, p. 1128.

28 Crémieux-Brilhac, *La France Libre*, p. 282.

29 *FRUS*, Conferences at Washington and Casablanca, memo. by Legal Adviser, Hackworth, 9 January 1942, pp. 396–8.

30 NAC, RG 25, vol. 2938, file 2984–40–C, Halifax to Eden, 25 December 1941, External Affairs memo to High Commissioner, Newfoundland, 26 December 1941; MAE, Londres CNF, vol. 117, tel. 3766A; Anglin, *St Pierre and Miquelon*, pp. 85–7.

31 *FRUS*, 1941, Europe, vol. II, Cordell Hull memo, 26 December 1941, pp. 557–8.

32 Paxton, *Vichy France*, p. 130.

33 PRO, CO 968/86/6, tel. 2782, Halifax to FO, 15 May 1942.

34 Burton, '"Nos journées de juin"', in Kedward and Wood, *Liberation*, pp. 229–30; PRO, CO 968/86/6, tel. 1328, Halifax to FO, 21 March 1943; FO 371/36034, Z4396/72/17, Sir Nevile Bland to Eden, 5 April 1943.

35 MAE, CNF Londres, vol. 117, CNF memo. for Tixier, 18 December 1941; de Gaulle to Muselier, 27 December 1941.

36 MAE, CNF Londres, vol. 117, France Libre memo. for Tixier, n.d., December 1941.

37 Paxton, *Vichy France*, pp. 125, 128–9.

38 *Memoirs of Cordell Hull*, II, p. 1130.

39 PRO, FO 892/117, tel. 1118, Tixier to de Gaulle, 26 February 1942; Munholland, 'The Trials of the Free French in New Caledonia', 562.

40 PRO, ADM 199/1281, Charles Peake to FO, 18 February 1942.

41 PRO, ADM 199/1281, tel. 183, COS to JSM, Washington, 9 May 1942; FO 892/127, tel. 238, FO to Halifax, 11 January 1942.

42 Munholland, 'The trials of the Free French', 563–79.

43 NAC, MG 26/J1, C-6808, WA 519, Canadian legation, Washington, to External Affairs, 2 April 1942; Munholland, 'The trials of the Free French', 565–7.
44 PRO, CO 968/86/6, Sir Ronald Campbell to W. H. B. Mack, 23 June 1942.
45 This became something of an 'orthodox view' following the 1947 publication of William Langer's *Our Vichy Gamble* (New York, Knopf, 1947). See also Kim Munholland, 'The United States and the Free French' in Paxton and Wahl (eds), *De Gaulle and the United States*, pp. 61–94.
46 Hurstfield, *America and the French Nation*, pp. 139–41. Regarding Roosevelt's attitude to de Gaulle in late 1942, see Robert Dallek, 'Roosevelt and De Gaulle' in Paxton and Wahl, *De Gaulle and the United States*, pp. 50–5.
47 PRO, PREM 3/121/5, PM/45/274, Alexander Cadogan to Churchill, 18 June 1945.
48 LHCMA, Dimoline papers VIII/5, Dimoline report, 'Account of the operations of 22 East African Brigade, 10 September–6 November 1942'.
49 PRO, PREM 3/265/1, Morton to Churchill, 17 February 1941; de Gaulle to Churchill, 16 December 1941.
50 PRO, PREM 3/265/11, Prime Minister's personal minute, 13 December 1941.
5 PRO, FO 371/31897, Z1750/23/17, Strang minute, 20 February 1942; COS(42)132, 27 February 1942.
52 LHCMA, Dimoline papers, VIII/1, notes by Lieutenant-Commander G. G. Butler, 'Operation Ironclad, the Madagascar operation', 11 July 1942.
53 SHAT, 1P34/D2, Conférence économique Africaine, Darlan note, 5 March 1942.
54 SHAT, 1P34/D6, Etat-Major des Colonies troisième bureau memo., 'Madagascar', 1 October 1940; PRO, ADM 199/874, Halifax to Eden, 10 May 1942.
55 Regarding Cayla's actions in Dakar, see Kent, *Internationalization of Colonialism*, p. 30; SHAT, 1P34/D6, troisième bureau memo., 1 October 1940.
56 PRO, WO 208/1518, Reneuve, 'La France Libre' Tananarive, to military intelligence, Cape Town, 16 October 1941; FO 892/147, Harlech to DO, 23 February 1942; AN, 560AP/27, René Pleven papers, Pleven to Tananarive, 10 May 1944.
57 PRO, CO 968/3/12, 'Operations of East Africa Command, 1941–1943', 31 March 1943.
58 SHAT, 2N246/D3, Marine, bulletin du haut commandement, 14 March 1938; on SOE activities see PRO, HS 3/28, Todd mission reports, 7 and 12 February 1942.
59 PRO, PREM 3/265/1, Churchill minute to Eden, 7 March 1942.
60 PRO, ADM 199/1277, Halifax to Eden, 5 March 1942.
61 PRO, WO 208/1518, WO intelligence report, B.J.102203, Vichy Secretariat of Marine cypher, 14 March 1942.
62 PRO, T 160/1146/17006/3, DO to Harlech, 18 December 1941; PRO, FO 371/31897, Z1602/23/17, Peake to FO, 19 February 1942.
63 PRO, FO 371/32002, H. Hopkinson, Cairo, to W. H. B. Mack, 29 August 1942.
64 Jean Van Der Poel (ed.), *Selections from the Smuts Papers*, VI. *December 1934–August 1945* (Cambridge, Cambridge University Press, 1973), pp. 354 and 360.
65 PRO, ADM 199/1277, CFR(42), misc. 3, 23 January 1942, CFR(42), misc.7, 13 February 1942 and CFR memo., 27 January 1942; PRO, HS 3/10, SOE memo., 10 February 1941.
66 SHAT, 1P34/D2, Conférence économique africaine, 18–20 February 1942.
67 PRO, PREM 3/265/2, Smuts to Churchill, 12 February 1942.
68 PRO, PREM 3/265/2, CFR meeting, 13 February 1942; FO 371/31897, FO to Harlech, 13 February 1942.
69 PRO, PREM 3/265/1, Harlech record of Sicé–Smuts meeting, 28 March 1942; PREM 3/265/2, Churchill to Smuts, 24 March 1942.
70 PRO, PREM 3/265/1, Churchill to Ismay, 30 March 1942.
71 PRO, WO 208/1520, 'Summary of Operation Ironclad', n.d., May 1942.
72 SHAT, 1P89/D3, Darlan report on Madagascar to Pétain, 2 June 1942.
73 Churchill to Roosevelt, 14 March 1942, in Warren F. Kimball (ed.), *Churchill and Roosevelt. The Complete Correspondence*, I (Princeton, N.J., Princeton University Press, 1984), doc. C-44; PRO, T 160/1146/17006/3, Finance Division summary of French events, 2–16 May 1942.

74 PRO, PREM 3/265/6, Churchill to Syfret, 14 May 1942.
75 PRO, FO 371/36138, Z8719/8/69, Consul Grafftey-Smith to Eden, 14 July 1943.
76 SHAT, 1P34/D6, EM-Col., 'Défense de Madagascar', n.d., March 1941.
77 LHCMA, Dimoline papers, VIII/3, Transcript of Dimoline interview with war correspondent, G. Kinnear, 6 November 1942.
78 PRO, PREM 3/265/6, Sturges to WO, 28 May 1942; PRO, ADM 199/874, Syfret to Admiralty, 28 June 1942.
79 PRO, PREM 3/265/6,Syfret to Admiralty, 14 May 1942.
80 PRO, PREM 3/265/6, Hollis to Churchill, 14 May 1942, Eden to Churchill, 18 May 1942; Laval discussed Japanese submarine operations from Madagascar with Japan's Vichy ambassador, Mitami; see Paxton, *Vichy France*, p. 313, n. 42.
81 PRO, PREM 3/265/6, Churchill to Syfret, 15 May 1942; PRO, FO 371/36138, Z8719/8/69, Grafftey-Smith to Eden, 14 July 1943.
82 PRO, PREM 3/265/6, Smuts to Churchill, 28 May 1942, Eden to Churchill, 29 May 1942.
83 PRO, PREM 3/265/6, COS note for Churchill, 30 May 1942.
84 PRO, ADM 199/937, Syfret, war diary, 3 June–9 July 1942. The Japanese mounted further attacks on merchant shipping in the Mozambique Channel in June.
85 PRO, WO 193/884, 203 mission, Pretoria, to WO, 21 June 1942.
86 PRO, CAB 66/33, W.P.(42)242, Cabinet Secretary note, 8 June 1942.
87 PRO, ADM 199/874, CFR(42) fourteenth meeting, 1 July 1942.
88 PRO, WO 193/884, Sturges to WO, 22 June 1942; PRO, ADM 199/1278, SOE, Durban station, to Admiralty, 16 July 1942.
89 PRO, ADM 199/1278, Eden to Grafftey-Smith, 30 June 1942.
90 PRO, ADM 199/1277, FO to Halifax, 22 August 1942; PRO, WO 193/884, Platt to Air Ministry, 5 August 1942.
91 PRO, ADM 199/1293, report on 'Streamline Jane', 6 October 1942; SHAT, 2P12/D5, Parisot to General Maggiolini, Turin, 11 September 1942.
92 SHAT, 1P34/D6, Annet to Ministry of Colonies, 23 September 1942; PRO, FO 371/32151, Z8463/8463/17, Platt to WO, 6 November 1942.
93 PRO, PREM 3/265/10, Smuts to Churchill, 26 September 1942.
94 PRO, PREM 3/265/10, Eden to Churchill, 29 August 1942.
95 PRO, PREM 3/120/6, Morton's record of meeting with de Gaulle and Pleven, 30 September 1942; Roshwald, 'Spears mission', 905–7.
96 PRO, PREM 3/265/10, Eden to Churchill, 29 August 1942.
97 PRO, ADM 199/874, CFR(42) thirty-fourth meeting, 6 October 1942.
98 Kersaudy, *Churchill and de Gaulle*, pp. 150–2; Roshwald, 'Spears mission', 907.
99 SHAT, 5P49/D1, General Juin, *Journal de marche*, 14 November 1942.
100 PRO, PREM 3/265/11, Eden to Churchill, 21 September 1942.
101 PRO, PREM 3/265/11, Eden to Churchill, 22 September 1942.
102 PRO, PREM 3/265/11, Churchill to Eden, 22 September 1942.
103 SHAT, 5P49/D1, Darlan to General Barre, 10 November 1942.
104 PRO, PREM 3/265/11, G. E. Millard to J. H. Peck, 24 November 1942.
105 PRO, FO 371/36138, Z8719/8/69, Grafftey-Smith to Eden, 14 July 1943.
106 PRO, PREM 3/265/11, Legentilhomme memo., n.d., October 1942.
107 PRO, DO 119/1151, Sturges to DO, 11 December 1942.
108 PRO, CAB 66/30, WP(42)518, Eden memo., 9 November 1942; PRO, FO 371/32151, Z8769/8463/17, FO memo., 15 November 1942.
109 PRO, FO 371/36138, Z8719/8/69, Grafftey-Smith to Eden, 14 July 1943.
110 PRO, ADM 199/1277, Platt to WO, 16 November 1942.
111 PRO, ADM 199/874, STO, Diego Suarez, to Admiralty, 31 October 1942, Lord Rennell report, 27 November 1942.
112 Regarding Muselier, see PRO, CO 968/87/7, Peake to Strang, 19 January 1943.
113 MAE, CNF Londres, vol. 88, Ludovic Chancel to de Gaulle, 28 December 1942. PRO, FO 371/36138, Z8719/8/69, Grafftey-Smith to Eden, 14 July 1943; PRO, FO 371/32151, Z8760/8463/17, minutes by Speaight and Strang, 19 and 20 November 1942.

114 MAE, CNF Londres, vol. 88, Bernard Cothier memo., 7 January 1943.
115 PRO, FO 892/176, Henry Hopkinson memo., 'The affair of Jibuti', 8 January 1943.
116 PRO, FO 371/32151, Z8760/8463/17, FO minutes, 19 and 20 November 1942.
117 PRO, FO 371/32153, Z9630/8463/17, Peake to Strang, 1 December 1942.
118 PRO, FO 371/32153, Z9615/8463/17, Lord Rennell memo., 22 November 1942.
119 PRO, ADM 199/1293, RN Mauritius station to Eastern Fleet HQ, 5 December 1942.
120 Allen, *Madagascar*, pp. 36–7, 45.
121 PRO, FO 371/36138, Z8719/8/69, Grafftey-Smith to Eden, 14 July 1943.
122 PRO, T 160/1151/17400/03, Strang record of meeting at FO, 13 May 1943.
123 Allen, *Madagascar*, p. 45.
124 PRO, ADM 199/180, FO to Halifax, 2 January 1943.

CHAPTER SIX

Operation Torch and Free French imperial supremacy in Africa, 1942–45

> Weygand has been arrested, after having refused the American high command's offer to join forces with them. Pétain has accused Giraud of disloyalty and duplicity. In Algiers, Darlan has stated that at the request of General Noguès, and in compliance with the Marshal's true wishes, he was taking command. There is no way I can make my way through this labyrinth of contradictions. [Edouard Daladier, 17 November 1942[1]]

Operation Torch and the Darlan interlude

The descent of General Eisenhower's two-pronged invasion force on Morocco and Algeria on 8 November 1942 was a great military success. Only thirty-six hours of fighting preceded a general cease-fire agreement between the invading forces and the Vichyite authorities in Algiers and Rabat. The political concessions made in order to secure this cessation of hostilities severely tested the relationship between Free France and the English-speaking powers. Immediately the invasion began, US plans to delegate political authority in French North Africa to a compliant French deputy were thrown out of kilter. This was the result of three problems.

The first of the difficulties arose from the misplaced confidence vested in General Henri Giraud. In the six months prior to Torch, under the direction of Robert Murphy, Roosevelt's itinerant envoy in North Africa, US consular officials in Morocco and Algeria worked to consolidate local support for Giraud.[2] Murphy's consuls later provided the core staff for American Office of Strategic Services (OSS) covert activity in the Maghreb. But, in 1942, their preliminary task was to reduce the risk of a serious military confrontation between Eisenhower's forces and the Vichyite administration across North Africa.[3] Cultivating support for Giraud promised many rewards. The general was an illustrious hero of the First World War and, after Weygand's dismissal in November 1941, none of the serving army officers in North Africa outranked him. Having been captured in humiliating circumstances during the battle for France, on 17 April 1942, Giraud restored his reputation as a soldier's soldier by escaping from imprisonment in Germany. In co-operation with General Louis Rivet's Service de Renseignements intelligence service and SOE operatives in France, Eisenhower's staff planned to transport Giraud to North Africa as part of the Torch landings.[4]

Superficially, the objective was simple. As a more senior commander than de Gaulle but free of substantial links with Vichy, Giraud seemed the ideal figure to rally the Armée d'Afrique to the Allied cause. Murphy reported that the Giraudist party in Algiers craved American direction. This relationship could develop only if the Free French played no part in it.[5] In consequence, Murphy and his officials ostracised the Gaullist underground, led from Algiers by the local Combat director, René Capitant. A large proportion of Capitant's activists in Algiers and Oran were Jewish – over 300 in Algiers alone. They had special reason to fear any local perpetuation of Vichy's odious antisemitic statutes.[6] With Darlan still in office, there seemed a genuine threat that the North African authorities would hound Free French supporters unhindered. This was a cruel irony, given that many of these Gaullists originally turned to Free France because of the official persecution meted out by the Algiers Government-General over the preceding two years.[7] Since Capitant was already in close contact with British SOE operatives, the suspicion persisted that Murphy and his consuls were engaged in a clandestine turf war with the British for control of a viable pro-Allied French underground in North Africa.[8] After conversations in July 1942 with Giraud's pre-eminent supporters – the so-called Algiers 'Group of Five' – OSS staff in Algiers advised the US Chiefs of Staff that the Allied invasion force should concentrate its initial assault upon Casablanca, avoiding a parallel assault on AOF 'like the plague'. Provided that Giraud could be flown into Algiers and that the British played no major role in the Allied landings, the Giraudist conspirators expected all Armée de l'Air squadrons to rally. They planned to neutralise the navy's coastal batteries in advance.[9] Commanders who remained outwardly loyal to Vichy, including the Group of Five supporters, Generals Charles Mast, Goislard de Monsabert and Emile Béthouart, who was also president of the French Armistice Commission in Morocco, could bow to Eisenhower's authority, knowing that support for Giraud need not involve endorsement of de Gaulle. This might conserve the prestige of the French authorities in the eyes of a local population subjected to two years of anti-Gaullist propaganda.[10]

Giraud and his American patrons were not interested in protracted witch hunts against former collaborators. The one imperative was to bring French North Africa over as a whole so that US forces could push eastwards without hindrance to engage German and Italian forces on the Libya–Tunisia frontier. Eisenhower was bound to support measures which facilitated US troop movements before German reinforcements arrived in Tunisia.[11] Once Eisenhower secured Algiers, General Juin's principal task as commander of the Armée d'Afrique was to induce his subordinate generals in Tunisia and eastern Algeria to follow his example in rallying to the Americans.[12] General Georges Barré's Tunisia garrison responded immediately to Juin's call. But the arrival at El Aouina airfield near Tunis on 9 November of Rudolf Rahn, Joachim von Ribbentrop's appointee as German delegate to the Tunis residency, left Admiral Esteva and his naval commander, Vice-admiral Louis Derrien, with little option but to submit to Axis control of Tunisia. In Vichy, Laval acquiesced in this on the night of 8–9 November under intense pressure from the German high command.[13] Even so, on 12 November, German commanders in Tunisia recorded 'the absolute refusal' of local French forces to collaborate with them. As it became clear on 10 November that Italian as well as German aircraft were landing at El Aouina, the Tunis Armée de l'Air command also refused to co-operate. Only the French naval units at Bizerta remained 'passive'.[14]

Putting Eisenhower's strategic requirements to one side, echoes of earlier US enthusiasm for Weygand were manifest in Washington's endorsement of Giraud. Drawn to an ostensibly apolitical figure with a prestigious military record, the Americans saw in Giraud the figure they wanted de Gaulle to be – a single-minded soldier profoundly grateful for US support and anxious above all else to pursue the fight against Hitler. Unfortunately for Giraud and his cabal of supporters in Algiers, neither the general's reputation nor his arrival in North Africa swayed the senior French commands in North Africa. This brought Eisenhower face to face with a second more serious problem – the prospect of armed conflict with French forces.

While the Allies made provision for the defeat of Armée d'Afrique units across North Africa, within hours of the first landings it became clear that the key to the situation was to find a means for the defending French units to lay down their weapons with dignity. This was not an empty concession to French pride. The circumstances in which the North African garrison surrendered were critical to the survival of the Vichy regime. If no resistance were offered, the German government was bound to exact immediate revenge upon Vichy France and, quite possibly, upon the families of the senior commanders involved. Yet, regardless of the circumstances of a French surrender in North Africa, German and Italian forces were always liable to sweep into unoccupied France in order to secure control of France's Mediterranean coast. Eisenhower was left with little room to bargain for a surrender of the garrisons in Morocco and Algeria. The solution to the difficulty proved to be a poisoned chalice. It was this third aspect of the political fall-out from Operation Torch that caused the more profound colonial damage.

Where Giraud had failed, Admiral Darlan succeeded. Anxious to secure a cease-fire and move on, Eisenhower agreed to parley with Darlan. This did not contravene established US policy. While Darlan was Minister of National Defence in the six months before Pierre Laval returned to power in April 1942, US representatives in Vichy broached the possibility of his changing sides.[15] The alacrity with which Darlan consolidated his political and military control in French North Africa through his chairmanship of a newly established Imperial Defence Council justified the 'Kingpin' code-name assigned to him by the Allies. Darlan went to North Africa in October to conduct a tour of inspection and visit his hospital-ridden son. His ability to bring over the Armée d'Afrique, and the possibility that he might also secure the remainder of the French Mediterranean fleet – de Laborde's Toulon squadron above all – ensured Eisenhower's endorsement of the 'Darlan deal'. This brought immediate results. At Mers el-Kébir, for instance, there was fierce initial resistance to attempted American landings, but Darlan's cease-fire order prevented the escalation of fighting both around the port and at the beach-head established by US forces at Fedhala.[16] In Morocco, General Noguès maintained contact with Pétain and was appointed replacement to Darlan once it became clear that the admiral had jumped the Vichy ship. Noguès stayed aboard a little longer, and, on the afternoon of 9 November, pressed the Moroccan sultan to take refuge at Meknès. He also offered shelter to General von Wuehlisch of the German Armistice Commission.[17] But Noguès's sympathy for Vichy had limits. In September 1942 he narrowly escaped an assassination attempt, organised by the Moroccan branch of Jacques Doriot's fascist Parti Populaire Français (PPF) as a protest at the general's less than enthusiastic collaborationism.[18] On 10 November, Noguès, too, turned his back on Laval's government. He accepted Darlan's order to cease fire once he received assurances that the Allies had not colluded with Franco's Spain over a partition of French Moroccan territory. A more militant Pétainist, Admiral Félix Michelier, the naval commander in Morocco, followed suit some hours later. By this point, Michelier had already locked up scores of suspected Giraudist supporters.[19] Although the newly appointed Minister of Marine, Admiral Jean Abrial, later appealed to Vichy naval commands in French

Africa to remain faithful to Pétain rather than Darlan, his plea fell on deaf ears. A typical reaction came from Admiral Collinet, naval commander at Dakar, who lamented that the eagerness of the AOF authorities to seek a compromise with Eisenhower's forces was too strong to resist.[20]

Clearly, Darlan's intervention was decisive in averting protracted hostilities. But to leave Pétain's former deputy in office in Algiers was hardly a triumph for the supposed forces of democracy and freedom. Indeed, Darlan also maintained contact with Vichy. Two weeks after his agreement with Eisenhower, Darlan wrote to Admiral René Godfroy, Pétainist commander of the 'Force X' cruiser squadron trapped in Alexandria harbour. Appealing to Godfroy to rally to the Allies, Darlan stressed that he, Giraud, Noguès and Abrial's replacement as Algiers Governor, Yves Châtel, were all quietly faithful to Pétain. But they could not ignore the American pledge to restore France's pre-war frontiers.[21] As Christine Levisse-Touzé puts it, this was nothing short of a *vichyisme sous protectorat américain*.[22]

The French National Committee was furious. Not only was it excluded from Torch planning, but the Gaullist network across French North Africa was treated with ill-disguised contempt by the US authorities on the ground. As Robert Murphy usually reported to Roosevelt direct, he bore the brunt of Free French criticism. But Murphy did not play the major role in finalising the 'Darlan deal'. From September 1942, Juin kept in contact with Murphy, largely via his *chef de cabinet*, Raymond Pédron. They discussed measures to prevent German landings in Algeria, and made plans to arrest PPF activists prior to any invasion – whether German or Allied.[23] Murphy visited General Juin secretly during the night preceding Eisenhower's landings and then met Darlan, too, at the Villa des Oliviers in Algiers. But Murphy did not arrange any secret accords with either man.[24] Previously, neither Murphy nor Juin had considered the possibility of Darlan taking office in Algiers. In fact, as an arrangement that was both militarily expedient and urgently required, the Darlan agreement was negotiated primarily through Eisenhower's command and the War Department in Washington.[25]

Though Eisenhower and the Combined Chiefs of Staff could plead strategic necessity, the French National Committee imagined darker forces lying behind the previous American endorsement of Giraud. Patrick Barclay, Foreign Office liaison officer with the Carlton Gardens foreign affairs commissariat, put this into context,

> To all of them [the US government] the principles proclaimed by the old marshal were in some ways more attractive than those of the Third

> Republic of the Front Populaire with which they were wont to be contrasted. It was perhaps not surprising, therefore, to find the President suppressing 'the elimination of Vichy' from among the political objectives of the North African campaign. This state of mind also accounts for the failure of the Americans to comprehend the emphasis laid by the Fighting French on the importance of the North African Administration disavowing all links with Vichy and repealing all Vichy legislation ... There is little doubt that there are some in Washington who hoped to see Giraud's Administration in North Africa take the form of a slightly modified version of Vichy, based on more or less authoritarian lines, and that they hoped that such an Administration would be able, thanks to the possession of a large American-supplied army, to play a predominant part in the liberation of France and so save the country from a de Gaullist régime closely allied to communism.[26]

This evaluation of US policy was certainly unfair. Where de Gaulle's lieutenants and their Foreign Office sympathisers tended to see studied American malevolence, there was more a nebulous dislike of both the doctrine and the methods of Gaullism. Alexis Léger, former Secretary-general of the Quai d'Orsay and the most influential among the French expatriate community in Washington, did much to inflame State Department distrust of de Gaulle. At root, Léger shared Cordell Hull's opinion that de Gaulle subordinated military leadership and Allied strategic requirements to his personal political advancement.[27] But neither Léger nor Cordell Hull played much part in the military decision to exclude the Free French from Torch. In fact, this derived from advice from the Washington Joint Intelligence Committee, which warned in September that Gaullist involvement would increase Eisenhower's military difficulties in North Africa.[28] Nevertheless, during the weeks that Darlan remained in office in Algiers in late 1942, the contradictions in US policy towards Free France and the French Empire became increasingly stark. It was inconsistent to criticise de Gaulle's dictatorial leadership and political cunning whilst Darlan kept his post; the admiral stood at the apex of an unreformed Vichyite administrative network across Algeria and Morocco. General Pierre Lejeune, a senior liaison officer to Giraud, captured the mood among French officials upon his arrival in North Africa in mid-November:

> When we finally got to Algiers the atmosphere was strange; the army like the [settler] population was Pétainist and anti-German, the arrival of the Allies had been greeted without hostility, but without enthusiasm. This provisional outlook was expressed to me by a captain to whom I mentioned my joy at the prospect of resuming combat and who replied, 'I certainly hope there will be no question of that'.[29]

The embarrassment inherent in this situation soon diminished. On Christmas Eve 1942 Darlan was assassinated. Giraud immediately took his place. Though not quite as intended before Torch, at least an unequivocal supporter of the Allied cause was now in charge in Algiers. But this left two obvious issues unresolved. How far was Giraud likely to go in transforming the politics of his subordinate administrations in liberated French North Africa? And when would Gaullist representatives be introduced to decision-making in Algiers?

North African nationalism before and after Torch

By the time Operation Torch commenced, the Vichyite regimes across French North Africa had long since suppressed nationalist parties in all three Maghreb territories. To do so, they merely extended the emergency powers enacted immediately after the war began in 1939. In Tunisia, for example, shortly before the French collapse in June 1940, the senior leaders of the principal nationalist party, Habib Bourguiba's Néo-Destour, were transferred to prisons at Teboursouk in the Tunisian Sahara and at Fort Saint-Nicolas in Marseilles. As a result, Tunisian politics descended into what one historian has termed a 'deceptive lethargy'.[30] With the Maghreb nationalist movements already decapitated, Vichy's approach to the Muslim population of North Africa rested upon a delicate balance between defence of settler interest, avoidance of extreme economic hardship and refusal to discuss significant political reform.[31] Between December 1940 and August 1942, in Algeria, the two moderate *élu* leaders, Ferhat Abbas and Dr Bendjelloul, repeatedly warned Governor Abrial and the Vichy government that Muslim rights could not be ignored indefinitely. They condemned the inequity of the dual college electoral system, the unfair restrictions upon civil rights and religious freedom, and the distortion of the economy in favour of *colon* interests – all themes which will be familiar to students of both pre- and post-war Algeria. What differentiated the Vichy period was that in Algeria – as in Morocco and Tunisia – only the most moderate representatives of the urban Arab elite were left at liberty to voice such concerns.

Messali Hadj's Parti Populaire Algérien (PPA) was dissolved on 26 September 1939, Messali having by this point spent several years in detention. Eager to exploit the propaganda potential of the French crackdown, Radio Berlin used its influential Arabic broadcast to relay news of the arrest of twenty-eight senior PPA figures on 4 October 1939. From December 1940 the German government co-ordinated its radio propaganda to French North Africa through a Paris propaganda bureau with individual sub-sections for the three Maghreb states, each staffed by prominent North African nationalists such as the PPA activist, Radjef Belqâcem. The Vichy authorities acquiesced in this even though their North African proconsuls were quick to stress the threat posed by capably directed radio propaganda. Like Radio Berlin, the Paris bureau seized upon details of Vichy's further clamp-downs upon North African nationalism.[32] In March 1941, a military tribunal in Algiers condemned twenty-seven senior PPA figures for sedition. The prison terms handed down ranged from three to sixteen years. Messali Hadj was sentenced afresh to sixteen years' hard labour.[33] In Morocco, the senior leadership of the pre-war Comité d'Action Marocaine (National Action Bloc) remained interned. In Tunisia, much the same fate befell Néo-Destour. Dr Habib Thameur, who became clandestine leader of the movement following Bourguiba's earlier detention, was himself arrested and sentenced to twenty years' hard labour in January 1941, a sentence which he did not actually serve.[34]

In the two North African protectorates, Vichy's extension of the *état de siège* martial law provisions enacted in 1939 allowed Resident Ministers Noguès and Esteva to employ military law to curb nationalist activity. With radical nationalists either jailed or driven underground, under Vichy rule, the Moroccan sultanate and Tunisia's beylical government assumed new importance as a focus of nationalist aspirations. In Tunisia, a strong-minded leader, Sidi Mohammed el Moncef Bey, acceded to the throne on 19 June 1942. The son of Naceur Bey, whose eighteen-point reform plan of 1922 provided a key foundation for the original Destour movement, Moncef Bey deliberately emulated his father's approach. On 2 August 1942 he issued a sixteen-point scheme for the 'Tunisification' of the country through constitutional reforms, free elections and increased public spending. The Bey insisted that Esteva should respect the tradition of indirect rule which was supposed to inform the government of the Tunisia protectorate.[35] Over subsequent months, the new Bey – popularly dubbed the *bey déstourien* – clashed frequently with Esteva. In one of his more erratic reports, Esteva suggested that Moncef Bey was in the grip of sectarian nationalism dominated by an unlikely coalition of Destour supporters, Freemasons, Jews and communists.[36] Esteva refused to consider the Bey's proposals for the creation of a Tunisian Consultative Council, Arab admission to senior administrative posts, equal pay for French and Arab functionaries and the introduction of Arabic in schools and administration. In a much-publicised incident, on 12 October, Moncef Bey snubbed Esteva at a public ceremony at Bardo. Protests in support of the Bey increased during Ramadan and Arab resentment at the frustration of reform was threatening to boil over by the time Axis forces arrived in November.[37] In the month prior to the

Torch landings, Esteva frequently discussed the worsening public order situation with his military and Sûreté chiefs, fearful that urban disorders might break out at any time.[38]

In contrast to Esteva's deteriorating position, in Morocco, Resident-general Noguès achieved greater success in managing the more conservative nationalism of Sultan Sidi Mohammed ben Youssef. This prevented the crystallisation of a more militant anti-French nationalism around the institutions of the sultanate.[39] It was thus a tremendous reverse for Noguès when the Sultan met Roosevelt at the ANFA conference in Casablanca on 23 January 1943 without having first cleared matters with the French residency in Rabat. Assured of US sympathy for Moroccan independence, Mohammed ben Youssef lent increasing support to nationalists such as Ahmed Balafrej and Mohammed el Yazidi who had stepped in to fill the vacuum left by the exiled nationalist leadership. This reached a violent climax in widespread demonstrations in January 1944.[40]

Since so many of these authoritarian measures originated in 1939–40 – the final year of the Third Republic – it was incumbent upon de Gaulle as the supposed inheritor of republican legitimacy to reverse them. But what of General Giraud? Was he similarly obligated? Giraud was not well suited to the role of colonial proconsul. Nor were his politics consistent with the image of enlightened imperial rule that both the Americans and the Free French hoped to foster. Before the ANFA conference convened in Casablanca in mid-January 1943, Giraud showed little wish to purge French North Africa of its remaining Vichyite officials. He was equally uninterested in dismantling the worst aspects of the Vichy legal system. But once Gaullist Governors were installed across North Africa, they, too, avoided major administrative purges. In Algeria, for instance, Catroux removed only three notoriously Vichyite prefects from Algiers, Constantine and Oran when he took over as Governor in June 1943.[41]

Immediately after his meeting with de Gaulle in front of the press cameras at the Casablanca conference, on 29 January Giraud proposed unity talks with the French National Committee. He made a show of an inconsequential meeting with René Capitant, and then appointed another Gaullist, Louis Joxe, to direct propaganda into occupied Tunisia.[42] Stirred by rising criticism, Giraud also took three immediate steps to reverse Vichy legislation. The 1872 Crémieux decree which afforded rights of citizenship to the Jewish population of the Maghreb was restored. Secondly, Giraud confirmed plans to release political detainees, including Gaullists, PCF activists and Spanish Republican exiles, from internment camps across North Africa. Finally, on 6 February Giraud established a War Committee (*comité de guerre*) to replace Darlan's Imperial Council of North and West African Colonial Governors. Only a titular change, this move none the less represented a definite break with the Vichy past. Though these were welcome measures, Giraud did not indicate that any further steps – including colonial reforms – were likely to follow.[43] Instead, he concentrated upon extending the call-up of North African reservists announced in November 1942, particularly in those regions traditionally most hostile to French rule, such as the Rif interior in Morocco and the Grand Kabylie in Algeria.[44]

It was against this background that Ferhat Abbas issued his landmark Manifesto of the Algerian People on 10 February 1943. The manifesto recounted the long history of French maltreatment and the broken promises made to Algerians since 1830. Drawing upon Catroux's promise to renegotiate the Syrian and Lebanese independence treaties, the manifesto ended with a plea for self-government based upon an Algerian constitutional settlement. This was to be constructed around six principles, including racial equality before the law, the end of discriminatory land tenure, recognition of Arabic as an official language and freedom of political and religious association.[45] In essence, the manifesto proposed a Franco-Algerian federation based on the twin pillars of Algerian autonomy and full equality for settlers and Muslims within the country. Having been rebuffed in an earlier attempt to contact Darlan and Giraud in December 1942, Abbas and Bendjelloul submitted the manifesto direct to the interim Algiers Governor-general, Marcel Peyrouton, who had replaced Yves Châtel soon after the Allied landings.[46] But an essential problem remained. Abbas effectively suggested a bargain between a greater Arab contribution to Algeria's war effort and broader emancipation of the Muslim population. This was an affront to French sovereignty in Algeria. It implied that the Algiers authorities could not mobilise the general population without nationalist assent. Furthermore, any linkage between reform and the effectiveness of the North African war effort was bound to interest the English-speaking powers, curbing French room for manoeuvre in the process.[47]

In spite of this, Peyrouton accepted the manifesto as 'a basis for reforms to come'. A Commission on Muslim Economic and Social Affairs was duly set up within Peyrouton's administration to study the manifesto proposals. But a further reform scheme, the *Additif au Manifeste* (Supplement to the Manifesto), received short shrift owing to its endorsement of national independence. The *Additif* was signed by twenty-one of the twenty-four Muslim members of the Délégations Financières – an elected committee with limited powers to scrutinise Algeria's annual budget. The fact that the elaboration of Abbas's original manifesto proposals was underwritten by a normally compliant group of Algeria's Muslim elite confirmed that demands for reform were hardening into pressure for outright national independence.[48] Still, neither the Giraudist administration in Algiers, nor the French Committee of National Liberation (FCNL) which succeeded it on 3 June 1943, showed much inclination to begin serious dialogue with Abbas or his colleagues while the war continued.[49]

Once Tunisia was liberated in May 1943, French Indo-China became the only substantial French overseas territory still technically loyal to Vichy. Liberation was a misnomer, since Giraud's administration was profoundly hostile towards Moncef Bey's earlier political reform plans for Tunisia. In theory, the Bey's brave refusal to collaborate with the Axis occupiers during early 1943 gave added gravitas to his proposals. Moncef Bey's actions tallied perfectly with Bourguiba's own earlier instructions to Néo-Destour supporters. Though still detained by the Vichy authorities, on 8 August 1942, Bourguiba instructed the party secretary-general, Dr Habib Thameur, to develop contacts with the Gaullist network in Tunisia. Bourguiba expressed his confidence in an eventual Allied victory and suggested that 'unconditional support' for the Allied cause would bolster Tunisian claims for independence at the war's end.[50] Unlike Morocco, where German radio propaganda had made some impact upon nationalist opinion with promises of Arab independence, Italy's claims to Tunisia always impeded a similar propaganda drive directed at Néo-Destour supporters.[51] Moncef Bey shared Bourguiba's outlook. Refusing to denounce the Allies, on 1 January 1943 he appointed a new National Union government under Mohammed Chenik. This was a mixed administration dominated by moderate supporters of the original Destour movement. Hence the paradoxical situation that, throughout the months of Esteva's collaboration with the Germano-Italian occupation, the Tunisian beylical government remained hostile to the Axis. Even the German bombardments of the towns of Kairouan and Marsa on 22 February and 14 March, ordered in response to the Bey's refusal to co-operate, did not sway the Tunisian executive.[52]

This made Giraud's subsequent reaction all the more crass. Accusing Moncef Bey of collaboration, on 14 May Giraud ordered his dismissal and exile. Giraud wished to be rid of a populist ruler whom he considered dangerously nationalistic. In July he forced the Bey to renounce the throne in favour of Sidi Lamine. Even the intensely conservative Juin recognised the folly of this action, although he helped enforce it in practice.[53] In another ill-advised measure, Juin maintained that Bourguiba was complicit in Axis activities and propaganda, a lie which reflected badly upon Fighting France across North Africa. For most educated Tunisians the Allied victory and the installation of General Charles Mast as new Resident-general proved a disappointment. Admittedly, Gestapo agencies were no longer in Tunis and Mast promptly abolished the arbitrary powers and 'special tribunals' of the pro-German *Phalange Africaine*. But the new French administration did not offer substantial political reforms to the Arab population. Instead, Mast attached utmost priority to a programme of rural development and agricultural investment intended to rally Tunisia's peasantry and so confine support for Tunisian nationalism to the country's major towns and cities.[54]

Unable to influence events in Axis-occupied Tunisia, after Darlan's murder, the Free French reserved their most violent criticism for General Noguès. In spite of his role in leading resistance to the initial American landings, Noguès kept the Moroccan residency, trading upon his experience as an efficient protectorate administrator with elaborate contacts with the sultanate.[55] Long after the Torch landings, Noguès remained an unreconstructed Pétainist. He justified his distaste for Gaullism by arguing that the Vichy loyalists deserved Allied credit for preserving France's Empire intact, having curtailed Germano-Italian access to North and West Africa and the Levant mandates. Noguès predicted that the American descent on North Africa would undermine French prestige whether or not the colonial authorities were co-operative.[56] The revelation of US military strength, the expansion of foodstuff supplies and the greater availability of US dollars were sure to leave Moroccans impressed by the relative weakness of France. This was Vichy orthodoxy. According to Noguès, limited collaboration remained defensible as a pragmatic response to French defeat. His policies had stymied German incursion into French Africa and undermined Axis encouragement of native rebellion. Forced to justify his actions at Eisenhower's Algiers headquarters, Noguès went still further:

> The Marshal had been consistently anti-German, as had M. Boisson and the Resident-General [Noguès] himself. All three had done everything they could to hamper the Germans, and he himself had always threatened to resign if they appeared in North Africa. There was no pro-German feeling among the French officers … Nor had German propaganda had the slightest effect on the natives. He had them well in hand and had given orders that any of them who tried to approach the German Armistice Commission or recognise any authority other than his own should be imprisoned.[57]

Noguès's status was one of the many issues that divided the Free French in London and the Giraudist administration in Algiers during the first half of 1943. Indeed, the course of the negotiations between the two Fighting French factions turned upon Giraud's willingness to make a decisive break with those officials upon whom he relied while he concentrated upon the military regeneration of the Armée d'Afrique.

The Giraud–de Gaulle unity talks

Alarmed at the speed with which Giraud imposed his authority after Darlan's murder, on 27 December 1942 de Gaulle visited Chequers to discuss the political situation in French North Africa with Churchill.[58] Throughout the subsequent half-year of stuttering negotiations between Gaullist and Giraudist representatives in Algiers and London, de Gaulle insisted upon the creation of a fully unified Algiers administration. Ultimately, this precluded the joint presidency of a single Fighting French movement. It also undermined American attempts to confine the unity talks to a military agreement between Giraud and de Gaulle. Cordell Hull was particularly anxious lest de Gaulle exploited a political settlement with Giraud as justification for the immediate creation of a provisional government in Algiers with full authority over the French empire – something which the British government was quite prepared to tolerate.[59] On 2 January 1943 de Gaulle lambasted the Allied powers for perpetuating the political uncertainty within French North Africa. Giraud merely compounded the problem: 'The reason for this confusion is that French authority has no basic point, following the collapse of Vichy, since the great force of national fervour, coherence and experience which constitutes Fighting France and which has already returned to the war and to the republic a large part of the empire is not officially represented in these territories.'[60]

French National Committee pressure for admission to North Africa intensified while the Allies made final preparations for the ANFA conference at Casablanca in the first fortnight of 1943. With long experience in dealing with Admiral Godfroy in Alexandria, the British Mediterranean Fleet commander, Admiral Andrew Cunningham, was sensitive to Giraud's dilemma regarding the pace of unity talks with de Gaulle. Writing from Algiers on 4 January 1943, he noted, 'De Gaulle is rushing things too much. First approaches must be made on a lower level. If Giraud received him now it would be said that having got rid of Darlan he hastened to make terms with his rival. The people here won't stand de Gaulle. Apparently all French officers are dead against him although Noguès told me he could handle him.'[61] Unconvincing as it was, the public reconciliation between Giraud and de Gaulle in the 'shotgun wedding' engineered by Roosevelt at Casablanca none the less indicated that the Allies would permit the French National Committee an expanding role in Algiers.[62]

But, over the subsequent month, Giraud refused to begin comprehensive negotiations with a Gaullist delegation. Instead, he continued to administer French North and West Africa in co-operation with Noguès, Peyrouton and Boisson. Catroux acted as de Gaulle's first key negotiator in Algiers. Ever charitable, he put the retention in office of so many former Vichyites down to Giraud's political naivety. In fact, the struggle for influence between Giraudists and Gaullists reflected profoundly different styles of governance. Throughout the unity talks, most of Giraud's senior backers were military figures who shared his disdain for democratic forms and liberal ideas. By contrast, the Gaullists showed greater political acumen and a deeper attachment to republican ideals. During March 1943 several factors combined to break the political log-jam in Algiers. After victory at Medenine in early March, the Allied advance through Tunisia rapidly gathered momentum. There were some 60,000 French troops deployed in Tunisia, but, as yet, there was little sign of an end to the bitterness and rivalry between Armée d'Afrique units and the Gaullist columns that arrived after an epic trans-Saharan crossing. Giraud was none the less desperate to expand the contribution of French forces to inter-Allied operations. It would be easier if talks with de Gaulle were going well. Unfortunately for Giraud, his rival seemed to command growing loyalty among Fighting French forces. This was confirmed by a sudden increase in voluntary recruitment to Free French units under de Gaulle's direct authority. Most spectacular was the conversion of some 350 crewmen aboard the former pride of Darlan's Vichy navy, the battleship *Richelieu*. But the conversion of former Vichyite sailors was offset by the continuing distrust between Juin's senior Armée d'Afrique commanders and de Gaulle's generals. This reached a climax during the Allied victory parade in Tunis on 20 May 1943. Leclerc openly snubbed Giraud and Juin by marching his mainly Coloniale troops alongside the British Eighth Army rather than with Armée d'Afrique troops.[63] While these abiding military tensions were important, Jean Monnet's appointment as head of the Giraudist negotiating team marked a more significant political advance. Monnet was well respected in Washington and London. He was neither a Vichyite nor a soldier and he shared a pragmatic view of the need for a Fighting French political settlement which endeared him to the British. As proof of his intentions, on his arrival from Washington in February, Monnet warned Giraud that the US government would not re-supply a French army tainted by reactionary and racist ideas.[64] Similarly, the clearer emergence of Catroux and René Massigli as principal Gaullist negotiators suggested that the posturing of the previous two months would give way to more reasoned discussion.[65]

Monnet's influence was quickly felt. He was largely responsible for Giraud's landmark 'New Deal' speech on 14 March by which the general at last promised to dismantle all vestiges of Vichy rule across French North Africa.[66] This commitment enabled Catroux to pursue a final settlement safe in the knowledge that Giraud was likely to defer to Monnet's political advice. In mid-April, de Gaulle and Giraud underscored their continued differences by endorsing opposing Governors in the newly rallied territory of French Guiana.[67] But, in Algiers, Catroux and Monnet drove the unity talks forward. Catroux insisted that de Gaulle and Giraud should accept some form of joint presidency of a unified Fighting French administration. This would balance the greater political expertise of French National Committee personnel against the military experience of Giraud and his senior army advisers.[68] In effect, the French National Committee and the executive of Darlan's former Imperial Council in Algiers were to merge. Giraud was to head a Fighting French military staff which would report to the new organisation. This arrangement was finally confirmed in a last round of intense discussions held at the Lycée Fromentin in Algiers between 31 May and 3 June. Although this culminated in the creation of a united French Committee of National Liberation, the rivalry between Giraud and de Gaulle continued much as before.[69]

Still influential in Washington, Alexis Léger insisted that neither the French National Committee nor the FCNL was a legally constituted authority. According to him, although the Free French movement claimed to be the guardian of the true French republican tradition, it ignored the so-called Trevaneuc Law of 1872 by which provison was made for the creation of an emergency government if the Third Republic faced a national catastrophe. De Gaulle was using specious arguments to justify his own autocratic rule. Léger's criticisms commanded greater interest in June 1943 because de Gaulle's first action as co-president of the FCNL was to oust Peyrouton and Noguès from their posts in Algiers and Rabat. Within weeks, the membership of the FCNL increased from seven to fourteen voting members. This gave de Gaulle a working majority. As Cordell Hull lamented, de Gaulle had 'pulled a fast one over Giraud' without any authority to do so.[70] In fact, in so far as the FCNL was more than a self-appointed body, its popular mandate derived primarily from the Conseil National de la Résistance, the executive of the principal metropolitan Resistance groups unified under Jean Moulin's direction in May 1943. Endorsement from the French Resistance certainly added to the popular legitimacy of the Fighting French movement. But it necessarily involved a *de facto* association with the communist Resistance in France. This was anathema to the Americans, who remained broadly hostile to de Gaulle.[71] In consequence, the US government still preferred to work with individual French colonial administrations on a case-by-case basis. This minimised the opportunity for Gaullist interference and avoided the risk of strengthening either the French authorities in Algiers or de Gaulle personally.[72]

This helps explain why negotiations over the future administration of AOF dragged on into 1943 in much the same fashion as the unity talks in Algiers. Darlan's co-operation with Eisenhower prompted a sharp rise in American influence upon Allied contacts with AOF once Boisson followed Darlan's lead in late November 1942. In January 1943 Eisenhower and Robert Murphy agreed that it made strategic sense to include Dakar within the jurisdiction of US civil affairs officers based in North Africa.[73] Not surprisingly, Boisson identified with Darlan, and then Giraud, both of whom relied upon American material support. Liaising with US representatives offered the perfect means to justify continued aversion to all things Free French while undertaking only superficial changes in what remained an essentially Pétainist administration across AOF.[74] The incumbent colonial Governors and the senior Vichyite garrison commanders across French West Africa retained their posts throughout the early months of 1943. Even General Falvy remained in place as army commander at Dakar, although he lived up to his nickname 'von Falvy', born of his earlier readiness to permit German access to the port's facilities.[75] But Boisson's efforts to keep his governorship by working with Darlan and Eisenhower were short-circuited by Lord Swinton's West African Supply Centre bureaucracy in Accra.

Whereas the Americans were the first to arrive in French North Africa, the British maintained an efficient economic infrastructure across West Africa. The success of Swinton's work in increasing West Africa's supply contribution to the Allied war effort ensured that the British remained top dogs in dealings with Boisson throughout the first half of 1943. If economic arrangements were made with AOF which cut across Swinton's previous work in British West Africa regarding shipping, produce quotas, price agreements and payments procedures, the raw material output of West Africa as a whole might be gravely affected. The logic of this was irresistible. Swinton was well established in West Africa and clearly intended to protect his jurisdiction as Minister Resident. As such, he was the only acceptable choice to lead negotiations with Boisson. Moreover, the negotiations, pursued intermittently between January and July 1943, were primarily economic rather than political. Swinton's first priority was to integrate

AOF into the economy of Allied supply requirements, not to make Boisson or his supporters enthusiasts for Free France.[76] In fact, the largely Vichyite staffs of individual AOF administrations escaped significant purge. Portraits of Marshal Pétain kept pride of place in government buildings, and in the Catholic Mission at Abidjan, capital of the Côte d'Ivoire, an heroic portrait of the defence of Dakar in 1940 hung defiantly during de Gaulle's visit to the town in January 1944.[77]

From July 1943, the profound animosity between Boisson's replacement as Governor-general, Pierre Cournarie, and the regional naval commander, Admiral Collinet, illustrated the continuing tension between Gaullists and unreformed Pétainists. This was exacerbated by Anglo-American jurisdictional squabbling. Swinton endorsed Cournarie, while the US military mission in Dakar, headed by Admiral William Glassford until April 1944, tended to prefer Collinet and his Vichyite subordinates.[78] In late January 1944, the British consul in Dakar, E. W. Meiklereid, reminded the Foreign Office that Cournarie faced an uphill struggle against the old guard. 'In both French Naval and Military circles, the stronghold of right-wing opinions, there is a very strong tendency to look upon all de Gaullists as upstarts from which category even the Governor-general and Madame Cournarie are not excluded. This is very evident at all Madame Cournarie's "at homes" where apart from two senior generals and their wives, senior service uniforms are noticeable by their absence.' Meiklereid was more blunt in his assessment of other influential sections of the French community across French West Africa, describing much of the clergy as ardent Pétainists, and the business classes of Côte d'Ivoire, Senegal and Dahomey in particular as 'inclined to hanker after the "good" days of the Vichy regime when the Germans were prepared to pay any price for their produce'.[79] Belatedly, Cournarie received stronger backing from the FCNL in Algiers. Though three Governors originally appointed by Vichy still remained in place, with the dismissal of Horace Crocicchia as Governor of French Guinea in early February 1944, the FCNL at last signalled its unwillingness to tolerate closet Pétainism in West Africa.[80]

The negotiations over the administration of a united Fighting French empire did not set relations between the Gaullists and the English-speaking powers on an entirely new footing. In October 1943 Churchill told Duff Cooper, newly appointed as Britain's ambassador-in-waiting to the FCNL in Algiers, that he still had strong reservations over de Gaulle's political style. US readiness to endorse the FCNL would depend on the committee's ability to set clear limits on de Gaulle's power.[81] As a result, Churchill was alarmed at the speed with which Giraud's residual power in Algiers was crumbling away. In early

September the FCNL undercut Giraud's authority in North and West Africa by denying him the power to supervise 'state of siege' regulations across individual colonies. Within weeks of this, the FCNL formally acknowledged de Gaulle as its political leader whilst confining Giraud's remaining military authority to those areas where Fighting French forces were actively engaged in operations. On 6 November Giraud resigned as co-president of the FCNL. In the subsequent reorganisation of the Algiers Committee, five remaining Giraudists lost their posts.[82]

Giraud's precipitous downfall did not ultimately tarnish the FCNL because it was generally assumed that the general fell victim to his own political inexperience. Duff Cooper simultaneously displayed great affection and considerable disdain for Giraud. In both respects, his attitude was typical of those French, British and American officials who came into contact with the general. As Duff Cooper noted, 'He is the *beau sabreur* whose unwrinkled brow has never been troubled by the painful process of thought.' Less flippant, Catroux none the less concluded that Giraud's overbearing patriotism and military fervour prevented him from grasping 'that war consisted of anything but front-line fighters'.[83] From Washington, Field-Marshal Dill, principal British representative on the Allied Joint Staff Mission, stressed that Eisenhower, too, had tired of Giraud, having 'completely failed to get any sense into his head' about the requirements of modern warfare and inter-Allied co-operation.[84] As it became clearer to Giraud that the British could not meet his requests for war material, so his badgering of the US service chiefs increased. This pressure was counterproductive and Eisenhower increasingly left it to his Chief of Staff, General Walter Bedell Smith, to manage Giraud as best he could.[85]

Though Giraud was sometimes overbearing, as a result of Juin's patient reorganisation of the French forces in North Africa, once US war material began to arrive in quantity it was quickly distributed among Juin's commands. By the start of the Italian campaign the French army was ready to play its first significant role in Allied operations since the limited, if sensational, victory of General Koenig's Free French brigade at Bir Hakeim in Libya a year earlier in June 1942.[86] By September 1943, 455,000 tonnes of US equipment – sufficient for four infantry and two armoured divisions – had been delivered to North Africa. The Armée d'Afrique, with over 150,000 troops, still provided the core of this new Fighting French army, though an additional 80,000 Coloniale troops were poised in AOF, and Generals Koenig and Leclerc still maintained an efficient Free French force of some 15,000 seasoned soldiers. Ironically, the pre-war conception of the French Maghreb's role within French imperial defence strategy was now realised. Belatedly, North Africa became the base for the revitalisation of the French military, preparatory to a liberation of metropolitan France. Inevitably, the major Allied armies still took the leading role. But, as Anthony Clayton has stressed, the creation of a French Expeditionary Force for service in the Italian campaign, and the later establishment of de Lattre de Tassigny's First French Army, which included Armée d'Afrique and Gaullist units, proved critical in dissipating intra-service tensions between erstwhile Vichyites, Giraudists and Free Frenchmen.[87] Although some personal rivalries persisted, the amalgamated French colonial forces in Italy and southern France in 1943–44 represented a tentative reconciliation between once divided compatriots. This was a key reason for the political importance attached to a high-profile presence for these units within France once the liberation got under way in 1944. In practice, it also meant that the loyal performance of African troops in Italy and France was sometimes downplayed in the interests of stressing French valour.

Once Allied forces began the push through southern Italy in the late summer of 1943, the strategic importance of the French North African territories began to decline. With the Italian surrender imminent, Franco's Spain anxious to mend fences with the United States, and German forces unlikely to return to North Africa, the Allied military administration in Algiers could be run down. These events provided the backdrop to Gaullist efforts to secure full Allied recognition of the FCNL as a provisional government-in-waiting. Much to de Gaulle's chagrin, Anglo-American plans for the second front in Europe were formulated with little reference to Algiers. In anticipation of France's liberation, on 2 June 1944 the FCNL re-launched itself as the Provisional Government of the French Republic (GPRF). But, on the eve of D-Day, the inter-Allied Joint Staff Mission in Washington remained closed to Fighting French influence. It was little wonder that de Gaulle's followers still displayed what Macmillan termed 'the French sovereignty complex'.[88] An obvious manifestation of this continued Gaullist insecurity was the heavy-handedness of French rule in North Africa during 1944 and 1945.

Gaullist rule in French North Africa

While Gaullists turned increasingly to the liberation of France, the transfer of Allied operations to Italy also enabled the FCNL to reassert French civil and military authority across the North African territories. Although covert and official Anglo-American contacts with the metropolitan Resistance were extended and improved over the winter of 1943–44, in Algiers FCNL mistrust of the English-speaking powers was undimmed.[89] The Lebanese crisis in November 1943 further convinced the FCNL that a show of strength was the essential prerequisite of reform in North Africa. After his appointment as Governor of Algeria as replacement for Peyrouton in June 1943, Catroux refined Maurice Viollette's earlier scheme for an extension of Muslim voting rights. The franchise for the Muslim electoral college was opened to the adult population aged twenty-one and over, and the right to vote for the more influential non-Muslim electoral college was extended to include Algerian ex-servicemen and Muslims with certificates of French secondary education. Though it was de Gaulle who announced these proposals in a speech delivered at Constantine in eastern Algeria on 12 December, the implementation of the plan fell to Catroux, who was by then acting as Commissioner of State for Muslim Affairs within the FCNL.[90] The Constantine proposals formed the basis of an ordinance completed in March 1944. Its underlying intention was to ensure no repetition of the Lebanese crisis within French North Africa, rather than to open the door to fundamental constitutional reform in Algeria. Catroux seemed a more sympathetic judge of Muslim concerns than the former Vichyite Peyrouton, who, as Resident Minister in Tunis in 1933, had initiated the official repression of Néo-Destour. Yet it was Catroux who in September 1943 first placed Ferhat Abbas and his fellow nationalist, Saïah Abdelkader, under house arrest and then intimidated other signatories of the manifesto into a humiliating public recantation of their proposals. Catroux then ordered the temporary disbandment of the Muslim Délégations Financières after the bulk of the Muslim delegates made plain their continued support for the *Additif au Manifeste*.[91]

This was a tremendous blunder. On 7 March 1944 the FCNL issued an ordinance for Algeria formulated by Catroux and his Secretary-general, Maurice Gonon. This limited scheme of reform stood no chance of success because by that point the Fighting French authorities had alienated the very people at whom the ordinance was directed – the moderate nationalists grouped around Ferhat Abbas. In addition, the ordinance was much criticised within the FCNL, not least by René Pleven, who, as Commissioner of Colonies, remained the most influential colonial specialist within the Algiers leadership.[92] The ordinance for Algeria was supposed to end legal discrimination against those Algerian Muslims who had acquired, or were judged eligible for, French citizenship. It increased the number of Muslims eligible to vote for the French-controlled Algiers electoral college by some 70,000. But, while the educational and religious restrictions upon French Muslim citizenship status were relaxed, the great majority of Algeria's Arab population did not stand to benefit from the measure.[93]

Ferhat Abbas condemned the proposal as a timid gesture unlikely to produce any meaningful Franco-Algerian assimilation. It was rejected out of hand by Messali Hadj, who was by now demanding complete Algerian independence. In danger of being outflanked, Ferhat Abbas immediately launched the Amis du Manifeste et de la Liberté (Supporters of the Manifesto and of Freedom, AML), a broad-based nationalist front which Catroux's administration treated with ill-disguised contempt. Much as in 1943, the failure to conciliate Ferhat Abbas caused a haemorrhage in Muslim support towards the more uncompromising nationalism of Messali Hadj's PPA.[94]

Less well publicised than the March 1944 ordinance, Catroux and Gonon also launched a plan for French economic investment in Algeria under the aegis of a special commission established in the Governor-general's office on 14 December 1943. With Muslim representatives, including Dr Bendjelloul and Dr Tamzali, head of the Muslim *délégués* from Grande Kabylie, the commission held twenty-seven sessions between 21 December 1943 and 8 July 1944. These were detailed meetings which produced precise plans for extended educational provision, public health improvements and support for industrial diversification. Final proposals were sent to the provisional government on 9 August 1944. As a result of its greater readiness to consult Muslim representatives on matters of social and industrial reform, Catroux's administration produced a socio-economic scheme which was both more ambitious and better thought-out than the political reforms embodied in the March 1944 ordinance. The real obstacle in this instance was not the failure of French political will but the provisional government's refusal to sanction the necessary expenditure for a plan scheduled for implementation over twenty years at a total cost of 21 billion francs.[95]

Though Catroux tried to rally support for the investment scheme during the brief experiment with a Ministry of North Africa during the winter of 1944–45, he only secured piecemeal grants to cover a handful of the measures originally put forward. In discussions preparatory to the 1945 budget, the Minister of the Interior, Adrien Tixier, and officials from the Ministry of Finance together stifled what remained of the original economic development plan. The failure of limited political reform and the provisional government's refusal to finance Catroux's scheme of economic modernisation in Algeria marked a decisive step towards the disorders that erupted in and around Sétif in eastern Constantine in May 1945.[96] But it was not Algeria that first erupted into violent protest against the timidity of Gaullist reform. This distinction went to Morocco.

When General Noguès was finally asked to retire from the Rabat residency in June 1943, the protectorate was not in good order. Never able to overcome Gaullist distrust, Noguès also resented the impact of American influence and largesse upon Morocco's politics, economy and people in the six months after the Casablanca conference.[97] Roosevelt's administration seemed little concerned if the presence of US forces in North Africa weakened the French hold upon the region. But Noguès's successor, Gabriel Puaux, the former High Commissioner in Syria, lacked the force of presence necessary to re-establish French prestige. More tactful diplomat than autocratic Resident, Puaux neither curbed the thriving Moroccan black market, nor tackled the emergence of what soon became Morocco's principal nationalist party, the Istiqlal. This was a movement which drew its inspiration from the Comité d'Action Marocaine that Noguès had banned six years earlier. Matters came to a head in January 1944. On 11 January the self-proclaimed Istiqlal leadership issued a manifesto calling for an independent Moroccan sultanate, Moroccan adherence to the principles of the Atlantic Charter and a seat for Morocco at an eventual Allied peace conference. The manifesto was signed by over fifty nationalist figures, many of them members of the original nationalist movement banned under the Popular Front. Having presented their manifesto to the US and British consulates in Rabat, the Istiqlal insisted that it wished to support the war effort by bringing Morocco full-square behind the Allies.[98]

The Allied consuls in Morocco were forewarned of the Istiqlal's intentions in December 1943. On 4 January Puaux further advised Britain's Rabat consul, Stonehewer-Bird, that the Istiqlal hoped to goad the French into the use of force in order to win US sympathy.[99] Over the subsequent fortnight, Puaux obtained assurances from US and British consular representatives that they would not encourage Istiqlal protest. A week after the party's manifesto was issued, the Sultan also agreed to instruct his subordinate *caids* to offer no support to Istiqlal demands. But Puaux undermined the success of his own backstairs diplomacy by again lashing out at the Allies and the Sultan for allegedly working to destroy his authority.[100]

For several months prior to the launch of the Istiqlal, Puaux turned down requests from French counter-intelligence officers for the detention of Axis agents, fascist sympathisers and their alleged contacts within the Moroccan nationalist movement. Once René Massigli arrived from Algiers to assess the breakdown in French civil control, Puaux abruptly reversed his decision. In late January 1944, the arrest and punishment of thirteen North Africans – of whom five were Moroccan – on spurious charges of espionage triggered mass demonstrations across Morocco.[101] On 31 January a French military tribunal handed down sentences on these detainees which varied from the death penalty in seven cases to terms of between one and twenty years' hard labour. Meanwhile, between 29 January and 2 February, sporadic and violent rioting broke out in several Moroccan cities. French troops were deployed in Rabat, Salé and Fez, but the disorders actually began in Rabat. Demonstrators, many of whom were students at Rabat's main Muslim college, gathered outside the Sultan's palace to protest at the detention of the local nationalist leader, Ahmed Balafrej. The Sultan's chief of protocol, Si Mammeri, failed to pacify the crowd and was set upon, beaten and castrated. After three French policemen were also killed, a mobile detachment from General Leclerc's second armoured division was called out, and French military police fired upon the demonstrators. In Salé and Fez this pattern was repeated: demonstration escalating to riot thereupon to be met by military intervention, civilian deaths and the imposition of curfew restrictions. Though estimates varied considerably, total deaths in the three cities were reckoned at 150 by the Allied headquarters in Algiers.[102]

It was widely assumed that Puaux would be replaced, but the first dismissals in consequence of the Moroccan disorders occurred within the native administration of the sultanate. A number of senior figures lost their positions, including the Pasha of Rabat, Si Abderrahman Bargach, and his son, Si Ahmed Bargach.[103] Although order was restored by mid-February, the Moroccan riots, coming so soon after the Lebanese crisis and the release from detention of several leading Algerian political leaders, including Ferhat Abbas and Saïah Abdelkader, destabilised French political control in the Maghreb. Following Balafrej's detention on the eve of the riots in January 1944 (on the grounds that he had allegedly spent 1941 in Germany), Mohammed el-Yazidi became de facto leader of the Istiqlal. The party only had some 4,000 members in 1944. But once the Sultan decided to support its nationalist programme more openly, the French authorities faced mounting pressure for reform throughout the last eighteen months of the war. Even in Tunisia, where political violence was less pronounced than in Algeria or Morocco, French relations with the new Bey, Sidi Lamine, were strained. By this stage, the FCNL had substantially altered the structure of indirect rule within Tunisia. Under the terms of decrees passed in June 1943 and March 1944, Tunisian administration was centralised under the authority of a French-appointed Secretary-general attached to the beylical administration. Throughout 1944–45 Maghreb nationalists appealed to the United States for support and looked increasingly to Egypt for both assistance and example. Both the Istiqlal and Néo-Destour appealed for Allied recognition at the San

Francisco conference in March 1945.[104] Disillusioned with the FCNL's refusal to contemplate greater autonomy for Tunisia, from 1944 Bourguiba achieved most success in cultivating such ties with the English-speaking powers.[105]

Bourguiba's quest for Allied support did not reap immediate rewards. By 1944 the FCNL formulated its North African policies with diminishing fear of British or US interference in the internal workings of French imperial control. Both the Istiqlal and Néo-Destour remained outcasts in the eyes of the provisional government in Paris. Yet one important external constraint remained. French North Africa still relied upon British financial and US material aid. This situation was the product of decisions taken in 1942. According to Gloria Maguire, by the end of that year, the outstanding Free French debt to the British Treasury amounted to £24,476,000. Monthly advances to Carlton Gardens increased markedly in the six months prior to Torch. Furthermore, from September 1942, Free French colonies became open recipients of American Lend-Lease and participated in the inter-Allied Reciprocal Aid programme. As a result, base facilities and primary produce in French North Africa were made available without charge to the United States in part payment for war material and other consignments of essential American supplies. Fortunately for the Algiers authorities, the Americans agreed to continue dollar payment for strategic raw materials, such as nickel, chrome and mica, all of which helped strengthen the currency reserves of Gaullist territories.[106]

Previous aid arrangements covering Free French AEF and Madagascar were dwarfed by the impact of the US military presence upon the economy of French North Africa. Impelled by Giraud's crusade to rebuild French infantry strength, the bulk of US Lend-Lease supplies was shipped direct to Morocco as part of the gradual re-equipment of the Armée d'Afrique. In contrast to the earlier agreements regarding black African territories, Roosevelt's government insisted upon cash payment for supplies of non-military goods.[107] But more important in the immediate aftermath of Torch was the economic impact of the arrival of a large US invasion force moving hastily from west to east, whose victualling requirements necessarily took precedence over the needs of the local population they had 'liberated'. In the short term, this reduced the supply of foodstuffs and consumer goods to North Africans. The dollar spending power of the US troops threatened to devalue the local currency. In practice, the real value of the North African franc, already subject to intense inflationary pressure, rested upon the twin pillars of a thriving black market – naturally enough, set in dollars – and an official rate of exchange agreed between the Algiers authorities and the US Treasury Department in mid-November 1942. Thankfully, the Casablanca conference set a revised rate of dollar–franc exchange (fifty francs to the dollar) in January 1943. The new rate was also applied to AEF and French North Africa and helped stabilise the currency in both federations. It was certainly not in the Allied interest to increase the economic privations of Africans and Arabs, so adding to popular disaffection with French rule, especially when the Americans had just underwritten an accord with Darlan which upheld it.[108]

On 8 February 1944 the FCNL signed a Franco-British financial agreement which replaced all previous financial arrangements between Britain and the Free French. There was obviously a need for a new arrangement unifying the rate of exchange between all territories under Gaullist administration. Under the terms of the February accord, the franc–sterling rate across the French Empire moved from 176.6 to 200 francs to the pound. The one exception was the Levant states, where the rate of exchange between sterling and the Syrian and Lebanese piastres remained unchanged pending the repatriation to Syria of the nation's gold reserves, removed by General Dentz in 1941. This deliberate postponement of financial change in the Levant effectively permitted the Syrian and Lebanese governments a direct role in any later arrangements made in response to currency adjustments decreed from Algiers.[109] The February 1944 agreement with Britain began the process of decoupling the French Empire from its British and American patrons. With the value of colonial francs reduced to a more competitive figure, the Empire was better placed to recover lost export markets once the war ended. This also promised a greater opportunity for colonial trade with metropolitan France as the Allied liberation proceeded.

Gaullist preoccupation with the reassertion of French sovereign control and the integration of French North Africa into the economic and military planning of French liberation left meagre time or resources available for the formulation of colonial reform. In late August 1944, the final transfer of de Gaulle's provisional government from Algiers to Paris carried an obvious symbolism understood by the settler and Muslim communities alike. By 1945 there was a stark contradiction between the restoration of liberty in France and the provisional government's stubborn refusal to act upon earlier promises of reform in the Levant and North Africa. Not surprisingly, the civil and military authorities across North Africa reported a growth in Muslim militancy and in support for pan-Arabism. This seemed immune to official propaganda which stressed the general improvement in economic conditions achieved since the end of Vichy rule.[110] The fact of the matter was that severe rationing continued, black market trade thrived and the superstructure of *colon* privilege remained intact. In late March 1945, some 5,000 Algerian women in Oran and Tlemcen used Governor Yves Chataigneau's tour of Oranie to protest against high food prices and a bread ration reduced to a daily limit of 250 g per individual. These demonstrations were reportedly orchestrated by PPA supporters.[111] As Anthony Clayton has stressed, within Algeria at least, the question was not whether nationalist protests and disturbances would break out, but whether such disorder would escalate beyond control.[112]

The Sétif outbreak

The Moroccan riots of 1944 were eclipsed by the appalling collapse of public order in eastern Constantine as the war in Europe drew to a close. In August 1944 de Gaulle advised General Henri Martin, the newly appointed army commander in Algeria, to be vigilant against nationalist protest in the months ahead whilst the provisional government was preoccupied with French reconstruction.[113] The initial spark of Muslim violence against French officials and settler families was a nationalist march in the town of Sétif, south-west of Constantine, on 8 May. It was stimulated in part by the French detention and planned deportation of Messali Hadj. This was a measure backed by Catroux which Governor Chataigneau had consistently opposed for the very reason that it might spark unprecedented protest. Other than Sétif, similar demonstrations in the larger cities of Bône and Constantine were quickly contained by gendarmes and troops but violence also erupted in Guelma, Kherrata and the rural interior of the Constantine department.[114]

The Sétif region was poor and thinly settled by *colons*. It had remained a centre of unrest since the Kabylie revolts of 1871 and 1916. The area was in the southern reaches of a key 'sensitive zone' identified by the military intelligence staff of General Martin's corps command in Algeria during a review of security in late October 1944.[115] The speed with which some twenty-nine Europeans were murdered in Sétif and the obvious complicity of so many Muslim townsfolk – both men and women – in the killings suggested a spontaneous outpouring of frustration and fury against French rule. In nearby Guelma and Kherrata a further eighteen Europeans were murdered and mutilated in separate outbursts. But the mob slaughter of *colon* farmers and isolated settlers over subsequent days was more redolent of a co-ordinated pogrom signifying the utter collapse of respect for colonial authority.[116]

French vengeance upon the Muslim population of eastern Constantine was immediate and massive. Where in the Muslim case the apparent hysteria attending so many of the hundred or so killings is horrifying, French retribution is most notable for its sheer scale. Minister of the Interior Adrien Tixier advised Georges Bidault on 22 June that the crackdown was 'proportionate' considering the gravity of the original outbreaks. Tixier drew this conclusion from what he admitted to be an approximate figure of 1,000 Algerians killed.[117] In fact, the sometimes indiscriminate application of firepower and the occasional encouragement offered to vigilante *colon* justice wiped out entire communities. The death toll remains hard to verify, partly because the majority of those killed died at the hands of settler mobs which often used mass graves to hide the extent of their crime. After a formal inquiry, the Algiers government produced an official figure of 1,340 Algerians killed, but it was certainly a gross underestimate. Almost 4,000 Algerian Muslims were arrested in sweep operations after the Sétif massacres. Many, including some notable future leaders of the Front de Libération Nationale (FLN), were detained until the announcement of a general amnesty in 1946.[118]

Aside from its intrinsic importance as a dreadful landmark in the history of French Algeria, the Sétif uprising perhaps exposed four issues of lasting historical significance. Firstly, the initial outbreak indicated that, in certain regions of Algeria, Muslim opinion was both more militant and less malleable than the leadership of Ferhat Abbas's AML or the Messalist PPA cared to admit. In this respect, the economic hardship and obvious injustices of a war economy which too often rewarded European profiteering surely contributed to a more populist Algerian nationalism which was less tidy than Ferhat Abbas's ideas about constitutional renovation and less doctrinal than Messalist thinking. Secondly, Sétif and its aftermath did permanent harm to the fabric of Franco-Muslim contact and co-operation in eastern Algeria. It was a signal event which shaped the nationalist outlook of a younger generation which came to prominence within the ranks of the FLN during the 1950s.[119] As a portent of future trouble, Sétif was notable in a third respect. Neither the original outbreaks nor the repression which followed caused much public reaction in France. The coincidence of Sétif with the end of war in Europe does not suffice to explain this. As the Indo-China war was soon to confirm, the centrality of Empire to the politicians and soldiers of the Second World War was not reflected in the lives of metropolitan French families, for whom defeat, occupation, resistance and reconstruction were more pressing concerns. This raises a final point – the lack of interest in Algeria, and North Africa more generally, which characterised the provisional government by May 1945. Certainly, the Damascus bombardment and the continuing struggle to restore French sovereignty in Indo-China were more critical to the survival of Empire in the short term. But it is hard to avoid the conclusion that de Gaulle's disdain for events in Algeria typified an outlook common amongst triumphant politicians and officials in Paris who had spent much of the war in detention, in resistance or in uniform and who were now relishing life at the heart of French politics.

Notes

1 Daladier, *Prison Journal*, p. 169.
2 Robert Murphy, *Diplomat among Warriors* (New York, Doubleday, 1964), pp. 109–23.
3 David A. Walker, 'OSS and Operation Torch', *Journal of Contemporary History*, 22 (1987), 667–70.
4 Arthur L. Funk, 'Negotiating the "Deal with Darlan"', *Journal of Contemporary History*, 8: 2 (1973), 95–101; Martin Thomas, 'The discarded leader: General Henri Giraud and the foundation of the French Committee of National Liberation', *French History*, 10: 1 (1996), 91–2.
5 PRO, HS 3/63, NR631, Murphy to Colonel Solborg, 5 August 1942.
6 Abitbol, *Jews of North Africa*, p. 110.
7 SHAT, 1P89/D4, Service des Contrôles Techniques, 'Renseignements sur les activités anti-nationales sous toutes leurs formes', 10 August 1942.
8 Martin Thomas, 'The Massingham mission: SOE in French North Africa, 1941–1944', *Intelligence and National Security*, 11: 4 (1996), 699–708.
9 PRO, WO 193/860, JSM to COS, 20 July 1942. The Group of Five consisted of a former diplomat, Jacques Tarbé de Saint Hardouin; the leading French royalist in North Africa, Henri d'Astier de la Vigerie; the industrialist, Jacques Lemaigre-Dubreuil; his assistant, Jean Rigault; and Colonel Van Hecke, leader of the 26,000-strong Chantiers de la Jeunesse in AFN. Both Lemaigre-Dubreuil and Rigault were supporters of the anti-republican Cagoulards before the war.
10 Charles Mast, *Histoire d'une rébellion. Alger, 8 Novembre 1942* (Paris, Plon, 1969), pp. 45–54. When Béthouart refused orders to fire upon US forces on 8 November, both General Noguès and his naval commander, Admiral Michelier, insisted that he should be tried for treason.
11 *FRUS, Conferences at Washington, 1941–1942, and Casablanca, 1943*, CCOS meeting, 15 January 1943, p. 573.
12 SHAT, 1K496, Campagne de Tunisie, Colonel Goutard report, 3 December 1945.
13 MAE, Vichy, Série P, vol. 12, no. 1695/RG, Esteva to section Afrique-Levant, 9 November 1942; SHM, TTA 3/Cabinet Militaire, 'Note au sujet du rôle de la marine française dans les événements d'AFN', n.d., November 1942; SHAT, 5P51/D5, EM-1, 'Rapport sur les opérations d'alerte générale en Tunisie', 1 December 1942; Paxton, *Vichy France*, p. 316.
14 PRO, HW 1/1100, CX/MSS/ZTPGM/3723, cipher intercept, 13 November 1942.
15 Funk, 'Negotiating the "Deal with Darlan"', 81–90.
16 PRO, HW 1/1070, NID intelligence summary, 9 November 1942. At Mers el-Kébir and Casablanca three French destroyers were sunk. A further six were immobilised, as was the heavy cruiser *Primauguet*. In addition, *Jean Bart*, the battleship anchored in Mers el-Kébir harbour, was heavily bombarded.
17 PRO, HW 1/1081, ZIP/KFL753, Abwehr, Vichy, cipher intercept, 9 November 1942.
18 Abitbol, *Jews of North Africa*, p. 53.
19 SHM, TTC 44/EMP, BCRA note, 22 October 1943; Crémieux-Brilhac, *La France*

Libre, p. 555.
20 PRO, HW 1/1168, Special intercept, no. 379, 28 November 1942.
21 SHM, Papiers René Godfroy, GG2 147/D7, Darlan to Godfroy, 23 November 1942.
22 Levisse-Touzé, 'L'Afrique du nord pendant la seconde guerre mondiale', 16.
23 Thomas, 'The Massingham mission', 707–8; SHAT, 1K496/D.AFN, Commandant d'Orange memo., 'Note relative aux événements du 8 November 1942', n.d., May 1943.
24 SHAT, Fonds Privées, Papiers de Maréchal Juin, 1K496, Mémoire/Journal de Marche, November 1942.
25 Maguire, *Anglo-American Relations*, p. 79; Mario Rossi, 'Les autorités militaires américaines et la France Libre de 1942 à 1944', *Guerres Mondiales et Conflits Contemporains*, 174 (1994), 179.
26 PRO, FO 660/15, Z 4596/117/69, Enclosure I, 10 March 1943.
27 Raoul Aglion, *Roosevelt and De Gaulle. Allies in Conflict* (New York, Free Press, 1988), pp. 289–95.
28 Rossi, 'Les autorités militaires américaines', 183.
29 SHAT, Fonds Privées, 1K650/D1, Général Lejeune, Témoignage, n.d., 1945.
30 Annie Rey-Goldzeiguer, 'L'occupation germano-italienne de la Tunisie: un tournant de la vie politique tunisienne', in Ageron, *Chemins*, p. 325.
31 Kaddache, 'L'opinion politique musulmane en Algérie', 95–6.
32 AN, F^{60}/187, Cabinet du Gouvernement Général, 'Situation politique indigène de l'Algérie au 15 février 1939'; AN, F^{60}/837, Service des Affaires Musulmanes, Bulletin de renseignements, 20 January 1945; Charles-Robert Ageron, 'Les populations du Maghreb face à la propagande allemande', *Revue d'Histoire de la Deuxième Guerre Mondiale*, 114 (1979), 17–20.
33 Kaddache, 'L'opinion politique musulmane', 103–4.
34 SHAT, 1K592/D1, Charles-Robert Ageron, draft paper, 'Les mouvements nationalistes dans le Maghreb pendant la deuxième guerre mondiale', p. 2. Dr Thameur was subsequently released in December 1942.
35 Rey-Goldzeiguer, 'L'occupation germano-italienne de la Tunisie', 329–30.
36 MAE, Vichy, Série P, vol. 12, Esteva to section Afrique-Levant, 28 September 1942.
37 SHAT, 1K592/D1, Ageron, draft paper, 'Les mouvements nationalistes', p. 3; Rey-Goldzeiguer, 'L'occupation germano-italienne de la Tunisie', p. 330.
38 MAE, Vichy, Série P, vol. 12, Lieutenant-Colonel Rosanvallon, Tunisia gendarmerie, report, 19 October 1942.
39 Hoisington, *Casablanca Connection*, pp. 183–4.
40 SHAT, 1K592/D1, Ageron, 'Les mouvements nationalistes', II, p. 4.
41 Lerner, *Catroux*, p. 269.
42 PRO, ADM 199/180, Algiers consulate to USFOR, London, 28 January 1943.
43 PRO, WO 193/844, tel. 9244, Eisenhower to CCOS, 6 February 1943; PRO, FO 660/64, no. 26, Macmillan to FO, 30 January 1943.
44 SHAT, 5P50/D5, EM-3, Alger, renseignement, 5 December 1942. Kabylie registered the lowest turn-out of reservists within Algeria during the first month of the call-up.
45 Jean-Charles Jauffret (ed.), *La Guerre d'Algérie par les Documents*, I. *L'Avertissement, 1943–1946* (Paris, Vincennes, 1990), pp. 31–8.
46 Jauffret, *Guerre d'Algérie*, EM-2, Constantine, bulletin, 15 March 1943, p. 39.
47 Mohamed Khenouf and Michael Brett, 'Algerian nationalism and Allied military strategy and propaganda during the Second World War: the background to Sétif' in David Killingray and Richard Rathbone (eds), *Africa and the Second World War* (London, Macmillan, 1986), pp. 262–3.
48 Crémieux-Brilhac, *France Libre*, pp. 662–4.
49 Charles-Robert Ageron, *Histoire de l'Algérie contemporaine*, II (Paris, Presses Universitaires de France, 1979), pp. 556–63.
50 Romain Rainero, 'La politique fasciste à l'égard de l'Afrique du Nord', 512–13.
51 Ageron, 'Les populations du Maghreb', 8–9.
52 Rey-Goldzeiguer, 'L'occupation germano-italienne de la Tunisie', pp. 332–9
53 Regarding the Bey's deposition, see Bernard Pujo, *Juin, Maréchal de France* (Paris,

Albin Michel, 1988), pp. 148–50; also cited in Anthony Clayton, *The Wars of French Decolonization* (London, Longman, 1994), p. 23.

54 SHAT. 2P14/D6, EMA-5, Lieutenant-Colonel Charles Dupuy note, 26 November 1942; MAE, Série Tunisie 1944–55, vol. 380, 'Notes sur la situation politique en Tunisie', n.d. In return for renouncing the Tunisian throne Sidi Mohammed Moncef Bey was transferred to Pau in south-west France, where he died on 1 September 1948.

55 Hoisington, *Casablanca Connection*, pp. 227–39.

56 *Ibid.*, pp. 241–2.

57 PRO, FO 660/27, F. W. G. Hamilton, AFHQ, to WO, 16 April 1943.

58 PRO, FO 660/13, Eden to Charles Peake, 28 December 1942.

59 PRO, ADM 199/180, WM(43), first meeting, War Cabinet conclusions, 4 January 1943.

60 PRO, FO 892/174, France Libre communiqué, de Gaulle statement, 2 January 1943.

61 LHCMA, Papers of Admiral Sir Gerald Dickens, WWII correspondence file, Cunningham to Dickens, 4 January 1943.

62 PRO, FO 660/23, Eden to Peake, 28 January 1943; John Charmley, 'Harold Macmillan and the making of the French Committee of National Liberation', *International History Review*, 4: 4 (1982), 557.

63 Charmley, 'Harold Macmillan', 561; Thomas, 'The discarded leader', 103. The vessel sailed from Dakar for a refit in New York after the rallying of AOF; regarding the Tunis campaign, see Clayton, *France, Soldiers and Africa*, pp. 139–40.

64 Crémieux-Brilhac, *La France Libre*, p. 465. For Monnet's role, see André Kaspi, *La Mission de Jean Monnet à Alger, mars–octobre 1943* (Paris, Sorbonne, 1971).

65 PRO, ADM 199/180, FO to Macmillan, 19 March 1943.

66 Jean Monnet, *Memoirs* (London, Collins, 1978), pp. 186–7; Maguire, *Anglo-American Policy*, pp. 84–5.

67 PRO, FO 371/36034, Z4633/72/17, R. L. Speaight minute, 11 April 1943. Giraud supported Governor Jean Rapenne; de Gaulle supported his own nominee, Berthaut.

68 PRO, ADM 199/180, FO to Macmillan, 15 April 1943.

69 De Gaulle, *Mémoires*, II. *L'Unité, 1942–44*, pp. 487–90; Lacouture, *The Rebel*, pp. 446–8.

70 PRO, ADM 199/180, copy tel., Halifax to Eden, 19 June 1943.

71 PRO, WO 193/192, copy tel., Z5513/5/O, Macmillan to Eden, 12 April 1943; Maguire, *Anglo-American Policy*, pp. 88, 163–4.

72 PRO, FO 371/36301, Z8225/8/17, French Section memo., n.d. July 1943.

73 PRO, WO 193/844, COS committee note, 'French West Africa', 2 January 1943.

74 Churchill College archive, Earl of Swinton papers, file SWIN II/5/8, tel. 547, Swinton to CO, 13 December 1942.

75 PRO, FO 892/173, tel. 23, Meiklereid memo. to Eden, 14 March 1943.

76 Swinton papers, file SWIN II/5/8, Halifax to Swinton, 14 May 1943.

77 Nancy Lawler, 'Reform and repression under the Free French: economic and political transformation in the Côte d'Ivoire, 1942–45', *Africa*, 60: 1 (1990), 91.

78 Akpo-Vaché, *L'AOF et la second guerre mondiale*, pp. 157–8.

79 PRO, FO 371/42150, Z1160/1769, Meiklereid to FO, 24 January 1944; Z417/17/69, Meiklereid to Eden, 12 January 1944.

80 PRO, FO371/42150, Z2587/17/69, Meiklereid to FO, 23 March 1944. The three remaining Vichy appointees were Governor Calvel in French Sudan and Governor Chalvet in Mauritania. The third, Jean-François Toby, Governor of Niger, was certainly a supporter of de Gaulle.

81 Churchill College archive, Duff Cooper papers, DUFC 4/4, Churchill to 'Duffie', 19 October 1943.

82 PRO, FO 371/42132, Z791/1/G69, Macmillan to FO, final report, 5 January 1944.

83 Duff Cooper papers, DUFC 4/4, Duff Cooper to Churchill, 8 February 1944.

84 PRO, WO 193/192, FM Dill to COS, London, 5 January 1944.

85 SHAT, 7P238/Colonies FFL, no. 892, Giraud to Bedell Smith, 20 September 1943.

86 SHAT, 7P238/Colonies FFL, EMG-1, compte-rendu, AFHQ, 17 August 1943.

87 Levisse-Touzé, 'L'Afrique du nord pendant la seconde guerre mondiale', 17–18; Clayton, *France, Soldiers and Africa*, pp. 141–5.
88 PRO, WO 193/192, COS to Eden, 3 May 1944; Macmillan to Eden, 12 April 1943.
89 PRO, WO 204/12595, AFHQ, French political intelligence report 3, 5 December 1943.
90 Lerner, *Catroux*, pp. 263–7.
91 Khenouf and Brett, 'Algerian nationalism', p. 263; Guy Pervillé, 'La Commission des Réformes Musulmanes de 1944 et l'élaboration d'une nouvelle politique algérienne de la France' in Ageron, *Chemins*, p. 358.
92 Lerner, *Catroux*, p. 273; Crémieux-Brilhac, *La France Libre*, pp. 666–71.
93 PRO, FO 371/42170, Z2216/87/69, Duff Cooper to Eden, 17 March 1944.
94 Khenouf and Brett, 'Algerian nationalism', pp. 272–3.
95 Pervillé, 'La Commission des Réformes Musulmanes', pp. 358–61.
96 Guy Pervillé, 'La Commission des Réformes Musulmanes de 1944', in Ageron, *Chemins*, p. 363; Anthony Clayton, 'The Sétif uprising of May 1945', *Small Wars and Insurgencies*, 3: 1 (1992), 3–4.
97 Hoisington, *Casablanca Connection*, pp. 241–3.
98 PRO FO 371/42170, Z1289/87/69, M. Abulafia memo., 'French North Africa – survey', 9 February 1944; WO 204/12595, Political intelligence report 12, 6 February 1944.
99 PRO, FO 371/42170, Z330/87/69, Gascoigne, Tangier, to FO, 31 December 1943; Z639/87/69, Stonehewer-Bird, Rabat, to FO, 4 January 1944.
100 AN, F^{60}/885, Lieutenant-Colonel Spillmann, report to Catroux, 6 April 1944.
101 PRO, WO 204/12595, AFHQ, French political intelligence report 12, 6 February 1944.
102 *Ibid.* The figure of 150 deaths contrasts with a much lower estimate of thirty-eight initially issued by the Rabat residency.
103 PRO, FO 371/42170, Z2152/87/69, M. Abulafia memo., 'Survey, North West Africa', 15 March 1944.
104 *DDF*, 1944, II, nos 26, 167.
105 SHAT, 2H129/D2, Résidence générale, Direction des Affaires Politiques, rapport politique mensuel, January 1944.
106 Maguire, *Anglo-American Policy*, pp. 118–9.
107 James J. Dougherty, *The Politics of Wartime Aid. American Economic Assistance to France and French Northwest Africa, 1940–1946* (Westport, Conn., Greenwood Press, 1978), p. 5.
108 Maguire, *Anglo-American Policy*, pp. 120–2.
109 PRO, FO 371/40299, E1126/23/89, Spears Mission, Political summary 97, 19 February 1944.
110 Jauffret (ed.), *Guerre d'Algérie*, Rapport du Capitaine Fraisse, Septième légion Garde Républicaine, 19–22 March 1945, pp. 160–2; SHAT, 2H129/D3, Résidence Générale, Section d'Etudes, Rapport politique, February 1945.
111 MAE, Série Afrique-Levant, 1944–55, Algérie, vol. 2, no. 637, Rachid Bencheneb report, 6 April 1945.
112 Clayton, 'Sétif uprising', 2.
113 Jean-Charles Jauffret, 'The origins of the Algerian war: the reaction of France and its army to the two emergencies of May 1945 and 1 November 1954', *Journal of Imperial and Commonwealth History*, 21: 3 (1993), 18.
114 Clayton, 'Sétif uprising', 7–8; Jauffret (ed.), *Guerre d'Algérie*, no. 768/S, Colonel Bourdila, Commandant, Sétif, 'Rapport sur le mouvement insurrectionnel du 8 mai 1945', 18 June 1945, pp. 244–6; AN, F^{60}/835, no. 3626/CIE, Chataigneau to Catroux, 27 April 1944.
115 AN, F^{60}/872, EMA-2, 'Notes succinctes sur le mouvement insurrectionnel du Sud-Constantinois', 21 August 1945; Jauffret, 'The origins of the Algerian war', 19–20.
116 Clayton, 'Sétif uprising', 7–8. The figures and local reports are from MAE, Algérie, vol. 2, B19, Tixier to Bidault, 22 June 1945.

117 MAE, Algérie, vol. 2, B19, Tixier to Bidault, 22 June 1945.

118 Clayton, 'Sétif uprising', 9–12. Jean-Charles Jauffret used a secret report by General Raymond Duval from the Vincennes military archives for his estimate of just under 3,000 Algerian fatalities: Jauffret, 'The origins of the Algerian war', 28, n. 8.

119 Tayeb Chenntouf, 'L'Assemblée Algérienne et l'application des réformes prévues par le statut du 20 Septembre 1947' in Ageron, *Chemins*, p. 367.

CHAPTER SEVEN

The fate of French Indo-China, 1940–45

> My governor-generalship of Indo-China lasted, in one piece, for almost five years (20 July 1940–9 March 1945). That, in itself, appears an exceptional historical fact, which should inspire in all those who wish to embark upon an impartial study of my proconsulate, if not indulgence, which I would not wish to encourage, then at least great caution. [Admiral Jean Decoux[1]]

As in the Levant states and French North Africa, so in the Far East the wartime combination of external intervention and uncompromising indigenous nationalism gradually undermined French imperial power. Indo-China was bound to be considered a special case by the Vichy regime and the Free French movement. A valuable colonial federation in peacetime, it was none the less considered virtually indefensible before the fall of France. The development of a coexistence policy between Jean Decoux's administration and the Japanese military was never equivalent to Vichy collaborationism in Europe and Africa. As a result, the Free French view of Decoux was more subtle than the wholesale criticism usually reserved for other pro-Vichy colonial Governors. Most significant, between late 1940 and 1945, the French administration in Indo-China was forced by circumstances to plough a distinctive furrow in order to survive intact. While Decoux's policies may have approximated to those of Vichy in many respects – not least the progressive extension of collaboration and the enthusiastic endorsement of a Pétainist national revolution – French rule in Indo-China was far more than an Asian mirror of the Vichy regime.

Fighting for survival: Decoux's first months in office

After the drama of General Catroux's final days in office in Hanoi in July 1940, his successor, Admiral Decoux, quickly stamped his authority upon the administration of French Indo-China. Indeed, Catroux was lucky to escape the federation. In early August, his temporary refuge at the Dalat hill station – a six-hour ride from Saigon – was under surveillance by Sûreté officials, and it was largely through the efforts of the British consul in Saigon that on 1 August Catroux smuggled out a message to the British authorities in Singapore offering co-operation if passage to London could be arranged.[2] Eager to utilise Catroux's standing in North Africa in a final bid to persuade General Noguès to recant his loyalty to Vichy, Churchill stated his readiness to go 'to any reasonable length' to get Catroux to Britain.[3] In the event, Decoux was undoubtedly glad to see him go.

By the time Catroux departed, Japanese pressure upon Indo-China was mounting fast. Though Decoux was to achieve perhaps the most thorough emulation of Vichy's national revolution within any of France's Pétainist colonies, the admiral was no friend of the Axis powers.[4] Throughout the exchanges between Japan, Vichy and French Indo-China in August and September 1940, the Governor proved far more tenacious than his political masters in France. Between 26 and 30 August, Tokyo ambassador Charles-Arsène Henry agreed a number of local concessions in return for a formal Japanese guarantee to respect French sovereignty in Indo-China. Unaware of the extent to which his negotiating position was already undermined, Decoux meanwhile resisted the demands put forward by General Nishihara's military mission to Hanoi.[5] On 4 September Decoux's military commander, General Maurice Martin, concluded an accord with Nishihara which imposed tight restrictions upon Japanese military transit rights through northern Tonkin. Pending the signature of a final working agreement, no Japanese soldiers were permitted to enter Indo-Chinese territory to occupy those frontier bases designated for their eventual use in a planned offensive against Chiang Kai-shek's Nationalist forces in southern China.[6] When this accord was breached by a limited Japanese incursion on 6 September, Decoux immediately broke off talks, incurring the anger of Vichy Foreign Minister Paul Baudouin in the process.[7]

The Japanese negotiators capitalised upon the growing rift between a Vichy government inclined to accept broad concessions and Decoux's military command which remained anxious to preclude direct Japanese supervision of Tonkin. Within the Vichy Foreign Ministry, Baudouin's senior advisers, François Charles-Roux and Jean Chauvel, suggested that a firmer line could be maintained without risk of an immediate Japanese occupation. Baudouin disagreed.[8] One of General Martin's staff officers recalled that the Japanese military mission exploited the differences between Vichy and the Indo-China command by encouraging frontier incidents along the Tonkin–China frontier between Japanese troops and the French garrison.[9] This emphasised Japan's overwhelming military superiority, making the exposure of the defending French units abundantly clear. Still Decoux tried to postpone a humiliating settlement. He calculated that firmer US diplomatic support for the French position might yet enable Vichy to withstand renewed Japanese military pressure for admission to Tonkin. This proved a misguided hope. Faced with a Japanese threat to invade unless agreement on transit rights and base facilities for up to 25,000 troops were swiftly reached, on 22 September Decoux gave way.[10]

Even more than the United States, both Britain and Nationalist China clearly had a vested interest in buttressing the French position. On 5 September, Chiang Kai-shek's representative in France, Dr Wellington Koo, relayed a Vichy plea for British assistance in escorting a contingent of 4,000 French colonial troops from Djibouti to Haiphong. On 8 September Decoux contacted Britain's China naval station in support of this request. In addition, the British were asked to lobby Washington for the release to Indo-China of several squadrons of recently purchased US fighters held aboard the French aircraft-carrier *Bearn*. This ship had been stranded at Fort-de-France in Martinique since the armistice. Acting on the advice of the Vansittart Committee on Foreign (Allied) Resistance, the British postponed any reply during the final stages of Decoux's talks with Nishihara.[11] Meanwhile, on 14 September Chiang Kai-shek indicated that Chinese troops might be made available to help defend Indo-China – a somewhat improbable proposal, given Japan's military grip upon China's Kwangsi province to the north-east of Tonkin. As Decoux realised, offers of British or Chinese support were a poisoned chalice, always more likely to provoke an outright Japanese take-over than to prevent it.[12]

In fact, Decoux's reluctant accommodation with Japan did not provoke any immediate British or Chinese response. Ironically, it was the Japanese themselves who undermined the 22 September accord. Encouraged by Emperor Hirohito's military emissary, Major-general Tominaga Kyoji, of the army staff operations section, units of General Rikichi Ando's fifth division deployed along the border between Tonkin and Kwangsi province deliberately ignored the Nishihara–Decoux agreement. They attacked French positions at Dong Dang and Langson, capturing the latter on 25 September.[13] Vichy immediately protested to Tokyo. Emperor Hirohito then intervened and the Kwangsi army withdrew. Its commanders were reprimanded and their over-zealous troops were evacuated via Haiphong.[14] Only a brief military engagement, the 'Langson incident' none the less proved that French Indo-China was entirely at Japan's mercy. Military commanders in the field might yet dictate whether or not French rule would be permitted to survive.[15]

Weeks later, in early November 1940, Charles Rochat, Director of Political Affairs in the Vichy Foreign Ministry, advised Decoux to acquiesce in widespread Japanese seizures of war material originally intended for onward shipment to the Chinese Nationalists. Although on 1 October the US and British governments belatedly stated that they would not block French reinforcement of Indo-China, what little forces were available in Vichy Africa could hardly affect the strategic balance in South East Asia. Decoux's sole option was to plead with General Sumita, head of the Japanese military mission to Hanoi, to exercise restraint.[16] Ultimately, the survival of Decoux's administration hung by the slenderest of threads – the forbearance of Japanese officers in Indo-China and South China.[17] In his original talks with General Nishihara, Catroux failed to secure any fixed term or precise demarcation for the activities of the Japanese Control Commission. This left Decoux powerless against further extensions of Japanese military influence. Though Sumita assured Decoux that Japan's Southern Region army headquarters did not plan to extend its occupation of northern Tonkin, he admitted that additional concessions might be required to meet Japan's strategic requirements. Hence the pattern of arbitrary Japanese demands and seizures of raw materials, including rice, coal, rubber and tin, continued into 1941. Though Decoux had tried to hold his ground in September 1940, for convenience alone, it was preferable for the Japanese military to settle matters directly with the Governor rather than have their demands raised at inter-governmental level between Tokyo and Vichy.[18] In late May 1941, for example, Japanese troops broke into two warehouses at Haiphong and loaded eight merchant ships with over 16,000 metric tonnes of US military equipment originally destined for Chiang Kai-shek's forces.[19]

The Franco-Japanese clash at Langson set another important precedent. The outbreak of hostilities was the catalyst to diffuse uprisings orchestrated by Vietnamese communists. Further outbreaks were directed by the pro-Japanese Phuc Quoc league, a movement organised in 1939 by Prince Cuong De, a royal pretender to Bao Dai's title as Emperor of Annam.[20] Phoc Quoc rebel strength increased from around 550 to some 1,500 after Japanese troops released several hundred *indigène* troops captured in September, even providing those who joined the Phoc Quoc with arms.[21] Previously, Japanese representatives encouraged the garrisons of Tonkinese tirailleurs at Langson and Dong Dang to mutiny against French rule. Japanese *agents provocateurs* also helped plan an abortive uprising by Trotskyite followers of Dr Nguyen Van Nha much further south in Cochin China.[22]

In October 1940 Decoux returned from a tour of Indo-China's colonial capitals convinced that the suppression of Vietnamese nationalism was fundamental to the continued exclusion of the Japanese.[23] As the Kwangsi army withdrew after the settlement of the Langson incident, so the French authorities could concentrate upon a vigorous, well directed crackdown upon disorder. French military repression was most severe in the wake of a further localised rebellion in Cochin China. This took place despite a strong warning from Indo-Chinese Communist Party representatives in Tonkin that the French could easily crush a premature local uprising in the south. It was a shrewd assessment. French Sûreté intelligence proved decisive in suppressing the rebellion, and Plan Dang Luu, the representative of the Cochin Chinese communists sent to liaise with his colleagues in Tonkin, was immediately arrested on his return to Saigon.[24] In spite of this early setback, concerted unrest began on 22 November with the seizure of a military post on the Cambodian frontier at Chau-Toc. It was soon followed by widespread rioting in Cang-Long, Vung-Liem, Tan-an Bentre and Hoc-Mon. Of the seventeen people killed by the rebels, eleven were *indigène* notables, including the head of Tranvinh province. A single French planter was murdered.[25] While the Sûreté prevented any uprising in Saigon itself, Foreign Legion units undertook severe repression within the interior of Cochin China. Numerous villages were burnt down and over 2,000 arrests were made.[26] Decoux initially attributed the outbreaks to communist infiltration and the inefficiency of the Cochin China administration. In December he refined his earlier opinion and blamed Caodaist religious sects above all. Decoux duly replaced the *résident supérieur* and the general commanding Cochin China-Cambodia and unleashed an official campaign against Caodaist organisations.[27]

Consolidation of the Decoux regime

After the uprisings in late 1940, an inverse equation was soon established. As Decoux's real power and room for manoeuvre diminished in 1940–41, so his determination to impose French authority upon Indo-China increased. Within Tonkin, military sweep operations continued in Langson province over the winter of 1940–41 in an effort to disperse any remaining rebel bands. Following an unsuccessful but violent mutiny of the *garde indigène* in Vinh province in northern Annam on 12 January 1941, Decoux had the perpetrators court-martialled within a week.[28] In mid-February, Decoux advised Platon that Cambodia and Laos were calm, and that violence within Annam was only 'episodic' and ill co-ordinated.[29] In fact, those leading the French pacification were clearly surprised by the ferocity of resistance they encountered. In Tonkin respect for French military capacity had evaporated. Commenting upon Foreign Legion repression in 1941, a senior officer noted, 'Indigenous soldiers who had fought very badly against the Japanese fought with courage against the Europeans.'[30] The principal victim in all this was the resident peasant population of northern Tonkin which, though certainly uncommitted to French rule, was not yet united in support of national independence. Returning French officers found the North Vietnamese peasantry gripped by the far more immediate problem of agricultural survival. As one garrison commander recalled, 'Across an entire province criss-crossed by [rebel] bands and striving to meet Japanese exactions, the population remained passive, greeting the revolutionaries or the French with the same fear whichever the case. Rare were the villages which sided with one or the other. There were few partisans, informers or guides [owing to] the fear of reprisal.'[31]

Tonkin remained the most volatile area of French Indo-China throughout the war. In spite of Decoux's undoubted willingness to tackle nationalist unrest militarily and politically, he never wholly contained communist-led subversion. The primary reason for this was the emergence and consolidation in 1941 of the Viet Minh nationalist coalition. This was directed surreptitiously by Ho Chi Minh, the inspirational Vietnamese communist leader whose personal resistance to colonial rule had already resulted in prolonged exile from Indo-China throughout most of the preceding decade. Ho and his closest associates, Vo Nguyen Giap and Pham Van Dong, worked together in South China during 1940 to prepare the ground for the revitalisation of communist support within Tonkin. But at the Indo-Chinese Communist Party's landmark eighth plenum, held at Pac Bo in early May 1941, Ho affirmed his adherence to a strategy of guerilla activity and Popular Front-style coalition politics. This temporarily subordinated ideological doctrine to the requirement for a broadly based nationalist movement. Over the next three years, the Indo-Chinese Communist Party took pains to conceal its guiding hand behind the multi-party image of the Viet Minh. In consequence, the movement attracted non-communist support whilst enjoying the benefits of communist expertise in organising underground activity.[32]

Always acutely conscious that French colonial authority was severely compromised, between 1940 and 1944 Decoux's government was the most actively repressive within the Vichy empire. Ironically, before the task of pacification in Tonkin was anywhere near complete, Decoux faced another source of foreign aggression. The French mounted fierce resistance in a brief campaign during November–

December 1940 against a Thai invasion west of the Mekong river. The Vichy troika of Darlan, Huntziger and Platon agreed in October 1940 that Thai claims could not be satisfied without irreparable loss of face. So, in contrast to Vichy dithering over Japanese incursion, Thailand's aggression met a firm response.[33] Though Darlan failed to meet Decoux's requests for submarine reinforcements from the Indian Ocean squadron based at Madagascar, Decoux's naval forces scored a notable success in mid-January 1941. In a surprise raid led by the ageing cruiser *Lamotte Piquet*, the Thai fleet was immobilised at Koh-Chang in the Gulf of Siam.[34] This was a chimeric victory. Though *indigène* units generally remained loyal during the fighting against the Thais, without the facilities or the officers to equip and train them more effectively it was clear that French military resources in Indo-China would gradually lose their residual value.[35] Once Japan effectively took the Thai side by imposing itself as 'mediator' in the conflict, Decoux was compelled to accept humiliating peace terms. In early March, he ceded to Thailand the Laotian district of Paklay, an area north of Battambang in Cambodia and the small island of Khong in the middle of the Mekong river channel (see map 5).[36]

Decoux tried to limit the political fall-out from his enforced capitulation to Bangkok. In an attempt to compensate the Laotian dynasty for its loss of territory to Thailand, Decoux and Platon agreed to confer upon the royal court at Luang Prabang a greater political and ceremonial role in the administration of Laos.[37] To prevent the alienation of Annam's influential merchant class, Platon also suggested that Decoux should spend more on education, civil courts and public health provision. This was intended to illustrate to those educated in Annam's French schools that Vichy administration was the direct antithesis of Japan's brutal colonialism in Manchuria, Korea and Taiwan.[38] It remains difficult to evaluate the extent to which the brief war against Thailand undermined Decoux's ability to challenge the emergent Viet Minh. Neither the Governor's office nor the Ministry of Colonies in Vichy appears to have considered that the Thai campaign significantly hampered the police actions under way across Indo-China after the Langson and Cochin China outbreaks of 1940. Rather, Decoux and Platon both took comfort from the spirited performance of French military units against Japanese-equipped Thai forces. Platon wrongly deduced that it would salvage local French prestige.[39] In fact, Vietnamese nationalists were largely unaffected by the Thai invasion far to the west. Meanwhile, the cession of Laotian land and the loss of rich agricultural resources in north-west Cambodia – albeit under Japanese pressure – made a mockery of France's self-appointed role as protector of those kingdoms.

For their part, during 1940–41, the Free French could do little to influence events in Indo-China. Having brought former Governor Catroux into the fold, it was hard to insist that the French community in Indo-China should rally to de Gaulle when their putative leader had fled the country. De Gaulle had more urgent matters to worry about in Africa and the Levant, and was uncharacteristically whimsical about the likelihood of the eventual liberation of Indo-China.[40] For the foreseeable future, the Free French seemed resigned to their dismal prospects in the Far East. In January 1941 the Empire Defence Council even agreed to lobby the British government to back Decoux's earlier pleas for a relaxation of blockade restrictions in order to permit the reinforcement of the Indo-China garrison.[41] Conversely, since Decoux was theoretically committed to recovering the French Pacific territories that had declared for Free France in 1940, de Gaulle took a considerable risk in supporting the Allied embargo upon the supply of strategic raw materials to Japan. As French Pacific territories had traditionally exported nickel to the Japanese, it was widely assumed within Carlton Gardens that Tokyo would cajole Decoux into action against New Caledonia in particular.[42]

During 1941 the Foreign Office made it plain to Carlton Gardens that Britain would not lend significant aid to the disparate groups of Free French supporters spread across South East Asia and China's main trading ports. To do so risked antagonising Japan for little reward. As a result, when Vichyite naval officers under Decoux's ultimate command began rounding up Gaullist sympathisers in Shanghai in April 1941, the British raised no effective protest.[43] During 1941, much of Britain's Indo-China policy was thus left to the Ministry of Economic Warfare, which attempted to increase British purchases of Indo-Chinese coal, rubber and rice in an unsuccessful attempt to loosen Japan's grip upon Indo-China's export trade.[44] Lacking useful British support and discouraged by Decoux's enthusiastic embrace of Vichy policies, over the spring of 1941 de Gaulle authorised an expansion of Gaullist propaganda to Indo-China. This was directed from a long-distance broadcasting station in the Gaullist enclave of Pondicherry in southern India.[45]

The Japanese increased their pressure on Decoux's administration following the end of Franco-Thai hostilities. On 14 July 1941 the Southern Army command demanded the extension of concessions covering military facilities and rights of transit from the northern reaches of Tonkin to cover Annam, Cochin China and Cambodia as well. In Vichy, Japanese ambassador Kato took up the same demands with Admiral Darlan, who had been serving as Deputy Premier and Foreign Minister since 10 February. Having failed to secure any firm

US support from Vichy ambassador Admiral William Leahy, both Decoux and Darlan feared that a refusal to agree terms with Kato would provoke Japanese landings in southern Indo-China.[46] In response to Anglo-American criticism that these further concessions contravened Pétain's pledge to defend the empire against all comers, the Vichy Foreign Ministry pointedly noted that British aggression in Syria and America's refusal to assist Decoux in 1940 compelled Darlan to negotiate the best conditions possible.[47] The result was the Darlan–Kato 'common defence' agreement of 29 July 1941, formally ratified in Hanoi five months later. Japanese forces entered Annam, Cochin China and Cambodia, advance bases were established for future Japanese operations against Malaya, Singapore and the Philippines, and secret provision was made for additional reinforcements upon specific Japanese demand.[48]

French Indo-China isolated

Although Japan's penetration of French Indo-China contributed to the breakdown of US–Japanese negotiations in 1941, as Stein Tonnesson, an outstanding historian of the wartime history of Vietnam, puts it, 'By 1942, Indochina had been largely forgotten; it lay far behind Japanese lines and could quietly enjoy stability under Decoux.'[49] In many respects the Indo-Chinese situation was unique. There was, for example, little room for compromise between de Gaulle and Admiral Decoux. Convinced that Free French propaganda only worsened his difficulties in containing the spread of communist support within Tonkin in particular, on 17 November 1941 Decoux announced an unprecedented round-up of suspected Gaullist sympathisers within the Indo-Chinese administration.[50] When Free France declared war on Japan on 8 December 1941 any hope of reconciliation with Decoux seemed to disappear. Since the admiral was ultimately beholden to the Japanese military for his survival, dialogue with the Free French risked his immediate overthrow. This situation was unlikely to change. The partial British naval blockade of Indo-China, supported by the authorities of the Dutch East Indies, also hardened Decoux's opposition to de Gaulle, even though the blockade came to an abrupt end with the collapse of Singapore in mid-February 1942. Over the preceding year and a half, British patrols certainly cut maritime trade between France, other Vichy territories and Indo-China. By September 1941 an average of only three Indo-China-bound vessels per month successfully breached the British naval screen in the Indian Ocean. But this only consolidated Japan's grip upon Indo-China's export trade.[51] In November 1941 the British intercepted a Vichy convoy bound for Indo-China from Madagascar. After this incident, the Secretariat of Marine was reluctant to sanction any major supply convoys to Indo-China.[52] Militarily powerless to resist Japanese requisitioning, Decoux relied upon the assurance of limited convoy supplies to strengthen his hand in economic dealings with the Japanese. The Darlan–Kato agreement and the reassertion of the British blockade in 1941 tipped the scales further against him. Far more serious, in September 1941 Decoux warned Vichy that extensive Japanese foodstuff requisitioning was bound to result in starvation across much of the Mekong delta.[53]

Japan's hold over Decoux increased as the country achieved victory after victory in the first four months of 1942. On the eve of Japan's capture of Singapore in February, Decoux faced renewed demands to permit the entry of further Japanese divisions to Indo-China and to renegotiate an already one-sided barter arrangement with Japan. Under the terms of this, Indo-China's principal mineral and foodstuff exports were offset against imports of Japanese manufactured goods of minimal use to Indo-China's peasant population.[54] Following his arrival in Saigon in late 1942, Yoshizawa Kenkichi, Japan's new Minister to Indo-China, kept the economic screws firmly applied. Furthermore, outside Cao Bang province in northern Tonkin (heartland of the emergent Viet Minh), the nationalist threat to French authority was increasingly diverse. While there was advantage in the fact that no single organisation held sway, the diffuse nature of opposition made it more difficult to contain. As Sûreté chief Louis Arnoux later conceded, the French security services were often preoccupied by the most pro-Japanese of the Vietnamese nationalist groups. These ranged from the nationalist Dai Viet and Phuc Quoc parties to the Caodaist religious sects.[55] A Sûreté clampdown in late October 1941 involving the arrest of over 500 suspects, including a large number of personnel from the administrations of Tonkin and Annam, indicated the scale of the problem faced. The detainees were variously accused of support for Japan's 'Greater East Asian Co-prosperity Sphere' and collusion with the Japanese Yasutai secret services and Kempeitei military police.[56] Sûreté suspicions were well founded, and were definitively proved following a French military inquiry initiated in October 1941. Neither the Tokyo government, Hanoi ambassadors Yoshizawa and Matsumoto, nor the senior military commanders in Indo-China offered much direct support to Vietnamese nationalists. But many of their civil and military subordinates did.[57] At various points between 1941 and 1945, in contravention of their undertakings to Decoux, Japanese officials either sheltered or advised pro-Japanese nationalists, including Ngo Dinh Diem, Tran Van An and Tran Trong Kim, as well as the Viet Minh leaders Tran Van Lai and Phan Khe Toai.[58] Similarly, the

Kempeitei offered intermittent support to the Caodaist leader, Tran Quang Vinh. Though never openly approved, these Kempeitei dealings with Vietnam's disparate political and religious groups were clearly intended to increase Japanese options should Tokyo require a compliant Vietnamese administration in place of Decoux.[59] Writing in 1978, Ralph Smith drew the following conclusion. 'The impression that emerges from all these fragments of information is that by the end of 1944 there was quite a number of Vietnamese nationalist groups which had contact with the Japanese and which were ready to collaborate with them if called upon to do so, but who were not necessarily in harmony (or even in contact) with one another.'[60]

As for those Viet Minh figures, including Ho Chi Minh, that were hostile to Japan, the partial Japanese occupation of Indo-China forced them to develop a more sophisticated clandestine network of support. So long as the Japanese remained, Ho's objectives were consistent with both US and Soviet policies. The Vietnamese communists were bound to profit – 'their national and revolutionary struggle against the Vichyite administration and the Japanese occupation integrated directly into the international strategy of war against fascism pursued by the communist movement. The rupture with the metropole had allowed Vietnam to participate independently in the war against Japanese militarism.'[61] The long-term consequences of this were profound indeed.

Having made no significant impact within Indo-China during the previous year, it was only in January 1942 that the French National Committee reconsidered the eventual dispatch of military forces to the Far East. So began a process of agitation for Free French representation with the regional British military commands in India and, later, South East Asia, which eventually bore fruit over the winter of 1944–45.[62] In February 1942, the British government agreed to maintain a five-man Gaullist military mission in Delhi led by Lieutenant-Colonel de la Valdene. But the precipitate fall of Singapore within days of this decision precluded any significant Anglo-Free French planning for covert operations or intelligence-gathering within Indo-China for the next eighteen months.[63] It remained the conventional wisdom within Whitehall and even Carlton Gardens that the French were no longer masters of their own destiny in Indo-China. Either they would be ousted by the Japanese or they would be restored by an Allied victory, provided, of course, that Roosevelt could be made to stomach the idea of a French return. The one element missing from this analysis was any real appreciation of how strong Vietnamese nationalism was becoming, catalysed by the pressures of Japanese occupation and Decoux's often arbitrary rule.

Lacking detailed sources of Far Eastern intelligence, the Free French remained blissfully unaware of the complexities of Indo-China's internal politics for much of the 1940–43 period. Until it decamped to Algiers in 1943, the French National Committee thus tended to concentrate its political analysis of Indo-China upon Decoux's administration alone. According to the Free French propaganda service within the Carlton Gardens information commissariat, Decoux compensated for his increased dependence upon Japan by cultivating settler loyalty through the promotion of Vichy's national revolution. To this end, he augmented administrative salaries and placed great emphasis upon recruitment to the *Légion des Combattants et Volontiers de la Révolution Nationale*. Finally, Decoux exploited a Vichy funding loan to ease the effects of Japan's partial occupation upon the settler elite.

In July 1942, a Franco-Thai frontier commission based in Saigon completed the demarcation of Thailand's extended eastern frontier. Diplomatic and commercial relations between Indo-China and Bangkok were resumed.[64] The limited economic benefits of this were almost immediately nullified by the British invasion of Vichyite Madagascar, which began on 5 May 1942. This snuffed out any residual hope of a resumption of Indo-China's trade with France or Vichy Africa. Since the Vichy authorities could do little to assist Decoux materially, on 30 December 1942 Premier Laval showed little compunction in accepting a special payments agreement with the Tokyo government which placed Indo-China within Japan's financial orbit. This established a system of reciprocal exchanges in 'special yen', based upon Tokyo's recognition of the Bank of Indo-China as the ultimate guarantor of trade payments to Japan.[65] Financially and militarily, Decoux was cut adrift, left to survive by his wits.

Despairing of Decoux's policies, what little Gaullist propaganda reached Indo-China during 1942–43 sought to provide the settler community with accurate and encouraging information upon the wider course of the war. In separate broadcasts intended for the indigenous population, French misrule was characterised as a purely Vichy invention. These were testing tasks for the most capable propagandist, and Japan's southward advance had ended Free French radio broadcasts from Hong Kong, Manila and Singapore. Without widespread rural networks of Gaullist support, it was near impossible to communicate directly with the mass of the population; harder still to convince urban Vietnamese that one sort of French governance was morally bankrupt while another offered salvation.[66] De Gaulle remained contemptuous of Decoux's tentative efforts to conciliate the FCNL from 1943 onwards. At the start of the year, Decoux dismissed his Secretary-general, Pierre Delsalle, whom he had earlier promoted to the rank of *rési-*

dent supérieur. Henceforth, Decoux set greater store upon the opinions of Claude de Boisanger, his chief diplomatic adviser in Hanoi. De Boisanger was more equivocal about continued loyalty to Vichy than Delsalle had been. He encouraged Decoux's efforts to begin a dialogue with Colonel Zinovi Pechkoff's Gaullist mission based with Chiang Kai-shek's administration in Chungking. The Governor's approaches went unacknowledged. In February 1943 the French National Committee had established a three-man Indo-China section, headed by Pierre Laurin, within René Pleven's Commissariat of Colonies. But Laurin and his staff did not consider immediate contact with Decoux worth while.[67]

In late 1943 Decoux resumed his efforts to contact de Gaulle, this time by direct liaison with the FCNL in Algiers. But over the intervening six months, perhaps his most pressing concern was to secure Indo-China's economic future. The colony's commercial survival was by now more closely tied to the East Asian economic region than to France. Decoux judged this reorientation in Indo-Chinese trade an unalterable fact. Though driven by Japan's wartime impositions, Decoux calculated that the economic relationship between France and Indo-China was fundamentally transformed. In a series of communications with Vichy in November 1943, he even raised the possibility of greater autonomy for Indo-China. This, and his economic proposals, were rejected outright on 19 November. Charles Rochat and the recently appointed Minister of Colonies, Rear-admiral Henri Bléhaut, agreed that Decoux's suggestions simply meant unnecessary concessions to Japan. The Vichy Foreign Ministry disparaged any binding statements regarding long-term plans for colonial reform.[68]

By this stage, Vichy's instructions to Decoux were little more than platitudinous rubbish. On 8 October 1943, for example, the military staff of the Ministry of Colonies reminded the Indo-China command that imperial policing should be its overriding concern. A show of French prestige was essential to contain 'the evolution in the mentality of our colonial subjects towards political emancipation'.[69] In spite of Vichy's apparent preference for truism over constructive suggestion, as Indo-China's economic plight worsened in 1944, Decoux tried once more to convince Laval's government that Indo-China had to pursue its interests in co-operation with Japan. Finally admitting its impotence, on 20 April, Laval's Cabinet invested Decoux with 'absolute powers' to enable him to pursue this objective. For months afterwards, Decoux maintained limited contact with Vichy. In July 1944 he warned Bléhaut that, in order to preserve *indigène* loyalty, the Government-General intended to publicise its plans for post-war reform. These would recognise the increasingly Asian orientation of Indo-

China's export trade. Though Bléhaut immediately raised this issue with Laval, the pace of the Allied advance across France meant that Decoux's proposals went unanswered.[70] The Vichy era in French Indo-China fizzled out, leaving Decoux's administration with precious little time to remould itself as a Gaullist Trojan horse before the eventual Japanese military take-over on 9 March 1945.

Plans for liberation

On 8 September 1943, Pierre Viénot, London representative of the FCNL, officially requested British permission for the dispatch of an enlarged Fighting French military mission to Admiral Louis Mountbatten's South East Asia Command (SEAC) in New Delhi. The Foreign Office and Chiefs of Staff were unenthusiastic; Churchill was positively discouraging.[71] The Prime Minister refused to antagonise his US partners by sponsoring Gaullist participation in the struggle against Japan. In principle, Churchill supported the French claim to participate in any Far Eastern settlement at the war's end. But, with the Moscow conference pending, and with preparations for Allied landings in north-west Europe gathering speed, autumn 1943 was not an opportune moment to begin arguing with Allies over the long-term future of Indo-China.[72]

The Chiefs of Staff and the Foreign Office Far Eastern department were less convinced that the issue of French sovereignty in Indo-China could be allowed to lie fallow. The timing of the FCNL's proposal was significant. By late 1943 it was clear that America's strategic control of the China theatre – exercised from the US command headquarters at Chungking – might prejudice the long-term security of French and British rule in South East Asia. In Chiang Kai-shek's Nationalist capital, neither General Joseph Stilwell nor his successor, General Albert Wedemeyer, showed much concern for British or French colonial interests.[73] Just as the American Office of Strategic Services was stealing a march on SOE's covert activities within Indo-China, so US support for Chiang Kai-shek threatened a situation in which Chinese Nationalist forces would be allowed a more prominent role in the eviction of the Japanese from northern Indo-China to the exclusion of SEAC and Free France.[74] On 3 October 1943, Ashley Clarke of the Far Eastern department summarised the problem:

> it may be possible to refuse French suggestions that they should participate in the Far East and it may be possible to evade any request for a statement of our attitude concerning Indo-China. But we have not only to organise and intensify our political warfare and undercover activities in respect of Indo-China, but we have also somehow to moderate simi-

> lar but unco-ordinated activities by the Chinese, the French and the Americans from Chungking, where there are two French missions completely outside our control.[75]

Having made no progress in London, in mid-November 1943 the FCNL clarified that the proposed military mission to SEAC would actually constitute a substantial force of troops trained in counter-insurgency. The mission was to be led by General Roger Blaizot, formerly a Coloniale divisional commander. He was to take charge of a *Corps Léger d'Intervention* (CLI) of between 500 and 1,000 men whose purpose was to engage in paramilitary activity, sabotage and intelligence-gathering behind Japanese lines in preparation for an eventual Allied liberation.[76] While the FCNL used its offer of military support and regional expertise to bargain with the British over Indo-China, the Gaullists took a more circumspect approach to Washington. Mindful of American criticism of French colonial policies, on 8 December the FCNL reaffirmed its commitment to liberate Indo-China from Japanese control. After this had been achieved, comprehensive – though poorly defined – reforms were promised. They were to strip away all vestiges of Vichy authoritarianism. Once that was done, an autonomous taxation and customs administration would be established to underpin a post-war investment programme tailored to the requirements of Indo-China's component territories.[77] The FCNL declaration effectively condemned Decoux and Vichy for the capitulations to Japan in 1940 and 1941, and for the first time suggested a possible basis of co-operation between the FCNL and the Viet Minh. This was only definitively rejected six months later by an Indo-Chinese Communist Party tract signed by Ho Chi Minh and the party Secretary-general, Truong Chinh. Their joint declaration, entitled *Pour l'indépendance complète de l'Indochine!*, mocked the limited French resistance effort in Indo-China and called for outright Vietnamese independence. On several occasions during 1944–45 the Viet Minh reiterated its own proposals for a common front with the Free French in its journal *Le Drapeau de la libération* (Flag of Freedom). But the essential condition was a prior Gaullist commitment to Vietnamese independence.[78] In July 1944, Ho appeared to relent somewhat when he passed on a list of revised Viet Minh demands to Jean Sainteny, head of the newly created French military mission at Kunming (Yunnanfou), the provincial capital of Yunnan in South China. But while Ho's proposals suggested Viet Minh acceptance of limited Vietnamese autonomy pending a final independence settlement, this seems to have been a purely tactical retreat designed to ensure the continuation of Allied material aid.[79]

In the period between the FCNL statement of December 1943 and the Viet Minh declaration the following June, at the Brazzaville conference between 30 January and 8 February 1944 the Free French again proposed a new constitutional relationship between France and Indo-China. Though the Indo-China federation was to remain politically subordinate to Paris and economically dependent upon French investment and trade, individual territories were promised substantial autonomy.[80] But Brazzaville was as much an exercise in propaganda and publicity as a serious forum for discussion of colonial reform. The expert officials led by Henri Laurentie, chief of the Political Affairs Section within Pleven's Commissariat of Colonies, who formulated most of the detailed proposals put forward at Brazzaville, were far in advance of the commissioners, Governors and former politicians who still determined the permissible scope of colonial reconstruction. Plenary conference sessions of conservative colonial Governors, many steeped in military tradition, were hardly likely to produce a clear-cut scheme of long-term imperial renewal.[81]

Not surprisingly, de Gaulle and his senior colonial administrators were more eager to secure French military participation in the liberation of Indo-China than to discuss the minutiae of political reconstruction. Indeed, apart from the generic pledge of future reform, the Brazzaville conference scrupulously avoided discussion of Indo-China in much the same fashion as reference to Arab territories was either averted or subsequently erased from the conference reports. In practical terms, during 1944–45 FCNL and, then, French provisional government policy towards Indo-China presupposed co-operation with Britain. With British support, the French looked to resuscitate their colonial authority through participation in the final stages of the conflict with Japan. Meanwhile, within the provisional government's Ministry of Colonies, Henri Laurentie and Léon Pignon, appointed in July 1944 to head the Ministry's new Indo-China division, carefully refined the planning of constitutional reforms for Indo-China.[82] The logic was simple. Once independent French control was restored to Indo-China, rapid implementation of reform offered the best means to consolidate French authority and so restore the legitimacy of colonial rule in American eyes.

By 1944, SOE operatives estimated that Coloniale forces across Indo-China numbered some 54,000, of which almost 30,000 were Annamite troops. Most of these were deployed along the Tonkin-Chinese frontier, making it easier to envisage their eventual liaison with Allied forces in southern China.[83] By mid-1944 SOE's French Indo-China section had trained a number of Fighting French units in resistance activities ranging from sabotage and demolition to wireless communication. The Indo-China section was composed of French and Vietnamese volunteers based at Calcutta under the leadership of Lieutenant-Colonel Jean Boucher de Crèvecoeur. The section was to provide the bridge between the internal resistance in Indo-China and incoming Free French support.[84] On de Gaulle's instructions, on 5 July 1944 his personal envoy, Major François de Langlade, was parachuted into Indo-China in the first of several missions to establish contact with the Gaullist resistance. At the time, this was covertly led by Decoux's army commander, General Eugène Mordant. The general had originally been appointed by Vichy as successor to General Maurice Martin in late 1940. But by 1944 Mordant was as disillusioned with Decoux as he was with Vichy.[85] At their initial meeting, Mordant passed on valuable information to de Langlade, warning that his garrison could not sustain an open rebellion against the Japanese without the prompt arrival of outside support. This confirmed the earlier conclusions of the French Indo-China section attached to SOE. De Crèvecoeur noted that the settler population was fatigued and demoralised. French and Indo-Chinese troops were hostile to the Japanese but dreaded mounting operations against them without far better equipment and the certain promise of immediate external aid. All in all, the loyalty of French colonial garrisons might waver if they were ordered into a hopeless struggle against the Japanese occupying forces.[86] Though Mordant was clearly well apprised of the local situation, he was useless as an intermediary between de Gaulle and Decoux since his relationship with the latter was extremely poor. Luckily, by the time Decoux replaced Mordant with his army deputy, General Georges Aymé, on 23 July 1944, neither the generals concerned nor Decoux himself regarded Vichy's writ as of any real importance in Indo-China. Mordant continued to control the French colonial garrison, Aymé proved equally willing to serve de Gaulle, and Decoux was desperate to distance himself from his own Vichyite past.[87]

De Langlade's missions to the French commanders in Indo-China were directed by SOE's Force 136, to which de Crèvecoeur reported. From April 1944, Force 136 operated from the relocated SEAC headquarters at Kandy in Ceylon. Suspicious of Mountbatten's overall control of Gaullist penetration to Indo-China, the US China command demanded a right of veto upon any extension of de Langlade's original contacts with Mordant and his followers.[88] Meanwhile, Roosevelt remained strongly opposed to French use of US Lend-Lease equipment in Indo-China. The President regarded it as tantamount to American complicity in the reassertion of colonial mastery by a power whose past record in Indo-China he considered utterly despicable. On several occasions from May 1942, the President vilified French policies in

Indo-China. His comments were often imprecise and were apparently thrown out in casual, almost scatter-gun fashion. But it seemed clear that Roosevelt could not be talked round by the State Department, let alone by any Gaullist delegation.[89] After Operation Torch in November 1942, French equipment requirements were handled piecemeal through a Joint Rearmament Committee in Washington. Following the liberation of Paris in August 1944, the French Committee of National Defence was quick to formulate rearmament proposals on a more global basis. Though Eisenhower raised few objections to this, Roosevelt did not want US war material used to rebuild a discredited colonial regime. Another American worry was that arms supplies to the French in Indo-China might become the thin end of a long wedge, particularly if the British seized upon any US arms deliveries as a precedent applicable to their own Asian colonies.[90]

Britain's firmer support for French provisional government requests for military assistance and a more prominent role in the war against the Japanese compounded the tension over Indo-China between Washington and Paris during the winter of 1944–45. In September 1944 the French Committee of National Defence promised to commit two colonial divisions to the Far Eastern theatre. In addition, a substantial cruiser task force led by the battleship *Richelieu* (fresh from a refit in New York), was offered for service in the Pacific.[91] The British responded favourably, prepared, it seemed, to back a fellow colonial power in the teeth of US opposition, both to support Britain's own claim to primacy in South East Asia, and in order to undermine Roosevelt's 'naive' anti-colonialism.[92] Broadly hostile to French colonialism in South East Asia, Roosevelt's views on the post-war status of Indo-China remained infuriatingly vague. The State Department failed in several attempts to delineate a clearer policy between 1943 and 1945.[93] In this respect, British support for the French was unproductive. Though Roosevelt showed less interest in Indo-China during his last months in office, and his special envoy Harry Hopkins made a notably successful visit to the French provisional government in February 1945, the Washington administration still refused to treat with Gaullists in Indo-China.[94]

Still, the French provisional government could not afford to turn its back on the United States. It became apparent in Paris only after the American recapture of the Philippines and the launch of the assault on Iwo Jima in February 1945 that US amphibious operations against the coast of Indo-China were not, in fact, a major element in American strategic planning. Prior to this, de Gaulle dreaded the prospect of US marines marching triumphantly into Saigon or Hanoi without any French regular forces alongside them. An SOE report of 7 December

1944 summarised the position. 'The French are afraid of a landing by the Americans in which no French troops will participate, and while politically they would very much rather work with us they are perhaps prepared to cut their losses and switch over to the Americans if it is the only way to get in on the liberation of Indo-China.'[95]

In October 1944 General Albert Wedemeyer was appointed as new American Chief of Staff to Chiang Kai-shek's China command. Wedemeyer refused to recognise the informal 'Gentlemen's Agreement' concluded between Chiang and Admiral Mountbatten in October 1943 under which the theatre boundaries of the China command and Britain's South East Asia command had been agreed.[96] Until the last days of the Pacific war, Wedemeyer contested Britain's right to direct French covert infiltration and eventual operations in central and southern Indo-China. Furthermore, the general was profoundly hostile to the Gaullist resistance inside Indo-China which he judged both corrupt and ineffective.[97]

In late January 1945, the British and French Joint Staff Missions in Washington remained pessimistic of any change in US policy: 'In our view, which is borne out by discussions on the planning level, the Americans will not associate themselves with the French resistance movement in Indo-China and are therefore averse to putting on record that S[upreme] A[llied] C[ommand] S[outh] E[ast] A[sia] is supporting the French or will continue to do so. In addition they would not wish it mentioned that the 14th United States Air Force [based at Kunming] utilises intelligence supplied by the French.'[98] As Roosevelt's health deteriorated, so America's Indo-China policy remained in stasis for much of early 1945. In late March, the US service chiefs advised their British counterparts not to expect any decisive intervention from Washington for the time being. Despite the high quality of information from its own OSS operatives throughout Indo-China, the US government failed to appreciate that, while the Viet Minh loathed the French, it feared Chinese expansionism still more. Ho Chi Minh was himself active in South China both at the beginning of the war and in early 1945. He sought both Chinese and, later, OSS support for Vietnamese resistance. But he had few illusions about Chinese irredentism.[99] Though, on occasion, the Viet Minh had been prepared to solicit aid from the Chinese, the prospects for peaceful coexistence with Nationalist China were not good. Backing Chiang Kai-shek to offset French or British regional dominance was a policy doomed to failure.

Liberation frustrated: the Japanese coup *and the end of the war*

During 1944 the Japanese Thirty-eighth Army command began a major reinforcement of Indo-China in readiness for a full assumption of power.[100] This acquired greater urgency once American forces attacked Luzon in the Philippines in January 1945. In conjunction with this, on 12 January Admiral William F. Halsey launched a brief naval raid along the Indo-China coast between Cam Ranh Bay and Qui Nhon, further to the north, in order to put the Japanese off the scent of Admiral Nimitz's advance upon Iwo Jima and Okinawa.[101] Japan's main Southern Region military command had transferred from Saigon to Singapore in May 1942. From that point until 1944, the Japanese garrison in Indo-China remained broadly static. The Thirty-eighth Army which occupied Indo-China was divided into two subdivisional commands – the 82nd Infantry Division, headquartered in Saigon, and the remainder of the army's 21st Division, based in and around Hanoi. In March 1944 a further mixed brigade was posted to the Tourane district in Cochin China and, in December, a further reserve brigade was created in anticipation of possible US landings along the coast of Annam. As the American liberation of the Philippines proceeded in early 1945, Japan's army chiefs anticipated eventual US assaults upon central China, Hainan and the China–Tonkin frontier or the island of Okinawa to the north. It was the Thirty-eighth Army's task to keep any US invasion force pinned down in northern Indo-China, so impeding a northward American advance towards Japan itself. To meet its expanded responsibilities, in February 1945 the Thirty-eighth Army was reinforced with additional divisions from Japan's South China command. Further troops were scheduled to return to Indo-China from Burma over the spring. These short-term strategic considerations governed Japan's decision to oust Decoux's regime. On 9 March 1945 a ruthless military take-over began. Though the Japanese military had contemplated a take-over from September 1944, the Supreme War Council only approved the so-called Meigo Sakusen (Operation Bright Moon) on 26 February 1945. Knowledge of the growing strength of the Gaullist resistance in Indo-China played, at best, a marginal role.[102]

Hanoi ambassador Matsumoto Shunichi conveyed three principal demands to Decoux. While the threat of US landings persisted, French forces in Indo-China were to be placed under Japan's sole command. The entire communications network, from railways and shipping to telegraph transmissions, was to serve the Japanese war effort. Finally, Decoux was to order the fullest possible collaboration with the Japanese authorities, who reserved the right to add to their demands on an *ad hoc* basis. In simple terms, this amounted to a complete transfer of power.[103] Decoux's refusal to comply ignited a hopeless, if heroic, military resistance to the Thirty-eighth Army in Hué, Hanoi and along the northern Tonkin frontier over the subsequent month. Warned of 'impending danger' on 8 March, General Gabriel Sabattier, land forces commander in Tonkin, placed his forces on alert. This had little effect. Many garrisons across Indo-China were almost immediately annihilated. One large force, the Saigon Mobile Group, was captured while trying to find a viable route for retreat.[104]

Only in the far north did Sabattier manage to evade the Japanese with some 6,000, mainly colonial, troops. De Gaulle instructed Sabattier to defend a pocket of territory in Tonkin which could then be used as the base for the subsequent reconquest of Indo-China. In fact, Sabattier's forces were forced to flee through the mountainous interior of Tonkin towards the frontier with Yunnan province, leaving the bulk of their equipment behind them. Though airdrops were attempted, SOE's Force 136 was unable to lend substantial material assistance to the retreating French troops.[105] Wedemeyer's Chungking command refused, in turn, to lend any significant support, although the remnants of General Sabattier's Tonkin division did find sanctuary in Yunnan, having evaded capture by the Japanese in late March. US aircraft then helped airlift elements of Sabattier's force to Kunming, where they came under the protection of French military mission 5, directed by Jean Sainteny, a capable figure who later served as the chief French representative in talks with the Viet Minh during 1945–46. In spite of Sainteny's energetic lobbying, for several months Sabattier's forces were too depleted and ill equipped to re-enter Indo-China.[106] Only the Viet Minh continued sporadic harassment of 21st Division units until Japan's final surrender in August.[107]

With Decoux and his senior administrators interned and French military resistance diffuse and crumbling, there were few immediate obstacles to the Japanese-sponsored declarations of independence in Vietnam, Cambodia and Laos between 11 March and 11 April. Japanese advisers were duly installed with the new puppet regimes, though only in Cochin China and the cities of Hanoi, Tourane and Haiphong did the Japanese briefly retain direct control.[108] In Hué, Emperor Bao Dai remained on the throne of a new Vietnamese state with a Cabinet directed by Tran Trong Kim and a Japanese special adviser, Yokoyama Masayuki, attached to the emperor's government. From late 1943, Tran Trong Kim, a former educational specialist in the Annamite administration, had been in exile under Japanese protection. Though the Japanese encouraged him to take office in order to facilitate the political transition from French rule to a quasi-autonomous Vietnamese state, the six-month life of Tran Trong Kim's government was dominated by bitter factionalism and an appalling famine which left some half a million Vietnamese dead.[109] Ironically, in May 1945 Bao Dai issued an imperial decree revoking the system of government purchase and distribution of rice that Decoux had approved two years earlier. But while the Annam government was certainly genuine in its efforts to increase rice supplies to the general population, the results were manifestly inadequate.[110]

In the renamed Cambodian state of Kampuchea, the Japanese again supported a monarchist elite loyal to Prince Norodom Sihanouk. Like Bao Dai's regime, Prince Sihanouk's government began by removing overt symbols of French dominion such as the compulsory use of romanised script and the employment of the Gregorian as opposed to the Buddhist calendar. Though not faced with the same famine conditions, Cambodia's royal regime was also overthrown in August 1945.[111] None the less, Prince Sihanouk's brief rule in 1945 consolidated his status among Cambodia's narrow elite, whose previous divisions both the Japanese and the French colonial authorities exploited during 1941–45.[112] In Laos, too, it fell to the monarchy – in the person of King Sisavang Vong – to declare independence. But, as in Kampuchea, the appearance of fundamental political reform was deceptive. By the second week of April, a Japanese occupation force controlled both Luang Prabang and the Lao royal capital of Vientiane, although King Sisavong was left in nominal charge.[113] Behind the royalist elites of Indo-China, the decisive figure remained Lieutenant-general Tsuchihashi, commander of the Thirty-eighth Army and new Governor-general of Indo-China.[114] Contrary to the wishes of Ambassador Matsumoto, General Tsuchihashi wanted to install Japanese military governors across Annam. He also suggested that more junior officers should be appointed to mayoral posts in all major towns. It was eventually agreed that Japanese civilian diplomats would take over these local administrative posts in Annam.[115]

As the US Navy took complete control of the South China Sea, so land communications between China and South East Asia grew in importance to the Japanese. Indo-China was again the principal bridge between southern China and the Malaya front. To the British Chiefs of Staff this made it imperative to secure Roosevelt's acquiescence in the dispatch of the *Corps Léger d'Intervention* to Indo-China as part of wider SEAC operations against the Japanese.[116] But Wedemeyer's opposition to SEAC control over the CLI found echoes in Washington, where the Combined Chiefs of Staff also objected to the dispatch of the CLI from Algiers to join General Blaizot at SEAC headquarters in Kandy.[117] After Yalta, Churchill was more willing to take issue with such obstructionism, having been persuaded by the War Office Directorate of Military Operations that CLI raids in Indo-China could inflict sufficient damage upon Japan's extended lines of overland supply to make a strategic impact upon the Malaya campaign. As the official appointee of the French provisional government, only Blaizot commanded sufficient authority to co-ordinate this diverse internal French resistance effectively.[118]

In addition to pressing London for a Far Eastern military deployment, the French provisional government also reiterated its commitment to post-war colonial reform in anticipation of the imminent change of leadership in Washington. Following a heart-felt broadcast by de Gaulle on 14 March in which the general promised to reverse the effects of the recent Japanese *coup*, ten days later Pleven's successor as Commissioner of Colonies, Paul Giacobbi, issued a landmark declaration on Indo-China. Indo-China's population would become eligible for a new form of imperial French citizenship, further political and electoral rights were to be assured through the operation of an Indo-Chinese Council of State, and unprecedented employment opportunities were promised under a new 'French Union'. The precise details of the planned French Union were still being debated by a commission of the French Constituent Assembly headed by Gaston Monnerville. But Giacobbi's specific mention of the project nevertheless implied that the French government intended to establish a more liberal imperial system as part of the post-war constitutional reconstruction of France. As proof of its good faith, the Ministry of Colonies appointed a commission of technical experts to the French military mission at Kunming to calculate Indo-China's immediate needs upon liberation.[119] Giacobbi sought to convince Indo-China's traditional elites that, despite the recent Japanese take-over, the French would return in a new guise as both liberators and reformers. This was an indirect challenge to the Viet Minh. Giacobbi's reference to French respect for regional autonomy disregarded nationalist plans for the unification of the three Ky (provinces) of Tonkin, Annam and Cochin China into a Vietnamese state. By the same token, his emphasis upon autonomous rights suggested that France would support the monarchies of Laos and Cambodia without demanding the same blind obedience expected by the Japanese.

As a conciliatory gesture, the 24 March declaration backfired. Far from undermining the appeal of Vietnamese nationalism, the proposed reforms suggested a return to the divide-and-rule policies of the Third Republic. Throughout the inter-war period, French authority in Indo-China had rested upon the continued political separation of the Vietnamese Ky and the Laos and Cambodia protectorates.[120] Certainly, the

French proclamation bore little relation to events on the ground in Indo-China, its release having been delayed by disagreement between the Foreign and Colonial Ministries over its terms. Though under Japan's thumb, Annam, Laos and Kampuchea were already nominally independent. So the French were already face-to-face with the fundamental contradiction of the French Union. As Martin Shipway has pointed out, it was quite impossible to trade liberal colonial reforms for the achievement of closer imperial unity in Indo-China.[121] Giacobbi's statement, issued from the comfort of liberated Paris to a colonial population still adjusting to Japanese dominion, was at once patronising and anachronistic.

While the provisional government publicised its commitment to reform, behind the scenes French pressure for the dispatch of the CLI to Mountbatten's command intensified. De Gaulle attached great importance to the information gathered in Indo-China by his envoy, François de Langlade. With SOE support, de Langlade completed a further crucial mission to General Mordant and Admiral Decoux in November 1944. Following a meeting with de Langlade on 19 November, Decoux agreed to conceal resistance preparations among the French garrison by continuing his outward co-operation with Japan. There seems little doubt that, had this not taken place, the Japanese occupation would have been ordered months earlier than March 1945, stifling the emergent Gaullist resistance movement among French units in the process.[122] Unfortunately for the French, the promising work of de Crèvecoeur's resistance networks, and the contacts built up with the French garrison forces over the winter of 1944–45, counted for precious little so long as there remained no immediate prospect of calling the CLI forward from Algiers. Resistance groups were established throughout Indo-China by March 1945. But without immediate external reinforcement they were bound to collapse or be driven underground.[123] Meanwhile, the American staff at Wedemeyer's China command clearly suspected that the close liaison between the French and British covert operations personnel – de Crèvecoeur's Service d'Action and SOE's Force 136 – concealed a host of secret politico-military arrangements deliberately kept from Wedemeyer and Chiang Kai-shek.[124]

As a whole, SOE's French Indo-China secton achieved only limited results in spite of the high quality of its personnel. The provisional government hoped to replicate in Indo-China de Gaulle's successful imposition of authority over the metropolitan resistance Forces Françaises de l'Intérieur. Control of a widely distributed resistance network inside Indo-China was bound to increase French political leverage with the Allies. In fact, this strategy disintegrated because, in this case, neither Britain nor the United States would lend adequate backing at a sufficiently early stage to make any real impact upon the internal politics of Indo-China. Moreover, the covert French resistance in Indo-China was always an essentially tangential phenomenon – closely linked with the British, but remote from the majority of Indo-China's population. There was never any likelihood that French resisters in Indo-China could unleash a popular uprising against the Japanese, nor was this ever seriously entertained.[125]

During the last three months of the Pacific war, French preparations for a resumption of authority in Indo-China rested upon four pillars above all. Firstly, the French still hoped that British forces under Mountbatten's command would play the leading role in the liberation of the colony and in the occupation administration bound to be established once the war ended. The former was increasingly unlikely, and plans for the latter were taken in hand only immediately prior to the Potsdam conference in July 1945. Secondly, de Gaulle's administration hoped US President Harry Truman would abandon the deliberate obfuscation of his predecessor. Truman was expected to clarify US acceptance of French authority in Saigon and Hanoi. The new President certainly followed State Department recommendations more closely and was less concerned about French colonialism than Roosevelt had been. But, during May and June 1945, Truman was antagonised by French intransigence over the Levant. He was also infuriated by de Gaulle's provocative instructions to General de Lattre de Tassigny's troops deployed in Stuttgart and in the francophone region of the Val d'Aosta in northern Italy.[126] As a result, the US administration saw little reason to accommodate de Gaulle. Critically, the French were excluded from the Potsdam conference, at which arrangements were made both for the temporary partition of Indo-China and for the joint Anglo-Chinese occupation of the region in order to disarm and evacuate the remaining Japanese forces.

A third element in French plans was the vital role assigned to Jean Sainteny's military mission in Kunming. From April 1945, Sainteny reported direct to the General Directorate of Planning and Research (*Direction Générale des Etudes et Recherches*), a covert intelligence organisation poorly controlled by the provisional government. An experienced resister, it fell to Sainteny to reorganise the French troops dispersed from Tonkin by the Japanese. More important, Sainteny also became the major point of contact between the Viet Minh executive in Tonkin and the French provisional government.[127] Though Sainteny was a capable intermediary, he had no mandate from Paris to pursue detailed contacts with Ho Chi Minh. More worrying, Sainteny was convinced by July 1945 that the French government did not appreciate the extent of Viet Minh power.[128] This brings us to the fourth aspect of French thinking on Indo-China over the summer of 1945. It was perhaps the most problematic. For the Paris government had to decide whether to trust in the military capacity of an expanded French Far Eastern expeditionary force being readied for August departure under General Leclerc, or to capitalise upon the Viet Minh's evident willingness to negotiate some form of compromise *modus vivendi*. This seemed likely to include a lengthy – perhaps even ten-year – period of French control prior to full Vietnamese independence. It was the gradual erosion of this policy of negotiation – the so-called *politique des accords* – over the subsequent year that formed that bridge between the end of the Pacific war and the beginning of the Indo-China conflict in December 1946.

It is hard to resist the conclusion that Gaullist strategic planning for Indo-China was improvised and often confused. Constrained by the obvious reluctance of the US government to support French authority in Indo-China, the Free French banked upon a British-led invasion of southern Indo-China in which the French could play a prominent role. This was stymied by three intractable problems which coalesced during the winter of 1944. Firstly, though the Foreign Office, the British Chiefs of Staff and Mountbatten's staff at SEAC agreed that the French CLI could prove pivotal to British plans to liberate Indo-China, Churchill was not prepared to press the British case until after the Yalta conference in February 1945. By that time it was too late to introduce substantial French forces to Indo-China before the Japanese acted to consolidate their own control. Secondly, the jurisdictional conflict between Mountbatten at SEAC and Chiang Kai-shek and his American chaperones in Chungking intensified after Wedemeyer's arrival in October 1944. Thereafter, several opportunities for constructive Anglo-American co-operation in Indo-China were missed. Both the resistance networks, often left waiting in vain for Allied air drops, and the French garrison troops forced into desperate retreat from Tonkin, paid a heavy price for this during March and April 1945. Finally, the mistaken belief that the Allies might provide material aid sufficient to enable the French to resume military and political control nourished the fatal complacency towards Vietnamese nationalism which characterised French governmental policy at the end of the Second World War. The work of Free French representatives with SEAC, and of their envoys and operatives inside Indo-China, was undone by the Japanese *coup*. Similarly, the abrupt nature of Japan's final defeat in August, which left large numbers of troops still in place in Indo-China, put the future of French authority in Hanoi in further doubt. Ultimately, the disastrous Allied partition of Indo-China at Potsdam in August 1945 set a match to the powder keg of frustrated Vietnamese aspirations and French impatience to resume unfettered colonial power.

Notes

1 Decoux, *A la Barre de l'Indochine*, p. 353.
2 PRO, FO 892/6, tel. 211, OAG, Straits Settlements, to FO, 1 August 1940; tel. 51, Saigon consulate to C-in-C, China, 2 August 1940.
3 PRO, FO 892/6, tel. 572, FO to Sir Walford Selby, Lisbon, 25 August 1940.
4 Lamant, 'La révolution nationale dans l'Indochine', 21–41.
5 John E. Dreifort, *Myopic Grandeur. The Ambivalence of French Foreign Policy toward the Far East, 1919–1945* (Kent, Oh., Kent State University Press, 1991), pp. 206–8. For a rather apologetic version of the Foreign Ministry's attitude to talks, see Charles-Roux, *Cinq Mois tragiques*, chapter 8.
6 Joseph C. Grew, *Ten Years in Japan* (London, Hammond, 1944), pp. 286–7.
7 Dreifort, *Myopic Grandeur*, pp. 208–9.
8 Charles-Roux, *Cinq Mois tragiques*, pp. 257–8.
9 SHAT, Fonds Privées, 1K401/C1, no. 171, 'Rapport du Lieutenant Pianelli', 5 May 1944.
10 Dreifort, *Myopic Grandeur*, pp. 209–12.
11 PRO, FO 892/30, FO Far Eastern Department, 'Memorandum for CFR', 8 September 1940.
12 Dreifort, *Myopic Grandeur*, pp. 210–11.
13 Hata Ikuhiko, 'The army's move into northern Indochina', in Morley, *The Fateful Choice*, pp. 193–203; George Paloczi-Horvath, 'Thailand's war with Vichy France', *History Today*, 45: 3 (1995), 36.
14 Decoux, *A la Barre de l'Indochine*, pp. 103–22.
15 See Sachiko Murakami, 'Indochina: unplanned incursion', in Hilary Conroy and Harry Wray (eds), *Pearl Harbor Reexamined. Prologue to the Pacific War* (Honolulu, University of Hawaii Press, 1990), pp. 141–8.
16 MAE, Série Asie-Océanie, 1944–55, vol. 30 Indochine, memo. 'Négociations franco-américaines pour la fourniture à l'Indochine d'avions et d'armes, octobre 1940–janvier 1941'; Série E, Vichy-Asie, vol. 261 Indochine, no. 8062, Charles Rochat to Colonies, direction politique, 7 November 1940.
17 Stein Tonnesson, *The Vietnamese Revolution of 1945. Roosevelt, Ho Chi Minh and de Gaulle in a World at War* (London, Sage, 1991), p. 37; Dreifort, *Myopic Grandeur*, pp. 212–13.
18 MAE, Vichy-Asie, vol. 261, copy tel., Decoux to Platon, 19 November 1940.
19 MAE, Vichy-Asie, vol. 261, tel. 642, Leahy to Darlan, 29 May 1941; tel. 380, Decoux to Platon, 3 July 1941.
20 The Viet Nam Phuc Quoc Dong Minh was strongly nationalist in sentiment but also drew upon Cuong De's long association with Japan, which dated to 1906; see Tonnesson, *Vietnamese Revolution*, pp. 37, 82, 104–5; Kiyoko Kurusu Nitz, 'Independence without nationalists? The Japanese and Vietnamese nationalism during the Japanese period, 1940–45', *Journal of Southeast Asian Studies*, 15: 1 (1984), 110.
21 Nitz, 'Independence without nationalists?', 112–13.
22 PRO, WO 208/661, Ministry of Information, Far Eastern Bureau, 'Analytic outline of political movements in Indochina', 25 April 1944; regarding French-educated Vietnamese Trotskyites, see R. B. Smith, 'The Vietnamese elite of French Cochinchina, 1943', *Modern Asian Studies*, 6: 4 (1972), 476–7.
23 MAE, Vichy-Asie, vol. 255, Decoux to Colonies, Vichy, 23 October 1940.
24 William J. Duiker, *The Communist Road to Power in Vietnam*, 2nd ed., (Boulder, Colo., Westview Press, 1996), pp. 67–8.
25 MAE, Vichy-Asie, vol. 255, no. 3343, Decoux to Platon, 29 November 1940.
26 PRO, WO 208/661, MOI, Far Eastern Bureau, 'Analytic outline of political move-

ments in Indochina', 25 April 1944; MAE, Vichy-Asie, vol. 255, no. 3833, Decoux to Colonies, 26 December 1940.

27 MAE, Vichy-Asie, vol. 255, no. 3597, Decoux to Colonies, 13 December 1940; Tran My-Van, 'Japan and Vietnam's Caodaists: a wartime relationship (1939–1945)', *Journal of Southeast Asian Studies*, 27: 1 (1996), 183–4.

28 MAE, Vichy-Asie, vol. 255, no. 161, Decoux to Colonies, 12 January 1941; no. 223, Decoux to Colonies, 17 January 1941.

29 MAE, Vichy-Asie, vol. 255, no. 541, Decoux to Colonies, 14 February 1941.

30 PRO, SOE Far East files, HS 1/86, Translation of FIC operational report, by Capitaine Borg, 'Opérations en nord Tonkin', 4 May 1944.

31 SHAT, 1K401/C1, memo. for Lieutenant-Colonel de Crèvecoeur, 'Opérations du nord Tonkin', 7 June 1944.

32 Duiker, *Communist Road to Power*, pp. 67–73.

33 SHM, TTA 2/Cabinet Militaire, Amirauté française, 'Réunion interministerielle', 5 October 1940.

34 SHM, TTA 102/EMM-3, FMF-3, no. 3881, 'Note sur l'activité de la Marine au cours de l'année 1941', 26 November 1941.

35 SHAT, 1K401/C1, Colonel Jacomey to Tonkin divisional command, 19 May 1941; General Boisboissel to Inspector of Colonial Troops, Royat, 5 January 1942.

36 PRO, FO 892/30, Sir Robert Craigie, Tokyo, to FO, 12 March 1941; Richard J. Aldrich, *The Key to the South. Britain, the United States and Thailand during the Approach of the Pacific War, 1929–1942* (Oxford, Oxford University Press, 1993), pp. 288–93. The Japanese did limit Thai demands for territory, and insisted on payment of a Thai war indemnity. But Decoux's position was certainly weakened.

37 MAE, Vichy-Asie, vol. 255, no. 1500, Platon to Decoux, 1 April 1941.

38 MAE, Vichy-Asie, vol. 255, no. 2070, Platon to Decoux, 2 April 1941.

39 SHAT, 1P118/D1, Secrétariat d'Etat aux Colonies, EMA-2, Bulletin mensuel de renseignements no. 4, 25 March 1941.

40 De Gaulle, *L'Appel*, p. 145; Martin Thomas, 'Free France, the British government and the future of French Indo-China, 1940–45', *Journal of Southeast Asian Studies*, 28: 1 (1997), 141–4.

41 MAE, CNF Londres, vol. 70 Indochine, Affaires extérieures, 'Memo. relatif à la situation en Indochine', 20 January 1941.

42 MAE, CNF Londres, vol. 70, Affaires extérieures, 'Memo. relatif à l'Extrême Orient', 24 February 1941.

43 PRO, FO 371/27841, F3330/2957/61, Sir G. Northcote, Hong Kong, to Far Eastern Department, 21 April 1941.

44 SHAT, 1K401/C5, memo. by Capitaine Caille, 'Généralités: attitude britannique vers l'Indochine', 1 June 1941.

45 MAE, CNF Londres, vol. 70, Affaires extérieures, 'Memo. relatif à l'Extrême Orient', 24 February 1941.

46 MAE, CNF Londres, vol. 70, Deuxième Bureau intercept, Direction Politique, Vichy, to Weygand, 14 August 1941. Darlan also directed the Ministry of the Interior between late February and July 1941.

47 Grew, *My Ten Years in Japan*, p. 351.

48 Tonnesson, *Vietnamese Revolution*, pp. 38–9.

49 Ibid., p. 156.

50 MAE, Vichy-Asie, vol. 255, Platon to Gongal, Hanoi, 24 July 1941; CNF Londres, vol. 70, Lieutenant-Colonel Tutenges, Bulletin de renseignements, 28 August 1942.

51 SHM TTA 102/EMM, FMF-3, 'Liaisons avec nos colonies', 10 September 1941.

52 SHM, TTA 102/EMM-3, no. 1110, FMF/SECA, 'Note intérieure', 8 May 1942.

53 MAE, Vichy-Asie, vol. 255, Decoux to Colonies, 2 September 1941.

54 MAE, CNF Londres, vol. 70, Affaires étrangères, Interrogation report 80, 16 February 1942.

55 Cited by Tonnesson, *Vietnamese Revolution*, pp. 39, 128; regarding Kempeitei – Caodaist collaboration, see My-Van, 'Japan and Vietnam's Caodaists', 184–90.

56 MAE, Vichy-Asie, vol. 255, no. 6420, Decoux to Colonies, 27 October 1941.

57 SHAT, 1P118/D1, EM-Col, Bulletin de renseignements 9, 10 November 1941; R. B. Smith, 'The Japanese period in Indochina and the coup of 9 March 1945', Journal of Southeast Asian Studies, 9: 2 (1978), 270–6.
58 Nitz, 'Independence without nationalists?', 115–16, 124–5; Pierre Brocheux, 'La question de l'indépendance dans l'opinion viêtnamienne de 1939 à 1945', in Ageron, Chemins, pp. 202–3.
59 My-Van, 'Japan and Vietnam's Caodaists', 185–8.
60 Smith, 'The Japanese period in Indochina', 274.
61 Quote from Grégoire Madjarian, *La Question coloniale et la politique du Parti communiste français, 1944–1947* (Paris, Maspero, 1977), pp. 118–19.
62 PRO, FO 371/31771, F614/582/61, W. Mack to Far Eastern Department, 17 January 1942.
63 PRO, FO 371/31771, F1945/582/61, FO to Clarke Kerr, 26 February 1942; HS 1/94, SOE memo., 'SOE operations – French Indo-China, December 1941–November 1944'.
64 MAE, CNF Londres, vol. 73, AFN 751, Chungking to France Libre, 16 November 1942; Bulletin de renseignements 64, 16 December 1942.
65 Smith, 'The Japanese period in Indochina', 269.
66 MAE, CNF Londres, vol. 70, Commissariat National à l'Information, 'Propagande sur l'Indochine', 8 August 1942.
67 MAE, CNF Londres, vol. 73, Chungking, Bulletin de renseignements, 36, 2 January 1943; MAE, CNF Londres, vol. 73, CNF Bureau d'Indochine, 2 April 1943.
68 MAE, Vichy-Asie, vol. 255, Affaires étrangères, Direction Politique Asie, Note, 24 November 1943. Bléhaut succeeded the former Governor-General of Indo-China, Jules Brévié, as Minister of Colonies on 26 March 1943.
69 SHAT, 2P12/D1, EM-Col., 'Note au sujet de l'organisation coloniale terrestre future', 8 October 1943.
70 MAE, Vichy-Asie, vol. 255, no. 975, Bléhaut to Laval, 4 July 1944.
71 PRO, FO 371/35921, F4870/1422/61, Minute by William Strang, 8 September 1943; PM/43/382, Cadogan to Churchill, 3 November 1943.
72 PRO, PREM 3/178/2, Churchill to Eden, 21 December 1943; Dreifort, *Myopic Grandeur*, pp. 225–6.
73 Christopher Thorne, 'The Indochina issue between Britain and the United States, 1942–1945', *Pacific Historical Review*, 45 (1976), 75–6. This article also appears as chapter 4 in C. Thorne, *Border Crossings. Studies in International History* (Oxford, Blackwell, 1988).
74 PRO, HS 1/94, SOE memo., 'SOE Operations – French Indo-China, December 1941–November 1944'.
75 PRO, FO 371/35921, F4881/1422/961, Minute by Ashley Clarke, 3 October 1943.
76 For details of the CLI see Claude Hesse d'Alzon, *La Présence militaire française en Indochine 1940–1945* (Paris, Vincennes, 1985), p. 148.
77 PRO, FO 371/35930, F6450/4023/61, Text of FCNL broadcast, 8 December 1943; Martin Shipway, *The Road to War. France and Vietnam, 1944–1947* (Oxford, Berghahn, 1996), p. 118.
78 Madjarian, *La Question coloniale*, pp. 121–3; Pierre Brocheux, 'La question de l'indépendance dans l'opinion viêtnamienne de 1939 à 1945', in Ageron, *Chemins*, pp. 203–4.
79 Duiker, *Communist Road to Power*, p. 85.
80 Andrew Shennan, *Rethinking France. Plans for Renewal, 1940–1946* (Oxford, Oxford University Press, 1989), pp. 146–8.
81 *Ibid.*, pp. 145–51; Shipway, 'The Brazzaville Conference', pp. 73–77.
82 Shipway, *Road to War*, p. 30, 120–1.
83 PRO, HS 1/94, SOE memo., 'SOE operations – French Indo-China, December 1941–November 1944'.
84 SHAT, 1K401/dossier Legrand, 'Détail de l'organisation de la section de sabotage du SA', December 1944; PRO, HS 1/321, Lieutenant-Colonel de Crèvecoeur, 'Memo. on the setting up of a plan of action and intelligence in Indo-China', 24 June 1945.

85 Dreifort, *Myopic Grandeur*, pp. 237–8; Tonnesson, *Vietnamese Revolution*, pp. 49–51.
86 SHAT, 1K401/C1, Memo. by de Crèvecoeur, 1 May 1944.
87 Tonnesson, *Vietnamese Revolution*, p. 50.
88 PRO, HS 1/106, Cipher tel, New Delhi, to AD, 5 August 1944; Charles Cruikshank, *SOE in the Far East* (Oxford, Oxford University Press, 1983), pp. 126–7. SEAC headquarters moved to Kandy in April 1944.
89 Thorne, *Border Crossings*, pp. 90–1.
90 PRO, WO 193/195, ZO 225, JSM, Washington, to War Cabinet, 19 September 1944; Maguire, *Anglo-American Relations*, pp. 149–51.
91 PRO, WO 193/195, SCAF 106, SHAEF HQ to CCOS, 16 October 1944; WO note, 'Participation of French naval forces in the war in the Pacific', 22 November 1944. The proposed task force consisted of the *Richelieu*, three heavy cruisers and five light cruisers with naval air support.
92 Maguire, *Anglo-American Policy*, pp. 151–2.
93 John J. Sbrega, '"First catch your hare": Anglo-American perspectives on Indochina during the Second World War', *Journal of Southeast Asian Studies*, 14: 1 (1983), 69, 73–4.
94 Thorne, *Border Crossings*, pp. 100–1; Irwin W. Wall, 'Harry S. Truman and Charles de Gaulle', in Robert O. Paxton and Nicholas Wahl (eds), *De Gaulle and the United States. A Centennial Reappraisal* (Oxford, Berg, 1994), p. 123.
95 PRO, HS 1/106, BB8 to AD4, 17 December 1944.
96 PRO, WO 203/5210, Report by Lieutenant-Colonel Carver, n.d., 1945; Thorne, *Border Crossings*, pp. 89–90.
97 PRO, CAB 122/1177, COS(45)143(O), FO memo., 'French Indo-China', 2 March 1945; FMW 16, Field Marshal Wilson, Washington, to COS, 10 March 1945.
98 PRO, WO 193/195, JSM 534, JSM Washington to AMSSO, 23 January 1945.
99 PRO, CAB 122/1177, FMW 33, Field Marshal Wilson to General Ismay, 27 March 1945; Duiker, *Communist Road to Power*, pp. 84–5.
100 Nitz, 'Japanese military policy towards French Indochina', 334–8.
101 Tonnesson, *Vietnamese Revolution*, pp. 190–3. In the process Halsey's ships destroyed the cruiser *Lamotte Piquet* at Cam Ranh Bay.
102 PRO, WO 208/3042, War Office Military Intelligence, MO2, 'Summary of changes occur[r]ed to the Japanese forces in Indochina (38th Army)', n.d., June 1945; Tonnesson, *Vietnamese Revolution*, pp. 220–2.
103 PRO, WO 208/3042, MO2, 'Summary of changes occur[r]ed to the Japanese forces in Indochina (38th Army)', n.d., June 1945.
104 Smith, 'The Japanese period in Indochina', 281–2; PRO, WO 203/5561A, HQ SACSEA intelligence collation file, 'French Indo-China in 1945', 3 September 1945.
105 MAE, Série Asie-Océanie, vol. 31, EMGDN, de Gaulle to Sabattier, 7 April 1945; PRO, WO 208/665, no. 7781, MI2 intelligence report, 'FIC – French colonial troops', 10 July 1945; PRO, HS 1/86, Force 136 memo., 'Clandestine operations in French Indo-China', 4 October 1945.
106 Smith, 'The Japanese period', p. 281; Jean Sainteny, *Histoire d'une paix manquée. Indochine, 1945–1947* (Paris, Fayard, 1967), pp. 25, 34–8.
107 Tonnesson, *Vietnamese Revolution*, pp. 349–51; Nitz, 'Independence without nationalists?', 124.
108 Nitz, 'Independence without nationalists?', 120.
109 Tonnesson, *Vietnamese Revolution*, pp. 281–4; Smith, 'The Japanese period in Indochina', 275, 288–9. Tran Trong Kim had been director of a boys' school in Hanoi until his retirement from administrative service in 1943.
110 Smith, 'The Japanese period in Indochina', 290–1.
111 David P. Chandler, 'The kingdom of Kampuchea, March–October 1945: Japanese-sponsored independence in Cambodia in World War II', *Journal of Southeast Asian Studies*, 17: 1 (1986), 80–2.
112 Pierre L. Lamant, 'Le Cambodge et la décolonisation de l'Indochine: les caractères particuliers du nationalisme Khmer de 1936 à 1945', in Ageron, *Chemins*, pp.

189–99.

113 Smith, 'The Japanese period in Indochina', 285.

114 The Vietnamese government even relied upon the Thirty-eighth Army's radio and telegraph service to announce its existence, see Nitz, 'Independence without nationalists?', 121.

115 Smith, 'The Japanese period in Indochina', 283–4.

116 PRO, WO 193/195, Note on COS(45)143(O), 5 March 1945.

117 PRO, CAB 122/1177, War Cabinet note to A. T. Cornwall-Jones, 26 February 1945.

118 PRO, WO 193/195, Directorate of Plans note on JIC(45)339, 18 March 1945; PRO, WO 203/5561/A, Esler Dening to Eden, n.d., January 1945.

119 Shennan, *Rethinking France*, pp. 151–3; MAE, Série Asie-Océanie, vol. 30, no. 3316, Laurentie note for President of Study Commission for Indo-China, 16 March 1945. Giacobbi's declaration is reproduced in full in Gilbert Bodinier (ed.), *La Guerre d'Indochine, 1945–1954, I: Le Retour de la France en Indochine 1945–1946* (Paris, Vincennes, 1987), pp. 141–3.

120 D. Bruce Marshall, *The French Colonial Myth and Constitution-making in the Fourth Republic* (New Haven, Conn., Yale University Press, 1973), pp. 134–7.

121 Martin Shipway, 'Creating an emergency: metropolitan constraints on French colonial policy and its breakdown in Indo-China, 1945–47', *Journal of Imperial and Commonwealth History*, 21: 1 (1993), 3–8.

122 PRO, HS 1/86, de Crèvecoeur note on de Langlade missions, 6 September 1945; Smith, 'The Japanese period in Indochina', 277.

123 SHAT, 1K401/C1, de Crèvecoeur memo., 'Plan d'opérations du SR pour mai et juin', 21 April 1945; Cruikshank, *SOE in the Far East*, p. 125.

124 PRO, WO 203/5210, CHBX 37689, Wedemeyer to Wheeler, 19 May 1945.

125 SHAT, 1K401/C1, Force 136 memo., 20 June 1944.

126 Wall, 'Harry S. Truman and Charles de Gaulle', pp. 119–23; John W. Young, *France, the Cold War and the Western Alliance* (Leicester, Leicester University Press, 1990), pp. 50–7.

127 Philippe Devillers, *Histoire du Viet-Nam de 1940 à 1952* (Paris, Editions du Seuil, 1952), pp. 133–5.

128 Jean-Marie d'Hoop, 'Du coup de force japonais au départ du Général de Gaulle', in Gilbert Pilleul (ed.), *Le Générale de Gaulle et l'Indochine, 1940–1946* (Paris, Plon/Institut Charles de Gaulle, 1982), pp. 142–3.

PART IV

Contrasting colonial policies

CHAPTER EIGHT

A new imperial order?

> The immense value of their colonial empire has been brought home to Frenchmen during this war. The majority of it rallied to de Gaulle at an early stage, and Brazzaville, 'la capitale de la Résistance', a town which most Frenchmen in 1940 had hardly heard of, became the imperial centre of French affairs and a very powerful Gaullist radio station. The French colonies have provided men and material for the reformed French forces and financial assets for the French government-in-exile. Therefore, at last Frenchmen are becoming alive to the immense importance of their empire whose social development, industrial exploitation and government will be discussed at the Brazzaville conference at the end of the month. [Allied Forces, Psychological Warfare Branch, French Political Intelligence Report[1]]

One irony of the turbulent history of France's wartime empire is that, while the Gaullist recovery was mounted from colonial territory, it was the Vichy state which made empire central to the ethos of its regime. Brazzaville and the post-war French Union notwithstanding, the imperial outlook that the Allied Psychological Warfare Branch detected among Free French supporters in early 1944 was not deep-rooted. Those most at home with colonial matters tended to be military men and colonial functionaries rather than experienced metropolitan politicians. Most of the soldier-administrators who married political responsibility with active military command at first remained loyal to Pétain – not surprisingly, since the soldier-administrator ideal epitomised by Marshal Lyautey reached its fullest development in the Arab territories of French North Africa and the Levant. From September 1941, members of Vichy's armed services were required to swear a new oath of loyalty to Marshal Pétain as head of state. Such was the importance attached to imperial defence by the Vichy government that those who tried to avoid service overseas by refusing to swear allegiance were obliged to complete their colonial tours of duty before facing a disciplinary charge in France.[2] Few of the genuine imperial enthusiasts serving in colonial governments and garrisons before the fall of France seriously contemplated joining de Gaulle. Many shared the bleak memories of the Third Republic that were so central to the appeal of Vichy. After all, the political immobilism and economic decline that sometimes characterised 1930s France was writ still larger in the inter-war stagnation of much of the French empire. For his part, Pierre Boisson believed that support for the treasonous Free French marked the thin end of a dangerous wedge. 'Dissidence is a very contagious disease for which the whites will pay in the end ... Movements that do not respect hierarchy carry within themselves the ferment of dissolution.'[3]

On the other side of the political divide, de Gaulle's supporters professed belief in the legitimacy of the Third Republic – if not in all its constitutional detail – and found themselves based in sub-Saharan Africa by force of circumstance, not by choice. In a speech delivered at Chatham House on 19 March 1942, René Pleven evoked the missionary zeal of de Gaulle's inner circles in Carlton Gardens and the AEF Government General in Brazzaville. But Pleven also indicated that Gaullist preoccupation with empire was merely a transient phenomenon:

> We have the very acute sentiment that Free France can never accept the idea that it is a static enterprise, which has now reached the limits of its growth. Our aim is to bring back into the war, by persuasion, or by force, all the territories constituting the French colonial empire, and when the time comes the French metropolitan territory itself and all Frenchmen. In other words, Free France can have no rest until it can drop the adjective and call itself France.[4]

AOF and AEF

Between 1940 and 1942 both Gaullist and Vichy propaganda emphasised the need to preserve imperial solidarity and a colonial patrimony for France. But on neither side were ambitious plans for political reform, economic rehabilitation or constitutional regeneration of the empire implemented to any great extent. Economic activity across Vichy Africa was severely affected by the loss of markets and, above all, by the debilitating effects of Britain's naval blockade. Once the Free French took full control of French Africa in 1943, Gaullist willingness to contribute colonial produce to the Allied war effort ended the economic isolation and stagnation experienced in Vichy AOF. But this did not generate significant improvements in living standards for African families and labourers. Wages continued to lag behind inflation and forced labour, though excused by Gaullist administrators as only an interim necessity, none the less remained intact in practice. As Michael Crowder has made plain, in AOF the notion that Free French administration drew a line in the sand against previous colonial exploitation was more propaganda myth than tangible reality.[5] Under Gaullist rule, French West Africans were compelled to assist France's struggle in a remote conflict much as they were previously obliged to accept the increased corporatism and authoritarian controls of Vichy planners.[6] Félix Eboué's November 1941 suggestion of the limited delegation of power to local notables within Free French AEF came to little in the short term. Pursued by a specially appointed Consultative Commission packed with AEF Governors under the chairmanship of Eboué's Secretary-general, Henri Laurentie, the plan to enhance the status of the so-called *notables évolués* was a very limited reform.[7]

In the closed world of Gaullist administration within Equatorial Africa and the French Cameroon, the white planter communities which had dominated the pre-war administrations of the French Congo, the Cameroon and Gabon still exerted powerful influence.[8] Eboué was reluctant to challenge this by encouraging the growth of a more closely regulated wage economy outside planter control. In fact, the Governor-general resisted the proletarianisation of black African labour, which he feared would have incalculable political side effects. With a romanticised attachment to peasant cultivation, Eboué considered respect for tribal hierarchy essential to facilitate French control. In 1941 he produced a tract on native policy in AEF in which he specifically identified the emergence of an urban African proletariat as a destructive evil which should be reversed. In this respect, as Frederick Cooper has pointed out, Eboué shared much in common with his arch political rival, Pierre Boisson.[9] Stimulated by the pressure of US anticolonialism, it was only in October 1943 that René Pleven suggested the requirement for a major imperial conference which would 'strengthen the awareness of our responsibilities and of our duties towards the African'. Even so, neither settlers nor indigenous peoples were directly represented at Brazzaville.[10]

The Vichy regime was always more assiduous in its colonial propaganda, more fervent in its colonial legislation and more inclined to theorise about the nature and purpose of empire than the French National Committee or the FCNL. Remarkably, the corporatist planning beloved of Vichy's colonial policy-makers survived for a full year after the collapse of Vichy authority in North Africa, AOF and Madagascar. Built around organisational committees set up for individual colonial industries and producers, and directed by the semi-official *groupements professionels coloniaux*, Vichy's colonial *dirigisme* envisaged the systematic modernisation of the economic structure and industrial organisation of French Africa. This was to be carried out through a ten-year programme of investment, labour reform and increased state direction. This was an ambitious scheme. But it was never fully implemented, even if the hang-overs of corporatism and economic mobilisation persisted in the minds of the many Vichy colonial officials who stayed in post after 1943.[11] In October 1943, for instance, the Ministry of Colonies military staff discussed proposals for the extension of Germany's compulsory labour service demands to the settler population of French Africa – a plan so unrealistic that one wonders whether the exercise was simply undertaken to appease the occupation authorities. Months earlier, the Vichy government also began an ambitious inquiry into the nature of long-term French financial investment in the colonies. This was part valedictory justification for the previous years of Vichy's colonial rule and part preparation for the defence of French imperialism at any post-war peace conference.[12]

In general, where Vichy looked southward towards a collapsing imperial position, Free France inevitably gazed northward to metropolitan France. Where Vichy dwelt upon imperial policy, Free France dreamt of the Liberation. This difference in emphasis was hardly surprising. Vichy was a quisling state which found in empire a refuge where it could govern relatively unfettered. In fact, the isolation imposed by blockade forced Vichyite Governors to intervene in all aspects of economic and social policy in order to sustain individual economies and contain potential dissent. By contrast, Free France was a metropolitan government-in-waiting temporarily confined to colonial territory. Hence the questions that suggest themselves are whether the reactionary Vichy state – the more enthusiastic legislator – did much that was constructive within the empire, and whether Free France in its preoccupation with liberating France did much to create a new style of French imperial rule?

During 1941 alone the Vichy government promulgated over 200 laws and decrees for application within the empire. Many of them simply concerned public order. But, taken as a whole, Vichy legislation created a distinctive imperial order based upon a more explicit assertion of French racial supremacy and the defence of settler interests. This 'racialisation' was, for instance, much in evidence in the French West Indies, where Creole whites, French officials and sailors were the mainstay of Admiral Robert's regime. Meanwhile, many Martiniquans regarded de Gaulle as a black liberation hero.[13] Vichy colonial policies marked less of a new departure than might be imagined. Designated areas for whites only, whether in buses, trains, cinemas or restaurants, and the conscriptive use of African labour to ensure the profitability of

European plantation agriculture, did not represent an abrupt reversal of pre-war practice. Nor did *de facto* segregation and forced labour disappear from Free French black Africa immediately the Gaullists took control.[14] None the less, Vichy rule was distinctive. In the fields of economic planning and judicial administration, new tiers of colonial administration were created, such as the Colonial Economic Agency and the Colonial Economic Bureau, established in February and July 1941 respectively. By May 1941 new controls were in place regarding the colonial press, labour service and employment provision, banking transactions and individual freedom of movement. Colonial subjects within Vichy France were denied access to the occupied zone to the north. Elective institutions were either suspended or suppressed and, within Algeria, the 1919 Jonnart citizenship law was revoked. In the largest single extension of authoritarian powers, in October 1941 colonial Governors were authorised to intern any individuals considered a threat to 'national defence and public security'. The immediate victims of this were Jews, Freemasons and Gaullist sympathisers. The bulk of those detained were transported to internment camps in southern Morocco and Algeria as well as a string of camps across AOF such as Louga, Sebikotane and Koulikoro.[15] As the British blockade bit harder, detention for 'economic crimes' such as resistance to forced labour or the hoarding of supplies became increasingly common. In the immediate pre-war years, despite earlier Popular Front efforts to control foodstuff price inflation, wage levels in North and West Africa had tended to lag behind the escalating cost of essential commodities. In Vichy AOF, the prohibitively high prices of rice, textiles, meat and oil, exacerbated by the effects of blockade and two years of widespread drought, left the Gaullist authorities with an overriding priority by 1944 – to restore some balance between wage levels and an exorbitant local cost of living across AOF's commodity-dependent economies.[16]

The severity of French colonial rule in black Africa was much affected by the local availability of cheap labour in individual colonies. Differing forced labour demands were themselves dictated by the labour intensity of plantation agriculture for the various staple crops within individual colonies. Throughout the inter-war period and the war years, AOF had a collective population over three times as great as that of AEF. But the latter territory was not correspondingly smaller in geographical extent, nor were AEF production targets far below those of AOF. Hence the financial and physical demands made upon the indigenous population of AOF tended to be less oppressive than in AEF. In French West Africa, serious manpower shortages were infrequent and generally short-lived. Furthermore, those pressed into forced labour in AOF were more likely to remain within their home region, sometimes within the confines of their local *cercle*. There were certainly numerous exceptions to this across West Africa and arbitrary labour demands remained a dreadful burden throughout the war years. In the Moshi tribal region of Côte d'Ivoire, for instance, prison terms were imposed upon local chiefs who failed to prevent their menfolk absconding into the Gold Coast. Similarly, in early 1942 entire village populations in French Guinea crossed into Sierra Leone in order to evade the anticipated arrival of French commissioners desperate to fill their quotas for African labour.[17] But in AEF the situation was still worse. French colonial overseers always faced shortages of personnel for the *prestation* system of forced labour in French Equatorial Africa. The terrible consequences of this emerge in the differing casualty rates among forced labourers in AOF and AEF. Between 1900 and 1945 long-term public works projects in AEF – such as the Congo-Océan railway project developed between 1921 and 1934 – sometimes resulted in casualties amounting to 45 per cent of the work force. In AOF, the most famous long-term infrastructural scheme – the Office du Niger irrigation project – registered average losses of 12.66 per cent. In both cases, these sorry statistics help explain the sluggishness in population expansion across francophone Africa in the thirty years before 1945.[18] In AOF the coffee, cocoa and banana plantations of Côte d'Ivoire and French Guinea demanded the largest numbers of forced labourers, though in both colonies the proportion of African-owned plantations was particularly high. But in Senegal, for example, the use of forced labour by European-owned agricultural consortia was much less pronounced.[19]

In AEF, then, there existed a more established French tradition of exploitative colonial rule, dominated by the burden of forced labour service being shared among a smaller overall population. How far did the Free French rulers of AEF take steps to reverse this? The influence of settler planters within the wartime politics of AEF and the prevalence of vast plantations in the Cameroon, French Congo and Gabon made an abrupt shift to less onerous labour practices unlikely. More important, beyond René Pleven's fledgling colonial office, most of de Gaulle's supporters in London were primarily interested in the export output of AEF. This was regarded as a vital means to convince the British of the region's value to the Allied war effort, while adding to the coffers of the French National Committee. The Free French thus placed additional AEF export capacity above any short-term consideration of political reform. For its part, the British government was slow to reward AEF's export contribution by supplying the Gaullist colonies with essential commodities. Instead, both the Colonial Office and the Spears mission simply hoped that Britain's wholesale purchase of AEF export produce would generate a beneficial trickle-down effect by increasing the purchasing power of the local population. This did not occur for the simple reason that the urgent import requirements of AEF outstripped even the increased export volumes of the Free French period. Although Allied funds undoubtedly poured into Brazzaville during 1940–45, the money very quickly flowed out again.[20] In early 1942 Japan's rapid advance through South East Asia denied the Allies access to key sources of raw materials. This, in turn, added to the economic importance of African primary produce such as tin, rubber and high-grade timber. With little convoy traffic to the Far East, additional shipping also became available for West and Central African exports. In consequence, the Free French export drive in black Africa intensified during 1942 and 1943. But still the colony ran a trade deficit which exceeded 200 million francs by 1944.[21]

In AOF export and labour trends were quite different. Stimulated by their alarm at unauthorised migration from French West African territories to neighbouring British colonies, and short of funds for major public works projects, the Vichyite administrations of AOF could claim with some justification that they limited their forced labour demands. In French Sudan, for example, the administration cut back its quotas, mobilising some 5.7 per cent of the black male working population for forced labour duties during 1942. Though frontiers were generally closed between individual French and British colonial territories, in general, the war made it easier for young men from AOF to flee into neighbouring British colonies in order to escape forced labour or military service. It was hardly in Vichy's interest to perpetuate the migration of French West Africans into British colonies, where they might add to the economic capacity of the British empire.[22] As Governor-general, Boisson had the clearest view of the extent to which forced labour could be used without in the process destroying the fabric of peasant society, breaking the hierarchy of tribal allegiance, undermining the birth rate in particular regions and risking serious political disturbance. Though he made no effort to dismantle the *prestation* system, Boisson recognised that the practice could neither continue indefinitely nor be expanded *ad hoc*.[23] During his last months in office in early 1943, Boisson refused to emulate the practices of AEF by increasing forced labour sharply in order to contribute more substantially to the West African export drive. Indeed, this was Lord Swinton's major criticism of the Dakar government.[24]

This is not to suggest that Boisson's administration deliberately avoided persecution. Technically, Vichy AOF was governed as a state under siege. In practical terms, the local military and police authorities possessed virtually unrestricted powers of arrest and detention.

According to Admiral William Glassford, the US special envoy to Dakar, by 1943 dissidents were often shot rather than interned.[25] Similarly, food and cloth rationing, coupled with high inflation, left many Africans across AOF facing unprecedented hardship during the years of Vichy rule. In Niger, Dahomey and French Guinea, for instance, by early 1942 the European residents, issued with special ration cards under the terms of product control decrees, had exhausted local supplies of cloth, refined tobacco and petroleum. This drove African families to seek these and other supplies from neighbouring British territories. In French Guinea, for example, by early 1942, African tobacco traders preferred to deal in British rather than French currency in order to enable them to make useful purchases in nearby Sierra Leone.[26]

There is no question that forced labour remained central to the operation of the AOF economies in the Boisson era, but there are grounds to claim that the later period of Free French administration brought no significant respite. During 1943–44, especially, severe forced labour demands continued. Boisson's successor as Governor-general, Pierre Cournarie was committed to reform of compulsory labour practices. So was André Latrille, from August 1943 the Gaullist Governor of Côte d'Ivoire, a region which suffered particularly heavy labour requisitions. They each decried the entire system of labour provision at the Brazzaville conference in 1944. Yet, in the short term, they buried their moral and political scruples about forced labour beneath the primordial requirements of increased war production. This was complicated by the fact that the pre-war system of voluntary labour migration had largely disintegrated. Many of the so-called *navétanes* – young men who moved from arid, inland *cercles* within French Sudan and Guinea to work seasonally on groundnut plantations in Senegal – no longer found the trip economically viable. This led Cournarie's administration to 'recruit' some 45,000 *navétane* labourers from French Sudan and Guinea during 1943.[27]

Between 20 and 21 December 1943, the council of the AOF Government General held its first full session since 1939. The colonial Governors, regional administrators and commercial representatives present debated plans for increased export production and the implementation of extended mobilisation for men aged between twenty and thirty-three. Only briefly did Governor-general Cournarie turn to social policy, congratulating his officials on the fact that, despite the weight of economic and military impositions, educational and medical services across AOF had not collapsed.[28] The overriding emphasis upon the export drive might not have been so damaging had the production quotas set for particular districts and *cercles* been more sympathetically – or sensibly – formulated. Instead, wholesale rises in quotas were set across AOF and AEF in 1943 in remarkable ignorance of the productive capacity and the agricultural complexion of individual regions. Furthermore, where European planters might satisfy the increased demands made upon them by greater recourse to forced labour, African producers were denied the same ready access to the *prestation* work force. The early results of the Gaullist export drive caused disappointment within Pleven's Commissariat of Colonies. Although AOF doubled its export output during 1943–44 from 572 million to 1, 197 million francs, the federation, much like AEF, still faced a net trade deficit in mid-1944.[29]

On Christmas Eve 1943, E. W. Meiklereid, the British consul-general in Dakar, reported to Anthony Eden, on a personal tour of four AOF territories conducted over the preceding three weeks. Meiklereid produced a shocking picture of arbitrary rule, systematic brutality and oppressive settler behaviour. In many colonies, the French had made vast increases to their labour requirement quotas from individual *cercles*. Village chiefs, who were traditionally expected to ensure that these manpower demands were met, faced 'severe punishments, not limited to imprisonment' when quotas were not satisfied. In Côte d'Ivoire, several district officers reported such a heavy depreciation of the local population of active black males that the birth rate had collapsed.[30] The exodus of young black men fleeing the French authorities continued unabated. In André Latrille's Côte d'Ivoire district commissioners issued local police with whips to help curb dissent. Clearly, in spite of the hand-over of power in Dakar, there was little change in administrative personnel throughout much of AOF. In a single *cercle* in French Guinea, close to the Sierra Leone frontier, over a thousand of those called up for labour service absconded into the British colony during 1943. It was a source of embarrassment to Leclerc and Pierre Cournarie that many French West Africans not only fled to British territory but then had the temerity to enlist with the British forces, rather than join the Fighting French military. Meiklereid did not mince his words:

> Though it is hoped that under the present [Fighting French] administration there may be some amelioration in the situation, the administrative class has become accustomed to employ severe measures of repression in their dealings with the natives and, with the demand for increased production by the Central Government, there will be a tendency for the system to continue. The average French administrator, planter or merchant is still inclined to regard the native as little more than a slave.

Nor did the consul see much ground for optimism. 'As regards the commercial community, the majority are strong supporters of the Marshal and are inclined to hanker after the "good" days of the Vichy regime, when the Germans were prepared to pay any price for their produce. They appear to be completely lacking in public-spiritedness and the war effort very definitely takes second place to their business interests.'[31]

Ruthless exploitation of French colonial resources was, of course, nothing new. Cocooned within the protection of quotas, tariffs and preferential clearing arrangements, and debilitated by an over-valued franc, for much of the inter-war period French industrial and agricultural producers, already fearful of intensifying European competition, regarded the colonies as entirely subservient to French economic requirements. This, too, should not surprise. But what distinguished French colonial rule in this respect was the absence of much sustained effort to improve living standards among subject populations. Put another way, inter-war France did not back up the rhetoric of colonial advancement with long-term investment sufficient to make a real difference. During the war itself, both Vichy and Free France lacked the funds required to meet the corporatist or reformist targets they set themselves. Pétainist French planters across AOF who saw Vichy as protector of their privileges and status were largely unaware of the developing corporatist ideas of Vichy's Ministry of Colonies planners.[32] Only with the creation of the colonial investment fund (Fonds pour l'Investissement et Développement Economique et Social, or 'FIDES') in 1946 did this position begin to change. The notion that the acid test of the French civilising mission should be a simple measurement of how living standards changed over time was largely confined to the French left, the Socialist Party in particular. Admittedly, the benefits of French education, culture and linguistic tradition were much stressed, but their value next to more basic economic needs was at best debatable.[33] Furthermore, as Popular Frontists in 1936–38, the Socialists were themselves deeply ambivalent about the merits of colonial industrialisation. A former Minister of Colonies, Marius Moutet, saw in rapid industrialisation and greater colonial self-sufficiency the beginnings of a black proletariat and mass colonial nationalism.[34]

With its high demands upon primary producers and inadequate capital for sustained investment, Free French colonial administration in sub-Saharan Africa signified a return to the recent past. But one profound change was inherent in the switch from Vichy to Gaullist authority. For many educated African *évolués*, Free French rule suggested at least an implicit commitment to reform. Cournarie and Latrille were taken at their word in their pronouncements regarding the eventual eradication of forced labour. The Brazzaville conference and the 'spirit' of reform it engendered were not allowed to ebb away unfulfilled. In August 1944, the legalisation of African trade unions – which mainly affected workers in the public utilities – gave new momentum to the creation of Western-style African political parties. Similarly, Gaullist co-operation with African planters in pursuit of greater export production increased the political voice of African agriculturalists. Nowhere was this better illustrated than in Latrille's collaboration with Félix Houphouët-Boigny and the Syndicat Agricole Africaine (SAA) founded in the Côte d'Ivoire in September 1944.[35] Latrille worked with the SAA to replace the *prestation* system with a commercial labour market in which African producers could compete for workers in a wage economy. This met Latrille's obligation to increase export output and helped the Governor prove his case against the manifest inefficiencies of forced labour. But in the longer term, the SAA acquired still greater importance. During 1945–46 it provided the platform for both the Parti Démocratique de la Côte Ivoire and the Rassemblement Démocratique Africain, two major political parties in post-war AOF. In this instance at least, Free French commitment to a greater colonial war effort and the rhetoric of Gaullist reform catalysed the growth of African political organisations which later proved pivotal to French decolonisation.[36]

Syria and Lebanon

To the Vichy government, the Levant states were never fertile grounds for the national revolution. Syria and Lebanon lacked a significant settler community capable of challenging the rising power of the Arab nationalist parties, although the Christian Maronites of Lebanon were always regarded as potential agents of French control. Hence, to Vichy, the Syrian mandate in particular seemed potentially disloyal. But the Free French quickly found that Gaullism was no more welcome in the Levant. Nor were Gaullists any more adept at managing inter-communal tensions once Fernard Dentz's Vichy administration was ousted. A few examples may illustrate the point. In late September 1941, Gaullist forces became involved in serious local disturbances in the Euphrates and Jezirah regions of Syria. Having tried to collect taxes by force, Free French troops participated in sporadic fire-fights with local villagers which resulted in at least seventeen deaths and scores of injuries. Once British forces were fired upon, the Middle East commander, General Auchinleck, asserted his authority over High Commissioner Catroux and insisted upon the imposition of British-supervised martial law. The principal Free French concern throughout was less to address the root cause of the unrest than to maintain the fiction of ultimate Gaullist control.[37] The French inclination to wield the big stick in order to bolster Gaullist authority continued unabated until its tragic climax in the bombardment of Damascus in May 1945. In November 1944, for example, following an incident in which a French civil official shot an Alaouite protester for tearing up a portrait of de Gaulle, the *Sûreté aux Armées*, the new appellation of the former *Sûreté Générale*, responded by ordering the deployment of 200 North African troops who duly imposed a terrifying martial law upon the town where the incident occurred.[38]

Within Syria and Lebanon, however, the French tendency to centralise imperial control was often reversed in pursuit of a looser administrative structure. Allowing special privileges and limited autonomy to Syrian and Lebanese minorities such as the Druzes and the Alaouites was supposed to prevent the development of national opposition to French rule. Quite apart from its divisiveness, this system perpetuated complex taxation and local trade arrangements which impeded the growth of the Syrian and Lebanese national economies.[39] In its efforts to cultivate the support of minority groups against the Sunni Muslim majority, Catroux's Levant administration tolerated certain organisations more suited to Vichy. Perhaps the best example of this was the Maronite *Phalanges Libanaises* (Lebanese Phalange). This drew its inspiration from fascist models, and had thrived under Vichy rule while developing a proto-nationalism hostile to French authority of any sort.[40] In April 1944 General Spears concluded that the *Phalanges Libanaises*, which actually dated from 1935, was certainly 'semi-fascist' in organisation and outlook, having been inspired in part by pre-war Italian propaganda from the Bari radio station. Although the Free French authorities outlawed the *Phalanges* and other less popular youth groups, the organisation continued to meet and produce its own newspaper. This French indulgence towards young Maronite extremists reflected the wish to cultivate Christian support against the growing strength of Arab nationalism. Though certainly not a new departure, it was a dangerous and reactionary policy, typical of an administration which felt embattled and exposed.[41]

The constant shortage of qualified administrative personnel nourished the sense of insecurity so evident in much Gaullist colonial administration. This was compounded by the remoteness of the colonial governments in sub-Saharan Africa and the Indian Ocean territories, the limited comforts of wartime colonial service and de Gaulle's deep mistrust of those not personally known or committed to him. But perhaps a greater difficulty was that de Gaulle refused to allow local administrative co-operation with the British to develop freely. The general clearly feared that the British governmental representatives attached to Free French territories under the auspices of the Spears mission would pursue a distinct political agenda at variance with long-term French imperial interests. Nowhere was this more evident than in the Levant. As Spears put it, 'The underlying fact is that as often reported previously, the Free French much prefer having doubtful Vichy elements in the key positions than reliable British.'[42] Though Spears was himself the principal cause of the malady he identified, the activities of Jean Baelen and Jean-Marc Boegner within the Beirut *Délégation Générale* – culminating in Jean Helleu's disastrous decision to arrest the Lebanese government in November 1943 – was proof enough that Free French administration in the Levant was blinkered and irretrievably divided. In February 1944, Helleu's replacement, General Beynet, arrived in Beirut. His new Secretary-general, Binoche, had been *chef de cabinet* to Pierre-Etienne Flandin during the latter's term as Vichy Foreign Minister in 1940–41 and had then worked with Admiral Esteva in Vichyite Tunisia. Binoche's appointment suggested that Free French administrative cohesion was impossible to achieve.[43]

There was nothing unusual in Gaullist reluctance to delegate any authority to British personnel. But the fact remains that the British were paymasters, arms providers, shippers and couriers to the Free French for much of the war. Had there been a more harmonious relationship between the Gaullists and their principal backers, there might have been scope for the temporary secondment of British personnel to Free French administrations. A pipe dream, of course. De Gaulle was certain to view any such contingent arrangements as typical of the empirical British approach to colonial administration that he so distrusted.[44] The British were wont to contrast their pragmatism with the lofty ideals and limited achievements of French colonial government. To de Gaulle, it was only a short step to Spears's – or indeed Roosevelt's – position; namely, that across large tracts of their empire, the French were no longer fit to rule. As it was, de Gaulle left in place numerous Vichyite administrators whose 'conversion' to Free France depended entirely upon the course of Allied fortunes in the war. More serious from the perspective of the long-term political development of Syria and Lebanon, French mandatory rule conspicuously failed to introduce educated Syrians and Lebanese to positions of administrative responsibility within their own country. Those Arab functionaries who did secure a place in local government or civil bureaucracy worked within a system where petty corruption and dull obedience were a better passport to advancement than genuine administrative skill.[45]

French North Africa

After June 1940, possession of the Maghreb territories was the single most important diplomatic lever remaining to the Vichy regime. Little wonder that Vichy legislation, antisemitic edicts and colonial propaganda were applied more intensively across North Africa – especially within Algeria – than in any other Vichy overeas territories. Quite apart from the strategic and economic importance of the Maghreb, and its historic role as the core of France's second empire, three further reasons help explain North Africa's pre-eminent position. First and foremost was Algeria's unique constitutional status as part of France, ruled as three distinctive overseas departments under Ministry of Interior jurisdiction. The change of regime did not alter this relationship. After all, the essential justification for it – the presence of by far the largest single community of French *colon* settlers – remained as before. Furthermore, this settler community produced fervent Vichyites, not least among the 'new French' of Spanish or Italian descent, many of whom saw in Pétain a benign mirror image of Franco and Mussolini. *Colon*-owned newspapers such as the *Dépêche de Constantine,* Pierre-Louis Ganne's *Dépêche Algérienne* and Alain de Sérigny's *Echo d'Alger* were not only Vichyite, they were frequently antisemitic and pro-Axis.[46] Nowhere was the Pétainist *Légion des Combattants et Volontiers de la Révolution Nationale* stronger than in French North Africa, where it drew heavily upon the pre-existing strength of ultra-rightist groups such as *Action Française,* and the *Parti Social Français* (PSF), itself the heir to Colonel François de la Rocque's *Croix de Feu.* Still more *Légion* volunteers combined their fervency for the *francisque* – the double-headed Frankish axe that became the symbol of the Vichy regime – with active membership of Jacques Doriot's pro-Nazi *Parti Populaire Français.*[47] Under the leadership of General François, in Algeria alone, *Légion* membership rose to almost a quarter of a million. Local leaders included Georges Hardy, Roger Le Tourneau and Augustin Ibazizen, all former doyens of the PSF.[48] From late 1941, many of these *Légion* enthusiasts were also inducted into the still more fascistic and antisemitic *Service d'Ordre Légionnaire* (SOL), set up on the initiative of the Interior Minister, Pierre Pucheu. As Jacques Soustelle famously commented in 1947, 'For the good of the French [settlers] in North Africa, if the national revolution had not existed, it would have had to be invented.'[49]

One measure of the depth of pro-Axis sympathy among French North Africa's settler community was the recruitment of volunteers to the *Légion Tricolore,* which fought alongside German forces. Affiliated to the *Légion des Volontiers Français contre le Bolshevisme,* its metropolitan forebear, the *Légion Tricolore* was created by Vichy decree, originally for service on the eastern front, on 18 July 1942. Over the next six months, recruitment to this organisation was conducted mainly amongst former Armée d'Afrique personnel. Though Generals Juin and Noguès did their best to curtail it, sporadic settler and *indigène* enlistment continued to the very eve of the Torch landings, encouraged by the growing popularity of the PPF and the intensification of German antisemitic propaganda broadcasts to the North African territories.[50] Directed by a Colonel Magnin, Commissaire-General of the *Légion Tricolore* in Algiers, some 800 volunteers enrolled during late 1942, the largest single proportion coming from Algerian *zouaves* and *spah*i battalions.[51] More significant was the level of recruitment to the *Phalange Africaine*, created by Vichy decree on 26 November 1942 for service in the Tunisian campaign as part of Rommel's Africa Corps. Counting on the use of large numbers of French North African ex-POWs repatriated from Germany via the Rivesaltes transit camp near Perpignan, the Vichy War Ministry remained certain in January 1943 that at least 7,000 volunteers could be found for a *Phalange* brigade. The eventual intention was to create a further mixed brigade from volonteers in Tunis, Sousse and Bizerta to bring total *Phalange Africaine* strength up to 18,000. After completing its duties inside Tunisia, the *Phalange* was then designated to form an elite force for attacks upon Gaullist colonies. The majority of settler volunteers were listed as active supporters of the PPF.[52]

The apparent confidence with which the Vichy War Minister, General Eugène Bridhoux, approached the recruitment of the *Légion Tricolore* and the *Phalange Africaine* in 1942–43 revealed a second basis for Vichy's attachment to AFN. The Maghreb territories were fertile soil for two of the central tenets of Vichy propaganda: racialism and the associated glorification of the martial virtues. A crude but effective means of colonial control for a regime short of prestige and military power was to emphasise an antisemitic message, reinforced by praise for the singular valour of Arabs and Berbers. Within the precise hierarchy of francophone colonial races delimited by Vichy, Maghreb Arabs were ranked directly below the French themselves. Only the Annamites supposedly displayed a comparable level of 'civilisation', but they were said to lack the moral fibre and fighting prowess of North African Arabs. West African Tirailleurs made excellent soldiers, but this was attributed in part to the greater 'brutality' of their indigenous culture. Where Algerians might aspire to become *constructeurs d'empire*, the highest achievement for Vichy's black Africans was to serve as *défenseurs d'empire*. These ideas drew heavily upon pre-war eugenicist thinking and, especially, upon the writings of a favoured theorist of the ultra-right, the *Action Française* figurehead, Charles Maurras.[53]

Another measure of the permeation of Vichy ideology within North African society was the strength of popular support for official repression of the 400,000-strong Jewish population. During August and September 1940 sanctions were imposed upon Jewish traders across French North Africa. Following a spate of PPF and Arab attacks on Jewish shops and businesses in Casablanca, Port Lyautey, Rabat and several smaller towns, some 153 Jewish 'speculators' were immediately arrested in Morocco alone. Noguès duly approved the construction of a Jewish detention camp near Azemmour. Apart from local detainees, this and other detention camps housed a large number of Jewish refugees from France. It was not straightforward repression. Noguès made it plain to Vichy that he wished to keep Jewish refugee families out of Morocco's major cities because he considered that Arab and settler antisemitism posed a grave threat to the internal stability of the country. Though an authoritarian figure and a Pétainist, the Resident Minister was no fascist. He looked upon the alarming popularity of Doriot's PPF among Morocco's *colons* with profound distaste. The PPF's September 1942 bomb attack on Noguès indicated that the dislike was mutual.[54]

The same pattern of limited official repression was evident in Tunisia, where there were some 90,000 resident Jews among a population of approximately 3 million. On 30 November 1940, the Tunisian residency approved its first *Statut des Juifs*. Two further statutes followed in June 1941 and March 1942. But though the legal forms existed, in general Vichy's antisemitic legislation was seldom enforced in Morocco or Tunisia with the same vigour as in France. In the two protectorates, native North African Jews were differentiated from Europeanised Jews and a rigorous purge of Jewish office-holders from North African administration was largely avoided.[55] One reason for this was the grudging recognition that North African Jews had been pivotal to several administrative and commercial offices before 1940. But a greater incentive was the recognition that official encouragement of antisemitism would give free rein to Muslim attacks on Jews and their property. After the Palestine revolt broke out in 1936, Arab antisemitism in Tunisia progressively increased. By 1941 the economic effects of the British blockade had added to the tension.[56] Much like Noguès in Morocco, in August 1940, Resident Minister Esteva justified his selective application of antisemitic legislation in Tunis as a pre-emptive measure intended to placate Muslim opinion. After a violent antisemitic attack in the port of Gabès on 19 May 1941, Esteva advised local Jewish leaders that he would make an outward show of enforcing antisemitic decrees while ensuring that the measures were actually enforced 'with more liberality than in France'. In October 1941 Esteva summarised his policy in a letter to Darlan: 'We have thus acted, with regard to Jews, with the firmness required against delinquents ['avec la fermeté qui s'impose contre les délinquants'], containing their illegitimate ambitions, but not falling into blind or systematic persecution.'[57]

This is not to make light of the Jewish experience of persecution in Vichy North Africa. The occasional restraint of the two protectorate administrations was not mirrored in Algeria. There, the abrogation of the Crémieux decree on 7 October 1940 was only the first of several repressive measures. On the initiative of Xavier Vallat's General Commission on Jewish Questions (Commissariat-Général aux Questions Juives), in August 1941 Vichy's earlier expansion of the existing *Statut des Juifs* was extended to cover Algeria. This confirmed the denial of citizenship rights to Algeria's Jewish population and led to their enforced exlusion from commerce, banking, public employment and secondary education. Vichy's confiscation of Jewish property was also applied to Algeria from 21 November 1941.[58] As Michel Abitbol puts it:

> Besides the fact that this fitted perfectly with the ideological orientation of the regime, the extension of anti-Jewish laws to North Africa was motivated by the aim of satisfying the long-standing wishes of the European population of the Maghreb and, incidentally, of gaining the support of the native population of the three colonies. Better than any other avenue, the abrogation of the Crémieux decree was to go a long way toward fulfilling these twin goals.[59]

Whatever Esteva or Noguès did to offset the impact of antisemitic statutes, the trend towards collaboration in Vichy France cast a long shadow over North Afirca's Jewish population during 1941–42. Similarly, the prospect of a German descent upon North Africa and Italy's identification of Tunisian Jews as leading opponents of Italian irredentism aroused deep concern. This intensified in early June 1941 in response to a Vichy decree ordering a census of French North Africa's Jewish population, the implications of which were obvious.[60] Axis propaganda also fomented increased tension between Arab and Jew in North African life. Once Rudolf Rahn's shadow Axis administration was established in Tunisia in late 1942, official persecution increased. The Jewish community was compelled to contribute to Axis occupation costs, Jewish savings were impounded and community leaders were effectively held hostage to ensure the compliance of their co-religionists. The antisemitic activity of the Tunisian branch of the PPF, led by Georges Guilbaud, also received official endorsement.[61]

The contradictions that emerged in the application of Vichy racial policy in North Africa were also evident in the mixed fortunes of the Pétainist national revolution within the Maghreb territories. This was the third pillar of Vichy's enthusiasm for French North Africa, since the Maghreb territories were the one colonial centre with sufficient manpower to implement the national revolution wholeheartedly. Numerous willing colonial officials were complemented by the large settler community, many of whom regarded themselves as pioneer farmers – the embodiment of the rural, patriotic, Catholic ideal envisaged by Pétain himself. Unlike the planters of tropical Africa, the smallholders of North Africa were less reliant upon the direct assistance of overseas administration – typified by the provision of forced labour – to eke out their livelihoods. Surely these were the sons of the soil whom Pétain considered fundamental to the moral regeneration of France? In late June 1941, Weygand's Algiers administration submitted ambitious proposals for industrial development in the Maghreb. On 2 July Weygand warned Pétain that French North Africa's rapid population growth, calculated at over 250,000 per year, made investment in industrial diversification imperative if mass unemployment and eventual social breakdown were to be avoided. The output of *indigène* agriculture could not keep pace with the advancing Arab birth rate. Though Weygand did not care to admit it, this was, of course, exacerbated by the fact that a tiny minority of *colon* landowners had long ago partitioned the bulk of French North Africa's prime agircultural land. To make his plans more attractive to Vichy, Weygand stressed that new industries and an electrification programme for the North African interior would create opportunities for a new generation of French pioneer settlers to re-build the industrial capacity of Greater France. The benefits of French colonial rule would be proven afresh. Somewhat fantastically, Weygand hoped to finance his schemes through the launch of a public subscription loan (*emprunt national*) in each of the three Maghreb territories.[62]

In fact, perhaps the major capital project to which North Africa's 'empire workmen' were assigned was the long-deferred project of a trans-Saharan railway. Throughout the spring of 1941 a series of Vichy press reports detailed the steps being taken to advance the railway scheme. Upon completion, the expanded network would link the Oran–Colomb–Bechar line, running north–south through Algeria, with the river Niger, so establishing direct overland communications between AOF and the Mediterranean coast. Although the German authorities endorsed the project, they were not willing to release the construction materials needed to finish it. With the limited equipment made available to them, by late 1942 the Vichy authorities had only managed to extend the existing Algerian line further south to Beni Abbes on the country's Saharan frontier. This was over 900 miles short of the Niger.[63] It was a typical instance of an ambitious colonial public works scheme frustrated by the reality of Vichy's increasing economic subordination to the Axis powers. With the German and Italian Armistice Control Commissions most entrenched and most interested in French North Africa, it is no surprise that capital projects in the Maghreb territories came under intense scrutiny.

Under Vichy rule, French North Africa remained starved of investment, weakened by the collapse of the export trade and pushed towards famine conditions by Axis foodstuff demands. Furthermore, the fall of Paris put an end to most of the vital remittances from Algerian workers living in French cities which traditionally helped keep Muslim families going in times of economic hardship.[64] Although Weygand's administration created a regulatory price commission in 1941, by the end of the following year, meat and fruit supplies were chronically short in many North African towns and cities, their distribution controlled by a black market which expanded during the Vichy period.[65] The settler community and armistice army garrisons derived most benefit from the American foodstuff supplies delivered to Moroccan ports from 1941. Little US material aid filtered down to the wider Muslim population. As the German government steadily increased its demands for North African cereals and livestock, so rationing which again favoured settlers over indigenous North Africans added to the hardships of Algeria in particular. Starvation and epidemic followed as soon as a particularly bad harvest was recorded. This occurred during 1942 when the combination of poor yields, increased Axis exactions and inflated black market prices produced widespread famine in Algeria and a chronic outbreak of typhus which affected some 200,000 Algerians.[66]

It seems cruelly ironic that, during 1941, the Vichy government attached greater weight to the relaxation of the military restrictions imposed under the armistice accords than to the alleviation of Axis foodstuff demands. Under the terms of a Franco-Italian economic accord signed in Rome on 22 November 1941, the Italian government agreed to relax its control over Vichy war material stocks and munitions production in return for a Vichy lump-sum payment of 2.6 billion francs. This money was to be used, in part, to defray the costs of the Italian Control Commission in North Africa, making it easier for the Italians to maintain their burgeoning control establishment within the Maghreb. General Vacca Maggoilini, the Italian Armistice Commission president, considered it a fundamental extension of

Vichy collaborationism, as was later confirmed by the wider economic agreements reached with both the Italian and the German Armistice Commissions at Wiesbaden on 21 December.[67] In sum, Darlan's decision to capitalise upon the Paris protocol agreements of May 1941 led to an extension of Axis control over the French North African economy by the end of the year. In the short term, the Germans and Italians were primarily concerned to re-supply their armies in North Africa. French North African raw material production was increasingly attuned to Axis requirements. One should not exaggerate the impact of this. Aware of the increasing likelihood of British military success in North Africa, in mid-February 1942 the Vichy government once again reversed its position and tried with mixed success to evade implementation of either the Rome or the Wiesbaden accords.[68]

The period of Fighting French control of French North Africa has been discussed in chapter six. But a couple of points perhaps bear emphasis here. It is worth recalling that, although Algeria was supposedly integrated into the metropolitan French administrative system, the similarities between rule within France and Algeria were always more apparent than real. Before 1914 the tensions between those colonialists who favoured closer assimilation and those prepared to tolerate looser administrative control, more akin to the situation in the neighbouring French protectorates, was played out through the changes made to the power of the Governor-general in Algiers. Looking back over Algeria's recent history, in 1947 the Ministry of Colonies Section Afrique recognised that this inconsistency had subsisted throughout the preceding forty years:

> The French government, in which a single representative – Marshal Clauzel – appears to have conceived the idea of organising Algeria into a real protectorate, has continued, throughout the course of [French] Algeria's history, to oscillate between two opposite poles: closer centralisation, inspired by ideas of assimilation of the indigenous population, and a higher degree of decentralisation intended to take account of the peculiarities of Algeria.[69]

This statement suggests that the period of Gaullist rule in French North Africa did not accomplish any significant overhaul. This raises a second point. The almost instinctual response to rising nationalist pressure in Algeria, and still more so in Morocco and Tunisia, was to attempt to isolate urban nationalists from the mass of the Arab rural population. In essence, this amounted to the formulation of ambitious and expensive plans of economic regeneration designed to ensure the loyalty of peasant cultivators and wage labourers. On 9 August 1945, Gabriel Puaux, the Moroccan Resident-general, reminded the government that the 'real' reforms he sought to implement were neither political nor constitutional. Far more important were the less sensational plans to improve rural living standards. In Tunisia, Puaux's fellow Resident-general, Charles Mast, followed the same principle.[70] But the Arab specialists within General Catroux's Commissariat of Muslim Affairs acknowledged in January 1945 that neither French electoral reform plans nor de Gaulle's promise of infrastructural investment in the French North African territories had made any significant impact upon the strength of support for Arab nationalism.

Indo-China

In Admiral Decoux's Indo-China the Sûreté became an essential guarantee of French political control. But Decoux did not simply resort to repression of Vietnamese nationalist groups in an effort to maintain French authority across Indo-China. Left to maintain French sovereignty with precious few resources, Decoux's administration sometimes preferred guile to heavy-handed repression. Typically the Sûreté worked quietly, preferring not to act against nationalist subversion until several key arrests could be made at once, as in its clampdown upon nationalists in Saigon in November 1940.[71] As Stein Tonnesson notes, 'Sûreté tactics throughout the period 1940–1945, towards nationalists and communists alike, consisted in permitting them to develop their activities up to a certain point, at the same time infiltrating them and registering all their doings – and then launching a sudden destructive raid against the organisation.'[72]

Having learnt a good deal from the abortive insurrections of September and November 1940, from 1941 French techniques of political coercion and control bore little resemblance to the indiscriminate oppression which followed the Yen Bay mutiny in 1930. Perhaps more important, Decoux was determined to challenge the Japanese claim to be more effective rulers of Indo-China.[73] In practice, this meant closer co-ordination of the work of village councils, accelerated advancement for loyal native civil servants and a concerted attempt to restore the prestige of the indigenous monarchies. As communications and trade with France diminished, Decoux became the clearest example of a Vichy Governor ruling by expedient with only the broad outlines of Vichy policy to guide him. For example, when pressed by Vichy to consider implementation of a workers' charter modelled on the corporatist ideas of the *groupements professionels coloniaux*, the Hanoi administration simply dismissed the suggestion as inappropriate to the Indo-China federation, where Decoux had already implemented tight controls regulating wage levels and the use of labour.[74] In hock to the Japanese, Decoux none the less accrued civil and military power, becoming an arbitrary ruler compelled to survive by his wits.[75]

As an administrator Decoux was more survivor than innovator. The admiral was not shy of reform, but he often lacked the wherewithal to carry it out. For instance, although Decoux proposed a major scheme to relocate the central bureaucracy of the Indo-China federation to a purpose-built administrative centre at Dalat in southern Annam, it was never carried through.[76] Rather than reorder the executive system of the Indo-China federation, Decoux simply ignored the advisory bodies that cluttered both the Government General and the subordinate colonial administrations. This avoided fundamental alteration of the autocratic French rule institutionalised under the federal system of French Indo-China in 1899. In general, Decoux preferred wholesale purges of central and regional administrations to any root and branch reform of governmental practice. Indo-China became the most authoritarian of Vichy's colonial regimes in part because those administrative and consultative bodies deemed inessential were dispensed with. The same applied to the staffs involved. Having temporarily suspended the Colonial Council in October 1940, a month later Decoux ordered the arrest of Indo-China's Inspector of Colonies, Cazeaux. This heralded a wider purge which included the dismissal of the Resident Superiors of Cochin China and Laos.[77]

Many of Decoux's administrative changes do not fit neatly into a coherent long-term scheme of colonial government. In November 1940 the admiral suspended Indo-China's major economic advisory council, the *Grand Conseil des Intérêts Economiques et Financiers de l'Indochine*. But this body was anyway becoming irrelevant as the Japanese economic hold upon the Governor-general increased. Furthermore, Decoux was careful to replace the *Grand Conseil* with a new federal council (*Conseil Fédéral*) in 1941. This even had an *indigène* majority by 1943.[78] Between May 1941 and January 1942 plans were announced to increase the number of *indigène* 'notables' represented within the communal administrations of Tonkin, Cambodia and Annam. Decoux also kept an advisory government council in place, though in December 1942 he reduced its membership from thirty-six to sixteen, restricted to the leaders of individual colonial administrations, the armed forces chiefs and the heads of the major spending departments within the Government General.[79] According to Decoux, these apparently piecemeal measures formed part of a broad policy intended to break down regional particularism in order to encourage *indigène* loyalty to French administration. Decoux certainly encouraged reciprocal visits and staff contacts between the individual colonial administrations of Indo-China. Similarly, he promoted student exchanges and the expansion of the University of Hanoi in an attempt to cultivate deeper attachment to France among Indo-China's French-educated elite. Most significant, Decoux championed the idea of Vietnamese national identity, even peppering his speeches and policy statements with the previously taboo word 'Vietnam'.[80] But it is hard to believe that such limited reforms affected popular support for Vietnamese nationalism.

In the individual territories of Annam, Tonkin, Laos and Cambodia, a subordinate Resident Superior, assisted by an advisory civil-military council, remained in place. Even in Cochin China – ruled directly as a French colony after the withdrawal of the region's traditional scholar-administrators in the decade after conquest – the local Governor still worked with Privy Councillors and a Colonial Council similar in composition to its pre-war equivalent. But only after Japan's defeat in 1945 did the French authorities promote a Vietnamese to the senior bureaucracy in Cochin China. Nguyen Van Tam, their choice as provincial administrator of Tan-an, went on to become Prime Minister of the associated state of Vietnam in 1952.[81] In sum, though he tinkered at the margins, Decoux could not resolve the abiding tension between French associationist ideas and the practice of arbitrary colonial rule across Indo-China.[82]

Under the terms of the Franco-Japanese agreements of 1940–41, Decoux surrendered a good deal of authority to the Japanese military. Japanese troops and officials controlled Indo-China's radio and telegraph communications, the output of Indo-Chinese mining and timber companies, water distribution and several major air bases and port facilities, including Cam Ranh Bay, Tourane and Saigon. Furthermore, the Japanese dictated the operations of Indo-China's railways and set limits to the equipment and deployment of Decoux's remaining land forces.[83] Japan's economic exactions, notably the imposition of rice, coal, ore and timber quotas, triggered price inflation which Decoux was hard pressed to contain. Despite the abrupt rise in prices which followed the 1941 economic agreement with Japan, Decoux struggled to avoid the imposition of rationing. The Hanoi Government General even managed to amass a 100 million piastre budgetary reserve during the latter part of 1941. Backed by a 310 million franc loan from Vichy, Decoux assuaged the worst effects of Japan's export demands in his 1942 budget. The Governor even extended his public works programme, increasing road-building and irrigation projects in Annam and extending the capacity of Haiphong port.[84] Here, too, lay the ambiguity characteristic of Decoux's policies as Governor-general. The avoidance of rationing was meant to conciliate the French community and the influential indigenous landowners of Cochin China and Annam. But at the core of the Indo-China–Japan economic agreement lay a barter system of no real benefit to peasant producers. Indigenous farmers had little incentive to increase agricultural production beyond immediate subsistence requirements. In the face of Japanese requisitioning, such personal needs were hard enough to meet anyway. With local rice supplies much diminished, the physical hardship endured by the majority of Indo-China's urban and town populations intensified. This was evinced by sharp increases in infant mortality during 1941, something Decoux's administration exploited in propaganda highlighting the effects of Japanese requisitioning.[85] Decoux's removal from office in March 1945 allowed him to dodge his proper share of responsibility for the famine which gripped northern Annam and Tonkin in 1945 after widespread crop failure, the breakdown in transport and the continuation of Japanese and French rice confiscation in the early part of the year.[86]

Decoux slipped easily into the role of Vichy authoritarian and proponent of an adulterated form of Pétain's national revolution. Though among the most isolated, the French settler community was thoroughly integrated into Vichy's *Légion des Combattants et Volontiers de la Révolution Nationale*. Between January and November 1942, for example, registered *Légion* membership rose from 2,637 to 6,576.[87] Settler children participated *en masse* in Vichyite youth and sports movements in the towns and cities of Annam and Cochin China, organised at Decoux's behest by Maurice Ducoroy. In his apologetic memoirs, Duroroy claimed to have established some 124 activity centres and over a thousand sports stadia across the federation by 1944.[88] As late as June 1943, settler enrolment to the *Légion* was increasing steadily. With an average of 50–100 new members joining month by month, total *Légion* strength rose to 7,057 by the middle of the year. But *Légion* membership was perhaps not that revealing. Many former adherents of *Anciens Combattants* groups moved naturally into the Vichy equivalent. Other veterans appear to have joined the *Légion* to avoid the prying eyes of local administrators and as a form of social release. *Légion* rallies, such as those held in Hanoi, Pnom Penh and Saigon over the early summer of 1941, were most remarkable for the prevalence of government employees among those waving *Légion* flags.[89]

A better indication of the official commitment to Vichy was that in a region where European antisemitism might be considered an irrelevance, anti-Jewish legislation was fully enforced by 1942. But Decoux is better remembered for repeated crackdowns upon Vietnamese and Gaullist political opposition. Ultimately, they were counterproductive. De Gaulle would have nothing to do with Decoux, and the Viet

Minh coalition responded to French and Japanese persecution by developing a more sophisticated underground network which, though sometimes reliant upon external support, remained deeply resourceful and hard to penetrate.[90] Even among erstwhile supporters of French rule, respect for French authority collapsed. In June 1945 General Pechkoff suggested from Chungking that most Vietnamese *évolués* counted on the Japanese to evict the French prior to an American descent upon Indo-China and a swift transition to independence.[91] Decoux's foremost 'accomplishment' was to keep French administration nominally intact. Encouraged by one of his many tours of inspection around the provinces of Indo-China, in a letter to Minister of Colonies Rear-Admiral Henri Bléhaut on 9 September 1943, Decoux congratulated himself on having kept public works, education and customs revenue outside direct Japanese control. He even anticipated a relatively smooth transition to peacetime rule when the war eventually ended.[92] Much to Japanese irritation, Decoux had extended direct state control over key sectors of Indo-China's economy, including rubber and cereals production. He also sponsored the operations of a national importers' federation.[93] This indirect resistance to Japanese economic control encouraged Japan's civil and police authorities in Indo-China to consolidate their own ties with diverse Vietnamese nationalist groups.

The Free French found it easier to promise reform for Indo-China than for France's African territories because until 1944 there was little prospect of significant Gaullist participation in the Far Eastern war. On 4 September 1942 a Free French delegation led by Pierre Laurin attended the opening of an Institute of Pacific Affairs conference in Washington. Laurin suggested that the Free French would revitalise France's civilising mission in the Far East by extending the suffrage, ending forced labour and setting Indo-China's relationship with France on a new footing. None of these pledges had yet been adopted as official policy.[94] Only in March 1945 did Minister of Colonies Paul Giacobi suggest a more binding French pledge to correct past colonial abuse and reorder the constitutional relationship between France and Indo-China within the terms of the new French Union. But, by this point, French influence in Indo-China was perhaps at its lowest ebb since 1940. The Japanese *coup* of 9 March swept aside French authority and the monarchist regimes of Annam, Cambodia and Laos were reinstalled as Japanese puppets. Much more serious in the long-term, US dominance of eastern Asia soon became an accomplished fact whilst, within Indo-China, the Viet Minh cultivated a popular resistance movement too deeply rooted for the French to destroy.[95]

To Brazzaville and beyond

In September 1943 the FCNL signed an agreement with the US government, negotiated by Jean Monnet in Washington over the previous month, which set new parameters to US military aid under Lend-Lease. Dollar payments for other non-military US supplies to French North Africa were also agreed. This accord altered previous arrangements for US–French empire reciprocal aid by including the provision of strategic raw materials within the aid programme. In simple terms, French colonies were now obliged to supply the Americans with raw materials for the Allied war effort without any longer receiving dollars in return. This was bound to have a damaging effect on the dollar reserves of those French colonies most heavily dependent upon mineral exports to America. Without evidence of buoyant dollar reserves, French colonial administrations found it harder to avert crises of confidence in the value of colonial francs.[96] This gave added importance to commercial links with Britain and British African colonies. Sterling trade and the rapidity of the French liberation during 1944 helped avert major economic crises across French Africa, even though the resumption of colonial trade with metropolitan France inevitably took considerable time. Following the establishment of a special technical mission under Laurent Blum-Picard, a former Inspector-general of Mines, in late 1943 and early 1944 the FCNL became increasingly preoccupied with the formulation of detailed plans for the post-war reconstruction of France, the limitation of Germany's industrial potential and a future western European customs union. Though de Gaulle hoped to make French Africa an adjunct of the new economic system his advisers envisaged, it was none the less clear that the empire's economic problems were a matter of secondary importance to the Gaullist leadership.[97]

By late 1943, then, empire was often treated as an afterthought to more pressing considerations of metropolitan recovery. This helps explain the muted reaction in Algiers to the developing Lebanese crisis provoked by Jean Helleu's order for the arrest of the newly elected Lebanese Cabinet in November. De Gaulle did not immediately refute Helleu's action but he none the less dispatched Catroux to Beirut to sort out the mess. Beyond the confines of the Levant itself, the FCNL responded to its humiliation in Lebanon by resurrecting Maurice Viollette's earlier proposals for an extension of citizenship rights to a narrow band of Algerian Muslims. This was hardly an inspiring new departure. Further evidence of the FCNL's limited interest in colonial reform emerged in late November 1943 when it was announced that colonial representation within the Algiers Consultative Assembly was to be increased from twelve to twenty-one representatives. The additional Assembly members were to be selected from the ranks of Gaullist supporters within the colonies of Tunisia, Morocco, Indo-China, French Oceania and AEF. But the FCNL devoted far more attention to the parallel increase in representation for communist supporters of the metropolitan resistance movement. Effectively a provisional Parliament-in-waiting established in parallel to the FCNL, the Consultative Assembly showed little interest in imperial affairs in the remaining two months before the Brazzaville conference got under way.[98] As communist representation within the Consultative Assembly increased, so de Gaulle faced the prospect of an increasingly left-wing and resistance-dominated Assembly shaping plans for the reconstruction of French government after the Liberation. Two such proposals were under consideration in January 1944. They were put forward on behalf of the FCNL by the socialist Vincent Auriol and by the Commissaire of Justice, François de Menthon. Both projects envisaged a reduction of de Gaulle's presidential power, partly in order to secure communist support.[99]

In November 1943 the PCF executive proposed that two of its members, Lucien Midol and Etienne Fajon, should join the FCNL as commissaires. Reflecting this increased communist and resistance influence, in the week before Christmas the FCNL levelled treason charges against Pierre-Etienne Flandin, Marcel Peyrouton and Pierre Boisson, among others. Reading between the lines, it seems clear that when the socialist Governor of Chad, Pierre-Olivier Lapie, opened a Consultative Assembly debate in January 1944 on colonial representation in post-Liberation France, many Assembly members were preoccupied with other matters. The reconstruction of parliamentary government in Paris, the trial and punishment of leading Vichyite collaborators and the growth of PCF influence within the politics of the FCNL – these concerns aroused more widespread controversy within the French political community of Algiers than imperial reform. When the FCNL discussed the forthcoming colonial conference in Brazzaville, it promptly agreed that not all the proposed reforms could be implemented at once. Budgetary constraints alone were bound to limit the implementation of ambitious public works schemes and the creation of new economic agencies, such as the Office du Bois (Timber Office) in AEF. Moreover, the proposed extension of imperial citizenship caused particular alarm, even though the FCNL merely registered its concern at the sweeping nature of the plans being being forward.[100] Argument over Lapie's ambitious proposals for a distinct colonial parliament whose members were to be chosen by an augmented electorate of 'imperial citizens' was confined to a small number of specialists and colonial enthusiasts within the FCNL, the colonial bureaucracy and the Consultative Assembly.[101]

Recently, two commentators have reiterated that the significance of the Brazzaville conference of January-February 1944 derived from French eagerness to be seen to be making 'a new departure', underscoring de Gaulle's insistence upon the legitimacy of a post-war colonial order in Africa. Having proclaimed their belief in liberal reform at Brazzaville, the FCNL and the provisional government which followed it were stuck with a commitment given real substance by the French Constituent Assembly in 1945–46.[102] Though Brazzaville held great symbolic importance, its proceedings were often uninspiring. Several short-term considerations help to explain this. Firstly, there was an obvious contradiction between the sophisticated proposals formulated by Henri Laurentie and his subordinate officials at the Commissariat of Colonies and the limited time allowed for the plenary conference of colonial Governors to debate them. Though Brazzaville's seven advisory commissions were supposed to refine policy options for ultimate consideration in plenary meetings, there was insufficient consensus amongst commission members and colonial Governors to permit definitive commitments to be made.[103] A series of meetings held over a ten-day period, with an agenda strictly regulated by René Pleven, was never likely to produce a comprehensive plan for a revitalised relationship between France and its black African empire. As the FCNL secretariat put it, the 'essential task' was to strike a balance between a spirit of generous reform and the need to produce viable, if 'modest', proposals. Furthermore the delegates were mindful of the limited authority of conference decisions which were closely defined as 'recommendations' rather than binding commitments.[104]

After Brazzaville, the same colonial Governors who set the tone of the conference itself chipped away at Laurentie's more ambitious reform proposals during protracted consultations with René Pleven in late 1944. Hence, for example, Cameroon Governor, Paul Carras, attacked the scheme for an extended African franchise, while Aimé Bayardelle, the new Governor-general of AEF, suggested stricter qualifications for those *évolués* to be accorded full voting rights. On a different tack, Cournarie reported from Dakar that existing male *évolué* voters were overwhelmingly hostile to any extension of the franchise to women, a view he felt compelled to support.[105] Another short-term problem was that neither de Gaulle nor Pleven showed much inclination to intervene decisively to settle the dispute between the protagonists and detractors of a federal imperial structure. As a result, there was no final agreement regarding the empire's precise constitutional relationship with France[106] This raised a further impediment to rapid decision-making – the fact that the war was still far from over. As Martin Shipway puts it, the conference took place within a 'political vacuum'.[107] With France not yet liberated, it was easier to put aside complex issues such as the permissible extent of colonial autonomy and electoral representation within the colonies for consideration by expert commissions.

Brazzaville is remembered in large part for the promises of wider citizenship offered to French colonial subjects. The first recommendation of the conference was to allow individual colonies a voice within a reconstructed Constituent Assembly which correlated with their relative standing within the proposed French Union. The provisional government further committed itself to this proposal on 20 February 1945, appointing a parliamentary commission under Gaston Monnerville to make detailed recommendations on this basis.[108] In this context, it is important to remember that, outside French West Africa and the scattered island territories of the first empire, the French were starting from a very low figure of colonial 'citizens' with voting rights. In Madagascar, there were barely 2,000 *autochtones* when Georges Mandel offered the prospect of citizenship rights to selected *évolués* in April 1938. In Annam there were under 3,000. By contrast, in AOF, with its four Senegalese *communes de plein exercice* whose original inhabitants were entitled to special citizen status, there were already over 70,000 French African citizens before war broke out. But in Senegal Vichy's destruction of Blaise Daigne's earlier African citizenship reforms threw the local situation into confusion, adding to the radicalisation of *évolué* opinion in the process.[109] As the FCNL secretariat had warned, there was much to be rectified before the Brazzaville recommendations could be implemented.

The contradiction between the French commitment to constitutional reform and the few colonial subjects actually affected by it was echoed in the wartime treatment of France's colonial forces. Within French Africa, military service could produce diametrically opposed results. Both the Armée d'Afrique and la Coloniale liked to portray military training as a key element in assimilating colonial manpower to the French way of doing things. But serving under the tricolour could leave native troops cut adrift from their cultural heritage. Returning troops, especially those from remote settlements, might prove valuable assets or dangerous trouble-makers once they returned home armed with a more intimate knowledge of French colonial politics than their neighbours.[110] Used to a certain status and income as French colonial soldiers, ex-servicemen and their families sometimes appeared isolated and vulnerable when the bulk of their compatriots turned to nationalism. Proud of their military experience and the status it conferred, many ex-servicemen, especially those who remained as professional troops beyond their compulsory service term, seemed deeply conservative, and acted as cornerstones of local colonial administration. In Martinique, for example, during 1941–42, black and mixed-raced ex-servicemen were conspicuously loyal to Admiral Robert and the Governor, Yves Nicol, even though their brand of Vichyism offered precious little to the local black population, the bulk of which was consistently hostile to their regime.[111] Equally, in Tunisia, birthplace of the pro-fascist *Phalange Africaine*, from November 1942, North African soldiers much influenced by the pro-Arab propaganda of Axis radio stations in Libya and Bari enlisted alongside PPF activists to form two volunteer companies attached to the Africa Corps.[112] In spite of this diverse wartime experience, colonial *Anciens Combattants*, many of whom were to a degree 'deracinated', were still regarded as the most trusted auxiliaries of French power in the conflicts of decolonisation which followed the Second World War.

De Gaulle's provisional government made a grave error in failing to highlight the pivotal contribution of colonial troops to the Free French military effort between 1940 and 1944. This was largely a product of the Gaullist effort to bring the French resistance to heel. As an act of political expediency, the removal of Tirailleurs from the première and neuvième colonial infantry divisions to make way for metropolitan troops drawn from the reorganised Forces Françaises de l'Intérieur was understandable.[113] Keen to conciliate and to control the metropolitan resistance fighters of the FFI, the Committee of National Defence pushed colonial troops aside in September 1944 in order to incorporate the more volatile personnel of the FFI into a disciplined French military force. There was even some compassion in the decision to spare colonial troops a harsh French winter by withdrawing Tirailleurs to garrison duties in southern France prior to shipping them onward to new postings in North Africa and Indo-China.[114] But delays in shipping out Senegalese troops, and the limited official recognition of their achievements during the victory celebrations in 1945, all added to tensions within colonial garrisons along the French Mediterranean coast. General de Lattre de Tassigny warned over the winter of 1944 that North African troops were beginning to consider themselves unfairly exploited and undervalued.[115] By this stage, a more dramatic indication of unrest among colonial troops had already occurred. On 1 December 1944, at Thiaroye transit camp outside Dakar, Tirailleurs who had been held as POWs in Europe protested over conditions and their right to back pay. During the violence which followed, thirty-five of the protesters were shot dead.[116] In his legal defence of the remaining protesters, Lamine Guèye, erstwhile leader of the Senegalese bloc within the French Socialist Party, lambasted French treatment of colonial soldiers. This helped maintain popular revulsion over the Thiaroye killings across AOF as a whole. The severity of the French response to Tirailleur unrest in 1945 bore witness to the failure of French political memory regarding its colonial soldiers.

The poor treatment accorded to some colonial troops suggested that previous Gaullist emphasis upon France's debt to its empire was empty rhetoric. But within the Ministry of Colonies, Henri Laurentie's gradual elaboration of the federalist schemes outlined at the Brazzaville conference precluded the abandonment of colonial reform as more pressing matters of domestic reconstruction and post-war planning consumed more governmental and parliamentary time. Laurentie remained wedded to a comprehensive programme of constitutional reform intended to rebuild the post-war French empire through the concession of political autonomy, backed by the promise of greater material aid from the metropole. During 1945–46, the disastrous climax of the Levant crisis, the unfolding drama of Japanese rule in Indo-China and the restored influence of numerous veteran Popular Front colonial reformers – including former Premier Léon Blum and ex-Minister of Colonies Marius Moutet – sustained political interest in imperial reconstruction even if the wider French public soon reverted to a more Eurocentric outlook.[117] The crises of the 1946 French Union and the calamitous 1947 Statute of Algeria lie outside the framework of this study. But it is worth reflecting that these measures were largely the work of Gaullist officials, ex-Popular Frontists and former Free French colonial administrators who remained united in their belief that the trauma of the Second World War should not be allowed to unravel the bonds of empire. Tragically, those Gaullists like Laurentie who saw no alternative but to begin an accommodation with emergent colonial nationalism were matched by other notable Free French resisters such as Thierry d'Argenlieu who considered the reassertion of imperial dominance fundamental to the Gaullist vision of a restored French Republic.

Notes

1 PRO, WO 204/12595, 16 January 1944.
2 SHM, TTA 2/Cabinet Militaire, no. 57/CAB, Darlan note, 24 September 1941.
3 Marshall, *The French Colonial Myth*, p. 79.
4 NAC, Vanier papers, vol. 14/6, Pleven speech, Chatham House, 19 March 1942.
5 This point is developed in Crowder's *West Africa under Colonial Rule* (London, Hutchinson, 1968), and *Colonial West Africa* (London, Frank Cass, 1978).
6 Cooper, *Decolonization and African Society*, pp. 156–7, 167.
7 Elikia M'Bokolo, 'French colonial policy in equatorial Africa in the 1940s and

1950s', in Gifford and Louis, *Transfer of Power*, pp. 179–86.

8 PRO, WO 202/73, Major J. G. C. Allen to Spears mission, London, 3 September 1942.

9 M'Bokolo, 'French colonial policy in equatorial Africa', pp. 173, 181–3; Cooper, *Decolonization and African Society*, pp. 147, 157.

10 Cited in Ollandet, *Brazzaville, capitale de la France Libre*, p. 129.

11 Cooper, *Decolonization and African Society*, pp. 142–3.

12 SHAT, 2P12/D2, no. 439, General Sarrat, Chef d'Etat-Major des Colonies note, 9 October 1943; Marseille, 'L'investissement français dans l'empire colonial', 410–11.

13 Burton, '"Nos journées de juin"', in Kedward and Wood, *Liberation*, pp. 228–9.

14 See, for example, the case of Côte d'Ivoire, described by Nancy Lawler, 'Reform and repression under the Free French', 88–110.

15 Pascal Blanchard and Gilles Boëtsch, 'Races et propagande coloniale sous le régime de Vichy, 1940–1944', *Africa*, 49: 4 (1994), 538–41; Martin Thomas, 'Captives of their Countrymen: Free French and Vichy French POWs in Africa and the Middle East, 1940–43' in B. Moore and K. Fedorowich (eds), *Prisoners of War and their Captors in World War II* (Oxford, Berg, 1996), pp. 90–1, 99.

16 Thioub, 'Economie coloniale et rémunération de la force de travail', 439–42.

17 PRO, ADM 199/1281, West Africa political intelligence bulletin, 27 March 1942.

18 Babacar Fall, *Le Travail forcé en Afrique-occidentale française (1900–1945)* (Paris, Karthala, 1993), pp. 290–5. In 1926 registered populations were 13,483,000 in AOF and 3,128,000 in AEF. The former figure had risen to 15,955,000 by 1945.

19 According to Nancy Lawler, by 1943 Ivoirien planters produced over 80 per cent of Côte d'Ivoire coffee and cocoa, see Lawler, 'Reform and repression', 92–3; Cooper, *Decolonization and African Society*, pp. 150–4.

20 PRO, WO 202/73, F. R. Cowell memo., 'Imports for Free French equatorial Africa', 5 January 1942; AN 560AP/27/D1, Pleven papers, no. 2103/AE, Pleven to Aimé Bayardelle, 21 April 1944.

21 Swinton papers, SWIN I/3/3, Lord Hailey memo., 'West Africa and the war', n.d., 1942; AN 560AP/27/D1, Pleven papers, 'Commerce extérieur des huit premiers mois, 1944'.

22 Fall, *Le Travail forcé*, pp. 294–5.

23 Cooper, *Decolonization and African Society*, pp. 147–8.

24 Swinton papers, SWIN I/3/3, Swinton to Lady Swinton, 21 March 1943; for the Swinton–Boisson accords, see Kent, *Internationalization of Colonialism*, pp. 111–16.

25 Churchill College archive, Spears papers, SPRS/1/137/2, tel. 272, Meiklereid to Eden, 24 December 1943.

26 PRO, ADM 199/1281, West Africa political intelligence bulletin 20, 27 March 1942.

27 Cooper, *Decolonization and African Society*, pp. 159–61, 178; AN, 550AP/27/D1, Pleven papers, Cournarie memo., 'Note au sujet des Navétanes', 14 April 1944.

28 PRO, FO 371/42150, Z416/17/69, Meiklereid to FO, 27 December 1943.

29 John D. Hargreaves, *Decolonization in Africa* (London, Longman, 1988), p. 79; Lawler, 'Reform and repression', 94–5; AN 560AP/27/D1, Pleven papers, Commissariat aux Colonies, 'Mouvement commercial des colonies, premier semestre, 1943–44'.

30 Churchill College archive, Spears papers, SPRS/1/137/2, tel. 272, Meiklereid to Eden, 24 December 1943.

31 *Ibid.*

32 Jacques Marseille, *Empire colonial et capitalisme français. Histoire d'un divorce* (Paris, Albin Michel, 1984), pp. 337–42.

33 See Ahmed Koulakssis, *Le Parti Socialiste et l'Afrique du Nord de Jaurès à Blum* (Paris, Armand Colin, 1991), pp. 265–91.

34 Ageron, 'La perception de la puissance française en 1938–1939', in Girault and Frank, *La Puissance en Europe*, pp. 229–30.

35 Ruth Schachter-Morgenthau, *Political Parties in French-speaking West Africa* (Oxford, Clarendon Press, 1964), pp. 178–88.

36 This argument is fully developed in Lawler, 'Reform and repression', 99–108.

37 MAE, CNF Londres, vol. 39, FO memo., 28 October 1941.
38 PRO, FO 371/40307, E7351/23/89, Spears to Eastern Department, 29 November 1944.
39 PRO, FO 371/35209, E1504/1504/89, 'Notes on Druzes families', 19 February 1943.
40 PRO, FO 371/40110, E1886/20/88, R. M. A. Hankey note, 'Phalanges libanaises', 11 February 1944.
41 PRO, FO 371/40111, E2305/20/88, Spears to Sir Maurice Peterson, 4 April 1944.
42 St Antony's College archive, SPRS IB/K7, Spears to FO, 24 September 1941.
43 PRO, FO 371/40299, E826/23/89, Spears to Eastern Department, 4 February 1944.
44 Catroux, *Dans la Bataille*, p. 99.
45 PRO, FO 371/40307, E7799/23/89, Spears final Beirut dispatch, 21 December 1944.
46 Khenouf and Brett, 'Algerian nationalism', in Killingray and Rathbone, *Africa and the Second World War*, p. 261; Abitbol, *Jews of North Africa*, p. 53.
47 Lacouture, *The Rebel*, p. 390. By the late 1930s the PPF had a power base in Oranie, see AN, F^{60}/187, Cabinet, Alger, 'Situation politique européenne, 1938'.
48 Blanchard and Boëtsch, 'Races et propagande coloniale', 533; Michel Abitbol gives a much lower figure of 150,000 Légion members in Algeria, see his *Jews of North Africa*, pp. 52–3.
49 Soustelle's quote appears in full in Abitbol, *Jews of North Africa*, pp. 49, 53.
50 SHAT, 2P14/D6, no. 1716, EM-I Juin to General Bridoux, 25 August 1942; no. 9628/POL, Affaires Politiques to General Bridoux, 13 July 1942.
51 SHAT, 2P14/D6, no. 2081, EM-I General Juin to Secrétariat d'Etat à la Guerre, 30 September 1942; Dix-neuvième région militaire – Etat numérique, Légion Tricolore, 15 September 1942. The Légion Tricolore was dissolved in January 1943.
52 SHAT, 2P12/D6, CAB, General Delmotte to Laval, 11 January 1943; EM-I note, Etat nominatif des officiers, 2 February 1943; D4/CAB, Colonel Pierre Lacombe memo., 'Le SOL Points au combat au Tunisie', n.d., July 1943.
53 Blanchard and Boëtsch, 'Races et propagande coloniale', 534–42.
54 MAE, Papiers Baudouin, vol. 9/Maroc, no. 773, Noguès to Baudouin, 13 September 1940; Noguès to section Afrique–Levant, 9 October 1940; Abitbol, *Jews of North Africa*, p. 42.
55 Daniel Carpi, *Between Mussolini and Hitler. The Jews and the Italian Authorities in France and Tunisia* (London, Brandeis University Press, 1994), pp. 205–6.
56 Rey-Goldzeiguer, 'L'occupation germano-italienne de la Tunisie', pp. 326–8.
57 MAE, Vichy Série P, vol. 12, no. 773/RG, Esteva to Darlan, 7 October 1941.
58 Abitbol, *Jews of North Africa*, pp. 60–3, 72.
59 *Ibid.*, p. 59.
60 Carpi, *Between Mussolini and Hitler*, pp. 201–3; Abitbol, *Jews of North Africa*, pp. 66–7.
61 Rey-Goldzeiguer, 'L'occupation germano-italienne de la Tunisie', pp. 332–3.
62 SHAT, 1P90/D2, no. 3537/SG, Weygand to Pétain, 2 July 1941.
63 Swinton papers, SWIN I/3/3, Lord Hailey memo., 'West Africa and the war', n.d., 1942.
64 Crémieux-Brilhac, *La France Libre*, pp. 663–4.
65 SHAT, 1P90/D1, Délégation Générale, conférence mensuelle, 28–30 May 1941.
66 Khenouf and Brett, 'Algerian nationalism', pp. 261, 268–9.
67 Rainero, *La Commission Italienne d'Armistice*, pp. 498–512.
68 Rainero, *La Commission Italienne d'Armistice* doc. 44, pp. 538–40.
69 ANCOM, Aff. pol., C2116/D2, Section Afrique, 'Note sur le statut de l'Algérie', n.d., May 1947.
70 AN, F^{60}/885, Puaux, statement to Comité de l'Afrique du Nord, 9 August 1945.
71 PRO, WO 208/661, Ministry of Information, Far Eastern Bureau, 'Analytic outline of political movements in Indo-China', 25 April 1944.
72 Tonnesson, *Vietnamese Revolution*, p. 104.
73 Japanese diplomats were shocked by the level of corruption which characterised French settler communities in Indo-China, see Nitz, 'Independence without nationalists?', 112.
74 Tonnesson, *Vietnamese Revolution*, p. 103; Cooper, *Decolonization and African Society*, p. 155.

75 SHM, TTA 102/EMM-3, FMF-3, Etude no. 24, 11 October 1942.
76 Smith, 'The Japanese period in Indochina', 270.
77 MAE, Vichy-Asie, vol. 255, Decoux to Colonies, Vichy, 23 October 1940; CNF Londres, vol. 70, 'L'invasion japonaise en Indochine', 21 August 1942.
78 Smith, 'The Vietnamese elite of French Cochinchina', 479.
79 MAE, CNF Londres, vol. 73, Bulletin de renseignements 64, 16 December 1942.
80 MAE, Vichy-Asie, vol. 255, no. 6942, Decoux to Colonies, Vichy, 20 October 1942; Shipway, *Road to War*, p. 122.
81 Smith, 'The Vietnamese elite', 467.
82 PRO, WO 208/661, FO memo., 'The policy and interests of France in the Far East', 26 March 1943.
83 Nitz, 'Independence without nationalists?', 114.
84 PRO, WO 208/661, MI2, 'Note on present position in FIC', 6 October 1944; MAE, Vichy-Asie, vol 255, no. 6942, Decoux to Colonies, Vichy, 20 October 1942.
85 MAE, CNF Londres, vol. 70, Commandant A. Duguey to Weygand, 'Situation des colonies', 14 July 1941.
86 Nitz, 'Independence without nationalists?', 119–20.
87 MAE, CNF Londres, vol. 73, Bulletin de renseignements 64, 16 December 1942.
88 Duroroy titled his memoirs *Ma Trahison en Indochine*, cited in Tonnesson, *Vietnamese Revolution*, p. 46.
89 PRO, WO 208/665, Military Intelligence intercepts, Mauritius listening station, Decoux messages to Vichy, 12 Feb, 6 May and 17 June 1943; F8378/8376/61, E. W. Meiklereid, Saigon consul, to FO, 24 June 1941.
90 MAE, Série Asie-Océanie, vol. 30, Laurentie draft comments on Indo-China for Ministry of Information, n.d., August 1945.
91 MAE, Série Asie-Océanie, vol. 31, no. 1293, Pechkoff to Affaires étrangères, 11 June 1945; Tonnesson, *Vietnamese Revolution*, pp. 45–6.
92 MAE, Vichy-Asie, vol. 255, Decoux to Colonies, Vichy, 8 September 1943.
93 Smith, 'The Japanese period in Indochina', 269–70.
94 MAE, CNF Londres, vol. 86, Insitut des Relations de Pacifique, 'Note relative à l'Indochine', 10 September 1942.
95 Madjarian, *La Question coloniale*, pp. 118–19.
96 Maguire, *Anglo-American Relations*, p. 127.
97 John W. Young, *France, the Cold War and the Western Alliance, 1944–1949. French Foreign Policy and Post-war Europe* (Leicester, Leicester University Press), pp. 11–14.
98 PRO, WO 204/12595, AFHQ, Psychological Warfare Branch, French Political Intelligence report 1, 21 November 1943. Resistance organisations increased their representation from forty to forty-eight Assembly members.
99 PRO, WO 204/12595, AFHQ, French Political Intelligence report 7, 2 January 1944.
100 AN, F[60]/889, Maurice Dejean reports, Secrétariat général, 'Note concernant la politique coloniale du Comité', 13 January 1944; AN, 560AP/27, Pleven papers, no. 31, Bayardelle, Brazzaville, to Pleven, 22 July 1944.
101 Shipway, *Road to War*, pp. 87–93.
102 Cooper, *Decolonization and African Society*, p. 182; Shipway, Road to War, p. 38.
103 Shennan, *Rethinking France*, p. 145.
104 AN, F60/889, Secrétariat Général, Note for de Gaulle, 5 January 1944; Ollandet, *Brazzaville, capitale de la France Libre*, p. 132.
105 James I. Lewis, 'The French colonial service and the issues of reform, 1944–48', *Contemporary European History*, 4: 2 (1995), 158; AN, 560AP/27, Pleven papers, no. 62/CAB, Cournarie to Pleven, 24 August 1944.
106 Shennan, *Rethinking France*, pp. 147–51.
107 Shipway, *Road to War*, p. 37.
108 Shennan, *Rethinking France*, p. 153.
109 Ageron, 'La perception de la puissance française', 235; Akpo-Vaché, *L'AOF et la seconde guerre mondiale*, pp. 245–6.
110 Akpo-Vaché, *L'AOF et la seconde guerre mondiale*, pp. 217–18.

111 Burton, '"Nos journées de juin"', pp. 228–9. It should be stressed that by 1943 the bulk of the Martiniquan ex-servicemen had become deeply opposed to Vichyite rule.
112 SHAT, 2P14/D6, Statuts – annexes à la loi du 26 November 1942; Rey-Goldzeiguer, 'L'occupation germano-italienne de la Tunisie', p. 334.
113 SHAT, Fonds Privées, Fonds Ziegler – Etat-Major FFI, no. 343/FILA, Commandment des FFI, 24 May 1944.
114 PRO, WO 193/195, SHAEF HQ to CCOS, London, 16 October and 1 November 1944.
115 Clayton, 'Sétif uprising', 7.
116 Myron Echenberg, 'Tragedy at Thiaroye: the Senegalese Soldiers' Uprising of 1944' in P. W. Gutkind *et al.* (eds), *African Labor History*, II (London, Sage, 1978); Tony Chafer, 'African perspectives: the liberation of France and its impact in French West Africa' in Kedward and Wood *Liberation*, pp. 244–5.
117 Shipway, *Road to War*, pp. 76–81, 90–2.

CONCLUSION

By 1945 post-Liberation France was too engrossed in discussion of domestic reconstruction, constitution-making and the closing stages of the war in Europe to pay much attention to matters of empire. In practice, this meant that within the country there was scarcely any public pressure for imperial reform.[1] Indeed, France as a whole was no more gripped by empire in 1945 than it had been in 1919. But the Sétif uprising, France's continuing humiliation in Syria and Lebanon, the uneasy return to Indo-China and the unfinished business of Brazzaville and the French Union – all kept imperial matters to the fore within de Gaulle's provisional government and the French General Staff. On 16 June 1945, the African section of French military intelligence submitted a coldly realistic analysis of the North African position to the Chiefs of Staff,

> In Algeria, the profound causes of malaise subsist, and nothing has been resolved. The implementation of pacification measures and the exposure of the PPA's insurrectionist organisation, which should put paid to this [Algerian] nationalism, may restore calm. But the sickness continues beneath the badly healed wound: a crisis of authority, of confidence, of morality as well.
>
> In Tunisia and Morocco, there is expectation. In the Levant, the British show of force has left France tethered, exposed to the claims of her local adversaries. There, too, nothing is settled ...[2]

Clearly, the Second World War caused a profound crisis of empire for France. It was made even more traumatic by the fact that French imperial territory became the battleground of several interlocking conflicts of authority. The developing contest between colonial ruler and subject population was for much of the war subsumed beneath the conflict between rival French authorities as Vichy and Free France competed for imperial control. This was, in turn, a struggle influenced and sometimes dictated by the overarching battle between the Allies and the Axis powers. In so far as the armistice agreements denied the Vichy regime the means to consolidate its defence of empire, so Free France stood to benefit, provided that de Gaulle could mould a viable and recognised political alternative. Among the Axis powers, only Japan gave vent to its imperial ambitions at French expense. But the threat that Germany or Italy might intercede in Vichy's defence against Free France, or that the fascist powers might unleash a land-grab across French Africa and the Levant, seemed real enough for much of 1940–42. In the event, Vichy's attempt to circumvent this by steadily increasing imperial collaborationism after Darlan's conclusion of the May protocols in 1941 only hastened the Allied descent upon French North Africa in November 1942.

Vichy was, of course, not alone in its effort to offset metropolitan weakness against continued colonial power. It is well to remember that the Free French movement had scarcely been in existence for three months before it could lay claim to authority over much of French Equatorial Africa. Much of the heroic achievement of de Gaulle's early converts in Africa lies in their temerity in seizing control with manpower and resources that were incredibly slight. This has perhaps generated a somewhat distorted picture of French North and West Africa in June 1940, where administrations with far greater military and economic means and more significant political expertise chose to abide by the armistice provisions. To enthusiastic Gaullists the conversion of AEF in August 1940 only confirmed the timidity of their Vichy rivals in Africa, a simplistic assessment which took little account of either local conditions or the positive allure of Pétain's call for loyalty in defeat. Less than a year later, in mid-July 1941, Gaullist forces replaced their Vichy rivals in Syria and Lebanon. But here one confronts the paradox of the Free French empire: it was a diffuse collection of territories dependent upon Allied military backing and ruled in the service of a movement whose cardinal aim was not the transformation of empire but the liberation of France. Gaullist colonies and mandates were neither economically self-supporting nor politically secure; indeed, Free French determination to 'enlist' these territories in the service of France's liberation generally made them less stable than previously. By 1943, in sub-Saharan Africa and Madagascar, the fact that Free French possessions benefited from British, and later US, financial support and economic supply encouraged an unscrupulous Gaullist colonial production drive intended to build up the political standing of Free France as an Allied power. Conversely, during 1940–42, Britain's land and sea blockade of Vichy Africa diminished the prospect of a peaceful conversion of Pétainist administrations to the Allied cause.

After the failure of the assault on Dakar in late September 1940, it became obvious that the French empire would long remain divided. Denied control of AOF, the Free French had even less chance of securing a foothold in North Africa. After the widespread arrests of Gaullist dissidents in late 1940, by 1941 nowhere was there a Free French network strong enough within an individual colony to topple the sitting authority. Determined to maintain Vichy control, in October 1940 Pétain's appointment of Weygand as his African supremo consolidated the loyalty of French North and West Africa. Until the successful invasion of the Levant in June–July 1941, the Dakar humiliation left de Gaulle at the mercy of British service chiefs who were deeply sceptical of either the intrinsic appeal or the military potential of Free France. Thereafter, the nature of Anglo-Gaullist imperial relations changed fundamentally. Whereas in the twelve months between August 1940 and July 1941 the Carlton Gardens administration sought to persuade its British hosts to support the expansion of Free French colonial control, after the Levant occupation Gaullist suspicions of British imperial power coloured subsequent colonial co-operation between the two. This reflected de Gaulle's basic imperial dilemma: while he needed Allied help to secure the larger French colonial prizes, he did not wish to compromise his political and military independence once Free French personnel were installed. The British and Americans were consistently reluctant to go to war with Vichy France. So they inevitably subordinated attacks on Vichy colonies to their wider strategic planning, and did not look lightly upon relatively straightforward operations against Vichyite colonies. As a result, there was never any likelihood that the Allies would readily hand over the reins of power to de Gaulle's representatives once the Levant, Madagascar, French North Africa or Indo-China was seized.

Although the political animosity generated by this clash of Free French and Allied objectives was at its most acute in Syria and Lebanon, the same problem made the British and Americans still more inclined to exclude the Free French from operations against Madagascar and French North Africa. Ostensibly, the basic Allied calculation seemed clear. Firstly, Free French forces were numerically too small to make a strategic impact upon the planned operations, and their introduction was expected to increase the determination of their Vichyite opponents to resist any invasion. Furthermore, to involve the Free French from the outset would inevitably reduce the political options available to the Allies, since it would preclude all dialogue or compromise with pro-Vichy administrations. Moreover, since the English-speaking powers never reconciled their respective policies towards Free France and Vichy, their preferred alternative was to avoid inter-Allied squabbling by sidelining de Gaulle. But the drawbacks of this deliberate obfuscation were made manifest in Indo-China. This was the colonial theatre where the Allies disagreed most sharply over the introduction of Gaullist forces and the assertion of Fighting French control. The net result was an inconclusive policy of delayed support for a Far Eastern Expeditionary Force whose arrival was eventually overtaken by events as Japan assumed ultimate control in Indo-China in March 1945.

In several respects, this shoddy treatment of Free France was far from the pragmatic, commonsense approach that the Allies claimed to be following. Before the launch of Operation Torch, Britain tried to undermine the Vichy empire through blockade, propaganda and limited covert action. But, unless strategic necessity intervened, as in the Syrian and Madagascan cases in 1941 and 1942, Churchill's government avoided open confrontation with Vichy colonies after September 1940. This enabled the US government to pursue contacts with Pétain's colonial regimes until increasing Vichy collaborationism and Weygand's dismissal from Algiers gradually destroyed this policy in the first half of 1942. As an imperial power, Britain upheld a double standard in its reluctance to acknowledge Gaullist insistence upon the role of empire within the projection of international influence. Adding insult to injury, from 1943 Churchill's administration abruptly reversed its position. By this point, Roosevelt's anti-colonialism and the possible coalescence of colonial nationalism and international communism generated greater British support for the French empire in those regions where Britain's imperial authority was under greatest threat – North Africa and South East Asia above all. But that did not amount to substantial Anglo-Gaullist imperial partnership. Indeed, where the continuation of French colonial control appeared inimical to British interests, the trend was quite different. Hence, Anglo-Gaullist acrimony in the Levant intensified after the Lebanese crisis of November 1943, a struggle so bitter that it poisoned Anglo-French relations beyond the war's end.

American attitudes to the Free French empire were equally ambivalent. Until 1942, Washington kept the French National Committee at a distance and did not care to advertise its contacts with Gaullist territories. After the creation of the FCNL in June 1943, Roosevelt's government also found it difficult to square its commitment to the liberation of France with de Gaulle's rising influence as head of a unified movement endorsed by much of the metropolitan resistance. In a colonial context, fruitless US efforts to woo Vichy and its overseas territories towards the Allied camp confirmed that official anti-colonialism would be given free rein only after the French empire was excluded from Axis influence. On a more practical note, most US politicians and military leaders, with the notable exception of Robert Murphy in North Africa, found France's colonial leaders an exasperating bunch. Noguès in Morocco, Muselier in St Pierre, Robert in Martinique, Thierry d'Argenlieu in New Caledonia and, ultimately, even Giraud in Algiers – all caused friction within and between various departments of state in Washington.

These Anglo-US pressures clearly indicate that the wartime French empire did not exist in a vacuum only occasionally and dramatically touched by the ebb and flow of the war. Equally, the experience of being cut off from metropolitan France did not result in individual colonies entering a suspended animation, awaiting the outcome of the conflict in Europe. Quite the reverse. By 1944 political protest in Syria and French North Africa posed a serious threat to French authority. Both the liberation of France and Allied victory in Europe brought a new immediacy to Arab nationalist demands. In the major French colonial federations, the economic stress engendered by the war acted as a catalyst to unrest and, in some cases, persecution. Whether in the form of stagnant trade, forced labour exactions, harsh rationing or alarming price inflation, the Levant states, Madagascar, French North Africa and AOF all faced incipient crisis by the time the Fighting French assumed control. Systematically drained of its resources by the Japanese, the economic situation in French Indo-China was still more appalling by 1945. Perhaps then we should be less surprised at the limited scope of Gaullist reform than at the apparent confidence with which the FCNL and the Paris provisional government contemplated the gradual introduction of a programme built upon the Brazzaville conference provisions. In North Africa and Indo-China above all, time was running out more quickly than de Gaulle's Ministers allowed. Only in the Levant was France's crisis of colonial authority seen as inescapable and pressing. But Catroux's attempts to limit demands for outright Syrian and Lebanese independence and Helleu's and Beynet's later efforts to reassert French sovereign control did not bode well for the prospects of dialogue between France and its subject peoples. May 1945, the occasion of final victory in Europe, was also the month of Sétif and the Damascus bombardment. After this last outburst, the French authorities were humiliated in Syria. The facade of re-established control in Algeria was also a fragile construction even if the shakiness of its foundations was not fully revealed until 1954. Beyond the sub-Saharan colonies to which the Brazzaville conference was devoted, it is significant that in all the major colonial federations in which the Free French fought either militarily or politically to assert their control during the Second World War, the transition to an era of decolonisation proved violent. In the Levant, the bloodshed was episodic and mercifully brief. But in Indo-China, Madagascar and French North Africa the breakdown in French colonial rule was of an altogether different order. The divided French empire of the Second World War never entirely recovered from the rifts that had opened up between rulers and ruled.

Notes

1 AN, F^{60}/837, Services des Affaires Musulmanes, Bulletin de renseignements, 20 January 1945.

2 AN, F^{60}/872, EMGDN, Section Afrique, Bulletin de renseignements 23, 15 June 1945.

BIBLIOGRAPHY

Primary sources

France

Ministère des Affaires Etrangères archive, Paris (MAE)
Foreign Ministry – correspondence files of the Free French National Committee: Guerre 1939–45, Londres CNF. Files consulted: AEF; AOF; Afrique du Nord; CFS/Djibouti; Indochine; Madagascar; Pacifique; St Pierre et Miquelon; Syrie-Liban.

Vichy Secretariat of Foreign Affairs: sections Afrique, Levant/Asie, Indochine.
Série E: Levant/Asie; Série K: Afrique; Série M: Maroc; Série P: Tunisie.
Sous-série: Amérique – Questions des Antilles/Relations avec les colonies françaises.

Post-Liberation files:
Série: Afrique-Levant, 1944–1955, Sous-série Algérie.
Série: Asie-Océanie, 1944–1955, Sous-série Indochine.
Série: Tunisie, 1944–1955.
Correspondence Politique et Commerciale: politique extérieure, questions militaires.

Private Papers:
Papiers d'Agents – Fonds René Massigli; Maurice Dejean.
Papiers 1940: Papiers Paul Baudouin.

Service Historique de l'Armée de Terre, Vincennes (SHAT)
Série 1P; Série 2P; Série 3P; Série 4P; Série 5P; Série 7P; Série 10P. Cartons consulted on the following subjects:
Vichy – Défense Nationale/empire – Défense: Etat-Major d'Armée premier bureau; deuxième bureau; troisième bureau.
Afrique Française: Afrique du Nord 1940–45; Algérie 1940–46 (19e Région Militaire); AOF 1940–44; AEF 1940–44; Maroc 1940–42; Levant – défense 1940–42.
Armée d'Armistice – plans de défense, organisation, effectifs, budget, potentiel militaire, missions militaires à l'étranger.
Armée Coloniale – organisation, effectifs, potentiel militaire, renforcement, Phalange Africaine.
Afrique Française Libre – EMA: opérations, renforcement, effectifs, empire économie.
Délégation Allemande de Contrôle/Délégation Italienne de Contrôle (Armistice Commissions – French North Africa/Levant).
Etat-Major Particulier, Général Giraud/Général Juin.

Série H: 2H, Tunisie; 3H, Maroc; 10H, Indochine.

Private Papers:
Série K: Archives Privées:
Alger deuxième bureau 1944; Fonds Général Emile Béthouart; Fonds Général Georges Catroux; Fonds Général Alphonse Juin; Fonds Général Paul Legentilhomme; Fonds Général Charles Luquet; Fonds Général Jean Richard; Fonds Général Maxime Weygand; Fonds Henri Ziegler (FFI).
Papiers du Général Marcel Alessandri; Papiers du Général Boucher de Crèvecoeur.

Service Historique de la Marine, Vincennes (SHM)
Série TT: Guerre 1939–1945.
Série TTA: Secrétariat à la Marine, Vichy: Cabinet Militaire; Forces Maritimes Françaises (FMF) premier bureau; deuxième bureau; troisième bureau.
Série TTC: Archives Forces Navales Françaises Libres:
Emile Muselier correspondence; FNFL service de renseignements; FNFL deuxième bureau.
Archives Personnelles: Sous série GG2, Fonds Amiral Sacaze; Papiers Godfroy.

Service Historique de l'Armée de l'Air, Vincennes (SHAA)
Série C – Forces aériennes françaises d'Outre-mer, CI Levant, CII Maroc, CIII Tunisie, CIV Extrême-Orient.
Série D – Armée de l'Air de 1939 à 1945.

Archives Nationales, Paris
Série F^{60} – Secrétariat Général du Gouvernement et Services du Premier Ministre (Premier's Office files).
Archives Privées: 560AP – Papiers René Pleven.

Archives Nationales Centre des Archives d'Outre-mer, Aix-en-Provence (ANCOM)
Papiers d'Agents: Robert Delavignette; Papiers Georges Mandel; Papiers Marius Moutet; Papiers Albert Sarraut.
Correspondence files of the Vichy Colonial Ministry direction des affaires politiques; North African administration files; Algeria – Algiers and Constantine departmental files (Série 1K).

Great Britain and Canada

Public Record Office, Kew
Cabinet
CAB 65 War Cabinet minutes.
CAB 66 War Cabinet memoranda.
CAB 69 War Cabinet Defence Committee.
CAB 79 Chiefs of Staff Committee minutes.
CAB 80 Chiefs of Staff Committee memoranda.

CAB 81 COS Sub-Committees (Joint Intelligence Committee papers).
CAB 84 Joint Planning Staff papers.
CAB 85 Committee on Foreign (Allied) Resistance Committee papers.
CAB 96 Far Eastern Committee files.
CAB 101 Cabinet Historical Section papers.
CAB 106 Cabinet Historical Section files.
CAB 121 Special Secret Information Centre files.
CAB 122 British Joint Staff Mission, Washington, files.

Admiralty
ADM 1 Admiralty Secretariat papers.
ADM 116 Admiralty and Secretariat cases.
ADM 199 Admiralty War History cases and papers.
ADM 205 First Sea Lord's papers.
ADM 223 Naval Intelligence papers.

Air Ministry
AIR 2 Air Ministry correspondence files.
AIR 8 Records of Chief of Air Staff.
AIR 9 Director of Plans archive.

Colonial Office
CO 323 General correspondence.
CO 865 Far Eastern Reconstruction, Original Correspondence.
CO 967 Private Office papers.
CO 968 Defence/Original Correspondence.

Dominions Office
DO 35 General correspondence.
DO 119 South African High Commission correspondence.

Foreign Office
FO 371 General correspondence: French Department, Southern Department, Western Department.
FO 413 Foreign Office Confidential Print Morocco and North West Africa.
FO 660 FO Ministers Resident papers.
FO 892 FO Mission to French National Committee files.
FO 898 Political Warfare Executive files.
FO 954 Avon papers (Sir Anthony Eden).
FO 959 Consular archives – French Indo-China (Saigon).

Special Operations Executive papers
HS 1 SOE Far East.
HS 3 SOE Middle East/Massingham Mission, French North Africa.

HW 1 Government Code and Cypher School – signals intelligence.

Prime Minister's Office
PREM 3 Prime Minister's Office correspondence and papers 1940–45.

Treasury
T 160 Finance Division records.

War Office
WO 32 War Office registered files.
WO 33 War Office reports/miscellaneous papers.
WO 106 Directorate of Military Operations and Intelligence.
WO 193 Directorate of Military Operations collation files.
WO 201 Military HQ papers: Middle East forces, 1939–45.
WO 202 Military Mission papers.
WO 203 South East Asia Command files.
WO 204 Military HQ papers – Allied Forces: North Africa.
WO 208 Directorate of Military Intelligence.
WO 216 Chief of the Imperial General Staff papers.
WO 219 Supreme Headquarters Allied Expeditionary Force (SHAEF) papers.
WO 259 War Office Private Office papers.

Churchill College Archive Centre, Cambridge
Major-general Edward Louis Spears papers.
Viscount Norwich (Alfred Duff Cooper) papers.
Earl of Swinton (Lord Swinton – Philip Cunliffe-Lister) papers
Admiral Sir James Somerville papers.
Lord Strang papers: Rougier mission, 1940.
Lord Lloyd papers: Colonial Office, 1939–40.
Air Chief Marshal Walter Cheshire: Allied Disarmament Commission, Saigon.
Theodor Harris: memoir of French Foreign Legionnaire, 1940–42.

St Antony's College, Oxford, Middle East Centre Archive
Major-general Edward Louis Spears papers (Middle East).
Diaries of first Baron Killearn (Sir Miles Lampson).
Nevill Barbour papers.

Liddell Hart Centre for Military Archives, King's College, London (LHCMA)
Papers of Major-general F. H. N. Davidson.
Papers of Admiral Sir Gerald Charles Dickens.
Papers of General Sir Douglas Gracey.

Rhodes House Library, Oxford, Manuscript collections
MSS. Afr. s. 940, A. A. Cullen, Report on visit to Cameroon, 1944.
MSS. Afr. s. 1085, Memorandum by L. C. Giles, 'First British Contacts with Eboué (1940)'.
MSS. Afr. s. 1252, Paul Singer, Memorandum on land tenure in Algiers and Tunis, 1919.
MSS. Afr. s. 1334(9–10), Diaries and papers of Sir Theo Chandos Hoskyns-Abrahall.

MSS Afr. s. 1754, Sir Gerald Halla Creasy, 'Diary of a Visit to West Africa, November 1943–January 1944'.

National Archives of Canada, Ottawa

RG 2 Cabinet War Committee minutes and documents.
RG 24 Department of National Defence, Naval Intelligence files.
RG 25 Department of External Affairs, 1940 series.
RG 25 Office of Under-secretary of State for External Affairs (Series A2).
MG 26 W. L. M. King memoranda and notes (Series J4/J13).
MG 30 Oscar Douglas Skelton papers (Series D33), vol. 5.
MG 31 Escott Reid papers (Series E46), vol. 5.
MG 32 Georges P. Vanier papers (Series A2), vols. 13–15.

Published document collections

La Délégation Française auprès de la Commission Allemande d'Armistice: Recueil de Documents publié par le Gouvernement Français, 4 vols, Paris, 1947 *et seq*.

Documents Diplomatiques Français, 1944, II, Ministère des Affaires Etrangères, Paris, Imprimerie Nationale, 1996.

Documents on Australian Foreign Policy, 1937–49, IV, *July 1940–June 1941*, Hudson, W. J., and H. J. W. Stokes (eds), Canberra, Australian Government Publishing Service, 1980.

Documents on Canadian External Relations, Part II, vol. 8, Murray, David R. (ed.), Ottawa, 1976.

Documents on German Foreign Policy, 1918–1945, Smyth, Howard M., *et al.* (eds), London, HMSO, 1957, *et seq*, series *D, VIII–XII*.

Foreign Relations of the United States, Washington, D.C., Government Printing Office, 1952–1964.

La Guerre d'Algérie par les documents, I: *L'Avertissement, 1943–1946*, Paris, Vincennes, 1990.

La Guerre d'Indochine, 1945–1954, I: *Le Retour de la France en Indochine, 1945–1946*, Bodinier, Gilbert (ed.), Paris, Vincennes, 1987.

Diaries, memoirs and contemporary studies

Baudouin, Paul, *The Private Diaries of Paul Baudouin*, English trans. London, Eyre and Spottiswoode, 1948.

British Military Administration in Africa, 1941–1947, London, HMSO, 1948.

Bullitt, Orville H. (ed.), *For the President. Personal and Secret. Correspondence between Franklin D. Roosevelt and William C. Bullitt*, Boston, Mass., Houghton Mifflin, 1972.

Cassin, René, *Les Hommes partis de rien. Le Réveil de la France abattue (1940–1941)*, Paris, Plon, 1975.

Catroux, Georges, *Dans la bataille de la Méditerranée. Egypte–Levant–Afrique du Nord 1940–1944*, Paris, Julliard, 1949.

— *Deux Actes du drame Indochinois*, Paris, Plon, 1959.
Chandler, Alfred D., *et al.* (eds), *The Papers of Dwight David Eisenhower*, vol. II, Baltimore, Md, Johns Hopkins University Press, 1970.
Charles-Roux, François, *Cinq Mois tragiques aux affaires étrangères (21 Mai–1er Novembre 1940)*, Paris, Plon, 1949.
Churchill, Winston S., *The Second World War*, 8 vols, London, Cassell, 1948–54.
Coutou-Bégarie, Hervé, and Claude Huan, *Lettres et notes de l'Amiral Darlan*, Paris, Economica, 1992.
Daladier, Jean, and Jean Daridan, *Edouard Daladier. Prison Journal, 1940–1945*, Boulder Colo. and Oxford, Westview Press, 1995.
Dard, Olivier, and Hervé Bastien (eds), *Henri Queuille. Journal de Guerre, Londres–Alger (Avril 1943–Juillet 1944)*, Paris, Plon, 1995.
Darlan, Alain, *L'Amiral Darlan Parle ...*, Paris, Amiot-Dumont, 1952.
Decoux, Jean, *A la Barre de l'Indochine. Histoire de mon gouvernement général (1940–1945)*, Paris, Plon, 1949.
De Gaulle, Charles, *Mémoires de Guerre*, 3 vols, Paris, Plon, 1954 *et seq.*
Deschamps, Hubert, *Roi de la brousse*, Paris, Berger-Levrault, 1975.
Giraud, Henri, *Un Seul But, la victoire. Alger 1942–1944*, Paris, Julliard, 1949.
Godfroy, René, *L'Aventure de la Force X à Alexandrie (1940–1943)*, Paris, 1953.
Grew, Joseph C., *Ten Years in Japan*, London, Hammond, 1944.
Hull, Cordell, *The Memoirs of Cordell Hull*, 2 vols, London, Macmillan, 1948.
Joxe, Louis, *Mémoires. Victoires de la nuit*, Paris, Flammarion, 1981.
Juin, Maréchal Alphonse, *Mémoires*, vols I–II, Paris, Fayard, 1959–60.
Kimball, Warren F. (ed.), *Churchill and Roosevelt. The Complete Correspondence*, vols I–III, Princeton, N.J., Princeton University Press, 1984.
Macmillan, Harold, *The Blast of War, 1939–1945*, London, Macmillan, 1969.
— *War Diaries. Politics and War in the Mediterranean, January 1943–May 1945*, London, Macmillan, 1984.
Mast, Charles, *Histoire d'une rébellion. Alger, 8 Novembre 1942*, Paris, Plon, 1969.
Monnet, Jean, *Memoirs*, London, Collins, 1978.
Murphy, Robert, *Diplomat among Warriors*, New York, Doubleday, 1964.
Muselier, Emile, *De Gaulle contre le Gaullisme*, Paris, Editions du Chène, 1946.
Palewski, Gaston, *Mémoires d'action, 1924–1974*, Paris, Plon, 1988.
Piétri, François, *Mes Années d'Espagne*, Paris, Plon, 1954.
Puaux, Gabriel, *Deux Années au Levant. Souvenirs de Syrie et du Liban*, Paris, Plon, 1952.
Robert, Georges, *La France aux Antilles de 1939 à 1943*, Paris, Plon, 1950.
Sainteny, Jean, *Histoire d'une paix manquée. Indochine, 1945–1947*, Paris, Fayard, 1967.
Sicé, Adolphe, *L'Afrique équatoriale française et le Cameroun au service de la France*, Paris, Presses Universitaires de France, 1946.
Spears, Sir Edward Louis, *Fulfilment of a Mission. The Spears Mission in Syria*

and Lebanon, 1941–1944, London, Cooper, 1977.
Van Der Poel, Jean (ed.), *Selections from the Smuts Papers*, vol. VI, *December 1934–August 1945*, Cambridge, Cambridge University Press, 1973.
Vigneras, Marcel, *Rearming the French*, Washington, D.C., US Army Department, 1957.
Weygand, Maxime, *Memoirs. Recalled to Service*, London, Heinemann, English trans., 1952.

Books

Abitbol, Michel, *The Jews of North Africa during the Second World War*, Detroit, Wayne State University Press, 1989.
Adamthwaite, Anthony, *Grandeur and Misery. France's bid for Power in Europe, 1914–1940*, London, Arnold, 1995.
Ade Ajayi, J. F., and M. Crowder (eds), *History of West Africa*, II, London, Longman, 1974.
Adès, Lucien, *L'Aventure algérienne, 1940–1944. Pétain – Giraud – De Gaulle*, Paris, 1979.
Ageron, Charles-Robert, *France coloniale ou parti colonial?*, Paris, Presses Universitaires de France, 1978.
— (ed.), *Histoire de l'Algérie contemporaine*, II, *De l'insurrection de 1871 au déclenchement de la guerre de libération (1954)*, Paris, Presses Universitaires de France, 1979.
— *Les Chemins de la décolonisation française 1936–1956*, Paris, Editions du CNRS, 1986.
— and Marc Michel (eds), *L'Afrique noire française. L'heure des indépendances*, Paris, Edtions du CNRS, 1992.
Aglion, Raoul, *Roosevelt and De Gaulle. Allies in Conflict*, New York, Free Press, 1988.
Akpo-Vaché, Catherine, *L'AOF et la seconde guerre mondiale. La Vie politique (septembre 1939–octobre 1945)*, Paris, Editions CNRS/Karthala, 1996.
Aldrich, Richard J., *The Key to the South. Britain, the United States and Thailand during the Approach of the Pacific War, 1929–1942*, Oxford, Oxford University Press, 1993.
Aldrich, Robert, *Greater Overseas France. A History of French Overseas Expansion*, London, Macmillan, 1996.
— and Isabelle Merle (eds), *France Abroad. Indochina, New Caledonia, Wallis and Futuna, Mayotte*, Sydney, Department of Economic History Occasional Publications, University of Sydney, 1996.
Alexander, Martin S., *The Republic in Danger. General Maurice Gamelin and the Politics of French Defence, 1933–1940*, Cambridge, Cambridge University Press, 1992.
Allen, Philip M., *Madagascar. Conflicts of Authority in the Great Island*, Westview Press, Oxford, 1995.
Alzon, Claude Hesse d', *La Présence militaire française en Indochine, 1940–1945*, Paris, SHAT, 1985.

BIBLIOGRAPHY

Andreopoulos, George J., and Harold E. Selesky, *The Aftermath of Defeat. Societies, Armed Forces and the Challenge of Recovery*, New Haven, Conn., Yale University Press 1994.

Anglin, Douglas G., *The St Pierre and Miquelon Affaire of 1941. A Study in Diplomacy in the North Atlantic Triangle*, Toronto, Toronto University Press, 1966.

Ansprenger, Franz, *The Dissolution of the Colonial empires*, London, Routledge, 1989.

Auphan, Paul, and Jacques Mordal, *The French Navy in World War II*, Westport, Conn., Greenwood Press, English trans., 1959.

Azéma, Jean-Pierre, *From Munich to the Liberation, 1938–1944*, Cambridge, Cambridge University Press, 1984.

— and François Bédarida (eds), *Le Régime de Vichy et les Français*, Paris, Fayard, 1992.

Balesi, Charles John, *From Adversaries to Comrades in Arms. West Africans and the French Military, 1885–1918*, Waltham, Mass., Crossroads Press, 1979.

Barker, Elizabeth, *Churchill and Eden at War*, London, Macmillan, 1978.

Beevor, J. C., *SOE. Recollections and reflections, 1940–1945*, London, Bodley Head, 1981.

Bell, Philip, *A Certain Eventuality. Britain and the Fall of France*, Farnborough, Saxon House, 1974.

— *France and Britain, 1940–1994. The Long Separation*, London, Longman, 1997.

Bessis, Juliette, *La Méditerranée fasciste. L'Italie mussolinienne et la Tunisie*, Paris, Karthala, 1980.

Betts, Raymond F., *France and Decolonisation, 1900–1960*, London, Macmillan, 1991.

Bey, Salma Mardam, *La Syrie et la France. Bilan d'une équivoque (1939–1945)*, Paris, Editions l'Harmattan, 1994.

Bidwell, Robin, *Morocco under Colonial Rule. French Administration of Tribal Areas, 1912–1956*, London, Frank Cass, 1973.

Biondi, Jean-Pierre, *Les Anticolonialistes (1881–1962)*, Paris, Laffont, 1992.

Blumenthal, Henry, *Illusion and Reality in Franco-American Diplomacy, 1914–1945*, Baton Rouge, University of Louisiana Press, 1986.

Bouche, Denise, *Histoire de la colonisation française*, vol. II, Paris, Fayard, 1991.

Carlier, Claude, and Guy Pedroncini (eds), *Les Troupes Coloniales dans la Grande Guerre*, Paris, Economica, 1997.

Caroff, C. F., *Le Théâtre Atlantique. Le Théâtre Méditerranéen*, Paris, SHM, 1958.

Carpi, Daniel, *Between Mussolini and Hitler. The Jews and the Italian Authorities in France and Tunisia*, Waltham, Mass., and London, Brandeis University Press, 1994.

Chalmers Hood III, Ronald, *Royal Republicans. The French Naval Dynasties between the World Wars*, Baton Rouge, University of Louisiana Press, 1985.

Chipman, John, *French Power in Africa*, Oxford, Blackwell, 1989.

Christian, William A., *Divided Island, Faction and Unity on St Pierre*, Cam-

bridge, Mass., Harvard University Press, 1969.
Clayton, Anthony, *France, Soldiers and Africa*, London, Brassey's, 1988.
— *The Wars of French Decolonization*, London, Longman, 1994.
Cogan, Charles G., *Oldest Allies, Guarded Friends. The United States and France since 1940*, London, Praeger, 1994.
Cohen, William B., *Rulers of empire. The French Colonial Service in Africa*, Stanford, Cal., Stanford University Press, 1971.
Cointet, Michèle, and Jean-Paul Cointet, *La France à Londres, 1940–1943*, Paris, Complexe, 1990.
Conroy, Hilary, and Harry Wray (eds), *Pearl Harbor Reexamined. Prologue to the Pacific War*, Honolulu, University of Hawaii Press, 1990.
Cookridge, E. H., *Inside SOE. The Story of Special Operations in Western Europe*, London, Barker, 1966.
Cooper, Frederick, *Decolonization and African Society. The Labor Question in French and British Africa*, Cambridge, Cambridge University Press, 1996.
Coquery-Vidrovitch, Catherine, *L'Afrique occidentale au temps des français. Colonisateurs et colonisés, 1860–1960*, Paris, Editions la Découverte, 1992.
Coutau-Bégarie, Hervé, and Claude Huan, *Darlan*, Paris, Fayard, 1989.
Cras, Hervé, *Les Forces Maritimes du Nord*, 3 vols, Paris, SHM, 1955.
Crémieux-Brilhac, Jean-Louis, *La France Libre. De l'Appel du 18 juin à la Libération*, Paris, Gallimard, 1996.
Crowder, Michael, *West Africa under Colonial Rule*, London, Hutchinson, 1968.
— *Colonial West Africa*, London, Frank Cass, 1978.
Cruikshank, Charles, *SOE in the Far East*, Oxford, Oxford University Press, 1983.
Dallek, Robert, *Franklin D. Roosevelt and American Foreign Policy, 1932–45*, Oxford, Oxford University Press, 1979.
Delavignette, Robert, and Charles-André Julien, *Les Constructeurs de la France d'outre-mer*, Paris, Presses Universitaires de France, 1946.
Delpha, François, *Montoire. Les Premiers Jours de la collaboration*, Paris, Albin Michel, 1996.
Dennis, Peter, *Troubled Days of Peace. Mountbatten and South East Asia Command, 1945–46*, Manchester, Manchester University Press, 1987.
Devillers, Philippe, *Histoire du Viet-Nam de 1940 à 1952*, Paris, Editions du Seuil, 1952.
— *Paris–Saigon–Hanoi. Les Archives de la guerre, 1944–1947*, Paris, Gallimard, 1988.
Dinan, Desmond, *The Politics of Persuasion. British Policy and French African neutrality, 1940–42*, Lanham, Md., University Press of America, 1988.
Dockrill, Saki (ed.), *From Pearl Harbor to Hiroshima. The Second World War in Asia and the Pacific, 1941–45*, London, Macmillan, 1994.
Doise, Jean, and Maurice Vaïsse, *Diplomatie et outil militaire, 1871–1991*, Paris, Imprimerie Nationale, 1987.
Dougherty, James J., *The Politics of Wartime Aid. American Economic Assistance to France and French Northwest Africa, 1940–1946*, Westport, Conn.,

Greenwood Press, 1978.
Dreifort, John E., *Myopic Grandeur. The Ambivalence of French Foreign Policy toward the Far East, 1919–1945*, Kent, Oh., Kent State University Press, 1991.
Dreyfus, François-Georges, *Histoire de la Résistance*, Paris, Editions de Fallois, 1996.
Duiker, William J., *The Rise of Nationalism in Vietnam, 1900–1941*, Ithaca, N.Y., Cornell University Press, 1976
— *US Containment Policy and the Conflict in Indochina*, Stanford, Cal., Stanford University Press, 1994.
— *The Communist Road to Power in Vietnam*, 2nd ed., Boulder, Col., Westview Press, 1996.
Duroselle, Jean-Baptiste, *L'Abîme, 1939–1945*, Paris, Imprimerie Nationale, 1982.
— and E. Serra, *Italia e Francia 1939–1945*, Milan, Instituto per gli Studi di Politica Internazionale, 1984.
Echenberg, Myron, *Colonial Conscripts. The Tirailleurs Sénégalais in French West Africa, 1857–1960*, Portsmouth, N.H., Heinemann, 1990.
Fall, Babacar, *Le Travail forcé en Afrique-occidentale Française (1900–1946)*, Paris, Karthala, 1993.
Favreau, Bertrand, *Georges Mandel, ou la Passion de la République, 1885–1944*, Paris, Fayard, 1996.
Ferro, Marc, *Pétain*, Paris, Fayard, 1987.
Folin, Jacques de, *Indochine 1940–1955. La Fin d'un rêve*, Paris, Perrin, 1993.
Funk, Arthur Layton, *The Politics of Torch. The Allied Landings and the Algiers Putsch, 1942*, Lawrence, University of Kansas Press, 1974.
— *Hidden Ally. The French Resistance, Special Operations, and the Landings in Southern France, 1944*, New York, Greenwood Press, 1992.
Gates, Eleanor, *End of the Affair. The Collapse of the Anglo-French Alliance, 1939–1940*, London, Allen and Unwin, 1981.
Gaunson, A. B., *The Anglo-French Clash in Lebanon and Syria, 1940–1945*, London, Macmillan, 1987.
Ghébali, V. Y., *La France en guerre et les organisations internationales, 1939–1945*, Paris, Mouton, 1969.
Gifford, Prosser, and William Roger Louis (eds), *The Transfer of Power in Africa. Decolonization, 1940–1960*, New Haven, Conn., Yale University Press, 1982.
Gillois, André, *Histoire secrète des Français à Londres*, Paris, Hachette, 1972.
Girardet, Raoul, *L'Idée coloniale en France, 1870–1962*, Paris, Editions Pluriel, 1972.
Gorce, Paul-Marie de la, *L'empire écartelé, 1936–1946*, Paris, Editions Denoël, 1988.
Haight, Jnr, John McVickar, *American Aid to France, 1938–1940*, New York, Atheneum, 1970.
Hargreaves, John D., *Decolonization in Africa*, London, Longman, 1988.
Harris Smith, Richard, *OSS. The Secret History of America's First Central Intelligence Agency*, Berkeley, University of California Press, 1972.

Harrison, Christopher, *France and Islam in West Africa, 1860–1960*, Cambridge, Cambridge University Press, 1988.
Hartley, Anthony, *Gaullism. The Rise and Fall of a Political Movement*, London, Routledge, 1972.
Hinsley, F. H., E. E. Thomas, C. F. G. Ranson, and R. C. Knight, *British Intelligence in the Second World War*, 3 vols, London, HMSO, 1981.
Hoisington, William A., *The Casablanca Connection. French Colonial Policy, 1936–1943*, Chapel Hill, University of North Carolina Press, 1984.
— *Lyautey and the French Conquest of Morocco*, London, Macmillan, 1995.
Hurstfield, Julian G., *America and the French Nation, 1939–1945*, Chapel Hill, University of North Carolina Press, 1986.
Hymans, Jacques Louis, *Léopold Sédar Senghor. An Intellectual Biography*, Edinburgh, Edinburgh University Press, 1971.
Joffé, George (ed.), *North Africa. Nation, State and Region*, London, Macmillan, 1993.
Johnson, G. Welsey (ed.), *Double Impact. France and Africa in the Age of Imperialism*, Westport, Conn., Greenwood Press, 1985.
Jones, Matthew, *Britain, the United States and the Mediterranean War, 1942–44*, Oxford, St Antony's, 1996.
Kaspi, André, *La Mission de Jean Monnet à Alger, mars–octobre 1943*, Paris, Publications de la Sorbonne, 1971.
Kedward, H. R., and Nancy Wood (eds), *The Liberation of France. Image and Event*, Oxford, Berg, 1995.
Kent, John, *The Internationalization of Colonialism. Britain, France and Black Africa, 1939–1956*, Oxford, Clarendon Press, 1992.
Kersaudy, François, *Churchill and De Gaulle*, London, Collins, 1981.
Khoury, Philip S., *Syria and the French mandate. The Politics of Arab Nationalism, 1920–1945*, Princeton, N.J., Princeton University Press, 1987.
Killingray, David, and Richard Rathbone, *Africa and the Second World War*, London, Macmillan, 1986.
Koulakssis, Ahmed, *Le Parti Socialiste et l'Afrique du Nord de Jaurès à Blum*, Paris, Armand Colin, 1991.
Krautkramer, Elmar, *Vichy–Alger 1940–1942. Le chemin de la France au tournant de la guerre*, Paris, Economica, 1992
Laborie, Pierre, *L'Opinion française sous Vichy*, Paris, Editions du Seuil, 1990.
Lacorne, Denis, Jaques Rupaik and Marie-France Toinet, *The Rise and Fall of Anti-Americanism. A Century of French Perception*, London, Macmillan, 1990.
Lacouture, Jean, *De Gaulle*, I, *The Rebel, 1890–1944*, London, Collins, 1990.
Lacroix-Riz, Annie, *Le choix de Marianne. Les Relations franco-américaines, 1944–1948*, Paris, Messidor, 1985.
— *Les Protectorats d'Afrique du Nord entre la France et Washington du Débarquement à l'Indépendance. Maroc et Tunisie, 1942–1956*, Paris, Editions l'Harmattan, 1988.
Langer, William L., *Our Vichy Gamble*, New York, Knopf, 1947.
Lasker, Michael M., *North African Jewry in the Twentieth Century. The Jews of Morocco, Tunisia and Algeria*, New York, New York University Press, 1994.

Lawler, Nancy Ellen, *Soldiers of Misfortune. Ivorien 'Tirailleurs' of World War II*, Athens, Oh., Ohio University Press, 1992.
Lerner, Henri, *Catroux*, Paris, Albin Michel, 1992.
Leygues, Jacques Raphaël, and F. Flohic, *Darlan–Laborde. L'Inimitié de deux amiraux*, Brest, 1990
Lynch, Frances M. B., *France and the International Economy. From Vichy to the Treaty of Rome*, London, Routledge, 1997.
Madjarian, Grégoire, *La Question coloniale et la politique du Parti communiste français, 1944–1947*, Paris, Maspero, 1977.
Maguire, Gloria E., *Anglo-American Relations with the Free French*, London, Macmillan, 1995.
Manning, Patrick, *Francophone sub-Saharan Africa, 1880–1985*, Cambridge, Cambridge University Press, 1988.
Marder, Arthur J., *From the Dardanelles to Oran. Studies of the Royal Navy in War and Peace, 1915–1940*, London, Oxford University Press, 1974.
— *Operation Menace*, London, Oxford University Press, 1976.
Marr, David G., *Vietnamese Anticolonialism, 1885–1925*, Berkeley, University of California Press, 1971.
Marseille, Jacques, *Empire colonial et capitalisme français. Histoire d'un divorce*, Paris, Albin Michel, 1984.
Marshall, D. Bruce, *The French Colonial Myth and Constitution-making in the Fourth Republic*, New Haven, Conn., Yale University Press, 1973.
Martin, Jean, *L'empire triomphant 1871–1936*, II: *Maghreb, Indochine, Madagascar*, Paris, Editions la découverte, 1990.
Masson, Philippe, *La Marine française et la guerre, 1939–1945*, Paris, Tallandier, 1991.
Michel, Henri, *Le Procès de Riom*, Paris, Albin Michel, 1979.
Michel, Marc, *L'Appel à l'Afrique. Contributions et réactions à l'effort de guerre en AOF (1914–1919)*, Paris, Publications de la Sorbonne, 1982.
Moneta, Jacob, *Le PCF et la question coloniale (1920–1965)*, Paris, Maspero, 1971.
Morley, James William (ed.), *The Fateful Choice. Japan's Advance into South East Asia, 1939–1941*, New York, Columbia University Press, 1980.
N'Dumbre, K. A., *Hitler voulait l'Afrique. Le Projet du Troisième Reich sur le continent africain*, Paris, Editions l'Harmattan, 1980.
Noguères, L., *Le Suicide de la flotte française à Toulon*, Paris, 1961.
Nora, Pierre, *Les Français d'Algérie*, Paris, Juillard, 1961.
Ollandet, Jérôme, *Brazzaville, capitale de la France Libre. Histoire de la résistance française en Afrique (1940–1944)*, Brazzaville, Editions de la Savane, 1980.
Paret, Peter, *French Revolutionary Warfare from Indochina to Algeria. The Analysis of a Political and Military Doctrine*, Princeton, N.J., Princeton University Press, 1964.
Paxton, Robert O., *Parades and Politics at Vichy*, Princeton, N.J., Princeton University Press, 1966.
— *Vichy France, Old Guard and New Order, 1940–1944*, London, Barrie and Jenkins, 1972.

— and Nicholas Wahl (eds), *De Gaulle and the United States. A Centennial Reappraisal*, Oxford, Berg, 1994.

Pearce, Robert D., *Sir Bernard Bourdillon. The Biography of a Twentieth-century Colonialist*, Oxford, Kensall Press, 1987.

Pedroncini, Guy, and Philippe Duplay (eds), *Leclerc et l'Indochine, 1945–1947. Quand se noua le destin d'un empire*, Paris, Albin Michel, 1992.

Pervillé, Guy, *De l'empire français à la décolonisation*, Paris, Hachette, 1991.

Pilleul, Gilbert (ed.), *Le Général de Gaulle et l'Indochine, 1940–1946*, Paris, Plon/Institut Charles de Gaulle, 1982.

Porch, Douglas, *The French Secret Services. From the Dreyfus Affair to the Gulf War*, London, Macmillan, 1995.

Prochaska, David, *Making Algeria French. Colonialism in Bône, 1870–1920*, Cambridge, Cambridge University Press, 1990.

Pujo, Bernard, *Juin, Maréchal de France*, Paris, Albin Michel, 1988.

Rainero, Romain H., *La Commission Italienne d'Armistice avec la France. Les Rapports entre la France de Vichy et l'Italy de Mussolini*, Paris, Vincennes, 1995.

Roshwald, Aviel, *Estranged Bedfellows. Britain and France in the Middle East During the Second World War*, Oxford, Oxford University Press, 1990.

Roulet, Louis-Edward, and Roland Blätter, *Les Etats neutres européens et la seconde guerre mondiale*, Berne, Editions de la Baconnière, 1983.

Rousso, Henri, *The Vichy Syndrome. History and Memory in France since 1944*, Cambridge, Mass., Harvard University Press, 1991.

Ruscio, Alain, *Les Communistes français et la guerre d'Indochine 1944–1954*, Paris, Editions l'Harmattan, 1987.

— *Vietnam. L'Histoire, la terre, les hommes*, Paris, Editions l'Harmattan, 1989.

Schachter-Morgenthau, Ruth, *Political Parties in French-speaking West Africa*, Oxford, Clarendon Press, 1964.

Schreiber, Gerhard, Bernd Stegemann and Detlef Vogel (eds), *Germany and the Second World War*, III: *The Mediterranean, South-east Europe, and North Africa 1939–1941*, Oxford, Oxford University Press, 1995.

Séguéla, Matthieu, *Pétain–Franco. Les Secrets d'une alliance*, Paris, Albin Michel, 1992.

Shennan, Andrew, *Rethinking France. Plans for Renewal, 1940–1946*, Oxford, Oxford University Press, 1989.

Shipley-White, Dorothy, *Black Africa and De Gaulle, From the French empire to Independence*, University Park, Pennsylvania State University Press, 1979.

Shipway, Martin, *The Road to War. France and Vietnam, 1944–1947*, Oxford, Berghahn, 1996.

Sivan, Emmanuel, *Communisme et nationalisme en Algérie, 1920–1962*, Paris, Presses de la FNSP, 1976.

Soley, Lawrence C., *Radio Warfare. OSS and CIA Subversive Propaganda*, New York, Praeger, 1989.

Stafford, David, *Britain and European Resistance, 1940–1945*, London, Macmillan, 1980.

Stora, Benjamin, *Nationalistes algériens et révolutionnaires français au*

temps du Front Populaire, Paris, Editions l'Harmattan, 1987.
— *Les Sources du nationalisme algérien*, Paris, Editions l'Harmattan, 1989.
Sweet-Escott, Bickham, *Baker Street Irregular*, London, Methuen, 1965.
Thobie, Jacques, Gilbert Maynier, Catherine Coquery-Vidrovitch and Charles-Robert Ageron, *Histoire de la France coloniale, 1914–1990*, Paris, Armand Colin, 1990.
Thomas, R. T., *Britain and Vichy. The Dilemma of Anglo-French Relations, 1940–42*, London, Macmillan, 1979.
Thorne, Christopher, *Border Crossings*, Oxford, Blackwell, 1988.
Tonnesson, Stein, *1946. Déclenchement de la guerre d'Indochine*, Paris, Editions l'Harmattan, 1987.
— *The Vietnamese Revolution of 1945. Roosevelt, Ho Chi Minh and de Gaulle in a World at War*, London, Sage, 1991.
Truchet, André, *L'Armistice de 1940 et l'Afrique du Nord*, Paris, Plon, 1955.
Vernet, J., *Le Réarmement et la réorganisation de l'Armée de Terre Française (1943–1946)*, Paris, Vincennes, 1980.
Vincent, Jean-Noël, *Les Forces françaises dans la lutte contre l'Axe en Afrique*, Paris, Vincennes, 1983.
Viorst, Milton, *Hostile Allies. F.D.R. and De Gaulle*, New York, Macmillan, 1965.
Wall, Irwin M., *The United States and the Making of Postwar France, 1945–1954*, Cambridge, Cambridge University Press, 1991.
Weinstein, Brian, *Eboué*, London, Oxford University Press, 1972.
Young, John W., *France, the Cold War and the Western Alliance, 1944–1949. French Foreign Policy and Post-war Europe*, Leicester, Leicester University Press, 1990.

Articles

Ageron, Charles-Robert, 'L'idée d'Eurafrique et le débat colonial franco-allemand de l'entre-deux-guerres', *Revue d'Histoire Moderne et Contemporaine*, 22 (1975), 446–75.
— 'Les populations du Maghreb face à la propagande allemande', *Revue d'Histoire de la Deuxième Guerre Mondiale*, 114 (1979), 1–39.
— 'La perception de la puissance française en 1938–1939: le mythe impérial', in René Girault and Robert Frank (eds), *La Puissance en Europe, 1938–1940*, Paris, Publications de la Sorbonne, 1984, 227–44.
— 'De Gaulle et les indépendances des Etats d'Afrique noire et de Madagascar', in Ageron and Michel, *Afrique noire*, 703–11.
— 'Vichy, les Français et l'empire' in Azéma and Bédarida, *Vichy et les Français*, 122–34.
Akpo, Catherine, and Vincent Joly, 'Les élites africaines face à l'administration gaulliste (1943–1946)', in Ageron, *Chemins*, 481–94.
Alexander, M. S., 'The Fall of France, 1940', *Journal of Strategic Studies*, 13: 1 (1990), 10–44.
Allain, Jean-Claude, 'Les emprunts d'état marocains avant 1939', in Ageron,

Chemins, 131–46.

Almeida-Topor, Hélène d', 'Les "termes de l'échange paysan" en Afrique occidentale française de 1938 à 1948: réflexions méthodologiques', in Ageron, *Chemins*, 117–30.

Alzon, Claude Hesse d', 'L'évolution des conceptions stratégiques du commandement français en Indochine entre 1940 et 1945', *Revue d'Histoire de la Deuxième Guerre Mondiale*, 138 (1985), 5–20.

Amadouny, V. M., 'The formation of the Transjordan–Syria boundary, 1915–32', *Middle Eastern Studies*, 31: 3 (1995), 533–49.

Anigniken, Sylvian, 'Les facteurs historiques de la décolonisation au Dahomey (1936–1956)', in Ageron, *Chemins*, 505–12.

Aouate, Yves C., 'La place de l'Algérie dans le projet anti-juif de Vichy (octobre 1940–novembre 1942)', *Revue Française d'Histoire d'Outre-mer*, 301: 4 (1993), 599–613.

Asiwaju, A. I., 'Migrations as revolt: the example of the Ivory Coast and Upper Volta before 1945', *Journal of African History*, 17: 4 (1976), 577–94.

Ayoun, Richard, 'Le décret Crémieux et l'insurrection de 1871 en Algérie', *Revue d'Histoire Moderne et Contemporaine*, 35: 1 (1988), 61–87.

Bastien, Hervé, 'Alger 1944, ou, La révolution dans la légalité', *Revue d'Histoire Moderne et Contemporaine*, 37: 3 (1990), 429–51.

Bell, P. M. H., 'Prologue de Mers-el-Kébir', *Revue Historique de la Deuxième Guerre Mondiale*, 9 (1959), 15–36.

Bergougnoux, Philippe, 'Le réarmement de la Marine Nationale (1934–1939)', *Revue Historique des Armées*, 4 (1985), 26–41.

Bézias, Jean-Rémy, 'Georges Bidault et le Levant: l'introuvable politique arabe (1945–1946)', *Revue d'Histoire Moderne et Contemporaine*, 42: 4 (1995), 609–21.

Binoche, Jacques, 'La politique extrême-orientale française et les relations franco-japonaises de 1919 à 1939', *Revue Française d'Histoire d'Outre-mer*, 86 (1989), 531–43.

Binoche-Guedra, J. W., 'La répresentation parlementaire coloniale (1871–1940)', *Revue Historique*, 280 (1988), 521–35.

Blanchard, Pascal, and Gilles Boëtsch, 'Races et propagande coloniale sous le régime de Vichy 1940–1944', *Africa*, 49: 4 (1994), 531–61.

Bou Assi, Maroun, 'La crise libanaise de 1941, ou, La bataille du Levant', in Ageron, *Chemins*, 307–24.

Bouche, Denise, 'Dakar pendant la deuxième guerre mondiale: problèmes de surpeuplement', *Revue Française d'Histoire d'Outre-mer*, 65 (1978), 423–38.

— 'Le retour de l'AOF dans la lutte contre l'ennemi aux côtes des alliés', *Revue d'Histoire de la Deuxième Guerre Mondiale*, 114 (1979), 41–68.

— 'L'ouverture de l'Afrique occidentale française au monde extérieur: la fin de l'empire et l'échec de l'Union française', *Relations Internationales*, 34 (1983), 173–85.

— 'L'administration de l'Afrique occidentale française et les libertés démocratiques (1944–1946)', in Ageron, *Chemins*, 481–94.

Bou-Nacklie, N. E., 'The Avenantaires: Syrian mercenaries in French Africa',

Middle Eastern Studies, 27: 4 (1991), 654–67.
— 'Les troupes spéciales: religious and ethnic recruitment, 1916–46', *International Journal of Middle East Studies*, 25 (1993), 645–60.
— 'The 1941 invasion of Syria and Lebanon: the role of the local paramilitary', *Middle Eastern Studies*, 30: 3 (1994), 512–29.
Brecher, F. W., 'French policy toward the Levant, 1914–18', *Middle Eastern Studies*, 29: 4 (1993), 641–64.
Brett, Michael, 'The colonial period in the Maghrib and its aftermath: the present state of historical writing', *Journal of African History*, 17: 2 (1976), 291–305.
Brocheux, Pierre, 'La question de l'indépendance dans l'opinion viêtnamienne de 1939 à 1945', in Ageron, *Chemins*, 201–7.
Brunschwig, Henri, 'L'impérialisme en Afrique noire', *Revue Historique*, 249 (1973), 129–42.
— 'De l'assimilation à la décolonisation', in Ageron, *Chemins*, 49–54
Burke, III, Edmund, 'A comparative view of French native policy in Morocco and Syria, 1912–1925', *Middle Eastern Studies*, 9: 2 (1973), 175–86.
Burton, Richard E., '"Nos journées de juin": the historical significance of the liberation of Martinique (June 1943)', in Kedward and Wood, *Liberation*, 227–39.
Ceva, Lucio, 'The North African campaign, 1940–43: a reconsideration', *Journal of Strategic Studies*, 13 (1990), 84–104.
Chafer, Tony, 'African perspectives: the liberation of France and its impact in French West Africa', in Kedward and Wood, *Liberation*, pp. 241–53.
Chalmers Hood III, Ronald, 'The French navy and parliament between the wars', *International History Review*, 6 (1984), 386–403.
— 'Bitter Victory. French Military Effectiveness during the Second World War', in Allan R. Millett and Williamson Murray (eds), *Military Effectiveness*, III: *The Second World War*, Boston, Allen and Unwin, 1988.
Chandler, David P., 'The kingdom of Kampuchea, March–October 1945: Japanese-sponsored independence in Cambodia in World War II', *Journal of Southeast Asian Studies*, 17: 1 (1986), 80–93.
Charmley, John, 'Harold Macmillan and the making of the French Committee of Liberation', *International History Review*, 4: 4 (1982), 553–67.
Chenntouf, Tayeb, 'L'Assemblée Algérienne et l'application des réformes prévues par le statut du 20 Septembre 1947', in Ageron, *Chemins*, 367–75.
Chieu, Vu Ngu, 'The other side of the 1945 Vietnamese revolution: The empire of Vietnam (March–August 1945)', *Journal of Asian Studies*, 14: 2 (1986), 293–328.
Clayton, Anthony, 'The Sétif uprising of May 1945', *Small Wars and Insurgencies*, 3: 1 (1992), 1–21.
Cohen, William B., 'The colonial policy of the Popular Front', *French Historical Studies*, 7: 3 (1972), 368–93.
— 'Legacy of empire: the Algerian connection', *Journal of Contemporary History*, 15: 1 (1980), 97–123.
Cointet, Jean-Paul, 'Les relations entre de Gaulle et le gouvernement britannique durant la seconde guerre mondiale', *Revue Historique*, 268: 2 (1982),

431–51.

Coquery-Vidrovitch, Catherine, 'L'impact des intérêts coloniaux: SCOA et CFAO dans l'ouest africain, 1910–1965', *Journal of African History*, 16: 4 (1975), 595–621.

— 'Vichy et industrialisation aux colonies', *Revue d'Histoire de la Deuxième Guerre Mondiale*, 114 (1979), 69–94.

Cornevin, Robert, 'Le corps des administrateurs de la France d'outre-mer durant la deuxième guerre mondiale', in Ageron, *Chemins*, 455–67.

Cornick, Martyn, 'The BBC and the propaganda war against occupied France: the work of Emile Delavenay and the European Intelligence Department', *French History*, 8: 3 (1994), 316–54.

Couture, Paul M., 'The Vichy–Free French propaganda war in Quebec, 1940 to 1942', *Canadian Historical Association Historical Papers*, (1978), 200–216.

Cox, Jafna L., 'The background to the Syrian campaign, May–June 1941: A study in Franco-German wartime relations', *History*, 72 (1987), 432–52.

Crowder, Michael, 'The 1939–45 war and West Africa', in Ade Ajayi and M. Crowder (eds), *History of West Africa*, London, Longman, 1974.

Dallek, Robert, 'Roosevelt and De Gaulle', in Paxton and Wahl, *De Gaulle and the United States*, 49–60.

Dalloz, Jacques, 'L'opposition MRP à la guerre d'Indochine', *Revue d'Histoire Moderne et Contemporaine*, 43: 1 (1996), 106–18.

Delmas, Jean, 'De Gaulle, la défense nationale et les forces armées: projets et réalités (1944–janvier 1946)', *Revue d'Histoire de la Deuxième Guerre Mondiale*, 110 (1978), 7–24.

Derrick, Jonathan, 'The "Germanophone" elite of Douala under the French mandate', *Journal of African History*, 21 (1980), 255–67.

Dreifort, John E., 'France, the powers and the Far Eastern crisis, 1937–1939', *Historian*, 39 (1977), 733–53

— 'Japan's advance into Indochina, 1940: the French response', *Journal of Southeast Asian Studies*, 13 (1982), 279–95.

Dubois, Colette, 'Internés et prisonniers de guerre italiens dans les camps de l'empire français de 1940 à 1945', *Guerres Mondiales et Conflits Contemporains*, 39: 1 (1989), 56–63.

Dumett, Raymond, 'Africa's strategic minerals during the Second World War', *Journal of African History*, 26 (1985), 381–408.

Duroselle, Jean-Baptiste, 'Une création *ex nihilo*: le Ministère des Affaires Etrangères du Général de Gaulle (1940–1942)', *Relations Internationales*, 31 (1982), 313–32.

Echenberg, Myron J., 'Paying the blood tax: military conscription in French West Africa, 1914–1929', *Revue Canadienne des Etudes Africaines*/Canadian Journal of African Studies, 10: 2 (1975), 171–92.

— 'Tragedy at Thiaroye: the Senegalese soldiers' uprising of 1944', in P. W. Gutkind *et al.* (eds), *African Labor History*, II, London, Sage, 1978.

— 'Les migrations militaires en Afrique occidentale française, 1900–1945', *Revue Canadienne des Etudes Africaines/Canadian Journal of African Studies*, 14: 3 (1980), 429–50.

— '"Morts pour la France": the African soldier in France during the Second

World War', *Journal of African History*, 26 (1985), 363–80.
— '"Promotion africaine": the africanization of military officers in French West Africa, 1945–1960', in Ageron and Michel, *Afrique noire*, 57–70.
— and Jean Filipovich, 'African military labour and the building of the Office du Niger installations, 1925–1950', *Journal of African History*, 27 (1986), 533–51.
Enders, Armelle, 'L'Ecole Nationale de la France d'Outre-mer et la formation des administrateurs coloniaux', *Revue d'Histoire Moderne et Contemporaine*, 40: 2 (1993), 272–88.
Evans, Martin, 'Algeria and the liberation: hope and betrayal', in Kedward and Wood, *Liberation*, 255–67.
Farrell, Brian P., 'Symbol of paradox: the Casablanca conference, 1943', *Canadian Journal of History*, 28 (1993), 21–40.
Fishman, Sarah, 'Grand delusions: the unintended consequences of Vichy France's prisoner-of-war propaganda', *Journal of Contemporary History*, 26 (1991), 229–54.
Fol, J. J., 'Le Togo pendant la Seconde Guerre Mondiale', *Revue d'Histoire de la Deuxième Guerre Mondiale*, 115 (1979), 69–77.
Frank, Robert, 'Vichy et les Britanniques, 1940–1941: double jeu ou double langage?', in Azéma and Bédarida, *Vichy et les Français*, 144–61.
Funk, Arthur L., 'Negotiating the "Deal with Darlan"', *Journal of Contemporary History*, 8: 2 (1973), 81–117.
Gaunson, A. B., 'Churchill, de Gaulle, Spears and the Levant affair, 1941', *Historical Journal*, 27 (1984), 697–713.
Gibbs, David N., 'Political parties and international relations: the United States and the decolonization of sub-Saharan Africa', *International History Review*, 17: 2 (1995), 221–40.
Giblin, James L., 'A colonial state in crisis: Vichy administration in French West Africa', *Africana Journal*, 5 (1994), 326–40.
Gras, Yves, 'L'intrusion japonais en Indochine 1940–1945', *Revue Historique des Armées*, 4 (1983), 86–102.
Guillen, Pierre, 'Une menace pour l'Afrique française: le débat international sur le statut des anciennes colonies italiennes (1943–1949)', in Ageron, *Chemins*, 69–82.
Halstead, C., 'Aborted imperialism: Spain's occupation of Tangier, 1940–1945', *Iberian Studies*, 7: 2 (1978), 53–71.
Headrick, Rita, 'African Soldiers in World War II', *Armed Forces and Society*, 4: 1 (1978), 501–26.
Heffernan, Michael J., 'The Parisian poor and the colonization of Algeria during the Second Republic', *French History*, 3: 4 (1989), 377–403.
Hess, G. R., 'Franklin Roosevelt and Indochina', *Journal of American History*, 59: 2 (1972), 353–68.
Hilliker, J. F., 'The Canadian government and the Free French: perceptions and constraints, 1940–44', *International History Review*, 2: 1 (1980), 87–108.
Hoisington, William A., junior, 'France and Islam: the Haute Comité Méditerranéen and French North Africa', in George Joffé (ed.), *North Africa, Nation, State and Region*, London, Macmillan, 1993.
Hoop, Jean-Marie d', 'L'Armée française de l'armistice de 1940 à la victoire de

1945: orientation bibliographique', *Revue d'Histoire de la Deuxième Guerre Mondiale*, 110 (1978), 103–14.
— 'Du coup de force japonais au départ du Général de Gaulle', in Gilbert Pilleul (ed.), *Le Général de Gaulle et l'Indochine, 1940–1946*, Paris, Plon/Institut Charles de Gaulle, 1982.
Ikuhiko, Hata, 'The army's move into northern Indochina', in J. W. Morley (ed.), *The Fateful Choice. Japan's Advance into South East Asia, 1939–1941*, New York, Columbia University Press, 1980.
Istasse-Moussinga, Cecile, 'La collaboration de guerre franco-britannique en Afrique noire, 1940–1945', *Guerres Mondiales et Conflits Contemporains*, 181: 1 (1996), 7–20.
Jauffret, Jean-Charles, 'The origins of the Algerian war: the reaction of France and its army to the two emergencies of 8 May 1945 and 1 November 1954', *Journal of Imperial and Commonwealth History*, 21: 3 (1993), 17–30.
Jessula, Georges, '1943: De Gaulle à Alger. Les "Carnets" d'Harold Macmillan', *Revue d'Histoire Diplomatique*, 105 (1991), 217–48.
Joffé, E. G. H., 'The Moroccan nationalist movement: Istiqlal, the sultan and the country', *Journal of African History*, 26 (1985), 289–307.
Johnson, Douglas, 'Algeria: some problems of modern history', *Journal of African History*, 5: 2 (1964), 221–42.
Joseph, Richard A., 'Settlers, strikers and *sans-travail*: The Douala riots of September 1945', *Journal of African History*, 15: 4 (1974), 669–84.
Kaddache, Mahfoud, 'L'opinion politique musulmane en Algérie et l'administration française (1939–1942)', *Revue d'Histoire de la Deuxième Guerre Mondiale*, 114 (1979), 95–115.
Khenouf, Mohamed, and Michael Brett, 'Algerian nationalism and Allied military strategy and propaganda during the Second World War: the background to Sétif', in Killingray and Rathbone, *Africa and the Second World War*, 258–74.
Khoury, Philip S., 'Factionalism among Syrian nationalists during the French mandate', *International Journal of Middle East Studies*, 13 (1981), 441–69.
— 'The tribal Shaykh, French tribal policy, and the nationalist movement in Syria between two world wars', *Middle Eastern Studies*, 18: 2 (182), 180–93.
Koerner, Francis, 'Les répercussions de la guerre d'Espagne en Oranie (1936–1939)', *Revue d'Histoire Moderne et Contemporaine*, 22: 3 (1975), 476–87.
Krautkramer, Elmar, 'Das Ringen um die Erhaltung der französischen Souveränität in Nordafrika im Zusammenhang mit Torch', *Militärgeschichtliche Mitteilungen*, 32: 2 (1982), 79–136.
Kurtovitch, Ismet, 'New Caledonia: the consequences of the Second World War' in Aldrich and Merle, *France Abroad*, 34–45.
Lafeber, W., 'Roosevelt, Churchill and Indochina, 1942–5', *American Historical Review*, 80 (1975), 1277–95.
Laffey, John P., 'French Far Eastern policy in the 1930s', *Modern Asian Studies*, 23: 1 (1989), 117–49.
Lamont, Pierre L., 'La révolution nationale dans l'Indochine de l'Amiral Decoux', *Revue d'Histoire de la Deuxième Guerre Mondiale*, 138 (1985), 21–41.

— 'Le Cambodge et la décolonisation de l'Indochine: les caractères particuliers du nationalisme Khmer de 1936 à 1945', in Ageron, *Chemins*, 189–99.

Lanné, Bernard, 'Le Tchad pendant la guerre (1939–1945)', in Ageron, *Chemins*, 439–54.

Lawler, Nancy, 'Reform and repression under the Free French: economic and political transformation in the Côte d'Ivoire, 1942–45', *Africa*, 60: 1 (1990), 88–110.

Lévisse-Touzé, Christine, 'La préparation économique, industrielle et militaire de l'Afrique du Nord à la veille de la guerre', *Revue d'Histoire de la Deuxième Guerre Mondiale*, 142 (1986), 1–18.

— 'La situation intérieure de l'Algérie pendant la Seconde Guerre Mondiale', *Histoire et Défense*, 25: 1 (1992), 5–22.

— 'L'Armée d'Afrique: armée de transition pour une grande révanche', *Revue Historique des Armées*, 188: 3 (1992), 10–19.

— 'L'Afrique du nord pendant la seconde guerre mondiale', *Relations Internationales*, 77 (1994), 9–19.

Lewis, James I., 'The French colonial service and the issues of reform, 1944–48', *Contemporary European History*, 4: 2 (1995), 153–88.

Loubes, Olivier, 'Jean Zay, Vichy et la Résistance: une mise en abîme de l'éclipse', *Revue d'Histoire Moderne et Contemporaine*, 43: 1 (1996), 151–67.

Maguire, Gloria Elizabeth, '"Notre mal de tête commun": Churchill, Roosevelt et de Gaulle', *Revue d'Histoire Moderne et Contemporaine*, 42: 4 (1995), 593–608.

— 'La nouvelle Grèce, la nouvelle Rome: Harold Macmillan et Dwight D. Eisenhower à Alger, 1943', *Frontières* (1995), 43–54.

Marseille, Jacques, 'L'investissement français dans l'empire colonial: l'enquête du gouvernement de Vichy (1943)', *Revue Historique*, 122 (1974), 409–32.

— 'Les relations commerciales entre la France et son empire colonial de 1880 à 1913', *Revue d'Histoire Moderne et Contemporaine*, 31: 2 (1984), 286–307.

M'Bokolo, Elikia, 'Forces sociales et idéologies dans la décolonisation de l'AEF', *Journal of African History*, 22 (1981), 393–407.

— 'French colonial policy in equatorial Africa in the 1940s and 1950s', in Gifford and Louis, *Transfer of Power*, 173–210.

Melka, R. L., 'Darlan between Britain and Germany, 1940–1941', *Journal of Contemporary History*, 8 (1973), 57–80.

Melki, James L., 'Syria and the State Department, 1937–47', *Middle Eastern Studies*, 33: 1 (1997), 92–106.

Merglen, Albert, 'La France pouvait continuer la guerre en Afrique Française du Nord en 1940', *Revue d'Histoire Diplomatique*, 106 (1992), 99–119.

Michel, Marc, 'La puissance par l'empire: note sur la perception du facteur impérial dans l'élaboration de la défense nationale (1936–1938)', *Revue Française d'Histoire d'Outre-mer*, 69 (1982), 35–46.

— 'La coopération intercoloniale en Afrique noire, 1942–1950: un néo-colonialisme éclairé?', *Relations Internationales*, 34 (1983), 155–71.

— 'Le Togo dans les relations internationales au lendemain de la guerre: prodome de la décolonisation ou petite "mésentente cordiale"', in Ageron,

Chemins, 96–108.
— 'Colonisation et défense nationale: le général Mangin et la Force Noire', *Guerres Mondiales et Conflits Contemporains*, 145 (1987), 27–44.
Mickelson, Martin L., 'Another Fashoda: the Anglo-Free French conflict over the Levant, May–September 1941', *Revue Française d'Histoire d'Outre-mer*, 63 (1976), 75–100.
Munholland, Kim, 'The trials of the Free French in New Caledonia, 1940–1942', *French Historical Studies*, 14 (1986), 547–79.
—, 'The United States and the Free French', in Paxton and Wahl, *De Gaulle and the United States*, pp. 61–94.
Murakami, Sachiko, 'Indochina: unplanned incursion', in Conroy and Wray, *Pearl Harbor Reexamined*, 141–9.
My-Van, Tran, 'Japan and Vietnam's Caodaists: a wartime relationship (1939–1945)', *Journal of Southeast Asian Studies*, 27: 1 (1996), 179–93.
Nitz, Kiyoko Kurusu, 'Japanese military policy towards French Indochina during the Second World War: the road to the Meigo Sakusen (9 March 1945)', *Journal of Southeast Asian Studies*, 14: 2 (1983), 328–53.
— 'Independence without nationalists? The Japanese and Vietnamese nationalism during the Japanese period, 1940–45', *Journal of Southeast Asian Studies*, 15: 1 (1984), 108–33.
Norindr, Panivong, 'Representing Indochina: the French colonial fantasmatic and the Exposition Coloniale de Paris', *French Cultural Studies*, 6 (1995), 35–60.
Olmert, Yossi, 'Britain, Turkey and the Levant question during the Second World War', *Middle Eastern Studies*, 23 (1987), 437–52.
— 'A false dilemma? Syria and Lebanon's independence during the mandatory period', *Middle Eastern Studies*, 32: 3 (1996), 41–73.
Paloczi-Horvath, George, 'Thailand's war with Vichy France', *History Today*, 45: 3 (1995), 32–9.
Paxton, Robert O., 'Anti-Americanism in the years of collaboration and resistance', in Lacorne *et al.*, *The Rise and Fall of Anti-Americanism*, 55–65.
Pennell, C. R., 'Women and resistance to colonialism in Morocco: the Rif, 1916–1926', *Journal of African History*, 28 (1987), 107–18.
Person, Yves, 'French West Africa and decolonization' in Gifford and Louis, *Transfer of Power*, 141–72.
Pervillé, Guy, 'La Commission des Réformes Musulmanes de 1944 et l'élaboration d'une nouvelle politique algérienne de la France', in Ageron, *Chemins*, 357–66.
Pithon, Rémy, 'Opinions publiques et représentations culturelles face aux problèmes de la puissance. Le témoignage du cinéma français (1938–1939)', *Relations Internationales*, 33 (1983), 91–102.
Porath, Y., 'Abdallah's Greater Syria programme', *Middle Eastern Studies*, 20: 2 (1984), 172–89.
Porch, Douglas, 'French intelligence culture: a historical and political perspective', *Intelligence and National Security*, 10: 3 (1995), 486–511.
Preston, Paul, 'Franco and Hitler: the myth of Hendaye, 1940', *Contemporary European History*, 1: 1 (1992), 1–16.

Pritchard, John, 'Winston Churchill, the military and imperial defence in East Asia', in Dockrill, *From Pearl Harbor to Hiroshima*, 26–54.

Queuille, Pierre, 'Le décisif armistice franco-italien, 23–24 Juin 1940', *Revue d'Histoire Diplomatique*, 90 (1976), 100–11.

— 'La politique d'Hitler à l'égard de Vichy', *Revue d'Histoire Diplomatique*, 97 (1983), 256–78.

Rabinovitch, Itamar, 'The compact minorities and the Syrian state, 1918–1945', *Journal of Contemporary History*, 14: 3 (1979), 693–712.

Rainero, Romain, 'La politique fasciste à l'égard de l'Afrique du Nord: l'épée de l'Islam et la revendication sur la Tunisie', *Revue Française d'Histoire d'Outre-mer*, 64: 237 (1977), 498–515.

— 'L'action de la propagande fasciste en direction de la Syrie et du Levant', in Ageron, *Chemins*, 297–306.

Rey-Goldzeiguer, Annie, 'L'occupation germano-italienne de la Tunisie: un tournant de la vie politique tunisienne', in Ageron, *Chemins*, 325–41.

Rivlin, Benjamin, 'The United States and Moroccan international status, 1943–1956: a contributory factor in Morocco's reassertion of independence from France', *International Journal of African Historical Studies*, 15: 1 (1982), 64–82.

Rolland, Denis, 'Jacques Soustelle: de l'ethnologie à la politique', *Revue d'Histoire Moderne et Contemporaine*, 43: 1 (1996), 137–50.

Roshwald, Aviel, 'The Spears mission in the Levant', *Historical Journal*, 29 (1986), 897–919.

Rossi, Mario, 'Les autorités militaires américaines et la France Libre de 1942 à 1944', *Guerres Mondiales et Conflits Contemporains*, 174 (1994), 179–94.

Sbrega, John J., '"First catch your hare": Anglo-American perspectives on Indochina during the Second World War', *Journal of Southeast Asian Studies*, 14: 1 (1983), 63–78.

— 'The anticolonial policies of Franklin D. Roosevelt: a reappraisal', *Political Science Quarterly*, 101 (1986), 65–84.

— 'Determination versus drift: the Anglo-American debate over the trusteeship issue, 1941–1945', *Pacific Historical Review*, 55: 2 (1986), 256–80.

Semidei, Manuela, 'Les socialists français et le problème colonial entre les deux guerres (1919–1939)', *Revue Française de Science Politique*, 18: 6 (1968), 1115–53.

Shipway, Martin, 'Creating an emergency: metropolitan constraints on French colonial policy and its breakdown in Indo-China, 1945–47', *Journal of Imperial and Commonwealth History*, 21: 1 (1993), 1–16.

— 'Madagascar on the eve of insurrection, 1944–47: the impasse of a liberal colonial policy', *Journal of Imperial and Commonwealth History*, 24: 1 (1996), 72–100.

Shorrock, William I, 'The Tunisian question in French policy towards Italy, 1881–1940', *International Journal of African Historical Studies*, 16: 4 (1983), 631–51.

Sivan, Emmanuel, 'Colonialism and popular culture in Algeria', *Journal of Contemporary History*, 14 (1979), 21–53.

Smith, Ralph B., 'The Vietnamese elite of French Cochin China, 1943', *Modern Asian Studies*, 6: 4 (1972), 459–482.

— 'The development of opposition to French rule in southern Vietnam, 1880–1940', *Past and Present*, 54 (1972), 94–129.

— 'The Japanese period in Indochina and the *coup* of 9 March 1945', *Journal of Southeast Asian Studies*, 9: 2 (1978), 268–301.

Smith, Tony, 'Patterns in the transfer of power in Africa: a comparative study of French and British decolonization' in Gifford and Louis, *Transfer of Power*, 87–115.

Smyth, Denis, 'Screening "Torch": Allied counter-intelligence and the Spanish threat to the secrecy of the Allied invasion of French North Africa in November 1942', *Intelligence and National Security*, 4: 2 (1989), 335–56.

Stora, Benjamin, 'La gauche socialiste révolutionnaire et la question du Maghreb au moment du Front Populaire (1935–1938)', *Revue Française d'Histoire d'Outre-mer*, 70 (1983), 57–79.

Swearingen, Will D., 'In pursuit of the granary of Rome: France's wheat policy in Morocco, 1915–1931', *International Journal of Middle East Studies*, 17 (1985), 347–63.

Taylor, Lynne, 'The Parti Communiste Français and the French resistance in the Second World War', in Tony Judt (ed.), *Resistance and Revolution in Mediterranean Europe, 1939–1948*, London, Macmillan, 1989.

Thioub, Ibrahim, 'Economie coloniale et rémunération de la force de travail: le salaire du manoeuvre à Dakar de 1930 à 1954', *Revue Française d'Histoire d'Outre-mer*, 81 (1984), 427–53.

Thomas, Martin, 'Plans and problems of the Armée de l'Air in the defence of North Africa before the fall of France', *French History*, 7: 4 (1993), 472–95.

— 'The Anglo-French divorce over West Africa and the limitations of strategic planning', *Diplomacy and Statecraft*, 6: 1 (1995), 81–106.

— 'The discarded leader: General Henri Giraud and the foundation of the French Committee of National Liberation', *French History*, 10: 1 (1996), 86–111.

— 'Imperial backwater or strategic outpost? The British take-over of Vichy Madagascar in 1942', *Historical Journal*, 39: 4 (1996), 1049–74.

— 'The Massingham mission: SOE in French North Africa, 1941–1944', *Intelligence and National Security*, 11: 4 (1996), 696–721.

— 'After Mers-el-Kébir: the armed neutrality of the Vichy navy, 1940–1943', *English Historical Review*, 112: 447 (1997), 643–70.

— 'Free France, the British government and the future of French Indo-China, 1940–45', *Journal of Southeast Asian Studies*, 28: 1 (1997), 137–60.

— 'Deferring to Vichy in the Western hemisphere: the St Pierre and Miquelon affair of 1941', *International History Review*, 19: 4 (1997).

— 'Captives of their countrymen: Free French and Vichy French POWs in Africa and the Middle East, 1940–43', in Bob Moore and Kent Fedorowich (eds), *Prisoners of War and their Captors in World War II*, Oxford, Berg, 1996.

Thorne, Christopher, 'The Indochina issue between Britain and the United States, 1942–1945', *Pacific Historical Review*, 45 (1976), 73–96.

Vinen, Richard C., 'The end of an ideology? Right-wing antisemitism in France, 1944–1970', *Historical Journal*, 37 (1994), 365–88.
Walker, David A., 'OSS and Operation Torch', *Journal of Contemporary History*, 22 (1987), 667–79.
Wall, Irwin, W., 'Henry S. Truman and Charles De Gaulle', in Paxton and Wahl, *De Gaulle and the United States*, pp. 117–29.
Wing Ray, Deborah, 'The Takoradi route: Roosevelt's prewar venture beyond the western hemisphere', *Journal of American History*, 2 (1965), 340–58.
Young, John W., 'The Foreign Office and the departure of General de Gaulle, June 1945–January 1946', *Historical Journal*, 25 (1982), 209–16.

Theses

Shipway, Martin, 'The Brazzaville Conference, 1944. Colonial and Imperial Planning in a Wartime Setting', M.Phil. thesis, Oxford, 1986.
Woolner, David B., 'Storm in the North Atlantic. The St Pierre and Miquelon Affair of 1941', M.A. thesis, Montreal McGill, 1990.

INDEX

'n' after a page number refers to a note on that page.